W9-AFY-552

4034
411
4/15

Negotiating Political Identities
Multiethnic Schools and Youth in Europe

DANIEL FAAS
Trinity College Dublin, Ireland

ASHGATE

© Daniel Faas 2010

All rights reserved. No part of this publication may be reproduced, stored in a retrieval system or transmitted in any form or by any means, electronic, mechanical, photocopying, recording or otherwise without the prior permission of the publisher.

Daniel Faas has asserted his right under the Copyright, Designs and Patents Act, 1988, to be identified as the author of this work.

Published by
Ashgate Publishing Limited
Wey Court East
Union Road
Farnham
Surrey, GU9 7PT
England

Ashgate Publishing Company
Suite 420
101 Cherry Street
Burlington
VT 05401-4405
USA

www.ashgate.com

British Library Cataloguing in Publication Data
Faas, Daniel.
  Negotiating political identities : multiethnic schools and
  youth in Europe. -- (Monitoring change in education)
  1. Multicultural education--Europe. 2. Minority youth--
  Education--Great Britain--Case studies. 3. Minority
  youth--Education--Germany--Case studies. 4. Ethnicity in
  children. 5. Nationalism and education--Europe.
  I. Title II. Series
  373.1'829-dc22

Library of Congress Cataloging-in-Publication Data
Faas, Daniel.
  Negotiating political identities : multiethnic schools and youth in Europe / by Daniel Faas.
      p. cm. -- (Monitoring change in education)
  Includes index.
  ISBN 978-0-7546-7844-1 (hardback) -- ISBN 978-0-7546-9664-3
(ebook) 1. Education--Social aspects--Germany--Case studies. 2. Education--Social
aspects--England--Case studies. 3. Education and state--Germany--Case studies. 4.
Education and state--England--Case studies. 5. Multiculturalism--Germany--Case studies.
6. Multiculturalism--England--Case studies. 7. Group identity--Germany--Case studies.
8. Group identity--England--Case studies. I. Title.
  LC191.8.G3F33 2010
  370.1170943--dc22

                                                                              2009046927
ISBN 9780754678441 (hbk)
ISBN 9780754696643 (ebk)

Mixed Sources
Product group from well-managed
forests and other controlled sources
www.fsc.org Cert no. SGS-COC-2482
FSC © 1996 Forest Stewardship Council

Printed and bound in Great Britain by
TJ International Ltd, Padstow, Cornwall

Contents

To my family, with love

List of Figures and Tables

Figures

Tables

Foreword

Questions of migration, ethno-religious belonging, nation-making and citizenship are key elements of today's rapid social and cultural transformations. These aspects of today's world are accompanied by pervasive feelings of anxiety, risk and dislocation, as well as new opportunity. The process of globalization means old polarities between First and Third World are less relevant and have been replaced with mass movements of capital, technologies and people. Shifting political mobilizations and the remaking of policies within these conditions of late modernity have witnessed a wider move from the politics of distribution to the politics of recognition, in ways that affect a diverse range of established migrants, faith communities, economic migrants and asylum seekers.

The fragmentation of social relations brought on by globalizing processes is reflected in the increasing range of social and cultural explanations of our rapidly changing social world. Much contemporary social and cultural theory examining these issues has been developed at an abstract level that is not embedded in 'old' institutional sites (such as workplaces or schools) or in individual subjects' lived realities. Herein lies the contribution of this book, which reconnects that which has become disconnected – schooling and social theory. The author's theory-led comparative methodology wonderfully narrates the centrality of modern European schooling for the making and remaking of societies around a dynamic and contested notion of multiculturalism.

Negotiating Political Identities presents a sociological analysis of the post-war historical relationships between national, European and multicultural political and educational agendas in Germany and England, and extends the findings to transatlantic discussions of immigrant incorporation. The research challenges, with a generous and creative reading, earlier work in the field of inquiry that has tended to focus on a more conventional approach in examining notions of citizenship, multiculturalism and belonging. Simultaneously, the author makes a substantial contribution to the field, offering real insights, at an epistemological level, into a contemporary understanding of discursive constructions of a multi-narrative sense of citizenship that explores the interconnecting social forces of school policies, peer groups, social class and the accompanying different histories of migration. His specific focus is a fascinating narrative centred on identity formation among young people – 15-year-old ethnic majority and Turkish minority students – located within schools. The book takes up an area in urgent need of critical exploration within conditions of late modernity, the institutional and self-positioning of ethnic majority and Turkish minority secondary students with reference to local, national, and European political agendas. This important book expands sociological understanding of contemporary youth by placing negotiated political identities at its centre. Even more impressively, the study serves to interrogate established theory at a macro-level by delving deeply into the reinforcement of national agendas within an English context, and contrasting it to Germany's prioritization of European agendas. There is a real sense here of a new generation of writing around the institutionally situated national/ethnic self, one which applies not only to European scholarship on immigrant incorporation, but to transatlantic dialogues around the integration of the second generation as well.

This challenging text, combining scholarship and accessibility, will appeal to multiple audiences, including academics, policy-makers, and the general reader.

Máirtín Mac an Ghaill
University of Birmingham

Acknowledgements

The idea for this project dates back to the late 1990s when I was teaching at King Edward VI Aston and Handsworth Schools in Birmingham. There I experienced life in multiethnic inner-city schools for the first time, since I had attended more rural and suburban white schools for my own education. While teaching in these schools, I became more and more interested in different levels of interaction and integration as well as how students from different backgrounds are positioned and position themselves, and decided to study these issues in greater depth. I have worked in five countries since doing my fieldwork for the project, labouring over this manuscript while living in Germany, Britain, Greece, Ireland and the United States. Spending time in each one of these countries has added to my own identity and what it means to be a European or global citizen in the twenty-first century. I have learned so much from listening to all of my respondents in this project and am forever grateful for their insights.

I am deeply indebted to a large number of colleagues and friends. First and foremost, I would like to express my profound gratitude to Madeleine Arnot at the University of Cambridge for her countless discussions, intellectual challenges, and meticulous attention to detail. While at Cambridge, I also benefited from the advice of Michael Evans, Edith Esch and Lynne Chisholm. I am grateful to Bob Ackerman, Jim Council and Tony Street for inviting me to try out some initial drafts at the Clare Hall Arts, Societies and Humanities Colloquia. During those years, my thinking also benefited from discussions with Deborah Youdell, Máirtín Mac an Ghaill, Anthony Adams, Avril Keating, Harriett Marshall, Stavroula Philippou, and Antonina Tereshenko. At the Hellenic Foundation for European and Foreign Policy, I benefited from several discussions and comments from Anna Triandafyllidou, Ruby Gropas and Loukas Tsoukalis. At the University of California, Berkeley, I owe many thanks to Irene Bloemraad, Jack Citrin, Aarti Kohli, Jorge Ruiz de Velasco, and Alex Street. Thanks to those who provided feedback at the Harvard University Migration and Immigrant Incorporation Workshop, especially Natasha Kumar Warikoo. At Trinity College Dublin, I would like to thank Ronit Lentin and James Wickham for facilitating a rather unusual research leave during my first year in the job. This ultimately speeded up the writing process and allowed me to publish this book despite a heavy teaching and administrative load.

I would further like to thank the many organizations that have financially supported me during this project. I gratefully acknowledge support from the British Economic and Social Research Council (PTA-030-2002-00853), the Cambridge European Trust, Clare Hall College Cambridge, the University of Cambridge Faculty of Education, the European Commission for awarding me a postdoctoral Marie Curie Intra-European Fellowship (MEIF-CT-2006-041636), the Commission for Educational Exchange between the United States, Belgium and Luxembourg for awarding me a Fulbright-Schuman Fellowship during which substantial rewriting of the initial text took place, and the University of California, Berkeley's Institute of Governmental Studies and Department of Sociology for sponsoring my research visits.

Thank you to previous publishers of my work. Parts of the analytical and empirical chapters originally appeared in the following Routledge Taylor & Francis journals: *Journal of Youth Studies* (volume 10, issue 2, pp. 161-81), *International Studies in Sociology of Education* (volume 17, issue 1, pp. 45-62), *European Societies* (volume 9, issue 4, pp. 573-99), and the *British Journal of Sociology of Education* (volume 29, issue 1, pp. 37-48). The London School of Economics and Political Science also allowed me to use parts of an article that first appeared in the *British Journal of Sociology* (volume 60, issue 2, pp. 299-320).

Several individuals also deserve special mentioning here. I would like to thank Willow Mata for her thorough editing and comments. At Ashgate, I owe many thanks to Claire Jarvis, Aimée Feenan and Kathryn Ely for all their editorial and marketing advice along the way. I thank my friends for at times serious, at times hilarious, luncheon and dinner conversations, especially during the Cambridge years, including Ong Seng, Weng Hong Teh, Soo Kien Chen, Miki Nishimura, Maiko Yamaji, Janny Leung, Beatrice Lok, Karen Lean, Bill Hollingsworth, Aun Shih Teh, Mun-Kit Choy and Siew-Kiang Ng. I especially thank my very best friend, Kai Sin Tan, for his continuing friendship, cultural and linguistic enrichment, and support – the friendship we have forged will last a lifetime!

Finally, my deepest thanks go to all those whom I interviewed at the four research sites, and to my family and my partner Teresa. I am immensely grateful for the time staff and students spent with me discussing the identity issues I was interested in. I found it inspiring that so many of my participants commented afterwards that this also benefited them by providing the space to reflect on where they felt they belonged and discuss it in groups for the very first time. As for my mum and dad, Adelheid and Oswald, they have made enormous sacrifices to support me and put up with all my absence and travelling. Their investment in my life has enabled me to overcome many hurdles and to be in the position I am today. To Benjamin and Irene, I thank you for always supporting and encouraging me. I dedicate this book to my family as a small token of my gratitude.

Chapter 1

Political Identities in a Multicultural Europe

Processes of European integration, globalization and migration are currently challenging national identities and changing education across Europe.[1] The nation-state no longer serves as the sole locus of civic participation and identity formation, and no longer has the influence it once had over the implementation of policies. Current trends show power moving both to the regional and supranational levels, for example through greater autonomy in how regions organize their school systems, and increasing involvement of European Union (EU) institutions in formerly national educational matters through the promotion of European citizenship and identity. At the same time that government power shifts levels, educational systems and schools face growing pressures to respond to migration and transform nation-centred approaches into more inclusive schooling processes. While the scale of change is clear, it is less clear how the national, European and multicultural agendas are intertwined at EU and national levels, or more importantly, how schools and young people interpret the development of these policy agendas. This book therefore relates a study of how EU and national policies connect to what is happening on the ground in two European countries. I argue that school-level actors mediate multiple levels of government policies, creating distinct educational contexts that shape youth identity negotiation and integration processes in quite different ways. By focusing on identity negotiation among immigrant youth, I provide evidence that expands discussions of youth integration beyond the traditional emphasis on educational outcomes.

In recent decades, EU institutions have become a major supranational player in education (e.g., Council of Ministers of Education 1993, 2007, European Commission 1995, 2002), with school-related issues shifting from a small concern of the EU to a major focus of the organization's activities. Only a few educational issues were mentioned in the 1957 Treaty of Rome, including provisions for vocational training and for the mutual recognition of diplomas and certificates (Phillips 1995). Not until 1971 was education first mentioned as an area of interest to the then European Community, when the European Commission set up two bodies focused on educational issues: a working party on teaching and education, and an interdepartmental working party on coordination (Hansen 1998, Ryba 2000). At this time, the European Ministers of Education stated that the provisions on educational measures in the Treaty of Rome should be complemented by increasing

---

1   There are other factors, such as devolution (e.g., Taylor and Thomson 1999, Wyn Jones 2001, Bond and Rosie 2002) and democratization, which have reshaped national identities but these are not the main focus of this book.

co-operation in education. The Ministers argued that the final goal was 'to define a European model of culture correlating with European integration' (Neave 1984: 6-7), recognizing for the first time the close relation between educational policy and European integration. Then in 1974, the Ministers argued for the need to institute European co-operation in education by emphasizing that the national diversity of education systems should be respected.

The institutionalization of education at the EU level took on ever more tangible forms in the mid-1980s, with programmes such as Erasmus (higher education exchange) and Lingua (language learning exchange). At the same time, EU policy debates saw a new emphasis on issues of identity and citizenship, with the Resolution of the Council and the Ministers of Education on the European Dimension in Education (1988: 5), prompting educators to 'strengthen in young people a sense of European identity and make clear to them the value of European civilization and of the foundations on which the European peoples intended to base their development today'. The Maastricht Treaty further provided the EU with a legal framework to involve itself in all levels of national educational systems (Council of the European Communities 1992). Importantly, EU policy documents have since emphasized that European citizenship should be viewed as supplementing national citizenship and not replacing it (see Council of the European Union 1997, 2007). Taken together, these activities and resolutions show an increasing EU involvement in national education systems, in both tangible and symbolic ways.

Other organizations have also worked to influence and reshape national identities through the promotion of European citizenship and identity, both inside and outside schools. For example, the Council of Europe,[2] a less influential but more diverse supranational organization than the EU, issued Recommendation 1111, which defined Europe 'as extending to the whole of the continent and in no way synonymous with the membership of any particular European organization' (Council of Europe 1989). The document further stressed the importance of encouraging the European dimension in teacher training and teacher exchange; giving more emphasis to the teaching of history, geography, citizenship and modern languages; and encouraging links between European schools through new information technologies (see also Council of Europe 1991). The Council's activities also include the Education for Democratic Citizenship programme, established in 1997 and still ongoing, which seeks to identify the 'values and skills individuals require in order to become participating citizens, how they can acquire these skills and how they can learn to pass them on to others' as well as identifying 'the basic skills required to practise democracy in European societies' (Bîrzéa 2000: 3-4). The EU, for its part, has launched an equally diverse range of

---

2   The EU currently has 27 member states, each of which has had to meet strict political and economic standards in order to gain entry. Membership of the Council of Europe is determined solely on the basis of political concerns, and, as a result, the institution has a larger and more diverse set of 47 members.

educational initiatives including defining eight key competences that education systems should foster, such as language learning and civic knowledge (Council of Ministers of Education 2006).

Despite these unifying calls for European identity and citizenship and a European dimension in education (see also the analyses in Lewicka-Grisdale and McLaughlin 2002, Soysal 2002a, 2002b), all EU countries presently govern education with nearly absolute autonomy, which complicates the development of a common approach to these policy agendas. EU actions therefore serve mainly to complement national level initiatives, for example through the increasingly important Open Method of Coordination (OMC),[3] an intra-European means of governance through which the EU identifies common challenges across the current 27 member states, pinpoints best practices, and encourages countries to review their existing national policies. Researchers debate the extent to which these initiatives penetrate national education systems. Some scholars argue that the promotion of a European dimension in education has helped transform nation-centred schooling approaches and curricula into more inclusive ones (see Schissler and Soysal 2005, Philippou 2007). Others, however, hold that the EU 'still adheres to some of the key components of the nationalist discourse it seeks to evade' (Hansen 1998: 15), pointing to the ways in which EU education policies assume the idea that a common pan-European 'culture' is inherent and inherited, despite the rhetoric of 'unity in diversity' and multiple identities. These debates leave unexamined the ground-level interpretations of EU-level policies by teachers and students in different countries. Given the growing size of the immigrant second generation across Europe, this study of how young people from different backgrounds relate to Europe as a political identity thus contributes important insights about how these macro-level policy debates play out on the ground, across national contexts.

In response to educational initiatives by the Council of Europe and the EU, some researchers have studied youth political identities and conceptualizations of Europe, but these studies have been mostly quantitative and therefore paid less attention to the discourses young people employ when positioning and repositioning themselves in relation to citizenship, Europe and cultural diversity (e.g., Angvik and von Borries 1997, von Borries 1999). For example, a series of six Eurobarometer surveys conducted on request of the European Commission (1982, 1989, 1991, 1997, 2001b, 2007) showed that being able to work, live and study in any of the member states were the three main advantages young people saw in European citizenship. Chisholm, du Bois-Reymond and Coffield (1995) explored the question 'What does Europe mean to me personally' with different groups of university students across Europe and found that some respondents saw a positive balance of perceived advantages (i.e., Europe as a multicultural adventure playground) and

---

3 The OMC rests on soft law mechanisms such as guidelines and indicators, benchmarking and sharing of best practice. This means that there are no official sanctions for laggards. The method's effectiveness relies on a form of peer pressure and naming and shaming, as no member state wants to be seen as the worst in a given policy area.

disadvantages (i.e., Europe as a bureaucratic and self-centred monster), and that national identities and nationalism generally were seen as dangerously suspect phenomena. In a more recent study, Grundy and Jamieson (2007: 663) surveyed the European identities of young adults aged 18-24 in Edinburgh and found that 'for many being European remains emotionally insignificant and devoid of imagined community or steps towards global citizenship'. Instead, most had strong Scottish identities and some had strong British identities. Moreover, the EU-funded project 'Orientations of Young Men and Women to Citizenship and European Identity' highlighted that both national location and schooling played an important role in shaping young people's responses to Europe. The study also found that European identity was most marked amongst German and Czech youth, and lowest in Spain and England (see Ros and Grad 2004, Fuss and Boehnke 2004). The findings of these studies raise important questions about the complexity of factors affecting identification with Europe and youth identity negotiations more broadly, questions addressed by this book.

Examinations of civic participation in the 1990s further investigate the level of active citizenship and political identities among multiethnic youth in Europe (e.g., Spannring, Wallace and Haerpfer 2001, Ogris and Westphal 2005).[4] Spannring, Wallace and Haerpfer (2001: 36) grouped participating countries into six geo-political regions and argued that there has been 'a general rise in civic participation' over the 1990s but also that 'the most astonishing growth in civic participation among young people is in the South-West [i.e., Spain] where it has increased from 9% to 35%'. This, they argue, shows a convergence in Western Europe in terms of civic participation and integration, while also demonstrating an increasing divergence between young people in these countries and those in the former Soviet Union and Balkan Peninsula, where civic participation has declined or only modestly increased in the same time period.

In addition to changes due to European citizenship and identity, national identities have also been challenged by the migration of people into and across Europe since World War II. According to Stalker (2002), there have been four main post-war phases of migration: refugees who were forced to resettle as a result of border changes (especially between Germany, Poland and former Czechoslovakia); economic migration from colonial countries to the 'motherland' (e.g., England) or under labour contracts (e.g., Germany); migration of family members after the 1973 oil crisis and recession; and asylum seekers and undocumented immigrants (see also Düvell 2009). Arguably, a fifth phase could be added here to account for

---

4   Ogris and Westphal (2005) conducted a European survey in eight countries (Austria, Estonia, Finland, France, Germany, Italy, Slovakia, Britain) and found that the 'majority is not very interested in politics, but there is hope that interest increases with age'. They also found 'evidence that identity is related to voting participation on the EU level: feeling as young European to a certain extent also means feeling obliged to vote at European elections'.

the intra-European flow of migrants from East to West following EU enlargements in 2004 and 2007.[5]

These migration flows have been shaped and controlled by national and European policies, with an increasing emphasis on EU-level involvement. For example, the 1999 Tampere European Council established the need for a common European policy on asylum and immigration (Council of the European Union, 1999). Ten years later, the European Pact on Immigration and Asylum (Council of the European Union 2008) outlined for the first time five basic supranational commitments: organize legal immigration to take account of the needs and priorities of member states; curb illegal immigration; establish more effective border controls; implement a European asylum policy; and create a partnership with the countries of origin to encourage synergy between migration and development.

While EU-level involvement in migration policies has been growing, national policies have been changing as well. National policies were relatively liberal during the 1950s and 1960s and have become more restrictive since the 1970s. Some countries (e.g., Britain, France, the Netherlands) accepted immigration from former colonies whereas others (e.g., Germany, Denmark, Switzerland) were without a colonial reservoir and recruited contract workers, so-called 'guest' or 'migrant' workers,[6] mostly from south and southeast Europe. In this book I dedicate two chapters to a discussion of the national policies of Germany (Chapter 2) and England (Chapter 5) to contextualize not only the school responses to diversity (and Europe) but also young people's political identities. These two countries are very interesting to look at because both are long-term immigration hosts, but have had different responses to diversity. Germany has traditionally adopted a more monocultural approach based on an ethno-cultural conception of citizenship while England has favoured multiculturalism (see Faist 2007, Modood 2007). The two EU member states also differ in that Germany has been at the forefront of the EU political integration project whereas England has viewed Europe in more economic terms. These legacies are likely to have different impacts on contemporary youth in schools, and how they see their identity in relation to their nation and Europe.

Taken together, these trends toward increasing migration and differing responses to diversity in schools point to an ethnic dimension at play across member states and education systems. The EU and the Council of Europe have responded to these changes with calls for multicultural (intercultural) educational initiatives (more on this below). At the same time, European political agendas

---

5   Ireland for instance has since tightened its citizenship legislation, adding ius sanguinis to the ius soli principle and only granting citizenship after five years of residence. The Department of Enterprise, Trade and Employment has revised eligibility requirements for new work permits for those entering the Irish labour market for the first-time from 1 June 2009. It is too early to comment on the implications of this for legal, let alone undocumented, migrants.

6   In the remainder of this book, I call this population 'migrant workers' because of their economic reasons for migration.

have polarized in ways that increasingly influence educational institutions. Indeed, many argue that processes of European integration and the legal and illegal migration of people into Europe have led to a rise of far-right parties in many European countries since the 1990s (e.g., Roxburgh 2002, Cheles, Ferguson and Vaughan 1995). For example, in the Dutch 2002 general elections, Pim Fortuyn's List came second on a campaign for border closure, obligatory integration, and measures against Muslim extremists. The Netherlands' restrictive asylum laws also led to a decrease in the number of applications from 43,000 in 2000 to 13,400 in 2003 (Duval Smith 2005). And the racist killing of the filmmaker Theo Van Gogh in 2004 has not only led to attacks on mosques, religious schools and churches, but also shows the contradictions in Holland's liberal society between legalizing euthanasia and the selling of cannabis, on the one hand, and applying restrictive and exclusionary asylum and immigration laws, on the other. Since 2005, Finland, Sweden, Denmark, the Netherlands, Belgium, Poland, Austria and France have also experienced a right-wing swing in their national governments, often on anti-immigration, anti-Muslim platform (see Koopmans et al. 2005).

These political developments have led to a new debate about multiculturalism in Europe and new research on attitudes towards migrants. In 2005, the European Monitoring Centre on Racism and Xenophobia (EUMC)[7] found that 60 per cent of respondents in the EU-15 felt multiculturalism had certain limits as to how many people of other races, religions or cultures a society could accept, compared with 42 per cent in the ten new member states.[8] There is considerable intra-European diversity on the issue, however, with Greeks, Germans, Irish and British most strongly supporting the view that there are limits to a multicultural society while the Spanish, Italians, Swedes, Finns and most of the new Eastern European member states being less critical. The report also showed that support for different forms of immigrant exclusion (i.e., resistance to multicultural society, opposition to civil rights for legal migrants, or support for repatriation policies) was more prevalent amongst older people with lower education levels. In other words, economic prosperity appeared to lessen the perceived threat posed by migrants, and young people exhibited less support for ethnic exclusion than older people. This supports Chisholm's (1997: 5) view that 'reservations in the presence of "foreigners" are at a low level' amongst young Europeans.

The increasing migration-related diversity in Europe has also been associated with increasing pressure on countries to transform their nation-centred and often Eurocentric curricula into more inclusive learning approaches (see Coulby and Jones 1995, Coulby 2000). Much of this pressure has come in the form of EU and

---

7   The EUMC was renamed European Union Agency for Fundamental Rights in 2007.

8   The EU-15 consisted of Austria, Belgium, Denmark, Finland, France, Germany, Greece, Ireland, Italy, Luxembourg, the Netherlands, Portugal, Spain, Sweden and the United Kingdom. On 1 May 2004, ten Eastern European countries joined the then EU-15 and, three years later, Romania and Bulgaria also joined to make it the EU-27.

Council of Europe (2002, 2003, 2005, 2007) guidelines. For example, in 2002, the Council of Europe launched a project called 'The New Challenge of Intercultural Education', which aimed to increase awareness of the necessity of including interfaith dialogue as an element of intercultural education, and focused on analysis of religion as a 'cultural phenomenon' (Council of Europe 2002). This was further highlighted in a project called 'Policies and Practices for Teaching Socio-Cultural Diversity' (Council of Europe 2005) whose main objective was to propose the introduction of common European principles for managing diversity at school. The Council highlighted that this should include the teaching of diversity through curricula, teacher training, and training for diversity in rural and urban areas. In 2007, ministers asked for the development of measures for inclusive education, particularly for the socio-culturally excluded; and called for the development of key skills for social cohesion including interculturalism, multilingualism and citizenship (Council of Europe 2007). Similarly, the EU has responded to the educational challenges arising from migration-related diversity by making 2008 the Year of Intercultural Dialogue (European Parliament and Council of the European Union 2006: 46) and adopting the Green Paper 'Migration and Mobility: challenges and opportunities for EU education systems' (European Commission 2008). The document lists earlier findings from international student assessment tests which show that migrants have lower educational achievement than their peers and that, in some countries, second-generation students have lower grades than first-generation students.[9] This clearly highlights the importance of schooling for migrant integration and educational achievement. The document also stressed learning of the host language as a way of creating social cohesion together with promotion of the heritage language as a way of respecting diversity. Such focus on early language learning contrasts with countries like the United States.

European initiatives for political integration and migration not only received different national policy responses across member states but have also been interpreted differently at the level of schools and youth. This suggests that youth identities are likely to vary within EU member countries, especially among migrants. As a result, a complex story of young people's political identities unfolds – a story that departs from more traditional two-way comparisons of either national versus European (e.g., Ryba 2000, Hinderliter Ortloff 2005) or national versus multicultural agendas (e.g., Wilhelm 1998, Graves 2002). This book delves into this story, exploring questions of what drives identity formation among ethnic majority and minority youth on the ground; how governments and schools respond to the challenges posed by globalization, European integration and migration; and what this means for the development of inclusive political and educational frameworks. Previous studies have tended to have a narrow emphasis on either white and ethnic

---

9   The tests the document draws on are the Programme for International Student Assessment (PISA), a triennial global test of 15-year-old's scholastic performance and the Progress in International Reading Literacy Study (PIRLS), a survey on literacy amongst fourth graders in primary school.

minority identities (e.g., Mac an Ghaill 1988, Dyer 1997, Sewell 1997, Waters 1999, Youdell 2003, Byrne 2006) or citizenship identities (e.g., Barrett 1996, Cinnirella 1997, Osler and Starkey 2001, Hussain and Bagguley 2005).[10] In contrast, this study adopts a more comprehensive approach to the study of youth identities, drawing on the insights of post-structuralist theories of identity.

Theorizing Political Identities

Scholars have conceptualized identity in various ways, including social psychological approaches that mainly draw on Tajfel's (1974) social identity theory; Turner's (1987) self-categorization theory; Moscovici's (1981, 1984) concept of social representation and acculturation models (e.g., Berry 1997, Cinnirella 1997, Barrett 2007, Nigbur et al. 2008); and post-structuralist approaches (e.g., Brah 1996, Nayak 1999, Rassool 1999). Social psychologists tend to assume that the nature of the person who is interacting with the world is 'a complete whole', a non-fragmented self, whereas post-structuralists see the subject as discursively constructed by the social context, such as government policies and school approaches. The work of Caglar (1997), Mac an Ghaill (1999), Tizard and Phoenix (2002), Dolby (2000, 2001) and Hall (1996), among others, is particularly important for the present study as as it shows that 'identity' is not a product, but a complex and multifaceted process of negotiation. Foucault (1980, 1988) and Derrida (1981) believe that there is no individual 'I' that interacts with the social context but that the only way an 'I' comes to exist is through the productive power of discourse. Post-structuralist approaches allow for multiple categories of identity and, most importantly, these do not have to be reconciled. A post-structuralist framework also challenges the idea of a single monolithic truth and identity (as opposed to the Enlightenment and modernity) and regards all absolutes as constructions.

Drawing on post-structuralist notions of multiple, fragmented and discursively produced identities, Hall (1992b: 275) argued that the 'post-modern subject' is conceptualized as 'having no fixed, essential or permanent identity, [and] is historically, not biologically, defined'. Brah (1996: 124) added that identity may be understood as 'that very process by which multiplicity, contradiction, and instability of subjectivity is signified as having coherence, continuity, stability; as having a core – continually changing core but the sense of a core nonetheless – that at any given moment is enunciated as the "I"'. Brah's conceptualization of identity leaves open the possibility for individuals to feel strongly about their identities, to construct subjects that can be 'spoken'. Hall (1996: 5) goes further to maintain that identity production also involves processes 'which attempt to "interpellate",

---

10   The only exception to this is perhaps Raymond and Modood's (2007) edited volume which compares and contrasts how ethnic (racial and religious) and political identities have become increasingly intertwined in the twenty-first century in Britain and France, notably following the 2005 communal violence in Birmingham and Parisian suburbs.

speak to us or hail us into place as the social subjects of particular discourses'. Hall (1996), among others, has also suggested that within a post-structuralist framework, identities can be understood as 'performed'. In this way, identities carry a sense of 'performativity' (see also the discussions in Butler 1997). The notion of performativity, relating to young people's negotiations of their identities, was important for the design of the study because performativity suggests that identities are a continual establishment and articulation of binaries. The linking of techniques of the self (Foucault 1988) and performance opens up an exploration of the ways in which the social context, such as schools and government policies, mediates how individuals deal with the lived realities of specific institutional locations (see Mac an Ghaill 1999, Papoulia-Tzelpi, Hegstrup and Ross 2005, Fülöp and Ross 2005).

The power of a post-structuralist framework for the study of young people's identities in schools is highlighted, among others, by Youdell (2003), Nayak (1999), and Haywood and Mac an Ghaill (1997). Youdell (2003: 3) demonstrates 'how the privilege associated with African-Caribbean identities within student subcultures is recouped and deployed within organizational discourse as "evidence" of these students' undesirable, or even intolerable, identities as learners'. She argues that the discursive practices of students and teachers contribute to the performative constitution of intelligible selves and others. Using a similar approach, Nayak's (1999) ethnographic case study in Newcastle-upon-Tyne argues that many white students perceive anti-racism as an anti-white practice; that the identities of the white majority need to be deconstructed with as much vigour as that of minority groups to avoid any future 'white backlash'; and that local history helps students better to understand what it means to be white in Newcastle. The advantages of a post-structuralist methodology for the study of young people's identities are also discussed by Haywood and Mac an Ghaill (1997) who distinguished between the philosophical positions of materialism and deconstructivism. The authors argue that in order to generate more comprehensive accounts of educational identities, critical analysis needs to engage with both philosophical approaches. For Haywood and Mac an Ghaill (1997: 267-68), deconstructionist approaches involve fluid and fragmented formations of identities:

> One of the shifts from a materialist to a deconstructivist position in examining the formation of educational identities has been to focus on the constitutive dynamics of subjectivity. (...) At a social level, this [deconstructionist] perspective suggests that having a singular "identity" is inadequate, because social situations produce varied subjective positions that may be occupied. (...) In this way, subjectivity is conceptualized as a process of *becoming*, characterized by fluidity, oppositions and alliances between particular narrative positions.

While materialist accounts of identity formation have positioned females, gays and black people as subordinated, deconstructivist strategies favour a discursive identity formation enabling, for instance, gay and lesbian students to occupy positions of power which allow the inversion and contestation of heterosexual power (Mac an Ghaill 1994). In other words, post-structuralist notions of deconstruction challenge the views of Enlightenment and modernity as well as the paradigm of acculturation studies that cultures and identities are fixed, static and of a binary nature (e.g., white/black, men/women) (Berry and Sam 1997), and instead perceive individuals as able to negotiate and renegotiate their identities discursively (see MacLure 2003). This study deconstructs the discourses of ethnic majority and Turkish minority youth and demonstrates how these socio-ethnically different groups of students – both of whom occupy positions of power at various times depending on the school context – negotiate their identities. However, other scholars have criticized deconstructionist accounts of identity formation 'for assuming that identities are available to everyone, with the opportunity to take up, reposition themselves and become powerful' (Haywood and Mac an Ghaill 1997: 269). A constant theme across materialist and deconstructionist identity epistemologies is the idea that educational institutions impact identity formation, a notion taken up by the present study. Indeed, as this book demonstrates, not only schools but also a range of other factors such as government policies, socio-economic background and immigrant status affect the formation of youth political identities.

The concept of 'identity/identities', meaning the communities young people feel they belong to, differs from the concept of 'identification' which refers to the reasons and discourses students employ to identify with a particular community such as Britain or Europe (Skeggs 1997). It is further important for the purposes of this study to distinguish between hybrid (e.g., Hall 1992, Tizard and Phoenix 2002) and hyphenated identities (e.g., Caglar 1997). Bhabha (1990: 189) maintained that, rather than being about the fusion of different identities, hybridity sets out to signify 'the third space which enables other positions to emerge. This third space displaces the histories that constitute it [and] gives rise to something different, something new and unrecognizable, a new area of negotiation of meaning and representation'. Similarly, Hall's (1992a) pluralization of the concept of ethnicity with his 'new ethnicities' stimulated possibilities for the loosening and destabilizing of ethnicity so that it could be investigated as something capable of temporal and spatial change and emphasizing its performativity and not its ascription. In other words, Hall (1992a: 252-53) observed a shift in black cultural politics from 'the language of binary oppositions [e.g., black/white] in which blacks were positioned as the unspoken and invisible 'other'' to a politics of representation which recognizes 'that "black" is essentially a politically and culturally *constructed* category' and that not all black people are the same. Linked with the new politics of representation is the pluralization of the concept of ethnicity (i.e., new ethnicities/new ethnic hybrid identities). For Hall, Europeanization and globalization play a central role because they have a pluralizing impact on identities, producing a variety of possibilities and new positions of identification, and making identities more positional, more political and diverse.

In contrast to hybridity, the idea of hyphenated identities, as understood by Caglar (1997), relates more to territorial or political identities, such as African-American, rather than the emergence of a new identity. Hyphenation implies that an individual continuously mediates between two disparate cultures and territories. Contrary to the binary oppositions that characterized modernization theory (e.g., white/black), 'no single mode has a necessary overall priority' in theories of hybridization and hyphenization (Pieterse 1995: 51). Instead, relations between cultures are conceptualized as flows that not only widen the field of identities but endow identities with a degree of fluidity. For example, both ethnic majority and minority youth in this study produced multi-layered identities that are constantly renegotiated and thus in a state of flux. 'Although hybridity [or hyphenization] ascribes cultures and identities with "fluidity", they remain anchored in territorial ideas, whether national or transnational' (Caglar 1997: 173). Also, Caglar (1997) observed that there is an assumption that hyphenated identities, such as German-Turks or British-Pakistanis, are potentially conflictual and problematic; that dual cultural 'membership' is a source of dual 'loyalties'. Implicitly, then, according to Caglar, culture posits a commitment and a loyalty to a 'people' and 'territory'. Such loyalties, the author argued, are incapable of true hybridization.

In order to explore how contemporary youth respond to national, European and multicultural political agendas, I draw on these post-structuralist notions of a fragmented society in which identities are hybrid and shifting. I contend that at a time of increasing globalization and migration-related diversity, it is useful to consider the post-modern subject as having fluid and situated identities.[11] Arguably, the fact that many young people in my study constructed their identities along ethnic and political dimensions, rather than mediating between two territories, suggests that the notion of hybrid identities is perhaps more accurate when analysing contemporary identities. Consequently, I avoided hyphenating by identifying for instance a 'Turkish-German' identity (which would refer to the territories of Turkey and Germany). Instead, I draw on the multiple ethnic, political and other categories elicited by the subjects themselves to allow for the emergence of new identities. As this book will show, young people (re)negotiate their identities within the world in relation to discourses available to them, rather than being born into a static identity tied with a particular territory.

Needless to say, for some readers, the distinction between hybridity and hyphenation and post-structuralist understandings of hybridity may sound all too simplistic.[12] Indeed, several theorists who acknowledge the fluid and multidimensional nature of identities have challenged notions of hybridity in

---

11   See Wetherell (1998) for a similar argument.

12   For example, Feminists and Marxists (e.g., Sarup 1993) have argued that post-structuralist intellectuals focus only on the heterogeneous, the diverse, the subjective, the relative and the fragmentary insisting that any general theory should be renounced and that life cannot be grasped from a single perspective. Such ambiguity, fragmentation and subjectivity can of course pose difficulties for practitioners and policy-makers.

identity formation processes. Modood (2000: 177), for instance, argues how cultural essentialism continues to underlie even some of the attempts to oppose it. Arguably, in terms of hybridity, cultures are still 'anchored in territorial ideas', whereby cultural essentialism is implicitly reinforced by being the norm to which hybridity is the exception. Modood thus maintains that hybridity offers only an illusory escape from essentialist modes of identity construction. Yuval-Davis (1997: 202) also warns of the possible danger of notions of hybridity and ambivalence to 'interpolate essentialism through the back door'. She argues that the supposed homogenous collectivities from which hybrid identities emerge invoke 'the mythical image of society as a "mixed salad"'. Before I move on to share a few methodological considerations underpinning the design of this study, I briefly introduce some of the analytical concepts and dimensions.

A Note on Europe, Multiculturalism and Citizenship

Politicians, academics and the media in countries in the EU and beyond debate the meaning of Europe (e.g., Neave 1984, Wallace 1990, Shennan 1991, Kuus 2004, Spohn and Triandafyllidou 2003). Many assume there is an absolute truth to be found, a definitive answer to the question 'What is Europe', but disagree on which criteria or historical evidence could or should be used to define Europe. Some researchers survey national discourses to show that Europe is a concept that has many facets and acquires new meanings in different countries (e.g., Malmborg and Stråth 2001). Others adopt a more historical approach and often conflate the term Europe with that of the EU (Dinan 2004). Still others concentrate purely on the EU itself, and discuss the system of EU governance, the political will of member states to adopt one or another type of governance, and the decision-making dynamics and challenges that lie ahead in terms of widening and deepening the European project (e.g., Tsoukalis 2003). One issue that has been especially controversial for this debate is the question of Europe's eastern boundaries, and the extent to which Russia and Turkey can be considered part of Europe. The question of Turkey's accession into the EU has given rise to fervent debates about the Christian roots of Europe, the compatibility of a predominantly Muslim country with the EU, and the eastern borders of Europe. As this study shows, Turkey's role in the debates over how to define Europe is particularly important for the negotiation of political identities among Turkish youth in Germany and England.

While disagreement on how to define Europe abounds among scholars and policy-makers, the experience of people in different countries demonstrates that there can be no single definition of Europe. Europe has assumed diverse meanings in history, and at the same time, Europe may have multiple meanings at any given moment depending on the perspective we adopt. Not only has the definition of Europe varied through the past centuries and even decades, but its content and meaning also varies in relation to the different realms of social life. There is a cultural Europe or a European civilization (e.g., Catholic South, Protestant North and Orthodox East), a political Europe, a social Europe, a historical Europe, and a territorial Europe. From a conceptual viewpoint, it is not possible to define a single Europe, drawing together all these meanings and perspectives into a single container. This is underlined, for instance, by Delanty and Rumford (2005) and Delanty (2005) who argue that 'being European' cannot be defined through distinctive European values, a European history, or a European polity. Instead, they put forth a cosmopolitan vision, maintaining that Europe is a multi-level polity with a plurality of centres and overlapping networks.[13] For the purposes of this book, the most important dimensions of this debate are the extent to which Europe is defined in inclusive (e.g., multicultural, multi-religious) or exclusive (e.g., Eurocentric) terms, and the implications these conceptualizations have for the identity formation of young people, particularly Turks, in different schools in Europe.

The concept of the European dimension in education is similarly contested. Researchers have taken up a broad sweep of projects, including describing and analysing EU and Council of Europe policy documents and directives concerning education in general and the European dimension in particular (e.g., Ryba 1992, 1995, 2000, Keating 2009); writing comparative accounts of European educational systems (e.g., Husén, Tuijnman and Halls 1992, Tulasiewicz and Brock 2000); and studying the meaning of European citizenship in education across various countries, subjects and sectors (e.g., Bell 1995, Davies and Sobisch 1997). In addition, Karlsen (2002) argued that the active use of symbols underlined the unity of the EU member states. Symbols such as the European flag (a circle of twelve golden stars on a blue background), Europe day (9 May), the common currency (euro), the European anthem (based on the 'Ode to Joy' from the Ninth Symphony by Ludwig van Beethoven), and a common motto (United in diversity) might help promote a sense of European identity and citizenship in young people. However, these potentially uniting elements have not yet found their way into many schools in Europe and are not part of European educational issues.

Another contested concept central to this book is multiculturalism, and the question of how it contrasts with interculturalism. Proponents of interculturalism emphasize communication, interaction and dialogue while those who favour multiculturalism argue that reciprocity, dialogue and civic integration are also central to most, if not all, contemporary accounts of multiculturalism. According to the United Nations Educational, Scientific and Cultural Organization (UNESCO 2006: 17-18):

> the term multicultural[ism] describes the culturally diverse nature of human society. It not only refers to elements of ethnic or national culture, but also includes linguistic, religious and socio-economic diversity. Intercultural[ism] is a dynamic concept and refers to evolving relations between cultural groups. It

---

13   A study by Pichler (2009: 13) provides evidence for this idea, finding that cosmopolitans identify more strongly with Europe and see more reasons for being European than non-cosmopolitan people that are more closely tied with (sub)national communities.

has been defined as the existence and equitable interaction of diverse cultures and the possibility of generating shared cultural expressions through dialogue and mutual respect. (...) Multicultural education uses learning about other cultures in order to produce acceptance, or at least *tolerance*, of these cultures. Intercultural education aims to go beyond passive coexistence, to achieve a developing and sustainable way of living together in multicultural societies through the creation of *understanding* of, *respect* for and *dialogue* between the different cultural groups.

European societies rely on different models to address cultural and religious diversity in education, with different potential consequences for the experiences youth have in schools. For example, Germany, Greece and Ireland prefer the term interculturalism and intercultural education. In contrast, Britain, the Netherlands, Canada, the United States and Malaysia, have historically worked with the concept of multiculturalism (see Nieto and Bode 2007). My view is that multiculturalism can be reconceptualized so that it addresses interaction and integration and thus redefines interculturalism as a form of inclusive or integrative multiculturalism.[14] I return to this point later.

According to Banks (1997), multiculturalism is a concept, an educational reform movement, and a process. For Banks, the intention of multicultural education is to create an environment offering equal education opportunities to students from different racial, ethnic and socio-economic backgrounds, thus preserving and promoting diversity while supporting students in becoming critical thinkers and responsible democratic citizens. To carry out these goals through multicultural education, Banks identified five crucial dimensions: content integration, knowledge construction, prejudice reduction, equity pedagogy, and an empowering school culture (see Banks 2004 for more about each dimension). These five components have a strong impact on the educational achievement of all students, not only ethnic minorities, and also improve intergroup relations among students and staff (Zirkel 2008).

At a time when many see a crisis for the concept of multiculturalism and its potential for integrating ethnic minorities (see the analyses in Modood, Triandafyllidou and Zapata-Barrero 2005), governments are increasingly emphasizing social cohesion and return to either an assimilationist approach which emphasizes national culture and values, or an integrationist approach which recognizes cultural diversity but often leans toward assimilation (see also Vertovec 1999, Olsen 1997). The Netherlands, for example, has been a forerunner in multiculturalism since the 1980s, but has shifted recently toward a more integrationist approach with the introduction of integration courses for newcomers

---

14   There are others (e.g., Lentin 2001, Malik 1998) who critique both multiculturalist and interculturalist politics as top-down policies. The ideology of multiculturalism, they argue, was developed not as eradication but rather as an accommodation of the persistence of inequalities despite the rhetoric of integration, assimilation and equality.

and a civics test to be undertaken by prospective migrants before departure from their country of origin (see Ter Wal 2007, Vasta 2007).[15] On the other hand, in the face of mounting civil unrest and social exclusion of second-generation immigrant youth, the French government reasserted its civic Republican integration model banning religious symbols from schools (see Kastoryano 2006, Guiraudon 2006).

In the debate over multicultural education and integration models, Germany and England pose uniquely interesting cases. Politicians in Germany recently officially acknowledged that it is now an immigration country and a multicultural society, but the restrictive implementation of the liberal citizenship law of 2000 has led to a decrease in naturalizations (see Schiffauer 2006, Green 2005). In contrast, Britain seems to be the only European country that has not abandoned multiculturalism as a public policy tool, although the Blair and Brown governments introduced a civic integration test and ceremonies in an attempt to revive community cohesion based on an inclusive understanding of Britishness. Meer and Modood (2009) term this a 'civic re-balancing' of British multiculturalism rather than a wholesale 'retreat' (Joppke 2004), or 'backlash' (Vertovec and Wessendorf 2010).

The idea of interculturalism, as distinct from multiculturalism, has hitherto more commonly been found in Dutch and German accounts of integration, particularly in the field of education (Gundara 2000). The British diversity debate has largely excluded any discussion of interculturalism (Gundara and Jacobs 2000).[16] According to Wood, Landry and Bloomfield (2006: 9) 'communication' is the defining characteristic of interculturalism. They argue that communication is the central means through which 'an intercultural approach aims to facilitate dialogue, exchange, and reciprocal understanding between people of different backgrounds'. Given the diversity of migrant countries of origin, the result is not communities but rather a churning mass of languages, ethnicities, and religions all cutting across each other and creating what Vertovec (2007) has called a 'super-diversity'. It is often argued that multiculturalism places too much emphasis on difference and diversity, on what divides us more than what bonds societies together (Goodhart 2004). This then leads to fragmentation and disunity which can be overcome through emphasizing inclusion and cohesion. This study demonstrates how schools differently interpret and work with the concept of multiculturalism (and interculturalism) and the repercussions this has for the identity formation of young people.

There are those who view multicultural education as a response to the diversity and fragmentation of European societies (e.g., Modood 1997), and others who

---

15   This 'retreat' from multiculturalism, as Joppke (2004) calls it, follows increasing tensions between national majorities and marginalized Muslim communities in Europe. Such conflicts have included the violence in northern England (2001), the civil unrest in France (2005) and the Danish cartoon crisis (2005).

16   In the late 1990s, a group of theorists around Kincheloe and Steinberg (1997) and May (1999) argued for a critical stance on multiculturalism. It could be argued that interculturalism needs a similarly critical perspective.

describe it as 'a critique of the Eurocentric and in that sense monocultural content and ethos of much of the prevailing system of education' (Parekh 2000: 225). The general ethos pervading the educational system, Parekh contends, highlights the glory and uniqueness of European civilization and underplays or ignores the achievements and contributions of others. A multicultural curriculum needs to satisfy two conditions, Parekh (2000) argues. Firstly, it should not be unduly narrow. Ideally, it should familiarize students with the major representative forms of the subject in question, concentrate on some of them, and so stimulate them that they follow up the rest on their own. Secondly, the way a curriculum is being taught is critical. The author suggests that it is not enough to include different religions, cultures and texts in the curriculum since these elements need to be brought into a dialogue. Multicultural education, Parekh concludes, neither undermines common culture and social unity, nor distorts history. Instead, it is committed to the basic values of liberal society, broadens them to include others, and helps create a plural and richer common culture. Moreover, it fosters social cohesion by enabling students to accept, enjoy and cope with diversity. I will return to this notion of balancing social cohesion and migration-related diversity later in the book.

The final concept informing this study is citizenship, which is also linked with notions of nationality and national identity (Pfetsch 1998). Citizenship is a concept that not only links the nation-state with belonging to Europe but is also important for migrants in the sense that it can be used as a political and educational tool for bonding together ethnic majority and migrant minority communities. Such an integrative or inclusive view of citizenship can be developed at local, national or supranational level. I return to this discussion later in the book. The difference between nationality and citizenship, according to McCrone and Kiely (2000: 25), is that 'the former is in essence a cultural concept which binds people on the basis of shared identity (…) while citizenship is a political concept deriving from people's relationship to the state'. Scholars dispute the relationship between citizenship and identity, with some claiming that citizenship involves a sense of group membership and 'imagined community', while others claim awareness of being a citizen is often no more self-defining than membership of other abstract bureaucratic categories (Jamieson 2002). Definitions of national identity and citizenship often overlap in these debates (see Werbner and Yuval Davis 1999).

Citizenship status continues to be largely granted by nation-states, with many academic commentators seeing European political identities as complementary to, or interacting with, national identities (e.g., Castano 2004, Citrin and Sides 2004, Risse 2004). Yet, according to Faist (2007), there has been a gradual shift from exclusive allegiance across most of the twentieth century to multiple allegiances of citizens at the beginning of the new millennium. Today, more than half of all states tolerate some form of dual citizenship. This shift is inextricably linked with processes of globalization, European integration, democratization, devolution[17]

---

17 Devolution describes the pooling of powers from central government to government at regional or local level. It differs from federalism in that the powers devolved

and migration (Beck 2000). Guibernau (2007: 50) observes that 'devolution has strengthened regional identity in Spain, Britain and Canada and, in all three cases, it has promoted the emergence or consolidation of dual identities – regional and national'. The governments of many emigration countries have also encouraged multiple citizenship as a means of maintaining contacts and transnational economic and political links with their diasporas abroad.

In contrast with national citizenship, post-nationalism links citizenship with rights and democratic norms beyond the nation-state, including European and global – or cosmopolitan – citizenship (e.g., Delanty 2000, Kastoryano 2002, Parekh 2008).[18] Transnationalism on the other hand refers to the cross-border lifestyles of citizens and the attempts by national governments to regulate these social formations (e.g., Bauböck 1994, Çaglar 2007, Smith 2007, Wessendorf 2007). Both schools of thought are relevant for understanding the discussions in this book because young people identify with political entities other than the nation-state and, in the case of migrant youth in particular, also develop transnational ties as a result of increased mobility between countries. Habermas (1994), a proponent of post-nationalism, argues for a citizenship model based on residence, a strong public sphere, and constitutional principles. Identity and affiliation, he maintains, are to have the constitution as their reference point (*Verfassungspatriotismus*) rather than the nation, culture or territory. Consequently, Habermas has also argued strongly in favour of a European Constitution. He imagines that when citizens are united by their common affiliation to constitutional principles and are members of a shared political community, citizenship becomes decoupled from national or socio-cultural practices. This conceptualization would allow for social multiculturalism as immigrants and others are not required to surrender their cultural traditions in order to be part of the community (Habermas 1992). Using a similar post-national approach, Benhabib (2005) argues that national identities are undermined by Europeanization, globalization and migration. She divides citizenship into three components: the 'collective identity' of those who are designated as citizens along the lines of shared language, religion, ethnicity, common history and memories; the privileges of 'political membership', in the sense of access to the rights of public autonomy; and the 'entitlement to social rights and benefits'. According to Benhabib, it is no longer nationality or origin but EU citizenship which entitles people to these rights. This gives rise to sub-national as well as supranational modes of identities, and this study demonstrates how ethnic majority and minority youth in Europe relate to these citizenship categories.

---

are temporary and ultimately reside in central government. In the United Kingdom, for instance, devolved government was created in 1998 in the Scottish Parliament, the Welsh Assembly and the Northern Ireland Assembly. Quebec and Catalonia are further examples of devolved regions.

18   Key authors in the post-national citizenship tradition include Habermas (1994, 2003), Benhabib (2004, 2005), Delanty and Rumford (2005) and Soysal (1994).

Research Design and Methodology

In recent decades, three major approaches have emerged within comparative research in education. Firstly, the detailed documentation approach which, at an early stage of the development of comparative education, established a respect for careful description of the different ways individual systems have for providing for the organization and delivery of education (Crossley and Broadfoot 1992). Secondly, a positivist approach driven by the desire to apply the scientific method in the search for generalizability (e.g., Holmes 1981). And thirdly, a more holistic approach arguing that 'the forces and factors outside the school matter even more than what goes on inside it' and that 'hence the comparative study of education must be founded on an analysis of the social and political ideas which the school reflects (...)' (Kandel 1933: 19). I drew on this latter holistic approach when designing this study.

The goal of comparative education, according to Broadfoot (1999: 26), is to:

> build on systematic studies of common educational issues, needs or practices as these are realized in diverse cultural settings in order to enhance awareness of possibilities (...) and contribute to the development of a comprehensive socio-cultural perspective. (...) The adoption of a comparative perspective establishes the socio-cultural organizational setting of the education system as the starting point to explore the way in which different approaches to the formal organization of education impact on the development of individual identity and learning.

For a study to be genuinely comparative and cross-national, according to Hantrais and Mangen (1996), researchers should set out to study particular issues or phenomena in two or more countries. In addition, researchers should compare the phenomena in different socio-cultural settings, using the same research methods. The authors argue that comparative studies can result in fresh insights and a deeper understanding of issues that are of central concern in different countries. Comparative studies may also point to possible directions for policy and change.

However, there are several methodological issues to consider while conducting exploratory cross-national comparative case studies, including that of *equivalence*, or how to study the same issue in different cultures and societies. Pepin (2005) defines conceptual equivalence as referring to the question of whether or not the concepts under study have equivalent, or any, meaning in the cultures which are being considered. This meant that to compare the different meanings of citizenship, Europe and multiculturalism (interculturalism) in the countries under study and look for commonalities and differences, I took measures to ensure that respondents understood exactly what was being examined and asked of them. To this end, I will relate the rather general discussions on Europe, multiculturalism and citizenship in this chapter to the specific German and English contexts in Chapters 2 and 5, thereby showing readers the ways in which I was attentive to local understandings of these broader concepts. Another problem identified by Pepin is that of linguistic equivalence and the issue of translation in particular. In this study, I had to be careful when translating interview schedules and questionnaires so that words and concepts did not change their meaning. I also had to be careful when comparing secondary sources such as official statistics. For example, data on the composition of the population of England and Germany are reported differently in the two countries: in England, a question on ethnicity has been part of the Census since 1991 and ethnic minority people are classified according to their ethnic origin despite holding a British passport; in contrast, in Germany, ethnic minority communities no longer appear in the statistics as Turkish Muslims, Italians and so forth once they are granted German citizenship.

Pepin (2005) also argues that adopting qualitative methodological approaches that compare like with like is not enough to achieve equivalence. Instead, Pepin points towards the importance of studying anomalies, or cases that do not compare with others. The study of anomalies is necessary 'in order to define the boundaries of our developing theories and thus help to deepen our understanding' (Pepin 2005: 48). For Pepin (2005), it is further important to explain what goes on in schools by making reference to differences in the English, French and German national cultural traditions; or, as Sadler (1964: 310) put it, 'in studying foreign systems of education (...) the things outside the school matter even more than the things inside the schools, and govern and interpret the things inside'. My project therefore paid attention to what happened within and outside schools. Specifically, I set out to explain ethnic majority and Turkish minority students' positioning in relation to citizenship, multiculturalism and Europe by referring to macro-political relationships between the national, multicultural and European agendas, impacting on students. However, the time I spent in the field (about three months in each country) might not have provided me with enough opportunities to become 'enculturated' which, according to Pepin, is likely to help in understanding the context under study and help to establish conceptual equivalence. Instead, my 'advance familiarity with the cultures under study' resulted from work and study periods in Germany and England prior to the study.

This book's argument draws largely upon sociological analyses of post-war historical relationships between national, European and multicultural political and educational agendas in Germany and England. The book's empirical core is a series of four case studies looking at how 15-year-old ethnic majority and Turkish minority students in secondary schools (two in each country) explore and negotiate their identities. The type of case study is important. Yin (2003) distinguishes between three types of case studies: descriptive case studies that provide narrative accounts; explanatory case studies that test existing theories; and exploratory case studies, which can be used to help generate new theories. My study emphasizes words, actions and records rather than statistics, perspectives and subjective interpretations rather than objective epistemology, and discovery rather than proving hypotheses or assumptions. Therefore, according to Yin's (2003) typology, my study is an exploratory case study.

The book draws on data from fieldwork carried out in 2004 which investigated how socio-economically and geographically different groups of young people constructed their identities. I focused on England (an old immigration host with a multicultural vision) and Germany (an old immigration host with a monocultural vision). Both countries are powerful economic and political players in Europe, but have put rather different emphases on issues of national identity, migration-related diversity, and European integration and globalization, as we shall see in Chapters 2 and 5. Since the responsibility for implementing European and multicultural educational initiatives rests primarily with local education authorities in England and with the sixteen federal states (*Bundesländer*) in Germany, I selected two boroughs in Stuttgart and London with a similar interest in European and multicultural issues. My choices were also driven by pragmatic considerations, including proximity to Cambridge where I was based at the time, and my hometown of Pforzheim, Germany. I then formally approached two German and two English schools and met with the liaisons once prior to fieldwork. I also took into consideration the different organizational structures of the two education systems: the English have a two-tier system consisting of comprehensive schools and some state grammar schools, and the German secondary school system has three tiers in the state of Baden-Württemberg. Consequently, I had to be especially careful to select schools with similar achievement levels and comparable levels of education. This was further complicated by the fact that German schools do not publish exam results. I therefore did not choose average German and English schools based on achievement, but rather schools with some interest in issues of citizenship, Europe and multiculturalism. Although the resulting four schools were dissimilar in size, they matched rather well in terms of the percentage of Turkish students, inner-city location, socio-economic background, and European and multicultural ethos, as summarized in Table 1.1.

The main data collection consisted of a questionnaire (see Appendix 2) as well as focus group and semi-structured individual interviews with Year 10 Turkish and ethnic majority students in all four schools (see Appendices 1 and 3). A majority of interviewees at Millroad School[19] in London (69.2 per cent) and Tannberg Hauptschule in Stuttgart (56.8 per cent) had skilled and unskilled parents, whereas more than half of 15-year-olds at Darwin School (57.8 per cent) and Goethe Gymnasium (54.2 per cent) had professional middle-class and routine non-manual parents. However, around one quarter of Turkish students at both Goethe (28.6 per cent) and Darwin (23.5 per cent) had skilled and unskilled parents compared with just one out of ten ethnic majority youth.[20] This indicates that the Turkish sample

---

19   The identities of all local education authorities, schools and students were protected from outsiders by using pseudonyms. The two English schools were therefore named Millroad School and Darwin School and the two German schools were named Tannberg Hauptschule and Goethe Gymnasium.

20   Parental occupations in the student survey were initially coded in seven categories: (1) professional middle classes; (2) routine non-manual; (3) skilled workers; (4) semi-

at Goethe and Darwin is somewhat 'less middle class' than the ethnic majority youth in these schools, and is very important to bear in mind because it brings to the fore other factors affecting identity formation, including school ethos, peer cultures, ethnic relations, and community experiences.

Table 1.1 An overview of the two German and English secondary schools

	Tannberg Hauptschule	Goethe Gymnasium	Millroad School	Darwin School
School population	320 students 18% Turkish	564 students 5% Turkish	1,204 students 26% Turkish	1,507 students 2% Turkish
Location	Working-class inner-city area	Middle-class inner-city area	Working-class inner-city area	Middle-class inner-city area
Citizenship issues	Discrete subject, community topics	Discrete subject, parliament visits	Theme days, part of 'Registration'	Cross-curricular, part of PSHE
Multicultural issues	Turkish mother-tongue teaching	Intercultural tolerance, displays	Turkish mother tongue-teaching	Exams in community languages
European issues				
(a) Languages	English only	English, French	French, Spanish	French, German
(b) Geography and History	Entire Year 7 Geography, half of Year 6 History	Entire Year 6 Geography, half of Year 7 History	One unit in Year 8 both in Geography and History	One unit in Years 7 and 8 Geography and History

Note: PSHE stands for Personal, Social and Health Education and is part of the National Curriculum in England. It covers aspects of health and personal growth.

skilled and unskilled workers; (5) unemployed; (6) housewives; and (7) occupations not stated. Fathers' and mothers' occupations were then recoded into four family class types: (a) families with at least one professional middle-class parent, (b) two routine non-manual parents, (c) a transition category comprising routine non-manual and skilled parents; and (d) families with skilled and unskilled manual parents.

The main reason for choosing Year 10 students was that my experience as a secondary school teacher suggests that 15-year-olds are able to develop personal opinions on a range of issues and challenge the opinions of those around them. Also, I did not want to disrupt the work of the schools in any way, and was thus cognisant of the fact that in England both Year 9 and Year 11 students are involved in public examinations. Although my main data collection took place with Year 10 students, the sample for the survey was the whole of Year 9 and 10 in Tannberg Hauptschule and Goethe Gymnasium (202 students aged 14-16) and a total of 208 Year 10 students in the two English schools. This was because the two schools in Germany were considerably smaller in size than the two English schools, and I feared that I would not get enough responses from Turkish students to be able to compare and contrast their views with that of ethnic majority students if I only included two Year 10 classes of about 25 students each. The aim of the questionnaire was to obtain broad insights into how students positioned themselves in relation to ethnic and political identities. Since questions on multiculturalism were potentially more sensitive for the students than those on the nation state and Europe, I placed them towards the end of the questionnaire. However, it was not clear from the survey alone what students actually meant by 'being British', 'Turkish' or 'European', and therefore my main data collection involved qualitative interviewing delving into how students constructed their political identities.

I used purposive sampling to ensure a gender and ethnic balance in each school. Regarding the focus groups and individual student interviews, I worked with the teachers to help me identify students who could express themselves sufficiently well in German and English. This meant of course that I did not tap the opinions of the introverted, passive, or shy students. However, I asked for students from all ability groups to be included in the sample. I conducted six focus groups of four to five students in each school (single-sex and mixed majority and Turkish youth) and I also interviewed eight students in each school (two boys and two girls from each of my ethnic groups). The main reason for interviewing majority and Turkish youth separately was that in an ethnically mixed group there might have been fewer possibilities of tapping the different discourses majority and Turkish students employed in their identity construction processes. I developed multiple conceptual themes associated with identity to design the focus group interviews, including positioning, integration and politics. I related the notion of positioning to the range of categories including national, ethno-religious and European that students drew upon to define their identity. Integration was defined as the acceptance of people in a society and it was thus helpful to look at interethnic friendships and social inclusion. The notion of politics related to young people's opinions about how societies are governed and who holds the power within these societies. The questions in the focus group schedule, as well as the sequencing, were similar to those in the individual student interviews. However, while the focus group method used group dynamics and interactions (e.g., Morgan 1988, Wilson 1997) to define terms such as 'citizen', 'Europe', 'England', and 'being English and British', the individual interviews included more personal questions on the role of the family. I also interviewed sixteen teachers (the principal, citizenship co-ordinator, the head of geography and the head of religious education) to gain insights into the role schools play in forming identities. All interviews were tape-recorded, transcribed and then analysed using a broadly inductive approach whereby the thematic categories and findings emerged from the deconstruction of the multiple meanings of these transcripts (MacLure 2003, Bryman 2008).

Although I had some *a priori* codes based on the interview schedules, I gradually adapted the thematic categories while reading through the transcripts. I looked at the ways in which students responded to questions and positioned themselves with particular discourses (e.g., European, national). When I tried to deconstruct the multiple meanings of these narratives I was guided by approaches from post-structuralist theories of identity, specifically MacLure (2003), who argued that one of the most commonplace ways people stitch together texts is through the setting up of binary oppositions (e.g., 'us' and 'them'). 'One "side" comes to meaning through its difference with respect to a constructed "other", which is always lacking, lesser or derivative in some respect' (MacLure 2003: 10). The space opened up by language or discourse, she argues, is an ambivalent one: it is both productive and disabling. Without distance, we would not be able to imagine others as distinct from ourselves. 'It's the spacing, the difference, that makes it possible for us to think truth, self, nature, etc. in the first place', she writes (McLure 2003: 165). This book deconstructs the multifaceted discourses of identity among 15-year-old youth. However, my analyses can only provide an account of my reading(s). Other researchers might put together the truths in different ways.

I further triangulated the interview data with documentary sources to enrich my analysis of the ways in which socially and ethnically different groups of young people negotiated their identities. At the macro-political level, which set the framework for schools, I analysed and compared European Commission and Council of Europe documents, as well as national German and English legislation and school guidelines dealing with notions of citizenship, Europe and multiculturalism. In each school, I also collected available documents on multiculturalism, Europe, and citizenship as well as school prospectuses. The prospectuses served to inform my analysis of how schools responded to these macro-level policies, which, I argue, affected the negotiation of young people's identities. In particular, I collected syllabi of citizenship education, geography, and history (see Appendix 4), because previous research has shown these subjects tend to demonstrate the promotion of national, European and multicultural identities especially clearly (e.g., Soysal, Bertilotti and Mannitz 2005). These are discussed in more detail later when I describe young people's identities in the four secondary schools.

The interviewer (and author) is a fluent speaker of German and English, and relatively young which, in terms of age at least, resulted in a fairly balanced power relation during the interviews. The strategies I used to be a non-threatening 'other' included introducing myself as someone who would like to learn more about other cultures and ways of thinking about people and society. I also decided not to dress too formally so that students were not put off by the image of having a teacher-like adult in the room.[21] Despite these strategies, there was a possibility that the respondents constructed their identities in response to my own identity (e.g. adult, German, middle-class) and the questions I was asking of them. It was difficult to determine the extent to which my own identity may or may not have interacted with the interviewees' self-perceptions.

Theories of identity suggest that identities are constructed through dialectical processes of negotiation between people and the larger social categories like nation-states within which they live. This project focuses on ethnic majority and Turkish minority youth in two national contexts and examines how the national context shapes identity constructions. It is especially fascinating to explore the shifting identities of Turkish students during a period when Turkey is getting politically closer to Europe. This is also the only ethnic minority group with sufficiently large numbers in both German and English schools, and it is a particularly under-researched and disadvantaged community. Enneli, Modood and Bradley (2005), for instance, argued that England's young Turkish Muslims are even more disadvantaged in housing, employment and education than the Bangladeshis (who are widely regarded as the least integrated community in England; see Modood, Berthoud and Lakey 1997). Research on the Turkish communities has been limited in European countries like Germany (e.g., Sauer 2007, Halm and Sauer 2005, 2007, Haug and Diehl 2005, Alt 2006, Şen and Sauer 2006) and England (e.g., Enneli, Modood and Bradley 2005, Issa 2005, Küçükcan 1999, Sonyel 1988), and research on the identity formations of Turkish youth has been especially limited. There are also relatively few comparative studies of young people's political identities with the exception of Convery et al. (1997a, 1997b) and Gordon, Holland and Lahelma (2000). The need for better understandings of pan-European youth experiences is increasing in importance as a result of social, demographic, economic, political and cultural changes in contemporary Europe, and this book is an attempt to fill this void.

Looking Ahead

The book is organized into two main parts. Part I (Chapters 2-4) discusses the impact of national, European and multicultural political agendas on the German education system and how these agendas are addressed by socio-economically and geographically different groups of youth. Part II (Chapters 5-7) adopts a similar approach by comparing how national, European and multicultural political agendas are combined in England, and what implications this had for the identity formation processes of young people in two London schools. I give each secondary school

---

21   My reflections were informed through readings of Kaye Haw's (1998) *Educating Muslim Girls* and Louise Archer's (2003) *Race, Masculinity and Schooling*.

a separate findings chapter to highlight the importance of schools in shaping youth identity, arguing that through ethos and peer cultures, schools play a more important role in the formation of youth identity than non-school factors such as government policies and immigrant status.

Chapter 2 highlights the role of education in Germany's shifting national political identities. Firstly, 'foreigner pedagogy' in the 1960s and 1970s was viewed as the key means of assimilating migrant children into a monocultural conception of Germany. Secondly, the subsequent Europeanization of schools and the curriculum aimed to construct a Europeanized German identity through education. Chapters 3 and 4 then look inside schools at the results of these policies. Chapter 3 shows that a predominantly working-class school in Stuttgart, Tannberg Hauptschule, mediated national agendas through a dominant European and at times Eurocentric approach, which led both ethnic majority and Turkish minority youth to develop ethno-national identities (i.e., Turkish German, Swabian German). In contrast, Chapter 4 demonstrates how a nearby predominantly middle-class German school, Goethe Gymnasium, promoted European values alongside multicultural values, with the result being that young people had cross-ethnic friendships and developed national-European identities.

Adopting a similar analytical approach, Chapter 5 looks at the role of education in England's national identity politics, arguing that the concept of Britishness, mediated through multicultural values, has remained primary in England despite recent 're-orientations' of multiculturalism along civic integrationist lines. Successive English governments have continued to emphasize the concept of nationhood and schools as being deeply implicated in the construction of national identity, over and above supranational European values and issues. Chapters 6 and 7 look at the cases of two British schools. Chapter 6 highlights how a predominantly working-class context (Millroad School) celebrated cultural and religious diversity, but had ethnic and racial conflict, with the result being that young people found safety in their national Turkish or English identities. In contrast, Chapter 7 shows how Darwin School, a more middle-class environment that tried to integrate students on the basis of common British citizenship, had a low level of ethnic conflict and young people who developed hybrid ethno-national identities such as being Turkish British.

The concluding chapter discusses some of the theoretical and political implications of this study. Firstly, there is the question how to create social cohesion in conflictual environments so as to balance and simultaneously promote diversity and solidarity. In my research, I have found that the politics of multiculturalism appears to have promoted integration in contexts where it is allied with inclusion. This goes some way toward adding an empirical basis to Modood's (2007) theoretical defence of multiculturalism, where he argues that instead of being opposed to integration, multiculturalism can be combined with integration to produce inclusive hybrid identities respectful of, and building on, the communities that people value. At the other extreme, my research also shows how celebrating diversity at the school level can result in more rather than less ethnic tension, and thus reinforce nationalistic views. On the other hand, given that the young people in this study intertwined the ethnic and political dimension of identity (sometimes privileging the former and other times the latter), I suggest that we need to reconceptualize the way we think about contemporary youth identities, offering a theoretical model for future studies. Finally, I indicate that some of the underlying themes in this book are not confined to specific European countries, even though my data stems from four schools in two countries. To illustrate this point, I make some relevant transatlantic comparisons around the educational challenges arising from migration-related diversity.

PART I
Germany

Chapter 2
The Europeanization of German National Identities

This chapter provides for a broad socio-historical account of how national, European and multicultural agendas have developed and been differentially privileged in Germany. This is useful in order to understand how the educational system might be shaped by the development of these three political agendas, and to contextualize the study of how ethnic majority and Turkish minority youth negotiate their political identities. It is also useful for interpreting broader debates around immigrant incorporation. As will become clear in the following chapters, the comparison of German and English responses reveals important differences in the weighing of these three agendas over time. The approach adopted to describe the German context is to consider the impact of Europeanism and multiculturalism on the national schooling agenda, especially its contribution to national citizenship. Analysing the relationships within education between notions of citizenship, multiculturalism and Europe is particularly difficult in Germany since each of the sixteen federal states is responsible for educational and cultural matters, and thus implements its own policies. For the present analysis of policy documents and research literature, I focus primarily on the directives issued by the Standing Conference of the Ministers of Education (*Kultusministerkonferenz*, KMK) because these national guidelines inform the development and implementation of regional policies.

Racialization of the Workforce and Foreigner Pedagogy: 1945-1973

When the Federal Republic of Germany was established in 1949, German national identity had just been shattered by the War and, according to Risse and Engelmann-Martin (2002: 314), 'it was no longer possible to relate positively to German nationalism, since it became identified with militarism, authoritarianism, and, ultimately, the Nazis'. Germany was a founding member of the European Coal and Steel Community in 1951, and the European Economic Community in 1958, and has been of central importance to the processes of European integration since the birth of the EU. Because of Germany's problematic national identity after World War II, it has shown a strong inclination to delegate national sovereignty to supranational institutions like the EU (Katzenstein 1997). Indeed, the conservative Christian Democratic government under Chancellor Konrad Adenauer (1949-1963) constructed what could be called a 'Europeanized German identity' after the Second World War. Goetz (1996: 40) observed that 'the Europeanization of the German state makes the search for the national, as opposed to the European, interest a fruitless task'. According to Goetz, 'the national and the European interest have become fused to a degree which makes their separate consideration increasingly impossible'.

The Christian Democratic Union (CDU) encouraged a new role for Germany in a European federal state. The policies of the Christian Democrats were based on a Christian view of Man and his responsibility before God. The principles and programme of the CDU further stated that the party 'is in favour of a free democracy based on the rule of law, a social market economy, the incorporation of the Federal Republic of Germany into the Western system of values and the Western alliance, the unity of the nation and the unification of Europe' (Christlich Demokratische Union Deutschlands 1994: 2-3). Chancellor Adenauer saw Germany as being positioned between two power blocs with antagonistic ideologies (the West and Soviet communism) and as a result he had to choose between the two, deciding to commit himself to the West (Schwarz 1975). But throughout the early 1950s, there was no consensus on the orientation of German foreign policy. The main debates at the time centred on the issue of whether German rearmament within NATO and German participation in the European Coal and Steel Community might hamper prospects for early reunification with Eastern Germany. In the 1950s, important segments of German industry were critical of Chancellor Adenauer's policy and not convinced that European economic integration would serve their interests well (Katzenstein 1997).

Opposition to Adenauer's politics of Western integration also came from the Social Democratic Party (SPD) which, at the time, took the view that Western integration foreclosed the prospects of a rapid reunification of the two Germanies. Founded on Marxist principles, the Social Democrats abandoned their socialist economic principles (i.e., calling for the nationalization of major industries and state planning) and adopted the principles of the social market economy in 1959. The revised SPD programme stated that 'we want a Europeanized Germany which is the engine of European unification and international co-operation. (...) We want freedom and social justice' (Sozialdemokratische Partei Deutschlands 1989: 3). During this period, the SPD became the first major German party to embrace the concept of a 'United States of Europe'. When it turned out that socialism was not the guiding principle of European integration, the Social Democratic leader Schumacher prioritized the prospects of rapid German reunification over Adenauer's politics of Western integration. The Social Democrats changed course after two consecutive election defeats so that, from the late 1950s on, a federalist consensus developed amongst policy-makers from the centre-right to the centre-left. This consensus outlasted the changes in government from the Christian Democrats to the Social Democrats in 1969. It also survived a major foreign policy change toward Eastern Europe, East Germany, and the Soviet Union under Willy Brandt (1969-1974).[1]

Two aspects of national identity were particularly relevant in the German context in this period: 'historical memories' or ways of understanding one's own past, and 'performances and achievements', which were considered as a model for others (Risse and Engelmann-Martin 2002). Bleek (1997) added that, because of the particular history of the Third Reich, differentiating between national consciousness (*Nationalbewusstsein*) on the one hand and nationalism (*Nationalismus*) on the other was a crucial part of the German national identity debate. As Bleek (1997: 26) wrote, 'national consciousness is a rather neutral category, with which ideas or ambitions are characterized, and which aims at the creation of a citizen's nation. In contrast, nationalism is a term for an exaggerated, mostly intolerant and militant ambition, aimed at the power and honour of the own nation'. Up until the 1980s, many Germans considered the goal of European unification so self-evident that they did not debate its advantages and disadvantages. As a result, there remained a stable consensus among German parties ranging from the centre-left to the centre-right that the processes of European integration were irreversible. The German national identity therefore became thoroughly European in the sense that a 'good German' was seen to equal a 'good European', supporting a united Europe (see Goetz 1996, Risse and Engelmann-Martin 2002).

While policy-makers and politicians were advocating Europe and avoiding the promotion of nationalism, they were presented with the changes brought by large-scale immigration, including the challenges to national identity. According to Bade (1993, 2000) and Marshall (2000), there were four post-war groups of immigrants which all brought their own challenges to German identity: refugees (*Flüchtlinge*), resettlers (*Aussiedler*), migrant workers (*Gastarbeiter*), and asylum seekers (*Asylbewerber*). The refugees and resettlers were of German origin (i.e., ethnic Germans); migrant workers and asylum seekers were 'foreigners', mostly Turks, Yugoslavians and Italians. The ethnic German immigrants were from the Second World War, when the mass deportation of citizens from former German territories in Czechoslovakia, Poland and Russia created an estimated 12 million refugees (see Hoff 1995). The resettlers were mainly people of German origin from the former Eastern bloc countries of the Soviet Union, Romania and Poland, many of them descendants of families who had emigrated to Eastern Europe and Inner Asia to settle in sparsely populated areas centuries before. Refugees and resettlers together made a large immigrant group between 1945 and 1950, when 8.3 million people from former German territories and Eastern Germany migrated to western zones (Herbert 2003). The war industries (e.g., submarine production, armaments and munitions industry) used around 7.7 million forced labourers and prisoners

---

1   The Brandt government introduced East policy (*Ostpolitik*) in 1969 but made clear that efforts at European integration had to be continued (see Hanrieder 1995). Europe was conceptualized as a stable, peaceful order capable of overcoming the continent's militant past, a democracy with human rights and a social market economy.

of war. After the war, German refugees and resettlers replaced these workers and contributed to the so-called 'economic miracle' (*Wirtschaftswunder*).

The third group of immigrants identified by Bade (1993, 2000) and Marshall (2000), the foreign migrant workers (*Gastarbeiter*), is the most important for this study. A German-Italian agreement of 20 December 1955 paved the way for the officially organized recruitment of mainly male, non-German workers to fill labour shortages in Germany and to rebuild Germany's traditional economy (Bade 2000). Subsequent agreements were signed with Spain and Greece (1960), Turkey (1961), Portugal (1964), Tunisia and Morocco (1965) and Yugoslavia (1968).[2] The recruitment of non-German manual workers became even more intense after the influx of refugees from eastern Germany ceased with the construction of the Berlin Wall in 1961. The first Turkish workers, many of whom originated from the economically underdeveloped rural southeast Anatolia region bordering Syria and Iraq, were recruited to work in Germany after 1961, and were greeted enthusiastically as temporary workers. The 31 October 1961 bilateral agreement between Germany and Turkey, which Şen and Goldberg (1994: 10) referred to as 'one of the most important milestones in the history of German-Turkish relations', stated that Turkish workers should return to their home country within two years. The German Government had no intention of employing migrant workers permanently but, because of the need for workers beyond the initially agreed-upon date, many of these young men stayed in Germany long beyond their initial two-year contracts, and were joined by their families in subsequent decades.

The influx of non-German workers in this period put the government in a difficult position in terms of education. On the one hand, no wholesale adjustments were made to schools, because no one wanted the migrant workers to stay in Germany. Yet on the other hand, many immigrants had children who needed an education, so schooling became compulsory for so-called 'guest worker children'. In 1965, the conservative-led coalition government under Chancellor Erhard passed a 'foreigner law'[3] (*Ausländergesetz*) granting limited rights to migrant workers including the right to send their children to school but excluding the right to citizenship.

However, despite provisions made for migrant children, the German Government assumed that immigrants would eventually return to their home countries. The German Government saw 'the presence of foreigners [as] a temporary problem, which [would] resolve itself over time' (Santel and Weber 2000: 111). Mostly, they were happy to have the labour. Throughout the 1960s, foreign labour migration

---

2   In addition to the recruitment of male manual workers, Germany also had a shortage of nurses during the 1970s and, in 1974, signed an agreement with South Korea to recruit nurses for three-year periods.

3   The 1965 law was not changed until 1990, when the German Parliament passed a new Foreigner Law, reaffirming the principle of ius sanguinis, by which only those of German 'blood' heritage receive automatic German citizenship. Naturalization procedures are made easier, yet dual citizenship is rejected.

was seen as benefiting all parties, from Germany's economy to immigrants and their home countries. Many saw labour migration as propelling economic growth and contributing to the return of Germany's economic strength. Because migrant workers took lower paid jobs, this economic system made possible an upward shift of a large part of the German labour force and their families (Herbert 2003). Indeed, between 1960 and 1970, 2.3 million German 'blue-collar workers' became 'white-collar employees', due to the constitution of migrant workers as a new 'sub-proletariat' (Herbert 2003: 214). As Kagitçibasi (1991: 32) commented:

> The migration of workers, which was desired by both country of origin [e.g., Turkey] and the host society [i.e., Germany], has nevertheless led to a marginalization of the immigrant workers. The unclear identity of migrants was emphasized by their temporary status as *guests* as well as their socio-cultural, psychological, political, religious [e.g., Muslim] and linguistic background. Immigration (…) has turned into a highly complex humanitarian phenomenon with far-reaching socio-cultural, political and psychological consequences.[4]

Although migration and European integration increasingly challenged national identity, educational debates in Germany throughout the 1950s and 1960s focused on citizenship education and whether it should be taught as a discrete subject or cross-curricular theme (Sander 2003: 113). A 1950 directive by the Standing Conference of the Ministers of Education argued in favour of citizenship as a cross-curricular principle and its introduction as a discrete subject (Kultusministerkonferenz 1950). Then the 1960s saw the development of new concepts of civic and political education (see Händle 2002). As a result, almost all German federal states introduced citizenship as a subject in political education. Sander (2003) identified three main factors for this reform. Firstly, many universities re-established political science as a discipline with the aim of encouraging political education in schools. Secondly, neo-Nazis vandalized several Jewish cemeteries in the 1960s prompting public calls for improving political education. And thirdly, a multidisciplinary concept of political education emerged in German schools, driven by the educator Kurt Gerhard Fischer, who argued that civic and political education should not simply be taught as a discrete subject, but rather across the curriculum. There was a consensus amongst educationalists of the time that civic education should be based on democratic values and principles, and should include learning about economic and social issues in addition to political institutions and processes.

By 1964, however, pressure was growing for educational policy-makers to respond to the presence of migrant children in German schools. Consequently, the Standing Conference of the Ministers of Education recommended that migrant children attend additional classes in German and other basic subjects (*Vorbereitungsklassen*), while also keeping the possibility of returning to their home country's school system. The educational approach of this time was largely based

---

4   Quote translated from German.

on an assimilationist model called 'foreigner pedagogy' (*Ausländerpädagogik*), which was closely related to special-needs education for mentally or physically disabled children (see Hoff 1995). In other words, migrant children were seen as having a handicap due to their lack of German language skills and inability to follow the German educational system. In subsequent years, politicians continued not to see Germany as a temporary immigration country, and consequently continued to renew the strategy of assimilating migrant children into the German school system while also preparing them for a possible return to their country of origin (Luchtenberg 1997).

Foreigner Politics and the Europeanization of Schools: 1973-1998

The 1973 Arab oil crisis prompted the Social Democratic-led coalition government under Chancellor Willy Brandt to put a hold on the further recruitment of migrant workers, leading to a shift in the German relationship between national, European and multicultural agendas. The image of immigrants was transformed from that of a welcome pool of cheap labour to a threat to jobs, and a drain on the welfare state. Immigrants were thus seen as unwanted 'foreigners' (Herbert 2003). Politicians adopted an increasingly reluctant and hostile approach to multiculturalism. Between 1974 and the early 1980s, three specific principles to manage immigration emerged under the Schmidt administration (Social Democratic Party): the 'integration' of those with the right to live in Germany, the continuation of the 1973 ban on recruitment of new migrant workers, and financial incentives to support the return of migrants to their countries of origin. Under the 1983 law for the 'Promotion of Readiness to Return' (*Rückkehrförderungsgesetz*), every migrant worker who voluntarily left Germany received an incentive of 10,500 deutschmark (5,400 euros). However, only about 250,000 migrants, mainly those of Turkish origin, responded to this opportunity (Santel and Weber 2000). Therefore the bulk of Germany's immigration policy focused on the migrant workers who had stayed. Until the late 1990s, state officials continued to distinguish between 'us' (Germans) and 'them' (migrant workers), and migrant workers were often perceived as socially and ethnically inferior. Politicians used terms such as 'guest worker' or 'foreigner' to refer to migrant workers, irrespective of the length of their residence in Germany. This was especially problematic given that migrant workers and their families were an increasingly important population group during this time. Indeed, by the end of the 1990s, the non-German 'foreigner' population in Germany was 8.9 per cent with the Turkish Muslims forming the largest minority, as shown in Table 2.1.[5]

---

5   The figures in Table 2.1 are based on citizenship (not ethnicity) and are the best available. As a result of the 1999 citizenship reform, the number of migrants decreased in subsequent years. In 2005, a new microcensus law tried to remedy this by including questions about the previous nationality of migrants. Results show that the non-German

Table 2.1 The ethnicity of residents in Germany in 1980 and 1999

Ethnic groups	Residents in 1980	Percentages in 1980	Residents in 1999	Percentages in 1999
Total	78,397,000	100.0	82,163,500	100.0
Germans	73,944,000	94.3	74,827,400	91.1
All non-German (im)migrants	4,453,000	5.7	7,336,100	8.9
Turkish	1,462,000	1.9	2,053,600	2.5
Yugoslavian	632,000	0.8	737,000	0.9
Italian	618,000	0.8	615,900	0.7
Greek	297,000	0.4	364,400	0.4
Polish	60,000	0.1	284,000	0.3
Croatian	n/a	n/a	209,000	0.3
Bosnia Herzegovina	n/a	n/a	190,000	0.2
Portuguese	112,000	0.1	132,000	0.2
Spanish	180,000	0.2	131,000	0.2
Other European	578,000	0.7	1,403,400	1.7
Asian	311,000	0.4	823,000	1.0
African	152,000	0.2	300,600	0.4
Other non-European	51,000	0.1	92,200	0.1

Note: Croatia and Bosnia Herzegovina were part of the Socialist Federal Republic of Yugoslavia until 1992 and hence no separate data is available for 1980.
Source: Federal Statistics Office (Statistisches Bundesamt 2008a, http://destatis.de).

Racial and religious discrimination, fuelled by youth unemployment following the fall of the Berlin Wall and the Iron Curtain, boiled over in the early 1990s into a series of anti-'foreigner' anti-Muslim violence in Germany. In 1992, three Turkish women were killed in an arson attack on their homes in Mölln, in the state of Schleswig Holstein. Then in May 1993, four young neo-Nazi German men set fire to the house of a large Turkish family in the western German town of Solingen in the federal state of North-Rhine Westphalia. Three girls and two women died, and 14 other family members were severely injured. The attack led to violent protests by Turkish Muslims in several German cities and to large demonstrations of Germans expressing solidarity with the Turkish victims. Conservative Chancellor Helmut Kohl was criticized at the time for neither visiting Solingen nor attending

---

'foreigner' population is constant at 7.3 million while the German population is now subdivided into those with a migration background (8 million resettlers and naturalised) and those without a migration background (67 million). The total current population with a migration background is thus estimated to be over 18 per cent.

the memorial services. He had denounced what he called the 'condolence tourism' (*Beileidstourismus*) of other politicians.[6]

Citizenship rights have been a particularly strong form of institutional discrimination against Muslim and other migrants in Germany (Wilpert 2003). Until 1999, Article 116 of the German constitution (*Grundgesetz*) defined a German citizen as a person who holds German citizenship, a spouse or descendant of persons who were settled in the German Reich (ethnic Germans), or a refugee with German ethnicity. While resettlers and refugees who came to Germany qualified for dual citizenship, migrant workers, many of whom were Turkish Muslims, did not have any right to German citizenship until 1993. Only in the aftermath of the Solingen attacks and protests was a right to citizenship granted to young immigrants between 16 and 23 years. This change created an exception to German naturalization tradition and gave legally resident 'foreigners' a right to citizenship under certain conditions. Specifically, the children of 'foreigners' between 16 and 23 years could be naturalized as German citizens if they had eight years of residence and six years of schooling in Germany, if they gave up their original citizenship, and if they were not registered as having a criminal record. On the other hand, adult 'foreigners' who had been legally resident for 15 years could become naturalized citizens of Germany if they applied before 31 December 1995, gave up their former citizenship, did not have a criminal record, and could support themselves and their families without relying upon unemployment aid or welfare.

This differential treatment between migrant workers on the one hand and resettlers and refugees (i.e., ethnic Germans) on the other did not initially occasion any major public debate about a multicultural German society. It was only in the 1980s, more than 25 years after the arrival of the first migrant workers, that a debate developed. Since then, German academics and politicians have debated the concept of multiculturalism. Some (e.g., Bukow et al. 2001) defined multiculturalism as commonplace in the age of globalization while others (e.g., Schulte 1999) emphasized the potential of multiculturalism for the democratization of society. Still others (e.g., centre-right and radical right-wing political parties) viewed multiculturalism as a threat. Demographic reasons for immigration were ignored in favour of the preservation of cultural and national homogeneity (Herbert 2003). The Christian Democratic government under Chancellor Kohl, who took office in 1982, largely perceived the national and multicultural agendas as incompatible, still maintaining that 'Germany is not an immigration country' despite the long tradition of immigration. Immigration at the time was widely seen as a threat and a burden. Instead of emphasizing the benefits immigrants brought to Germany, the

---

6 Most recently, in February 2008, nine Turkish women and children died in a blaze in Ludwigshafen, a town in the state of Rhineland-Palatinate. Although the cause was said to be an electrical fault, it brought back strong memories of Solingen and renewed the tensions between Germany's largest Muslim minority and state authorities while many ordinary Germans expressed their solidarity with the victims.

Kohl government reinforced the perception of 'foreigners' as 'Other', for instance by reaffirming the principle of *ius sanguinis* (citizenship by birth) in citizenship legislation while rejecting the notion of dual citizenship.

By the 1980s, the concept of multiculturalism – or interculturalism as it is more commonly referred to in Germany – had taken over the educational debate in Germany. Intercultural education, according to Hoff (1995), attempts to address all children in order to prepare them for a life in a multicultural society, emphasizing cultural identity, mother-tongue teaching, and modifications to curricula towards a multicultural representation of values. The German debate during this period also included the notion of anti-racist education (*antirassistische Erziehung*).[7] Anti-racist education took the burden away from the immigrant as the person who must integrate into school and society at large. Instead, educational institutions were expected to develop an awareness and understanding of the 'racist' structure of German society itself, its laws, its hierarchy and its institutions. Auernheimer (1990) strongly argued for co-operation between the anti-racist and the intercultural/ multicultural approaches in education since intercultural education, in his view, failed to address power inequalities in the education system.

A popular method of funding studies in multicultural education was the use of experimental models of schooling. One such example is the 'Krefelder Modell', named after a city in the Rhineland industrial region (see Dickopp 1982).[8] Three primary schools were at the centre of a project which aimed to provide bicultural education for ethnic minority children and to concentrate resources by creating two Turkish German schools and one Greek German school, responding to the representation of migrants in the town. Other primary schools in the area would be run as German-only schools. The schools involved provided intensive mother-tongue teaching and studies of the national culture. In first grade, only mathematics, sports, arts and music were offered in the integrated classrooms. In fourth grade, all subjects were taught in German for all children, except for eight hours of mother-tongue teaching. The project succeeded in addressing the needs of culturally diverse groups of migrant students, and teachers as well as additional schools and communities wanted to continue it. However, the project was discontinued because regional politicians, in the 1980s, by and large showed little interest in migrant communities (Hoff 1995).

As a result of the federal structure of the German educational system, no general document on multicultural and anti-racist education was issued other than the guidelines published by the Standing Conference of the Ministers of Education. The 1996 guideline 'Intercultural Education at School' (*Interkulturelle Bildung*

---

7   This was, however, more prominent in other European countries such as Britain (see Archer 2008).

8   Later projects include that of Ingrid Gogolin (2000) focusing on the subject of German. Gogolin differentiated between migrant children who have knowledge of two languages and non-migrant children, arguing that both groups of students needed to be valued in German lessons.

und Erziehung in der Schule) (Kultusministerkonferenz 1996) argued that federal states should:

> Overhaul and further develop their curricula and guidelines of all subjects with regard to an intercultural dimension; develop teaching materials which address intercultural aspects as an integral part of school and education; only allow school textbooks that do not marginalize or discriminate against other cultures and include texts and pictures that give non-German students an opportunity to identify with; facilitate the employment of non-German teachers in all subject areas and intensify the collaboration between mother-tongue teachers and other staff; and include intercultural aspects in teacher training courses.[9]

Several of the 16 German federal states subsequently developed an intercultural dimension for their schools, in part as a result of the above recommendations by the Standing Conference of the Ministers of Education. For example, the curriculum guidelines of the state of North-Rhine Westphalia stated that teaching had changed because of the fact that children with different ethnic backgrounds and different cultural norms and traditions were taught together. Living and learning together was to be exploited to allow 'intercultural experiences and learning processes' (Der Kultusminister des Landes Nordrhein-Westfalen 1985). In 1995, the Education Commission of North-Rhine Westphalia argued that 'reflective living together in a multicultural school and society demands an intercultural education in all school types and the support of equal opportunities for minority ethnic students' (Bildungskommission Nordrhein-Westfalen 1995: 117).

The intercultural guidelines and teaching materials that were developed in the mid-1990s in several federal states were based on recommendations by the Standing Conference of the Ministers of Education in Germany. Thematic aspects which were recommended included 'the teaching of characteristics and developments of different cultures and societies; similarities and differences between cultures and societies; the reasons for racism and xenophobia; the causes and significance of prejudices; human rights and their meaning in different cultural settings; and the living together of minority and majority ethnic communities in multicultural societies' (KMK 1996: 8). Following their recommendations, the KMK offered didactical guidelines showing how these thematic aspects could be taught in subjects such as citizenship, geography, religious education, and history. This was an important local effort, but in general the implementation of multicultural education in mainstream curricula still lacked official support in many German federal states.

Since this study investigates the interface of the national, multicultural and European political and educational dimensions, work on the possibilities of combining the multicultural and European educational agendas (Boteram 1993;

---

9   Quote translated from German.

Luchtenberg 1996, 1997) was particularly relevant. Luchtenberg (1997: 138) argued that:

> Most migrants stem from European countries; multicultural and European education are implemented in similar subjects though European education is more prominent in geography than multicultural education; the same teaching materials are often used, such as games, stories or songs; as far as Germany is concerned, both approaches mainly stress mutual understanding by playing down conflicts.

Besides these similarities between multicultural and European, Luchtenberg referred to several difficulties posed by European education. Firstly, she argued that the limitation to Europe could result in Eurocentrism which neglects countries beyond Europe. Secondly, by concentrating on a Christian European world picture, the European dimension could widen the gap between 'accepted' countries, people and languages, and those that are 'non-accepted'. Thirdly, a European dimension could simply be understood as an 'add-on' part of education, leading to a mere addition to an otherwise unchanged nation-centred curriculum. These ideas are important because they relate to the inclusivity (or not) of terms such as Europe and multiculturalism as well as respective curricular approaches. My study unravels the implications of such schooling and teaching strategies for the identity formation processes of different groups of 15-year-olds.

In Germany, unlike in some other European countries, the European agenda had already begun to impact education during the 1970s and 1980s. Building on various earlier initiatives to implement a European dimension in German schools (e.g., 1978 'Europe in the Classroom' document), the Standing Conference of the Ministers of Education published the revised document 'Europe in the Classroom' (*Europa im Unterricht*) in 1990. This document came in response to the 1988 Resolution of the Council of Ministers of Education, discussed earlier.[10] Europe in the Classroom not only underlined the enthusiastic approach German policy-makers and educators had toward Europe, but also highlighted the perceived role of education in shifting national political identities towards a more European agenda. The directive (Kultusministerkonferenz 1990) stated that the goal of education must be:

> To *awaken* in young people the consciousness of a *European identity*; to prepare them to be aware of their responsibilities as citizens of the European Community; to provide as many students as possible with the opportunity to learn several

---

10   The 1978 document was the first attempt to determine how notions of Europe should be tackled in German schools. In 1983, a Resolution on a Policy for Europe emphasized the link between concrete progress in policy on behalf of Europe and the teaching of the idea of Europe in schools. Most recently, in 2008, the KMK reinforced the documents from 1978 and 1990 entitled 'Europe at School' (Kultusministerkonferenz 2008).

foreign languages; and to promote mutual learning with young foreigners to foster the ability to feel mutual solidarity and to live together peacefully.[11]

The document stressed the political justification for a European dimension in education, arguing that Europe was more than just a geographical term and that the painful experiences of two World Wars as well as the developments in Western and Eastern Europe since 1945 had given Europeans every reason to reflect upon their common origins. The task of the school was also seen as conveying insights into geographical diversity, political and social structures, formative historical forces, and the history of the European idea. In 1992, the Standing Conference of the Ministers of Education in Germany published a further review of progress and recommendations. The particular areas for development were identified as foreign languages as part of vocational qualifications, political and cultural education, and school and teacher exchanges (Kultusministerkonferenz 1992). Since 1990, European Schools (i.e., schools that particularly emphasize the European dimension in education) have been set up across the country (see Bell 1995).

The impact of the above guidelines by the Standing Conference of the Ministers of Education has since been investigated by educational researchers (e.g., Hauler 1994, Kesidou 1999, Natterer 2001, Hinderliter Ortloff 2005, Engel and Hinderliter Ortloff 2009). Research on the European dimension in the curriculum and school textbooks, for example, described how Europe became part of the German secondary school curricula and textbooks. Youth studies at the time focused particularly on young people's attitudes towards Europe and European integration (e.g., Weidenfeld and Piepenschneider 1990, Glaab 1992). Weidenfeld and Piepenschneider (1990: 117) conducted a representative survey among 15 to 24-year-olds and identified five different responses to Europe that were typical of young Germans. Firstly, the 'enthusiastic European' (14 per cent) who is in favour of a unified Europe and feels strongly addressed when people use the term 'the Europeans' in an ordinary discussion. Secondly, the 'interested European' (47 per cent) who is in favour of a unified Europe and feels partly addressed by the term 'the Europeans' and would regret it if the European project failed. Thirdly, the 'indifferent European' (14 per cent) who is in favour of a unified Europe and feels partly addressed by the term 'the Europeans' and would not regret it at all if the European project failed. Fourthly, the 'sceptical European' (8 per cent) who is in favour of a unified Europe but does not feel addressed when people talk about 'the Europeans'; and finally, the 'anti-European' (16 per cent) who is against a unified Europe.

While social and educational researchers in the 1990s continued to look at Europe and the European dimension, reunification created new political challenges for the country which resulted in a more pragmatic and less visionary approach to Europe. With the costly addition of the poorer regions of eastern Germany and mounting public concern over who would foot the bill for Europe's future

---

11   Quote translated from German.

projects, such as enlargement, Germany responded more cautiously to European initiatives. Emmanouilidis (2009a) talks about a 'normalization' of Germany's European politics, determined by national interests. Despite this, Katzenstein (1997: 48) commented that 'it is highly improbable that German political elites will turn their back on European institutions that have served German interests so well both at home and abroad'. One particular challenge came from the Party of Democratic Socialism (PDS), the successor to the former Socialist Unity Party (SED) of the German Democratic Republic. The PDS was critical of the ways in which Germany's major parties addressed European political issues, and was the only party to vote against the Treaty of Maastricht and Amsterdam in the German Parliament. Anderson (1997: 104) argued that '[re]unification did not precipitate a major domestic re-evaluation of Germany's role in Europe (...) and it is still possible to interpret Germany's approach to the EU in terms consistent with the pre-unification period'. In other words, for Anderson, 'Germany's exaggerated multilateralism and culture of restraint have endured'.

Since German policy-makers and politicians remained ardent proponents of widening and deepening the EU, it was not surprising that there was widespread support for the introduction of the euro as a single currency across Europe. Chancellor Kohl (1982-1998) attached his support for the single currency to the Europeanized German identity. He wanted to be remembered as the person who forced through the euro and made a closer EU inevitable in the hope to prevent any future return to nationalism in Europe.[12] This stance effectively silenced critics of the euro (e.g., Bandulet 1998, Hankel et al. 2001), who suggested that the single currency would never reach the stability of the German currency. But supporters of the euro (e.g., Bofinger, Collignon and Lipp 1993), who emphasized that the single currency would be as strong and stable as the deutschmark, faced challenges in Germany in the 1990s because of what Katzenstein (1997: 22) and Risse and Engelmann-Martin (2002: 307) called 'Deutschmark patriotism' (*Deutsche-Mark-Nationalismus*). This term refers to the value the deutschmark acquired as a national symbol of Germany's prosperity and economic strength.

Despite the pro-European approach of many policy-makers, national identification remained ambivalent in this period. For decades, a 'gap' existed between the constitutional ideal of one German national identity and the reality of two German states. Erich Honecker, leader of the Socialist Unity Party (SED) in the former German Democratic Republic (GDR), tried to create a separate sense of national identity by inventing a separate historical tradition for the regions which it occupied. Popular identification with the country was supposed to be cemented by the massive investment in sporting prowess. Prussian heroes such as Martin

---

12   See Karolewski and Suszycki (2007) for a more detailed analysis of the causal relationship between nationalism and European integration across a wide range of European countries. This volume mainly addresses the question of when and to what extent European integration has been a catalyst for nationalist developments, and when and to what extent it has put a damper on nationalism in European nation-states.

Luther and Frederick the Great, whose statue was placed on East Berlin's main boulevard (*Unter den Linden*), were retrospectively turned into East Germans by virtue of the fact that they had worked or lived in areas subsequently occupied by the GDR. Yet in retrospect, according to Evans (1997: 214), this sense of a separate East German identity ran 'no more than skin deep'. The reunification of Germany entailed a crisis of national identity in various ways. For West Germany, it was a crisis as it regained full political sovereignty and thus had to reinterpret its role in European and world politics. For East Germany, it was a crisis as it had to come to terms with economic, social and ideological changes created by a new political union of two national identities whose historical paths had been diverging (Piper 1998).

The lack of a properly developed national consciousness in contemporary German society and politics was commented on by 30 journalists and academics writing in *The Self-Confident Nation* (1995). In this document, the historian Rainer Zitelman argued that the self-confidence of the German nation was still broken as a result of the Nazi past; others (e.g., Karl-Eckhard Hahn) called for a recovery of a German sense of 'belonging' (*Heimatgefühl*), of the word 'fatherland' (*Vaterland*), and of an unbroken national identity. None of the authors wanted Germany to leave the European Union and most argued explicitly in favour of remaining. Hahn's main argument seemed to be that Germany's central geographical position gave it a particular responsibility for integrating the eastern European states into the Union. The furthest anybody went in criticizing the processes of Europeanization was to argue, as did Manfred Brunner, against the euro and to call for a confederal rather than a unitary European state. The extent to which the fractured German national identity became Europeanized is clearly revealed by the positions laid out in this document.

Yet, in the early 1990s, there were signs of a resurgence of German nationalism when incidences of racial discrimination culminated in a series of organized, violent and murderous attacks on 'foreigners' (particularly Turks, Travellers and Poles) by poorly educated, young, male, neo-Nazi skinheads in the western German cities of Mölln and Solingen, and the eastern German cities of Hoyerswerda and Rostock-Lichtenhagen. Evans (1997) argued that in some instances at least, these attacks were openly tolerated by the police. Public reaction, however, was swift, and across Germany, millions of people joined in peaceful mass demonstrations, carrying candles and holding hands in a symbolic affirmation of solidarity with the victims. According to one analyst (Watts 1999), this increased xenophobic aggression amongst German youth in the early reunification phase was brought about as a result of fear of competition from 'outsiders', youth unemployment, the expansion of aggressive youth subcultures, and the right-wing view that 'foreigners' were a threat to German welfare and culture.

Right-wing intellectuals and politicians grew more prominent in the 1990s, and increasingly advanced the belief that national, European and multicultural agendas were incompatible with each other. For example, the Republicans (REP), who were disappointed by what they perceived as the shallowness of the conservative turn (*Wende*) promised by Chancellor Kohl (see Olsen 1999), consistently called for an end to the one-sided guilt thesis of Nazi Germany, a get-tough policy on crime by foreigners, an ethnic understanding of German identity, and a promotion of the German self-determination seen as threatened by the EU. Like other right-wing parties during this period, the Republicans viewed German ethnicity and nationhood as a non-contingent, fundamental basis of identity. Similarly, with the backing of young, often unemployed people, the German People's Union was able to make some stunning electoral gains in the early 1990s. While the Far Right denounced a multicultural German society, some Christian Democrats at the time began to step up their attacks as well, from Bavaria's ruling Christian Social Union's (CSU) claim that multiculturalism endangered the stability of the Federal Republic, to an insertion into its party programme stating that Bavaria and Germany would not allow multiculturalism.

The Politics of Integration and the Rise of Muslimophobia: 1998-2009[13]

A marked shift in relationship between migrants and German policy-makers occurred in 1998 with the election of the Social Democratic-Green coalition government under Chancellor Gerhard Schröder. His administration broke with the mantra repeated since the 1970s that Germany was not 'a country of immigration', but at best a temporary home for 'foreigners' (Martin 1994, Bade 2007). The administration reformed citizenship laws, arguing that Germany should do more to attract high-skilled workers. In addition, they established an influential commission on immigration under the progressive CDU politician Rita Süssmuth, and passed the country's first explicit immigration law in 2005 (see the report of the Süssmuth-Kommission 2001).[14] The leadership of the conservative CDU/CSU also adjusted and appointed integration ministers at the regional level (such as Armin Laschet in North-Rhine Westphalia), as well as a Commissioner for Migration, Refugees and Integration in the federal government.

---

13   Although my empirical data collection in schools took place in 2004 (and this chapter is primarily designed to set the context for the two school case studies that follow), I analyse macro-level developments through 2009 here, as well as in the chapter on England. The main reason for this is that the book also engages in larger (intra-European and transatlantic) political and educational debates around immigrant incorporation, and the insights from the more recent events are thus useful for contextualizing the findings.

14   The immigration law refers to 'Zuwanderung', a newly-invented word that was preferred to the direct translation 'Einwanderung' which would have entailed a stronger rebuttal of the earlier insistence on being 'kein Einwanderungsland'. The description of migrants as 'Ausländer' or foreigners also remains prevalent although the concept of 'person with a migration background' has gained importance in recent years, particularly through its adoption by the Census authorities. In contrast with the United States, there has been little academic debate over the conceptual basis of the new census language, or of its possible contribution towards 'defining' social groups (see Lee 2008).

There is now a broad consensus on the need to promote integration and the grand-coalition government under Angela Merkel has hosted three so-called integration summits (*Integrationsgipfel*) with political and societal representatives to discuss issues of German language learning, education and job opportunities. Several additional Islam conferences (*Islamkonferenz*) have sought to focus on the interaction between the national majority and Muslim minorities, addressing religious topics, German law and values, and employment policies. This appears to reflect recognition that 'people with a migration background' will play a large role in shaping the country's future, an important change since around one third of the children now entering German schools have a migrant background (Schäfer and Brückner 2008). Academics and politicians agree that current policies must make up for the 'mistake' of ignoring integration in the past. Bade (2007) for instance speaks of 'catch-up integration' (*nachholende Integration*). However, this recognition is not leading to straightforward acceptance of migrants. Rather, these people are increasingly called upon to demonstrate that they are 'willing' to integrate and, until now, there has been a deadlock between the two main political parties over the meaning of 'integration' – the SPD views naturalization as a precondition of successful integration whereas the CDU mostly views integration as a precondition for naturalization. This has impacted on several policies, including citizenship.

After years of impasse in citizenship for migrants, many described the 2000 citizenship reform as having 'historical' importance (e.g., Koopmans et al. 2005, Green 2000). In addition to reducing the standard waiting period from 15 to eight years of residence, the reform introduced provisional dual citizenship for children born to foreign parents in Germany (children would have dual citizenship until age 23, then have to choose a single citizenship). Researchers see the change as a shift away from an exclusively 'ethnic' conception of German identity, whereby citizenship was accessible only by descent, to a more territorial definition of citizenship (see Brubaker 1992). Alongside the principle of *ius sanguinis* (citizenship by birth), the reform introduced the concept of *ius soli* (citizenship by territoriality). But in recent years, a number of commentators have argued that the practical implications of the citizenship reform are limited (e.g., Green 2005, Howard 2008, Thränhardt 2008), mostly because few people have taken advantage of easier access to citizenship. One study (Schiffauer 2006) argued that the reform of citizenship legislation and general restrictions on dual citizenship led to a decrease in naturalizations. Data from the Federal Statistics Office also show a declining number of naturalizations with return migration of resettlers peaking in the mid-1990s following the fall of the Iron Curtain, as summarized in Figure 2.1:

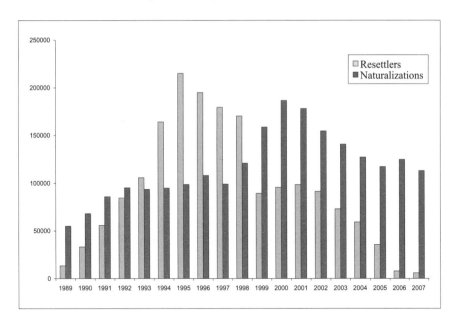

Figure 2.1 Naturalizations and return migration 1989-2007
Source: Federal Statistics Office (Statistisches Bundesamt 2008b, http://destatis.de).

Arguably, the low citizenship uptake, especially among Turkish-origin residents who make up the largest group of 'foreigners', is mainly due to the restriction on dual citizenship (Skrobanek 2009). Ethnic Germans and refugees have always been granted dual citizenship for life, whereas migrant workers have to choose a single citizenship by the age of 23. Some fear that forcing people to choose a single citizenship by the age of 23 could make the children of immigrants reject German citizenship altogether, perhaps out of a desire to retain their cultural identity and/ or out of solidarity with their parents who cannot access German citizenship (see Sayad 2004). As one interviewee on a recent radio programme put it: Germans call their country the fatherland (*Vaterland*), and Turks call theirs the motherland (*Mutterland*), and if you force people to choose between mother and father they tend to chose their mother (Westdeutscher Rundfunk 2009).

In 2002, the German Parliament approved new immigration legislation, but it was then fiercely opposed by the Christian Democrats in Germany's upper house (*Bundesrat*). The Christian Democrats employed populist tactics by using slogans such as 'children instead of Indians' (*Kinder statt Inder*) to oppose the introduction of green cards, thus mobilizing xenophobic sentiments.[15] A further

---

15   The slogan was coined by Jürgen Rüttgers, a leading conservative politician, to imply that Germany should train its own computer workers instead of recruiting them from countries such as India.

two years passed before an agreement was reached to pass Germany's first Immigration Act (*Zuwanderungsgesetz*). Under the Immigration Act of 2005, new immigrants and repatriates were expected to attend language and culture courses free of charge. This law was then amended in 2007 to allow the migration of spouses and integration courses (Bundesministerium des Innern 2004, 2007). Failure to participate in these integration courses could result in sanctions on migrants' right of residence. Ethnic minority people already residing in Germany are also obliged to attend such integration courses insofar as places are available; breach of this obligation can be punished with a reduction in social benefits for the duration of non-attendance as a sanction under social law. Spouses from non-EU countries that need a visa (e.g., Turkey, Middle East, Africa) are only allowed to come to Germany when they are at least 18 years old and have sufficient linguistic knowledge. This is seen as a move to prevent arranged marriages. Paradoxically, the regulation does not include spouses from non-EU countries that do not require a visa (e.g., South Korea, Japan, Australia, United States) and thus raises important questions of equality.

Paradoxically, although the German Government removed the main impediment to integration by granting citizenship to most born in Germany from 2000 on, politicians and social groups have increasingly questioned migrants' civic participation, from demanding new loyalty tests, to intensifying government surveillance of Muslim associations. This reflects the tensions between the ethno-cultural vision of German citizenship that predominated until recently (Brubaker 1992), and a new desire to address the realities of a culturally and religiously diverse society. In early 2006, several federal states governed by the conservative Christian Democrats (Baden-Württemberg, Hesse, Lower Saxony and Bavaria) announced citizenship tests with 30 to 100 questions on German language, history, culture and post-war values. These questions played on stereotypes of Islam and Muslim beliefs, attempting to screen views of gender equality, domestic violence and Israel's right to exist, as well as tolerance for homosexuals, Jews and blacks. Muslim organizations soon started to challenge these so-called 'Muslim tests'.[16] The conservative interior ministers proposed a nationwide values test, in addition to a language test, but Social Democratic interior ministers rejected this plan. In May 2006, the national conference of interior ministers compromised on some national standards allowing for the 'discussion' of democratic values and a 'role-playing' exercise in civic knowledge if this was deemed necessary.

The 2000 citizenship law was implemented in stages, with amendments regarding linguistic knowledge coming into force in August 2007. Then amendments

---

16   Question 15, for instance, asked applicants if one would allow one's daughter to participate in sport and swimming classes at school. Question 16 asked if one would allow one's child to participate in class trips with overnight stay. In Question 30, the applicant had to say what he or she thought of homosexuals taking public office. And Question 24 asked about the applicant's position is on 'honour killing' of women when they have an 'unvirtuous way of life'.

regarding knowledge of cultural, political and historical aspects of Germany came into force in September 2008. The reformed law allows federal states to carry out background checks of applicants, and also introduces mandatory integration courses on democracy, themes of democracy, conflict resolution in democratic society, rule of law, gender equality, basic rights and state symbols. There is a test at the end which costs 25 euros. Migrants with 'appropriate foreknowledge' of Germany may petition to opt out of the course and still take the test. Applicants who have successfully completed an integration course are now eligible for naturalization after seven years of residence (instead of eight), and those who demonstrate evidence of integration are eligible after six years. The federal state of Baden-Württemberg (where the two case-study schools are located) is the only state continuing to hold additional naturalization discussions with applicants, including questions on convictions. The traditionally-conservative government in this state views a strict definition of integration as a precondition for naturalization, thereby adopting a particularly harsh stance which might further alienate Muslim migrants.

The reorientations of Germany's approach to managing migration at the national level in this period also included a youth integration summit (*Jugendintegrationsgipfel*), bringing together young people from diverse backgrounds to discuss their ideas about language and education, local integration and cultural diversity. A National Integration Plan was also launched at the second integration summit in 2007, consisting of ten thematic priority areas such as improving integration courses, promoting early German language learning, integration through sports, using the diversity of the media, and strengthening integration through civic commitment and equal participation (Bundesregierung Deutschland 2007). In this respect the German Government, like its counterparts in North America and elsewhere, appears to be taking a new interest in civil society organizations. In Germany, this interest appears largely instrumental however, since the government is arguing that civil society organizations should be encouraged not so much because membership is of intrinsic value, but because they facilitate government influence over processes that are hard to steer from above. Jann (2003) describes this as a new style of governance in Germany. The National Integration Plan, for example, states that it is not possible to legislate for integration, but goes on to list over 100 commitments on the part of various levels of government and non-governmental organizations.

Some sceptics argue that unless the government provides serious funding to support relevant activities, this new focus on civil society may end up casting migrants as responsible for their own problems of integration (see Ha 2009, Riesgo Alonso 2009). As in other European countries that received labour migrants in the 1960s, the German state arranged for their assistance through existing institutions of social welfare. Migrants from Southern Europe were assigned to the welfare institutions of the Catholic Church, those from orthodox Greece were assigned to the Protestants, and those from Turkey to the Workers' Welfare Association (*Arbeiterwohlfahrt* which is linked to the unions). Representatives of migrant organizations commonly complain that it is still harder for them to receive state assistance than it is for such pre-existing organizations. For example, not a single Islamic organization has yet been granted the same legal status that allows the established churches not only wide-ranging tax exemptions but even allows for the state to collect tax revenues on their behalf.[17] As yet, the National Integration Plan does not seem to have added much funding to that provided by the previous government for integration courses for newly-arrived migrants and certain resident foreigners.

The German Government did introduce comprehensive anti-discrimination legislation in 2006, but this was the result of two European Commission directives (Council of the European Union 2000a, 2000b) rather than domestic impetus. The directives stipulated protection against discrimination on the basis of gender, sexual orientation, age, disability, race, or religion/worldview, and applied to the labour market and to the exchange of goods and services, with stronger protections foreseen in the former. But the preliminary evidence is that the new legislation has had a limited impact. The national law should have been in place by 2003 but was delayed because of the opposition of major political and social interests (Bielefeldt and Follmar-Otto 2005). These opponents insisted the rules would have unintended effects such as prohibiting churches from employing co-religious preachers. Early studies show little evidence of such effects (Priddat and Wilms 2008). But the resulting legislation is widely seen to be weak by western European standards. Indeed, in December 2008 the European Commission announced plans to take Germany to court because of incomplete implementation of the directives (Pagels 2008). One common complaint, especially from 'ethnic German' migrants from the former Soviet Union, is that the German Government and employers do not recognize many foreign qualifications.

At the same time, policy-makers and politicians at the regional level, particularly in conservative-controlled federal states, have continued to perceive national and multicultural agendas as largely incompatible. The aforementioned 'Muslim tests' provide evidence for this, but more important evidence comes from legal challenges to wearing the Muslim headscarf. In 2003, Germany's highest constitutional court found that the state of Baden-Württemberg was wrong to ban Fereshta Ludin (a German teacher of Afghan descent) from wearing a headscarf in school, but declared that states could in principle legislate on such issues (Bundesverfassungsgericht 2003). Unlike in France, the other major European country to recently legislate against headscarves in schools, in Germany there was no serious question that students have the legal right to wear headscarves (see Wallach Scott 2007, Weil 2004). School authorities in Baden-Württemberg argued that the headscarf could be seen as a political symbol, and is thus inappropriate in a public classroom. The teacher in question argued that she should be allowed to

---

17   Such funds have allowed the Catholic and Protestant churches, between them, to employ around one million Germans, making them among the biggest employers in the country.

wear the headscarf on the basis of her constitutional right to freedom of religious expression, and further that public schools should mirror the pluralism of German society rather than imposing secularism (Joppke 2007: 329).

The states of Baden-Württemberg, Bavaria, Bremen, Thuringia, Lower Saxony, North-Rhine Westphalia, Saarland and Hesse subsequently introduced legislation banning teachers from wearing headscarves. This is important because it privileges the Christian cross over other religious symbols in schools and society at large and is therefore counterproductive to integration efforts. For example, in April 2004, the Baden-Württemberg parliament added the following paragraph to the law on education:

> Teachers in public schools [...] may not make statements on politics, religion or ideology that could endanger the neutrality of the State with respect to children and parents, or which may disturb the peaceful operation of the school. In particular, it is forbidden to behave in such a way as to give children or teachers the impression that the teacher is opposed to the constitutional guarantees of human dignity, equal rights according to Article 3 of the Constitution, the rights to personal and religious freedom or the liberal-democratic basis of the State. The transmission of Christian and western educational and cultural values is not affected by [these stipulations]. The requirement of religious neutrality does not apply to religious education, following Section 1 Article 18 of the Constitution of the state of Baden-Württemberg.[18]

This paragraph is remarkable in several ways. The first sentence evokes the image of female teachers in headscarves posing a 'danger' to pupils and school order. The second sentence encompasses many of the arguments commonly used against wearing a headscarf, including the idea that it is an insult to human dignity and that it is likely to have been imposed upon the woman in question by a patriarchal religion.[19] The third and fourth sentences ensure it will still be acceptable for a crucifix to hang in classrooms in Baden-Württemberg and for nuns to teach wearing the habit. This was justified on the grounds that German educational and cultural values are fundamentally Christian. Most of the other German states that have introduced legislation banning headscarves include a similar provision to make clear that Christian (and Jewish) symbols are *not* affected (see Joppke 2007). Only in Berlin does the reform in question explicitly apply to all religions. In Berlin the ban applies not only to teachers but also to other higher-level state officials; this is also true of the headscarf ban in the state of Hesse. In no part of Germany were there substantial numbers of teachers actually wearing headscarves when the legislation was passed. During the past decade, Muslims have been quite

---

18　This is my own translation, and omits some of the cross-references to articles and paragraphs in other sections of constitutional or civil law.

19　For a prominent argument to this effect see the work of Germany's most famous feminist, Alice Schwarzer.

successful in claiming rights and, at the same time, Germans have been more willing to concede these rights which are further signs of the ideological shifts that have occurred during integration. However, as evidenced by the legislation in Baden-Württemberg, policy-makers and parts of the general population are finding it hard to accept this accommodation of Muslim rights (see Faas 2010).

The most recent incident showing Muslimophobia[20] in the general population happened in July 2009, when a German stabbed a pregnant woman of Egyptian origin in a Dresden courtroom. The woman, Marwa al-Sherbiny, was suing the man for insulting her for wearing a headscarf. Marwa al-Sherbiny's killing has not only raised many questions regarding interracial relationships and co-existence in Europe, but has sparked a controversy that includes the German police and government. A German security officer shot and seriously injured the husband who was trying to save his wife, which led to questions as to why that policeman did not target the attacker. Soon after, the Chairman of the Central Council of Muslims in Germany, Ayub Axel Köhler, called on German politicians to 'finally take seriously the issue of Islamophobia'. The case attracted much media attention in Egypt (where newspapers dubbed the victim a 'martyr of the hijab') and across the Muslim world, prompting German Chancellor Merkel and then Foreign Minister Steinmeier to reassure migrant minorities that there is no room for xenophobia in Germany. It remains to be seen how effective these calls will be.

The 'headscarf debate' and general rise of Muslimophobia in this period has also been part of a wider debate about national pride and xenophobia. In 2001, for instance, senior members of the Christian Democratic Union (CDU) demanded that every public person in Germany must confess to be proud of Germany. This revival of the ghost of nationalism comes at a time when economy, culture and most areas of society have already moved beyond the national level towards supranational integration. Although the main right-wing parties have been unable to surmount the 5 per cent hurdle necessary for representation in the German Parliament in Berlin, they nevertheless managed their highest percentage of the vote (a combined 3.3 per cent) in 30 years in the 1998 federal elections, then dropped back to a combined 1.8 per cent in the 2002 federal elections, before rising again to a total of 2.2 per cent in the 2005 elections. Since 2005, Finland, Sweden, Denmark, the Netherlands, Belgium, Poland, Austria and France have all experienced a right-wing swing in their national governments, often on an anti-immigration, anti-Muslim platform. In contrast, at a regional level, the extremist German People's Union received 6.1 per cent of the vote in the 2004 state elections in Brandenburg, while the right-wing National Democratic Party received 9.2 per cent in the 2004 state elections in Saxony, and 7.3 per cent in the 2006 state elections in Mecklenburg-Western Pomerania. There has been a resurgence of

---

20   The current tensions between Muslim migrant minorities and the national German majority might not necessarily be rooted in religion, but in education and other cultural areas which is why the term 'Muslimophobia' might be better in this case than 'Islamophobia' (see Erdenir 2010 for a discussion of Islamophobia and Muslimophobia).

radical parties that support nationalistic ideas and oppose immigration and the inclusion of Turkey in the EU, but the majority of radical parties concentrate in the East, where people have expressed disillusion with the slow socio-economic reforms following Reunification (Olsen 1999). In 2008, the populist Citizens in Anger (BIW) party won a seat in the federal state of Bremen, having obtained 5.3 per cent of the vote in the city of Bremerhaven.

A combination of intercultural and anti-racist education has been Germany's prevailing educational response to such xenophobic incidents and diversity in general. Some states (e.g., Saarland, Thuringia) have developed intercultural teaching units and others (e.g., Berlin, Hamburg, Schleswig Holstein) introduced intercultural education as a cross-curricular theme. Still others (e.g., Bremen, Hesse, Rhineland-Palatinate) have carried out intercultural projects during special project days in school and some (e.g., Baden-Württemberg, Bavaria, Brandenburg) have taken a combined approach of the above. North-Rhine Westphalia and Hamburg were amongst the states that took a leading role in implementing intercultural education. Hamburg's revised school law today states that 'schools have the task to educate for a peaceful living together of all cultures and the equality of all human beings' (Behörde für Bildung und Sport 2003: 9). Baden-Württemberg, where Tannberg Hauptschule and Goethe Gymnasium are located, delivers intercultural education in a range of subjects, including geography and history. Moreover, as a result of the poor performance in international student assessment tests, and the particular underachievement of Turkish and other migrant youth (see OECD 2006), the Standing Conference of the Ministers of Education agreed on national educational standards to improve education (Kultusministerkonferenz 2004a, 2004b, 2004c) and also revised the standards for teacher training to enhance 'knowledge of the social and cultural backgrounds of students and the role of schools in responding to increasingly diverse populations' (Kultusministerkonferenz 2004d: 9).

Although schools in this period have continued to privilege European agendas over and above multicultural and national agendas, the European dimension has a surprisingly low priority in citizenship education (Derricott 2000). Instead, citizenship education and community studies emphasize the federal democratic structure of Germany, including local political decisions, political participation, and democratic culture in Germany (see Phillips 2001). The curriculum only marginally addresses aspects of the new European or international citizenship dimension. For instance, in the vocational-track secondary schools (*Hauptschulen*), there is only one teaching unit about the EU in Year 8 (age 13-14) and another on international politics in Year 9 (age 14-15). Similarly, at the end of schooling in secondary modern schools (*Realschulen*), there is one teaching unit on European integration in Year 10 (age 15-16). In contrast, the concept of Europe is particularly integrated into geography and history. For example, in the geography curriculum of Baden-Württemberg, the entire Year 7 (ages 12 to 13) in extended elementary schools deals with Europe; in university-track secondary schools (*Gymnasien*), three out of four teaching units in Year 6 (ages 11 to 12) deal with Europe (see Table 8.1). The main purpose of citizenship education seems to have been to continue to remind young Germans that their country is a federally-organized parliamentary democracy, indicating the still ambivalent relationship to their past and national identity.

One of the latest educational debates in Germany (which has also been addressed at the Islam conferences organized by the Interior Minister since 2006) has focused on the country's religious diversity, particularly the approximately 2.6 million Turkish Muslims. As shown in Table 2.2 below,[21] non-German students made up 8.5 per cent of the 2004/05 total school population (the year the fieldwork was conducted), with Turkish students forming nearly half of the 'foreigner' school population:

Table 2.2 The ethnicity of students in German schools in 2004/05

Ethnic groups	Total number of students 2004/05	Percentages of students 2004/05
Total	13,530,198	100.0
Germans	12,387,500	91.5
All non-German (im)migrants	1,142,698	8.5
Turkish	488,766	3.8
Italian	82,956	0.6
Serbia Montenegro	66,280	0.5
Greek	41,200	0.3
Croatian	27,825	0.2
Bosnia Herzegovina	26,511	0.2
Polish	25,404	0.2
Portuguese	16,648	0.1
Spanish	9,443	0.1
Other European	141,308	1.0
Asian	140,206	1.0
African	44,762	0.3
Other non-European	31,389	0.2

Source: Author's calculations from 2004/05 Federal Statistics Office data on general and vocational schools in Germany (http://www.destatis.de).

As a result of the large number of Turkish Muslim students in German schools, several federal states have begun providing Islamic religious education in German (*Islamunterricht in deutscher Sprache*) for students of Muslim origin alongside the

---

21 Figures should be treated with caution because Germany, like France, has recorded nationality rather than ethnicity and the total number of non-German migrant students was 13,303 higher in 2001/02 (9.2 per cent in total). This 'decline' is mainly due to naturalizations after the 1999 citizenship law reform and not the result of emigration (see Table 2.1).

Protestant and Catholic religions in German state schools. One concern regarding this debate has been that offering Islam as a subject alongside the mainly Christian religions in state schools could lead to a 'ghettoization' of Muslim children and hamper integration. However, without Islamic religious education in German state schools, groups could offer their more radical interpretations of Islam in private lessons; and more and more Muslim students might attend mosque-based Koran schools (Siedler 2002).[22] Arguably, one of the main advantages of providing Islamic instruction in the German language in state schools is that Muslim students from different countries and cultures can learn their shared religion together. The question of the content of Islamic lessons and the extent to which Islamic organizations and communities should be allowed to shape the curriculum has been at the centre of this continuing debate about multiculturalism in Germany. The third Islam conference in March 2008 agreed that all German state schools should offer Islamic religious education in German and that Muslim community leaders should work out a legally binding agreement with the state. However, this is likely to take several years given that Muslims in Germany were represented by no less than 15 different organizations and individuals at the conference.

Arguably, a more inclusive approach would have been to merge the subjects of religious education and ethics and teach the major world religions to all students in the same class. In fact, in 2006, the SPD and PDS coalition government of Berlin introduced compulsory ethics classes, intended to ensure that children get the kind of ethical instruction that might otherwise be the focus of religious education. Conservative parties recently initiated a referendum to replace the ethics classes with compulsory religious education, but the vote failed by a large margin in April 2009. All these controversies are part of a continuing debate in Germany over religion and national identity.

Another challenge arising from migration-related diversity over the past years has been the educational underperformance of migrant students. The 2001 PISA study, administered by the OECD, came as a shock to the German public. It demonstrates that the German educational system is performing poorly, and that second-generation young adults, particularly Turks and Italians, experience pronounced disadvantages compared to their German peers (see also Kristen and Granato 2007). A review report which built on data from the 2003 PISA study shows that, on average, in mathematics, 15-year-olds with a migrant background trail their native peers by 40 points, an educational deficit of about one year of study. In Germany, the gap between second-generation students and native students is nearly twice as big (93 score points) and reaches 120 score points between Turkish students and German students – the equivalent of about three years of study (OECD 2006). The 2006 PISA study confirmed many of these findings, albeit with a focus on science (OECD 2007). Kristen and Granato (2007)

---

22   In Berlin, home to most Turks in Germany, some 17 per cent of Turkish children already attend Koran schools after school. In Bavaria, Islamic instruction classes were set up in the 1980s but were only available in the Turkish language.

and Heath (2007) attribute this to the somewhat socially-conservative German educational system which appears to perpetuate differences in socio-economic status over generations.[23] In most of the country, children are separated into a three-track education system at the age of ten or eleven. The decision whether a child will attend an 'academic' school intended to lead to a university degree, or a school leading to vocational training, is made largely by teachers, rather than on the basis of aptitude testing. Migrant children are concentrated in the lowest tier, which may be due in part to the prejudices of teachers and the relative infrequency with which foreign-born parents (who may not speak good German) contest the teachers' recommendations. Overall, around 1.5 per cent of Germans without a migration background have no formal qualifications compared to around 9 per cent of the population with a migration background (Birg 2009). Seibert (2008: 3) shows similar differences even for people of migrant origin who were educated in Germany.

Another controversial issue raised by migration is the provision of mother-tongue education, and the perceived value of the linguistic and cultural capital that migrants bring into the school community. Until the 1980s the children of migrants were sent to separate schools for 'foreigners' so that they could retain linguistic and cultural ties to their countries of origin, and be prepared for their eventual return. This educational strategy has shifted however, and policy-makers now emphasize integration and German language acquisition, typically to the exclusion of mother-tongue education. The swing from one policy extreme to the other largely ignores the findings of many academics, who argue that mother-tongue language ability complements, rather than competes with, the process of learning German (e.g., Boos-Nünning 2005, Gogolin and Neumann 2009). In addition, proficiency in the mother tongue has also been found to provide a source of stable 'identity', which is important for success in school (Krumm 2009).

Germany has seen a wave of familial disputes between first-generation parents (representing the traditional Turks) and second-generation liberal Turks, mostly girls. Between October 2004 and June 2005, eight Turkish women who broke with their family traditions and lived according to Western values (e.g., non-marital sex, own living quarters, relationships, combined job and family life) were murdered by male family members who felt that their *namus* (honour and dignity) and *seref* (reputation and prestige of the family) had been compromised (Banse and Laninger 2005). Since 1996, more than 40 girls and women of Turkish or Middle Eastern origin who had lived in Germany for all, or most, of their lives were murdered for the same 'crime'. Many of these so-called 'honour killings' were largely ignored by the media until 23-year-old Hatun Sürücü, born in Berlin, was shot dead in the open street on 7 February 2005 by three of her brothers who felt that she had brought dishonour on her family (Peil und Ernst 2005). Officially,

---

23   See Faas (2010) for a more detailed discussion of the structural and cultural factors affecting educational performance. For example, recently, some federal states have decided to abolish the tripartite secondary education system.

she became the sixth victim among Berlin's 200,000-strong Turkish community. Her killing not only intensified the German debate about integration (e.g., German language courses in kindergartens and primary schools), but also sparked a new discussion about the necessity of introducing compulsory lessons on morals and ethics, following approval of the killing by several Turkish youth at a local school (see Grote 2005, Beckmann 2005).

Despite these controversies, there is general recognition and valuation of the Turkish subculture that has emerged in Germany. This is particularly the case amongst the large Turkish community who have combined a commitment to their ethnic and cultural background with openness to the German society. A thriving and colourful literary and cinematic Turkish German subculture sprung up, with over a thousand works written in Turkish and dealing with Sunni and Alevi experiences in Germany (Riemann and Harassowitz 1990). In 2004, the German Turkish film 'Head-On' (*Gegen die Wand*), which tells the story of a marriage of convenience between two Turkish Muslims in Hamburg, won the Berlinale Golden Bear and was awarded Best European Film. There are also an increasing number of elected politicians and candidates with a migration background. However, there exists little published research on this development. In 2007, the journalist Mely Kiyak published a book '10 for Germany' (*10 für Deutschland*), which has portraits of ten Turkish-origin elected politicians from all the major German parties. The most prominent of her interviewees is Çem Özdemir, who was first elected to parliament for the Green party in 1994 and subsequently held a seat in the European Parliament. In November 2008, Özdemir was elected to be one of two chair-persons of the party. What is striking is that the Greens and the communist Left party (*Die Linke*) have relatively high numbers of migrant candidates on their lists. The two main parties have been slower to promote migrant candidates, perhaps for fear of alienating core supporters who dislike any suggestion that migrants get extra assistance. The proportion of candidates with migrant backgrounds, at around 2 per cent, is well below the share of migrants and their descendents in the German population (Fonseca 2006). The same holds true for teachers, where less than 1 per cent has a migrant background (Verband Bildung und Erziehung 2006).

To sum up, in spite of paradigm shifts from 'foreigner politics' to a 'politics of integration' during the past decade, Germany is still struggling to leave behind the image of the third-generation 'foreigner' (*Ausländer*) or 'foreign citizen' (*ausländische Mitbürger*). This has to do with the ideological power struggle between the two main political parties. At the same time, the struggle to change how immigrants are seen is related to the ingrained insensitivities formed over five decades of politicians and policy-makers rejecting the notion of Germany as an immigration country. One of the challenges now lying ahead is how to balance the country's renewed national pride and Europeanized identity with migrant values. This detailed socio-historical analysis of the impacts of national, European and multicultural political agendas on the German education system serves as a rich context for broader European and transatlantic debates on immigrant incorporation and inclusive citizenship and educational policies, and aides our understanding of the identity formation processes among 15-year-olds in schools. Tannberg Hauptschule and Goethe Gymnasium are affected by these macro-policy approaches and are mediating these debates in rather different ways. In turn, the different school approaches impact on the identity formation processes of young people.

Chapter 3
Eurocentric Education at
Tannberg Hauptschule

Tannberg Hauptschule, a vocational-track school, is located in a residential area on a hill on the edge of an inner-city, multiethnic, mainly working-class, borough in Stuttgart. A majority of students (56.8 per cent) have skilled and unskilled parents. Less than two out of ten students have routine non-manual and professional middle class parents. The school has 320 students, 191 (62.4 per cent) of whom come from migrant minorities. Turkish youth form the largest group (54 students) followed by Italians (30 students), Serbs and Montenegrins (24 students), Croatians (18 students) and Greeks (14 students). Ethnicity did not appear to play a major role in terms of grades students received in early 2004, with Germans having the same average as Turkish students (2.9), and Italians (2.8) and Yugoslavians (3.0) being marginally above or below their German classmates.[1] Tannberg Hauptschule has an overall exclusion rate of 4 per cent (14 out of 320 students) per academic year.[2] However, the rate is higher for ethnic minority students (6.3 per cent or 12 students) than Germans (1.5 per cent or two students), and boys (ten boys) are more often excluded than girls (four girls). Only one of the 14 exclusions during the fieldwork year was permanent; the others were for three days only.

The school system in Germany is more or less under direct control of the regional government and each type of secondary school (e.g., Hauptschule, Gymnasium) has a mandatory curriculum for all ages and levels. This leaves little room for schools to design their own curricula and principally ensures that all schools and teachers within a federal state (*Bundesland*) teach a similar curriculum. The differences between schools are thus largely the result of local interpretations of macro-level policies as well as school dynamics including ethos and peer cultures. Like all other Hauptschulen in this state, Tannberg Hauptschule provides a broad curriculum which, in Years 9 and 10 (age 15-16), consists of religious education, German, geography, history/citizenship education, English, mathematics, physics, biology/chemistry, physical education, music, art, and information technology. Students can additionally choose between technology and domestic science. Tannberg Hauptschule provides Turkish mother-tongue teaching and also sends

---

1   In the German grading system, grade 1.0 is the highest and 6.0 the lowest grade. The average grade was obtained by adding up the grades of those 100 students who completed the questionnaire in this school.

2   The exclusion rate represents the percentage of pupils expelled from school during an academic year.

migrant students to German language preparation classes (*Vorbereitungsklassen*) for one or two years in a neighbouring school before integrating them into the mainstream classes. However, apart from one external Turkish teacher who comes into the school once a week, there is no teacher among the 34 permanent staff with a migration background despite Tannberg Hauptschule's culturally diverse intake. Because of the predominantly working-class background of its students and the limited financial resources to travel, Tannberg Hauptschule has no European exchanges or partnerships. It does, however, promote a European and international educational dimension, for instance, by displaying European maps, posters of the names of French months, English posters saying 'Peace and freedom for the world', Japanese schoolbooks and Japanese geographical data resulting from an exchange with Shizuoka on a teacher level, and by offering one-week trips to London or New York.

Although there had been a controversy in the past over the building of a new mosque in the catchment area of Tannberg Hauptschule, I did not see any conflict or gang fights between resident communities during my fieldwork. The city of Stuttgart also seemed to have been spared the sorts of violent disputes between first-generation parents and second-generation Turkish girls in Berlin that were described in the previous chapter. The relatively congenial community relations outside the school could partly be the result of Stuttgart's successful local integration policy called 'Pact for Integration' (*Bündnis für Integration*) which was adopted by the city council in 2001 and earned them the 2004 'Cities for Peace' prize by the United Nations Educational, Scientific and Cultural Organization (Landeshauptstadt Stuttgart 2003). The Pact for Integration is a coalition that spans politicians and administration in the public sector, special interest groups and businesses in the private sector, and associations, sport clubs, community groups, and non-governmental organizations representing civil society. The Pact highlights four main areas of activities: firstly, language and education including the promotion of German as a lingua franca among all residents in Stuttgart; secondly, neighbourhood integration through initiatives such as political participation, information about civil rights, conflict mediation programmes, and community centres; thirdly, support of pluralism and diversity in all social realms including the German-Turkish Forum; and, finally, a strengthening of the city's self-perception as a multicultural place. In the past few years, while promoting diversity, Stuttgart has been keen to integrate all people on the basis of the common German language. Nevertheless, the identity formation processes in the two schools were rather different and dependent on a range of factors, notably school policy approaches as well as socio-economic backgrounds.

Working with Different Citizenship Agendas

Tannberg Hauptschule mediated national citizenship agendas through a dominantly European and arguably, at times, a Eurocentric approach. The teachers I interviewed claimed that the school aimed to create self-confident, critical, tolerant and informed citizens. However, the school was a 'flashpoint school' (*Brennpunktschule*), meaning one with a substantial 'at-risk' student population, because of its location in a low-income neighbourhood and the associated problems of poverty and neglect.[3] Teachers believed students had linguistic difficulties and a lack of social skills. As a result, in the view of Mr. Müller, the deputy principal, it was difficult to put theoretical conceptualizations, such as the notion of an informed and active citizen, into practice. The teachers admitted that they frequently had to address extracurricular concerns before meaningful learning and teaching could take place. According to Mr. Müller, only about half of the prescribed curriculum could be taught, whereas the remaining time was spent on improving students' social and civic skills, including the ability to live together in peace, the development of mutual feelings, and problem-solving strategies.

Community studies (the title of citizenship education in the state of Baden-Württemberg) formed part of the compulsory curriculum from Year 6 (age 11-12) on and was being taught for one hour per week in Tannberg Hauptschule during the period of this study. Mr. Koch, the community studies co-ordinator, felt that this was not sufficient time to engage students in debates surrounding Germany's conflictual relationship with the past. He wanted to teach about civil rights and the values of democracy:

DF: What do you think about the overall attention given to citizenship in the curriculum?

MR. KOCH: Very low priority in the curriculum, very low. Religious education seems to be more important, honestly.

DF: What could be the reasons for this?

MR. KOCH: Lack of resources, the willingness to engage with the past, with politics, political apathy in general. I used to be a very critical person, was a member of a political party, part of the trade union. Today, after all what our government's been doing, I'm not interested any more. When I see politicians' attitudes towards money, I'm beginning to understand my students. It's a pity and I fear that we will get more and more religious and political radicalization here. A lot of violence is the result of a lack of teaching about basic rights and democracy. (…) One hour per week, that's a joke. You can't teach all that in one hour. And there is no citizenship and history exam any longer. Gone.[4]

---

3   Schools are classified as 'flashpoint schools' by the Baden-Württemberg Ministry of Education if there are particular educational and pedagogical tasks for teachers, resulting for instance from poverty.

4   The interviews at Tannberg Hauptschule and Goethe Gymnasium (Chapter 4) took place in German and were transcribed in German and subsequently translated into English.

Besides the teaching of community studies as a discrete subject from Years 6 to 9 (ages 11 to 15), the school actively involved its students in the community by encouraging one to two students to run for the Stuttgart youth council, or participate in a conflict mediation programme (*Streitschlichterprogramm*) similar to the one promoted in the Stuttgart Pact for Integration.⁵ Further extra-curricular citizenship activities, such as trips to the European Parliament, were extremely difficult because of the lack of (financial) resources mentioned by the community studies co-ordinator. Mr. Koch argued that the Hauptschulen had a very low reputation and position in the German public and political discourse. 'I wanted to visit the Berlin Parliament with my students and contacted our local MP and they said "The Gymnasium has priority". I once had an invitation to go to Berlin and then it was cancelled because of budgetary constraints. Later on, I found that our neighbouring Gymnasium students were in Berlin. They got our slot to visit the Parliament'. These negative experiences not only explain the frustration and pessimism of the community studies co-ordinator, but also indicate the marginal status of Hauptschulen in this tripartite German secondary school system.

While civic education texts emphasized the federal democratic structure of Germany (e.g., local decisions, political participation, and democratic culture in Germany), the European agenda was privileged over and above national and multicultural agendas in curriculum subjects like geography and history. For example, in Geography, the entire Year 7 (ages 12 to 13) was spent looking at Europe, with a geo-political overview of Europe followed by study of either France or Britain, the physical and human geography of northern and southern Europe, and the changing landscape of Europe. In Year 9 (ages 14 to 15), Europe was one of five cross-curricular themes of the Hauptschule curriculum, with one further geographical teaching unit on the EU (see Appendix 4). Mr. Koch, the community studies co-ordinator, maintained that there was no alternative to the European dimension and that it was essential to deal with Europe in school:

> DF: Citizenship, as well as other subjects, should include experiencing the European dimension. What do you make of that?
>
> MR. KOCH: Must, must; not should. The curriculum must have a European dimension. We are living in a united Europe, a multicultural society, especially here at this school and the European spirit must be promoted stronger than ever before. There is no alternative to that. The only problem we have is that we do everything on a theoretical level. For example, it's very problematic when I visit

---

5   This programme gives students the chance to solve smaller conflicts their peers have without teacher involvement. It works on the principle that a non-partisan trained mediator (one of the students) steps in and sets up a frame within which the conflicting parties develop and negotiate solutions. This might be one contributing factor for the relatively low overall exclusion rate of 4 per cent (14 out of 320 students) per academic year in Tannberg Hauptschule.

Strasbourg with my Turkish students; they need a visa. Same problem occurs when I want to travel to England; I have a lot of trouble at the border. That shouldn't be the case in a united Europe; all countries should have the same rules. But it's absolutely necessary to deal with Europe in school.

The head of geography, Ms. Brandt, also maintained that 'the EU is not only important because nearly all students come from a European country, but also has governmental institutions that are more important than the national ones. For example, students should be able to debate why a country should join the EU or not'. Although teachers strongly advocated a European dimension in education, they argued that it was difficult at times to strengthen in students a sense of European identity, particularly because of a lack of funding and students' socio-economic background. The deputy principal maintained that 'my dream would be to take my students to Turkey or to our neighbouring country Poland, which has just joined the EU [on 1 May 2004]. Few Hauptschulen have achieved this. But there's always the problem of how to get money for this'. Mr. Müller went on to describe a sailing trip that the school organized with a group of students, off the Dutch coast. 'We got in touch with the local people and being on a boat helped strengthen values such as honesty, punctuality and responsibility'. In theory, the teachers I interviewed agreed that a European dimension was compatible with a national and multicultural dimension. However, their classroom experience showed that Hauptschule students had difficulties understanding the European and global dimensions:

> DF: To what extent do you think that a European dimension is actually compatible with a national and multicultural dimension?

> MR. MÜLLER: The problem is the linguistic dimension and I have to say that some of our students have enormous deficits, perhaps even intelligence deficits. That's why it's difficult to integrate these students into a European and global community as I'd have it in mind, a sense of free movement and communication with others in other countries. Nevertheless, I try to educate them by taking them to the European Parliament in Strasbourg and I also go and visit concentration camps in France or elsewhere. And then they start raising questions "why France and what about the French and German histories?" And then I teach them how European history actually works and what pivotal role France and Germany have played to create the EU and to bring Europe into a new dimension. That's very important but the question is to what extent they are actually capable to understand that.

The European ethos of Tannberg Hauptschule was also visible within the classrooms and along the corridors where I saw maps and posters of Europe and the EU. By contrast, the school appeared to do little to address the diversity of its predominantly working-class population. Ms. Brandt, the head of geography, argued that 'perhaps we should have more cultural events. So far, we only do that every two years when, during our school festival, parents from different countries cook their national dishes. But there's nothing more; well, there's one Turkish mother-tongue teacher'. Also, in some of the classrooms, there were a few Turkish pictures of traditional food, prophets that appear in the Koran, the Hajj pilgrimage, Islam clothing, information on India, and a sub-Saharan Africa map that included the independence days of various African countries.

Despite some intercultural teaching, the teachers I interviewed appeared to struggle to combine the notion of multiculturalism with the dominant European agenda. For example, while eating with the students in the canteen, I witnessed cultural insensitivity amongst some Tannberg Hauptschule teachers towards Turkish Muslim students (although these might not necessarily be their espoused values). On that particular day, there was pork and beef sauce available for the students and the teachers on duty told a male German student who wanted to help himself to some beef sauce that this is 'Muslim sauce' (*Moslemsoße*) and that he should rather take some 'non-Muslim sauce' and when the German student asked why he should not eat beef sauce the supervising teacher replied that 'you will get impotent from that'. I also sat in some lessons where teachers occasionally spoke German with a foreign accent (*Ausländerdeutsch*), and thus either intentionally or unintentionally ridiculed some ethnic minority students in class. These examples indicated how some teachers marginalized migrant students.

Although there was no obvious hostility towards Turkish students at Tannberg, there were other suggestions that Turkish people were still considered strangers and not part of the European project. For example, Ms. Klein, the head of religious education, referred to the Christian roots of Germany and Europe and established a racial/religious hierarchy which privileged the Christian cross over the Muslim hijab. She also showed little understanding for the dilemma Muslim teachers faced in German schools:

DF: How do you feel about wearing headscarves or crosses in school?

MS. KLEIN: I think that we are still Christian Occidental [i.e., white western and European] here with our basic values. I am of the opinion that if a religious symbol was allowed in class then it should be the cross. Islam, for me, has both a religious and political dimension and I'm not allowed to wear the cross in a Muslim context. Then why should we allow things, despite being a democracy, that are not possible in other countries either. I mean, I can only argue from my religious viewpoint. When children wear the headscarf I have no problem with that but I think that as a teacher I have a political function. As our constitution demands neutrality, and teachers are meant to be role models, I cannot accept that. And if teachers were allowed to show their religious-political background, then it should be the cross and not the headscarf.

The deputy principal, Mr. Müller, felt that 'you've got to see that there could be a loss of values within our German culture by allowing everything. I want my students to go swimming together, to travel together and don't want anything that separates them. Sometimes [Muslim] students are not allowed by their parents to attend swimming lessons. I mean, where are we?' The remarks of Mr. Müller here resemble those of Ray Honeyford, the Bradford ex-headmaster, who promoted notions of educational nationalism in Britain in the 1980s (see Tomlinson 1990). The difference, of course, is that notions of nationalism were replaced with Eurocentrism at Tannberg. Arguably, such a Eurocentric educational approach and ethos made it very difficult for students, and Turkish students in particular, to identify with the concept of Europe. Let us now take a closer look at how young people in this school environment talked about themselves.

Comfort, Friendship and Interaction

Both ethnic majority and Turkish minority students, all of whom were born in Germany (i.e., second-generation), appear to have had cross-ethnic friendships and felt safe in the German society. However, as we shall see, there were also tensions between the ethnic communities and the Turkish youth were subject to verbal abuse and discrimination because of their cultural and religious 'otherness'.

To examine Turkish students' attempts to integrate, I asked them about their comfort level with German society. While the Turkish boys I interviewed tended to explain their comfort in the German society in terms of the economy, work and their future, Turkish girls in this sample talked more about their social life, their societal role and relationships. The discussion I had with the Turkish male and female interviewees revealed the extent to which this group had adapted to the German way of life. This was particularly evident in the case of Umay who was allowed to go out in the evenings, just like most German girls, whereas this would be more problematic for her if she lived in the rural area of Turkey where she originated from:

DF: How comfortable would you say you feel in Germany?

YELIZ: I feel comfortable here and in Turkey, there's no difference. Turkey is chaotic, loads of people want, because it's a southern country and in the evenings, loads of parties and stuff.

UMAY: I feel much more comfortable here because I can go out late in the evening whenever I want. When I come home from school and don't fancy going out but wanna go out at nine or ten, then I'm allowed to do that. In Turkey, it's different; and where I live everybody knows everybody and when I go out at ten there are only men and boys gossiping about you and I don't like that. I have to be home at seven in Turkey.

UGUR: I feel most safe here, in terms of work, security, and we have a future here I would say.

TAMER: Well not completely. I don't feel completely safe here.

YELIZ: Yes, I feel more comfortable here too than in Turkey.

In ways not dissimilar to Turkish students, who compared their experiences of Germany with their country of origin, the ethnic majority students often compared their level of comfort in Germany with other countries such as Israel and England. For example, Peter argued that 'in contrast to Israel, Germany is a safe country because there are no suicide bombers here. People don't fight for their religion as they do there. People there dress differently, Germans rather solve things diplomatically'. While Peter referred to the low level of violence in Germany and the local community of Tannberg Hauptschule, the ethnic majority students who took part in the mixed-sex focus group focused their discussion on Germany's environmentally-friendly politics. Only Andrea drew on ethnic diversity to explain her partial discomfort in the German society arguing that 'I have seen fights between people of different nationalities here and stuff like that and theft (…) I feel comfortable yes and no, the police should do more'.

Both ethnic majority and Turkish minority students said their parents engaged in their education. For example, Ralf maintained that 'they help me find a job, yes, and say I should study a lot (…) They search the newspaper for apprenticeship places'. Peter added that 'they give me something to eat and a place to sleep, that's the most important thing. My brother tells me where to find a job and my mum helps me with my schoolwork'. Peter's remarks not only indicate his disadvantaged socio-economic background, with his parents not being able to afford homework tutoring or computer equipment, but also contrast sharply with the experiences of students in Goethe Gymnasium, which we shall see in the next chapter. Discussions with various students underline that the support parents could offer largely depended on socio-economic status:

ANDREA: Yes, of course, they help me whenever they can. They plan things for me, like getting news from job centres and stuff. Look that I get advised, that I have addresses of schools for further education or apprenticeships, that this info get sent to me. I don't know, my parents just help me wherever they can. […]

BÜLENT: Yes, they do, my parents always say that I should study hard cos it's important. They always tell me to study, because when I was in Year 4 (ages 9 to 10), I was bad at school; I got a 4 in German (equivalent to grade D) and I didn't deserve that, but today it's different and my parents tell me to study. […]

SEMA: My dad always wanted me to go to a "Realschule" (secondary modern school) but I said that I wouldn't be able to make it, I said that I'd prefer to get a good "Hauptschulabschluss" (a qualification below GCSE level), that's more important to me and he accepted that. But he was really sad about that.

Both Andrea's and Sema's parents wanted their children to continue with their education and get a higher qualification. What is particularly interesting is that there were no apparent gender differences in parental support and that Sema was encouraged to study hard and find a good job as much as Bülent and Andrea. Not only does this indicate a rather progressive attitude amongst Turkish parents, but also shows the extent to which this group of second-generation Turkish students are integrated into the German society. Other studies have revealed similar findings. Şen and Goldberg (1994) and Şen (2000) compared the level of integration of first- and second-generation Turks, concluding that while many first-generation Turkish Muslims (i.e., parents) had a relatively poor educational background with limited knowledge of German and strong identification with their home country, most second-generation Turks (i.e., first-generation children born in Germany) identified to a similar extent with both Germany and Turkey and had partly adapted to German society and values.

Cross-ethnic friendships further showed second-generation Turkish students' attempts to integrate in my study. When I observed some of the lessons, I noticed that students mixed fairly well and I also saw cross-ethnic friendship groups, including groups consisting of Greek, Turkish, Thai and Syrian students; others with Russian, Italian, Turkish and German students; and yet another group of Albanian, Turkish and Italian students. Age seemed to have been a more important factor in the formation of groups than ethnicity. Most second-generation Turkish students I talked to had mixed friendship groups. However, there was a tendency amongst some respondents to favour non-German classmates of mainly European origin. Generally, this study did not find that ethnicity played a major role with regard to choosing friends:

DF: Could you tell me a bit about your friends, where they come from?

CENGIS: Italy, Croatia, Serbia, Greece. I've different friends from different countries and we all get on well.

BÜLENT: I've got friends that are half Greek and half Turkish although Greece and Turkey had an argument initially, only in the past. The citizens (of Turkey and Greece) sometimes argue with each other and stuff.

HAKAN: They're all our friends. It's humanity. There are people who say things against Albanians and stuff, they make jokes about them.

ZEHEB: Yes, or in the United States, black people were called niggers and stuff.

The four nationalities mentioned by Cengis were also the largest ethnic minority groups other than Turkish in Tannberg Hauptschule (only about one-third of students were of German origin, 37 per cent). Hakan's reference to humanity might indicate that, for him, personality was more important than ethnicity. The non-German mixed European friendship groups could, however, also indicate that the sample of Turkish students felt more at ease being friends with other ethnic minority classmates with whom they shared their migrant children status in the German society. We have seen in Chapter 2 that, until the late 1990s, politicians and policy-makers deployed a distinction between Germans and non-Germans. Migrant workers from all countries, but particularly of Turkish origin, were often perceived as socially and ethnically inferior and addressed with oppressive terms such as 'guest worker' or 'foreigner' irrespective of their length of residence in Germany.

Similarly, a majority of ethnic majority interviewees had mixed friendship groups. However, there were also a few German students in this sample who employed racialized and exclusionary discourses towards ethnic minority people, and Turkish youth in particular. These were counterproductive to the integration attempts of Turkish students (and the Stuttgart integration policy) and resulted in divisions between some respondents which, as we saw earlier, were reinforced by the hostile remarks of some of the teachers at Tannberg Hauptschule. For example, the male and female ethnic majority interviewees discriminated between Germans and 'foreigners', a term which Benjamin and Sebastian seemed to equate with 'being Turkish':

DF: Could you tell me a bit about how mixed your friendship groups are?

FRANZISKA: I have only Germans in my group. I won't let any foreigners in.

TOBIAS: No, that's not the case with me. But foreigners do have other opinions and stuff.

FRANZISKA: We've enough foreigners here in Stuttgart. We don't need anymore as friends. I don't know, it's not that I hate foreigners. It depends where they're from.

SEBASTIAN: No, I wouldn't say that, every human being is different.

BENJAMIN: I've recently seen in a chat show, there was a "Southerner" and he sat down and said that Germans were ugly and stuff like that and started like "you have small dicks" and stuff. He said that his wife would only be in the kitchen, exactly the kind of Turk that we have here. And when you pass by them they say "What are you looking at? You wanna be beaten up?" They say things like that.

SEBASTIAN: They make so many children here. I hardly see a Turk who doesn't have a brother or sister, always five family members or more.

JESSICA: That's good though cos if we didn't have the foreigners we would be few people here. Germans only have one or two children and that's not enough. We need foreigners, we just have to get used to the facts.

The use of the word 'foreigner' by these youth has several different connotations in Germany. Firstly, it refers to the different citizenship status between ethnic majority and ethnic minority communities.[6] We have learnt in the previous chapter that the concept of German citizenship has been organic and ethnicity-centred and, until 1999, migrant workers had limited or no right to German citizenship. Only since then has 'ius sanguinis' been complemented by a 'conditioned ius soli'. In addition, the use of such isolating terms by ethnic majority youth sent a strong message to ethnic minority communities that they are different, unwanted and not part of Germany. However, because the term 'foreigner' or 'foreign citizen' has been used frequently throughout Germany, some Turkish youth, as we shall see below, have come to terms with their status and even use the word themselves. Finally, in purely linguistic terms, the word 'foreigner' can mean someone who comes from a foreign country or someone who is not a member of a group (i.e., who is an outsider). While it is not necessarily always clear in official public discourse which meaning is referred to, the sample of ethnic majority students at Tannberg mostly associated 'foreigner' with 'outsider' (see also Bagnoli 2007). As we saw above, Franziska described herself as having only German friends, 'I have only Germans in my group. I won't let any foreigners in'.

The discussions I had revealed that the tensions between groups were expressed verbally rather than in gang fights. Many Turkish interviewees felt that their community was not included in the German concept of nationhood and that they were subject to discriminatory remarks because of their Muslim religion and cultural differences. Similar to my study, Auernheimer (1990) also observed that young Turks in Germany are being marginalized and discriminated against, and face three problems: firstly, the culture of origin looses meaning; secondly, family strategies dominate individual lifeplans (familism); and thirdly, individuals acquire a marginal identity and positioning in relation to both cultures of reference. In Germany, Auernheimer argues, Turkish youth share the first two problems with young people from other ethnic backgrounds, whereas they experience

---

6   While ethnic Germans who migrated to Germany qualified for dual citizenship, migrant workers did not have any right to German citizenship until 1993. In spite of the new legislation of a conditioned ius soli in 1999, some discriminatory practices remain as ethnic Germans are granted dual citizenship whereas migrant workers have to make a choice between German citizenship and the citizenship of their country of origin. For more, see Chapter 2.

particular conflicts in relation to the third issue (acquiring a marginal identity) as a consequence of their positioning within racist discourse.

According to Auernheimer, the marginality of young people of Turkish origin in Germany became evident when they found themselves disparagingly identified as *almanci* (German Turks) on their visits to Turkey. Boos-Nünning (1986) maintained that second-generation Turkish adolescents in Germany face a reference group problem. Where they privilege the validity of their own individual perspectives, they find themselves rejected by their minority community and subject to pressures to conform to German culture and society. Those who are prepared to conform in this way, according to Boos-Nünning, run into problems with their families, but cannot count on being truly accepted into German society either because of their cultural and religious 'otherness'. The statements of Turkish students who took part in the mixed-sex discussion group in this study echoed this finding, emphasizing that it is above all members of the Turkish community who are referred to as 'foreigners' in Germany. They noted that Turkish students in Tannberg Hauptschule were singled out by teachers and classmates because of their Muslim religion and customs:

DF: Have you ever experienced any form of discrimination or prejudice?

BÜLENT: Yes, I have. People say "they're Turks" and stuff; and the women because of their headscarves.

HAKAN: The Germans call the Turks "foreigners", not so much any of the others. [...]

YELIZ: When my mum and my auntie were on the tram one day, a German approached them, stared at my auntie and she said "why are you staring at me like that?" And then he said "why do you walk around here wearing a headscarf?" My mum doesn't wear a headscarf but my aunt does and my mum found that guy really silly cos the Germans used to wear headscarves too; they used to go to church wearing a headscarf, I mean, we're not the only ones wearing headscarves.

TAMER: And some people say "fuck the Turks". There are many who don't really like us'.

UMAY: I was once waiting for the tram together with my sister. An old woman came to us and said something stupid, said "shit religion".

While some (Turkish) students I interviewed argued in favour of wearing the hijab, others rejected the idea. The following statements of Cari and Bülent on the one hand, and Tamer and Iris on the other, indicate how deeply divided this school community was over the issue of headscarves; and how prominently this topic figured in (Turkish) students' experiences of discrimination and prejudice.[7]

> CARI: Wearing a headscarf is not that bad. There's been a case recently where a Muslim woman wanted to teach with a headscarf. I found it stupid that she wasn't employed because of her headscarf, I mean, if she speaks the language fluently I think it's ok to become a teacher even with a headscarf cos not only Turks wear it but nearly all Muslims. […]

> BÜLENT: I don't find the headscarf that bad. Some Punks dye their hair and stuff and nobody says anything to them. But when they see someone with a hijab then they all say something.

> TAMER: I'm totally against headscarves. My mum doesn't wear one either and I don't like it at all; I don't know what's good about wearing that. I really don't. […]

> IRIS: It's getting on my nerves. In Turkey, women hardly wear headscarves, I've been to Turkey once but here they all wear it. I think it's good that they banned it, it's just impossible that people wear headscarves here in school.

The ethnic majority interviewees were also subject to verbal abuse and reported experiences of prejudice because of both their nationality and socio-economic status.[8] For example, Ralf argued that 'sometimes they say something about Germany that it's a stupid country or so; and then I say go back to your own country and stuff'. Both Peter and Andrea added that 'my friends, all the foreigners, they sometimes call me "potato" and stuff, just for fun. But I don't care. (…) We then say "you foreigner" and things like that. But we only say that for fun'. The term 'potato' here refers not to the vegetable, but to a 'couch potato', a person sitting or lying on a couch. Typically, couch potatoes are seen to be overweight or out of shape. While ethnic majority students called their ethnic minority peers 'foreigners', the Turkish and other ethnic minority students called their white peers 'potatoes'. Both terms imply a sense of racial/ethnic hierarchy and are a means by which these 15-year-olds reassert their racial superiority. I return to and elaborate on this notion of racial/ethnic hierarchy in my discussions of Turkish and African Caribbean youth at Millroad School in Chapter 6. I shall now move on to look at

---

7   Cari referred to the prominent case of the Afghan Muslim teacher Fereshta Ludin, discussed in Chapter 2, who was banned from teaching in Baden-Württemberg because of her headscarf. This example underlines Cari's awareness of the current German societal debate and thus suggests her degree of social integration.

8   I am not suggesting here that the terms of abuse were necessarily equal across the countries and schools discussed in this book.

young people's knowledge of politics which, in addition to Tannberg's ethos and peer cultures, also impacts on the formation of their identities.

Political Positioning and Ethno-National Identities

The predominantly working-class background of students at Tannberg may have been a reason why many engaged in a discussion about local and national political issues. The group of four ethnic majority boys I interviewed were happy to talk about unemployment, apprenticeship places and tax reform, and also mentioned the job competition they face with 'foreigners'. Arguably, some of the discriminatory remarks against Turkish youth described earlier in this chapter were linked with the fear of economic competition, as the following quotation demonstrates:

> DF: What do you see as important political issues nowadays? What interests you?
>
> JAN: Well, the war and stuff. There was a war in Iraq. If an Iraqi lives here, then there'll be prejudices again although he can't do anything that he's Iraqi.
>
> MICHAEL: I haven't watched the news for half a year.
>
> FLORIAN: I don't know what's going on in politics. I mean, the things that I need to know, apprenticeship places and stuff like that, I know. But other things don't bother me. And even if it interested me I couldn't do much about it anyway. So, I just can't be bothered.
>
> DOMINIK: Well, I haven't watched any news either for the past week. I'm only interested in unemployment, that the foreigners get a job and take our jobs away. They work for less money, on the black market and stuff, and take the chances away from others.

These young people did not perceive European and global political topics to be particularly relevant to their lives (except for the war in Iraq). Also, there was a difference between the voices of some of the male and female ethnic majority interviewees as Julia argued that 'family politics is most important. Families need more support. It's not important to raise a child with all the expensive branded clothes and stuff'. In contrast, none of the boys in the study talked about child and family politics.

What was noticeable in my discussions was the ways in which the Turkish youth linked politics to current ethnic issues, such as the issue of Turkish EU membership and the current situation of the Kurdish people. Without being able to engage fully in the discussion because of their lack of political knowledge, the group of four Turkish girls nevertheless referred to both Turkey's situation in the EU and welfare support:

DF: What do you see as important political issues nowadays?

SERPIL: Nothing.

AZIZE: Nothing either.

ZERRIN: I am for politics but I don't really have much knowledge. I can't understand it, when I watch the news. I don't understand many of the things they're talking about. But I'm interested so that I don't have prejudices. (...) Turkey wants to join the EU, they're thinking about it and talk.

SEMA: Well, income support and what they do with that is important. I was wondering how to monitor that those who have a job don't get additional welfare support. Those things are interesting.

Zerrin indicated that it was difficult to understand the complexity of political issues as well as the language with which politicians and the media convey their information. Language difficulties, particularly on the part of some Turkish respondents, might be one of the reasons why the majority of Turkish interviewees mentioned Turkish television as their main source of political information. For example, Bülent stated 'I watch Turkish news but also German television'. Turkish students in this school seemed to draw on the facilities and structures provided by their own ethnic community.

The school itself was also mentioned by a majority of respondents as a source for political information and thus helped shape students' political identities. Both ethnic majority and Turkish minority students I interviewed said that they have been provided with information on the Iraq war, the headscarf debate, job opportunities, the Turkish EU membership debate and the special tax on alcopops (alcoholic soft drinks) introduced by the government in 2004 to limit alcohol abuse amongst young Germans. Peter, a German student, referred to the new alcopops tax, arguing that the school taught him that 'kids start drinking that, it's the number-one drug and so on; smoking, too, is one of the entrance drugs and that you can get addicted to that and have a breakdown'. The fact that many students at Tannberg mentioned the school as a source of political information might be a result of compulsory politics lessons in the German education system along with informal conversations taking place in the school.

The Turkish 15-year-olds mostly argued from a German viewpoint when talking about the possibility of a Turkish EU membership, which was not only suggestive of their familiarity with contemporary national socio-political debates but also indicated the ways in which they brought together ethnic identities with national identities. The Social Democratic-Green coalition government (1998-2005) had argued in favour of full Turkish EU membership whereas senior members of the Christian Democrats prefered a 'privileged partnership' (see İçener 2007).[9] A similarly distant approach was adopted by both Sema and Zerrin, who thought of Turkey as a largely backward country and not only distanced themselves from those Turkish people who live in Turkey and who, according to them, know little about life in Germany, but also rejected some of the customs associated with the Muslim religion:

> DF: How do you feel about Turkey joining the EU?

> SEMA: I don't want Turkey to join the EU.

> ZERRIN: Me neither.

> SEMA: Germany, Turkey is bankrupt anyway. What do they want in the EU? In Turkey, they think that everything is fine in Germany. Turkish people approach me and ask me where I was from and when I say "from Germany" they ...

> ZERRIN: (interrupting) They want to marry you, want to follow you to Germany and lead a better life here. That was the case with my brother-in-law too. Well some things are better here (...)

> SEMA: Some Germans also think that the Muslim religion is a bit stupid. I find it stupid too. The fact that you can't eat pork or have a boyfriend, which is the case amongst Turks, I mean you are only allowed to have a boyfriend when you're engaged. That's just nonsense.

In contrast, some Turkish boys in Tannberg who are part of the study were either neutral or in favour of their country of origin joining the EU, which may be a result of their stronger Turkish identity. There was a tendency amongst the group of 15-year-old boys at Tannberg to consider their ethnic background as more important than their German identity, while the group of Turkish girls identified with Germany and Turkey to an equivalent extent. Bülent says that it would be good for Turkey to share the knowledge of the European community whereas Tamer maintains that it would be financially beneficial for Turkey to join the EU:

---

9   The German Christian Democrats (CDU/CSU) are the most vocal supporters of the idea of a privileged partnership. In addition, Austria and France have announced referenda on Turkey's EU accession. Proponents of this position (e.g., Angela Merkel, Nicolas Sarkozy) cite the incapacity of the EU to absorb Turkey without foreclosing future integration. Others (e.g., Valéry Giscard d'Estaing) argue that Turkey is simply not a European country.

BÜLENT: Well, I would say if more Turkish people come to Germany it wouldn't be good, I mean, there are advantages and disadvantages. It's good if Turkey joins because it's a community and the others know a lot; that's good. (…) I think that the human rights situation has changed a lot, not everything but many things. […]

TAMER: I find it quite ok, but also not. I wouldn't find it good if lots of people come from Turkey to Germany. But many want to improve their social position and that's good. (…) Turkey would get support if they joined the EU and then it would perhaps be better for the country than now.

The ethnic majority students I interviewed were similarly ambivalent regarding a possible EU membership of Turkey. While some drew on EU political discourses advocating membership, others conceptualized the Turkish students as dangerous fundamentalists with a potential for violence. For example, the group of German boys argued that 'They'd have to change a lot of cultural things and stuff (…) They'd have to change their penal code; people still get beaten there'. Similarly, Peter thought that 'I don't mind Turkey joining but they have to abolish death penalty', and Andrea added that 'I have nothing against Turkey joining the EU but the EU itself said that Turkey would have to change a few things. They'd have to pay more attention to human rights and equality'.

In contrast, in the wake of the terrorist attacks on the United States on 11 September 2001, the male and female ethnic majority interviewees were a lot more sceptical and employed xenophobic discourses when comparing Turkish Muslims with terrorists. While Benjamin and Franziska felt that a Turkish EU membership would make little difference, Sebastian and Jessica argued that terrorism could spill over more easily into Europe with the new EU then bordering to Iraq and other Arab Muslim countries:

DF: What do you think about a possible Turkish EU membership?

BENJAMIN: I think that not much would change. Many Turks are already here so that I don't think there'd be much of a change.

FRANZISKA: Yes, I mean, plenty are already here. Why should they still join? They've already joined. That's how I see it.

SEBASTIAN: It would be the first Muslim country though. Right now, that wouldn't be such a good idea; perhaps terrorist attacks would then also come to Europe and so. That would be a disadvantage; on the other hand there would be better access to all the Arab countries. If there was another war in Iraq or in that region there'd be a country where we could have a military base. That's an advantage.

JESSICA: (interrupting) Oh, I just remember that, because of terrorism, Turkey has a lot to do with terrorist attacks so to speak. All these Muslim attacks in Iraq and so on. And I think if we get them to join the EU, terrorism will come closer to Europe and there could be terrorist attacks here too.

Although both ethnic majority and Turkish minority youth engaged in a discussion about the possibilities of Turkish EU membership, their general knowledge about Europe and the EU seemed to be rather limited, as measured by the student survey I conducted. This despite the school's promotion of strong European agendas and identities. The student survey showed no statistically significant differences between ethnic majority and Turkish minority students, and both groups referred to Europe as a political and monetary union. The Turkish students at Tannberg listed some concepts including 'the euro', 'the EU', 'western world' and 'advanced rich countries', but were unable to engage in a wider discussion about Europe and the EU. Tamer, for example, alluded to the 'United in Diversity' motto of the EU and Ugur referred to the EU's peace-keeping role:

DF: What do you know about Europe, about the European Union?

TAMER: It's a community.

YELIZ: That's what I think too.

UMAY: I don't know. I'm not so sure.

TAMER: It's a community of different countries.

CARI: EU, countries that belong together; they talk about politics of different countries; they have negotiations and debate what they can do. It's a strong, political team.

YELIZ: If a country needs help then the other EU countries will help. They have treaties with each other.

UGUR: The European Union is a good thing; we don't have war today.

Ethnic majority students in the study also revealed some factual knowledge about Europe during the interviews. For example, the group of boys and girls referred to power as well as transatlantic and inner-European relationships. Not only was Sebastian aware of the strength of the common currency, but he and Tobias also alluded to the political and economic benefits of a united Europe. Drawing on the dispute over the Iraq war in 2003, Jessica reminded the boys that Europe still does not speak with one voice:

DF: What do you know about Europe and the EU?

FRANZISKA: The euro.

TOBIAS: I think it's better now when it's Europe than when the countries were alone. We are too weak. We would have no chance, for example, against America. The euro strengthens everything, of course. And the English always say "travel to Europe"; they still think they are on their own. That's a bit silly what they think, I just find that the wrong attitude.

SEBASTIAN: Well, I think the deutschmark used to be weaker than the dollar. Now the dollar's become weaker than the euro. And when you're together, when you're a community, you're a lot stronger than on your own.

JESSICA: Lots of languages, lots of cultures, well, I think that Europe is really a comprehensive image although the countries don't always stick together. You could see that with the Iraq war and America, some countries supported America. Germany didn't. And that's where you can see that the countries don't really always stick together.

Some of these glimpses of factual European knowledge amongst 15-year-olds might be the result of European teaching units in compulsory subjects such as geography, history and community studies in Baden-Württemberg secondary schools. In other discussions, Bülent maintained that 'the EU was founded on the good relations between France and Germany', thus alluding to the 1950 proposal of the French Foreign Minister, Robert Schuman, to unite the German and French coal and steel industry. The group of four German girls referred to the country's geographically central location in Europe and also mentioned that Germany and Italy were amongst the six nations that signed the Treaty of Rome in 1957, establishing the European Economic Community:

DF: How would you describe Germany's relationship with Europe?

MANUELA: Well, I think we're in a fortunate position. Germany is at the heart of Europe, because of our central location and stuff.

JULIA: Mmh, that's right.

ANDREA: Well, Germany is one of the first countries of the EU too.

VERENA: (clearing her throat) I think that Italy was one of the first countries too.

Given the country's decade-long commitment to Europe and European politics, it was not surprising that nearly all 15-year-olds interviewed in Tannberg Hauptschule thought that Germany should get closer to Europe. Ralf, for instance, favoured European multilateralism over American unilateralism arguing that 'in the States, Bush has too much power and control and he does what he wants. Here, more countries have a say, they come together and discuss things which is better'. In contrast, Peter reminded us that 'Europe and Germany are dependent on the USA, I mean, Germany is an exporting country' and he called for a more global political approach saying that 'it would be best to include Japan, I mean, Asia, America, Africa and Australia, to have relationships everywhere'. However, an anti-American stance figured prominently in students' European political discourses, likely due to unilateralist policies under the Bush administration (2000-2008), including the Iraq invasion in 2003 that were not supported by Germany:

DF: To what extent should Germany get closer to Europe or America?

TOBIAS: You can't compare that, I think, Europe is different.

JESSICA: America has more land, they have enough. They've oilfields, they can stand on their own. They've resources we don't have. That's why we're more dependent than the USA or so.

BENJAMIN: I think you cannot compare Germany with Europe *and* America. America is not part of Europe, it's thousands of kilometres away from Germany; that's why there's not much reason for comparing them. Germany, for me, only really belongs to Europe and never to America.

FRANZISKA: Only to Europe cos it's part of the EU and everything.

JESSICA: During the Iraq war, that's what I heard, Germany did not participate. They didn't want to follow America.

BENJAMIN: But what is now. Now, the whole world should pay and support. Now, we've to pay to rebuild Iraq. But who's getting all the building contracts there? Who rebuilds the houses? The Americans, as always, cos they send their workers there and we've to pay.

Many Turkish interviewees at Tannberg also argued that Germany should get closer to Europe and, in so doing, positioned themselves within Germany's political discourse. For example, Tamer thought that 'Germany belongs to Europe, we are the EU, Europe, I think' whereas Cari was slightly less emphatic saying that 'the US is fierce. I think it's ok the way it's right now'. Tamer used the inclusive first person plural form 'we' to describe Germany's relationship with Europe, thus revealing his level of integration and the extent to which he adapted to the German way of life and thinking.

Paradoxically, despite having some knowledge about Europe and being able to talk about Germany's role in Europe and the possibilities of a Turkish EU membership, neither the ethnic majority nor the Turkish minority students I interviewed saw themselves as 'European'. Arguably, the Eurocentric approach of some of the teachers at Tannberg (and the predominantly working-class background of Tannberg students) made it very difficult for 15-year-olds to relate positively to Europe as a political identity. Some teachers clearly constructed Turkish youth as originating from a non-European Muslim country. Europeanness, for these students, was not separate from the concept of being German – 'being German' in other words equals 'being European'. Most of the Turkish students I interviewed argued that they felt European only 'because I live here in Germany … we are Germans and Germany is part of the EU'. In contrast, each of the four Turkish boys in one focus group claimed that 'I don't think I feel part of Europe … I feel more Turkish'.

Similarly, most ethnic majority students I interviewed at Tannberg Hauptschule also only felt European 'because Germany is part of the EU and Europe'. One group of students, for example, argued that 'if you go to a foreign country and you say that you are European and not German, you are perhaps treated a bit better'. This remark can only be understood in light of Germany's particular history of the Third Reich and the subsequently ambivalent relationship with its past and national identity, as we saw in Chapter 2. A small minority of respondents felt rather proud about their German identity in contrast to Europe, saying 'I feel German; I don't know what all these countries have in common'.

When asked what they associated with Germany, the group of five Turkish boys and girls referred to 'education' and 'rights' as well as the changing economic situation:

DF: What do you associate with Germany?

UGUR: Education.

CARI: Well, it used to be a safe country, economy, really and you could live here the way you wanted to, and it's not only that, but today it's not like that anymore; for example with apprenticeship places, job places, that all people get unemployed; loads of people are unemployed. Since we got the euro, it's all been going downhill really and that's why nothing is safe anymore.

DF: And what does that mean for you?

YELIZ: Germany has no future either, I suppose.

UMAY: Nothing. No country has any future really. You just participate where you get the ok sign.

CARI: People have human rights.

TAMER: Yes, people have more rights, I think, compared to Turkey.

UGUR: Yes, more rights here in Germany.

YELIZ: Germany is a free country in contrast to Turkey. Some things just don't matter too.

The group's awareness of German economic history has to do with their parents' migration to Germany following the German-Turkish agreement of 31 October 1961 to recruit non-German workers to fill labour shortages partly resulting from the construction of the Berlin Wall and Germany's booming economy at the time. Cari's use of the pronoun 'we' was suggestive of the ways in which these Turkish students positioned themselves within German national discourses as a result of being born in Germany and benefiting from the better opportunities associated with Germany (e.g., education, rights, jobs) as opposed to Turkey.

In contrast, nearly all discussions I had with groups of ethnic majority students centred on Germany's ethnic minority populations and the presence of Turkish Muslims in particular. Some students employed a positive approach to multiculturalism (e.g., 'there are all kinds of nationalities with whom I can be friends') and others, such as the group of four German girls, drew on the divisive theme of 'us' (Germans) and 'them' (Turkish youth) to distance themselves from Turkish people and their culture:[10]

DF: What comes to your mind when you hear the word "Germany"?

MANUELA: Well, I constantly have to think about World War One and Two.

JULIA: Yes, for example, that's what I often think about.

(murmurs of agreement)

---

10   These findings were corroborated by the fact that, in the student survey, the sample of Turkish students associated notions of Christianity (i.e., monoculturalism) very strongly with Germany while ethnic majority respondents had a higher mean score for 'white people'. The survey also revealed that both ethnic majority and Turkish minority students associated European concepts (e.g., part of Europe, language and the euro) most strongly with Germany.

MANUELA: Always having to feel the guilt although we have nothing to do with that any more. And those, Turks, they say shit Germans and shit Nazis and stuff.

VERENA: That's really strange, you get blamed from people who are voluntarily in your home country. But when I then say "If you don't like it here, fuck off" then I only get to hear "I would, but I can't". (…)

JULIA: Recently they collected signatures here cos they wanted to build a mosque in the area; loads of Germans voted against that. Otherwise they would have built a mosque here!

VERENA: That's what they can do in their own country. That's their culture! Let them go back to their own country and do such things there.

ANDREA: You won't find a Catholic or Protestant church in Turkey.

MANUELA: You're really racist. Really bad.

Being in a context in which ethnic majority youth held these opinions created considerable tensions between 'being Turkish' and 'being German' for Turkish 15-year-olds. Although their family was Turkish, most Turkish interviewees seemed to identify with Germany, claiming that Germany was more important than Turkey. It was fascinating to listen to the ways in which the group of Turkish girls balanced their hybrid identities. Hybridization produced a third space allowing other identities to emerge (e.g., Turkish German, Swabian German). However, there is some evidence in this data that 'the language of binary oppositions [i.e., German or Turk]' (Hall 1992) has evolved into one of tertiary oppositions (i.e., German or Turk or German Turk) which also constructs, for instance, the German Turks as 'Other'. The following quotation shows for instance the dilemma Sema and Zerrin face as a result of their ethno-national (i.e., Turkish German) identities. In Germany, they are positioned as 'foreigners' and in Turkey people refer to them as Germans, which is precisely what Boos-Nünning (1986) called a 'reference group problem' and what Auernheimer (1990) referred to as individuals acquiring a marginal identity and positioning in relation to both cultures of reference:

DF: Where do you feel you belong to?

SEMA: As a citizen I feel I belong to Germany. But when people ask me, I mean, when I am here then people call me "foreigner". When I go to Turkey, they call me "German" there.

ZERRIN: Yes, I don't feel I belong to anything. I don't think that I am German and I don't think that I am Turkish. I don't know. When I go to Turkey, then they say "Oh, look at the German"; and here I am a foreigner. Great. So, who am I? Where do I belong to?

SEMA: As a citizen, I can say I belong to Germany.

ZERRIN: I can say that I'm a German citizen but I'm not German. German citizen, I think, means that I have to adapt to this country, I try to adapt myself, and then I think about the laws and everything. I know a lot more about Germany so that I am a German citizen, but I'm not German. But, I'm not Turkish either if you see what I mean.

SEMA: I know Germany better than Turkey. I could never ever imagine living in Turkey.

Zerrin's questions 'Who am I? Where do I belong to?' highlight the ongoing process of identity formation, the struggle between 'being a German citizen' which is based on residence, and 'being German' which is based on blood and race. During the course of the conversation, Sema further justified her feelings, saying that she could not speak Turkish that well and that she did not have any friends back in Turkey. Also, she preferred the freedom of Western societies to dress however you want and distanced herself from those 'typically Turkish women who just sit around all day long not doing much apart from knitting and gossiping about others'. Clearly, Sema, but also Zerrin and others from cities such as Antalya or Istanbul, rejected this traditional Muslim image of women, which is particularly strong in the rural villages of the southeast Anatolia region bordering on Syria and Iraq. This partly accounts for why Sema and Zerrin did not strongly identify with Turkey.

Other Turkish students I interviewed also had hybrid identities. For example, the group of Turkish boys argued that they felt slightly more Turkish than German because 'although we were born in Germany, our origin and family background is in Turkey'. However, their struggle for social acceptance was also highlighted in the experience that 'here [in Germany] we're foreigners and in Turkey we are also foreigners, basically we're foreigners everywhere'. Arguably, the tendency that some boys identified more strongly with Turkey than girls might have to do with their different roles in the Turkish society, where women often have a more domestic role while men carry on their family name, and thus their honour and identity. It could of course also have to do with girls wanting and seeking out the freedoms for women allowed in the German society.

While the group of Turkish students constructed their identities around ethno-national (Turkish and German) communities, they could not easily relate to the regional Swabian identity because of their unfamiliarity with the Swabian dialect, customs and traditions. Swabia was an administrative region in Germany and is today still used in popular culture as an ethnic identity for those living in the Württemberg part of the federal state of Baden-Württemberg, including Stuttgart. However, as a result of being born in Stuttgart, some Turkish students, notably the group of Turkish girls, were able to imitate the Swabian dialect fairly well, saying 'Ah, des koscht du jetzt net mache, gel' (Oh, you can't do this now, can you?). The use of the word 'gel' in this sentence was particularly suggestive of the girls' familiarity with the Swabian dialect. Generally, however, Turkish interviewees at Tannberg argued that 'I feel more part of Stuttgart than Baden-Württemberg'. For young Turkish people who were born in Stuttgart, but not fully exposed to the Swabian culture, this was a rather distant and unfamiliar community.

Some of the ethnic majority respondents linked the notion of 'being Swabian' with concepts of blood and family which, arguably, excluded Turkish students since their families were born in Turkey. The following passages, taken from individual interviews with two German students, show that Ralf and Verena privileged their Swabian over their German identity:

DF: To what extent do you see yourself as Swabian or German?

RALF: Swabian, rather Swabian, yes. Because there are also those in the East and I am rather Swabian. My mum was born here, and my dad, and me too and we are totally a Swabian family, yes. [...]

VERENA: I was born and grew up in Stuttgart, in Baden-Württemberg, and when I was younger I always spent the day at my grandma's place, cos my mum was at work, and she raised me like a Swabian, so.

However, there were also those German 15-year-olds, such as Sebastian, who argued that 'I feel first German and then Swabian, I have a German passport and not a Swabian one'. Despite varying emphases on local, regional and national identities, what emerges from these data is that most of the ethnic majority respondents in Tannberg Hauptschule employed ethno-national (i.e., Swabian German) identities, indicating the multidimensional and complex nature of young people's identities.

Some of the ethnic majority students I interviewed in Tannberg Hauptschule offered what I would describe as a 'chain of identities' by maintaining that the local, regional, national and supra-national European citizenship levels were interlinked and all partly relevant in the processes of negotiating identities:

DF: Where do you feel you belong to?

DOMINIK: Stuttgart, or Germany.

JAN: Stuttgart, Germany and Europe.

DF: Why?

DOMINIK: Don't know.

JAN: Stuttgart belongs to Germany and Germany is part of Europe.

MICHAEL: Well, I mean, I was born in Stuttgart, grew up in Germany and Germany belongs to Europe.

FLORIAN: I live here and when somebody lives in a country, then he's a citizen of that country and that's why we also belong to Europe, Stuttgart and Germany.

JAN: If someone asks me, then I say, I am now living in Stuttgart but I was born in Berlin. I've hardly said European really. Maybe that's just a habit that you don't really say that yet, but when you are more used to it (Europe), then you would say that.

Despite the promotion of European agendas over and above national and multicultural agendas, it appeared to be very difficult for a school like Tannberg to educate its working-class population about the concept of Europe since there were more important issues for students to come to terms with (e.g., low level of education, socio-economic and ethnic marginalization, and worries about jobs). This analysis of the ways in which young people in a predominantly working-class school in Stuttgart construct their political identities highlighted the importance of school dynamics, local context (rather than the school curriculum *per se*), peer group interaction and political knowledge for the construction of young people's hybrid identities. I shall now move on to analyse the ways in which ethnic majority and Turkish minority youth in a predominantly middle-class environment in the same inner-city Stuttgart borough understand the relationships between national, European and multicultural agendas and what messages they receive from the school. Despite a similar curriculum emphasis on Europe, the three political agendas were mediated in rather different ways, producing different identities.

Chapter 4
Liberal Politics in Goethe Gymnasium

Goethe Gymnasium, a university-track school in a more middle-class neighbourhood within the same borough of Stuttgart, was established in 1818 as a single-sex school for girls. In this school, given its academic programme, there was a much stronger emphasis on student performance. As early as 1818, students were taught five lessons of French a week and in 1853 this was supplemented by three hours of English per week. In 1972, the school became coeducational but has maintained its surplus of girls, currently consisting of two-thirds girls (377 girls) and one-third boys (187 boys). Only 135 (24 per cent) of its 564 students come from ethnic minority communities with Italians (31 students) forming the largest group followed by Turks (26 students). Goethe Gymnasium has an exclusion rate of fewer than 2 per cent (eight out of 564 students) per year. Like at Tannberg, boys are more often excluded than girls (seven boys compared to one girl) and ethnic minority students have a higher exclusion rate than their German peers (4.4 per cent compared with 0.5 per cent). The figures are much lower than Tannberg Hauptschule, however. In 2004, ethnic majority students had an average grade of 2.6 – half a grade better than Turkish students (3.1), who had the lowest score.

Goethe Gymnasium, like Tannberg Hauptschule, promoted European values but this time alongside rather than instead of multicultural values. Socio-cultural and ethnic differences were mediated in this school through notions of tolerance, liberalism and a strong sense of community as teachers tried to integrate students on the basis of what I am calling 'multicultural Europeanness'. In this liberal and inclusive school environment, where the relationships between different communities appeared to be congenial, young people privileged what I call national-European (e.g., German European) identities. Like all other Gymnasium type of schools in Baden-Württemberg, Goethe Gymnasium is obliged to deliver a balanced curriculum which, in Years 9 and 10, comprises religious education, German, history, citizenship education (only from Year 10 onwards as a discrete subject), mathematics, physics, chemistry, biology, physical education, music, art, English and French. Additionally, students must choose between Italian and Latin as their third foreign language, or they take more physics lessons. The European dimension of Goethe Gymnasium is not only visible in the teaching of French and English as compulsory modern foreign languages for all students, but also in the range of exchange programmes with France, Italy and Poland. Additionally, the European dimension comes through in citizenship education, which includes a visit by all Year 11 students to the European Parliament in Strasbourg, followed by one plenary session and a talk with a European Member of Parliament. This is an example of how Goethe Gymnasium incorporates its European dimension in the delivery of citizenship.

The school's European and international profile is a result of its particular location and local community. Although there is no mother tongue teaching, the school values the fact that ethnic minority students have an additional language and regards this as an asset. In religious education, for instance, students visit synagogues, mosques and churches alike and the school also has contacts with a Buddhist teacher who is frequently invited to discuss her religion with students. These initiatives were aimed at promoting intercultural tolerance, mutual respect and a sense of community. Like Tannberg, this school was also affected by the initiatives of the 'Pact for Integration' (Stuttgart's integration policy). Not only did Goethe Gymnasium encourage students from all ethnic backgrounds to stand for the youth council of the city of Stuttgart, but it also set up a conflict mediation programme that was similar to that promoted in the Stuttgart Pact for Integration. Because of the diversity of students on roll, who came from no less than 29 countries, Goethe Gymnasium appeared to have adopted a liberal interpretation of the notion of Europe, one that was multiethnic and multifaith. Fewer teacher insensitivities and a higher awareness of cultural diversity compared with staff at Tannberg Hauptschule further contributed to this inclusive European approach.

The Politics of a Multicultural Europe

Unlike at Tannberg Hauptschule, community studies (or civic education) only played a minor role in promoting the multicultural and European values of Goethe Gymnasium. Like in all Gymnasium schools in that state, community studies formed part of the compulsory curriculum for Year 10 (age 15-16) and was taught as a discrete subject for two hours per week. Mr. Meier, the community studies co-ordinator, not only felt that more curriculum time should be allocated to this subject, but also called for a cross-curricular citizenship theme as 'it's very important to give students a sense of political education and passion at a young age'. Given the limited curriculum space allocated to community studies in Germany (one to two hours a week depending on the year and type of school), it appeared that other dimensions including European and multicultural agendas were prioritized. In fact, the most problematic dimension, for most of the teachers, was the national dimension. Miss Fischer, the school principal, commented:

> DF: What kind of national identity should the curriculum promote?
>
> MS. FISCHER: Well, we Germans have difficulties with our identity, much greater difficulties than other European countries because of our past, the Third Reich, and insofar we're actually born to be Europeans because our national identity is very subordinate. Right-wing extremists don't like that and what's worrying me is that some young people are supporting extremist ideas.

Therefore, I'd say that young people are looking for certain rules, role models and a national consciousness because otherwise they wouldn't support that. Young people have an interest in the German past including the Third Reich but they don't show a feeling of guilt and remorse any longer; they just see it as a part of history like Bismarck. They want to know about World War II and find it horrible but it's the past for them (…) I feel European anyway and I think, of course I am German but I don't feel German. I am only aware of my German nationality when I'm abroad sometimes.

The head of religious education, Miss Weber, also had an ambivalent relationship toward German national identity arguing that, in her lessons, the national element was always underdeveloped. 'I have no access to any national values and when I hear that word I've already got a problem with it. But international or general cultural values play an important role in my lessons'. She argued that she is German just because she speaks German and her parents were born there. But apart from that, Miss Weber, like the principal, was not particularly interested in German identities, instead choosing to promote Europe.

DF: Citizenship, as well as other subjects, should include experiencing the European dimension. What do you make of that?

MS. WEBER: Very important, of course. I don't teach national religious education. There's not just a European but a liberal way of seeing things. I mean it's obvious that you also debate with your students what Europe could mean and whether it's an advantage to have a united Europe, as it promotes peace, human rights, or a disadvantage in terms of excluding some religions and countries. Is a united Europe an advantage for the rest of the world or a disadvantage? That's the kind of ethical questions we also deal with. (…)

MR. MEIER: That's an important question. On 1 May this year is the Eastern expansion of the EU; and then we have Europe Day. I mean, it's not very difficult for us because our school ethos is very European. We have school partnerships, theatre, literature and music projects in France, Italy and Poland. We have even had exchanges with Latin America and have provided our students with a dimension that is part of our everyday lives and teaching. We've long been part of Europe and our students feel they are part of Europe.

However, some teachers at Goethe Gymnasium admitted that it is difficult to 'teach' a sense of European identity, arguing that European identity develops more through experiences like travelling, school partnerships and exchanges, as well as modern foreign language learning. While young people at Goethe Gymnasium had access to all these European activities because of their privileged socio-economic background, students at Tannberg Hauptschule were largely deprived of such opportunities. The principal, Miss Fischer, problematized the notion of

European consciousness, arguing that 'the fact that there are still problems in getting educational and vocational qualifications recognized in other European countries is counterproductive for a European identity. Things should be much more compatible, I mean, like it is in higher education'. Here, she alluded to the Bologna Process[1] which was initiated in 1998 as an intergovernmental process outside the EU framework with the aim of creating a 'European Higher Education Area' in order to facilitate greater mobility, employability and competitiveness.

The fact that Goethe Gymnasium promoted European values alongside (rather than instead of) multicultural values became even more evident in the school prospectus which stated that:

> The ethos of our school is characterized by mutual respect, confidence and tolerance towards other people. Our students, who come from diverse backgrounds, practice intercultural tolerance and community; they learn the full range of European languages, cultures and mentalities and can thus develop their own identity within our school. The internationality of our school community alongside its location next to libraries, museums, opera houses, archives, theatres and galleries characterize our profile. Europe as a cultural area is one of our guiding principles.

The school principal felt that, because of the liberal and inclusive interpretation of the concept of Europe at Goethe Gymnasium,

> we don't really need to have loads of strategies in place [for our ethnic minority students]. I've been Head here since 1970, with a break of three years, and I've always seen this school as a multicultural, tolerant, very progressive and liberal school; liberal in the Anglo-American sense. For example, Turkish students are given time off during Ramadan and my colleagues respect that. I tell every student from a non-German background to value the fact that he or she has an additional language. I support German students as much as I support Turkish, Italian or Yugoslavian students.

The notion that multiculturalism and liberalism were 'lived' in Goethe Gymnasium was further underlined by Mr. Meier, the community studies co-ordinator, who had a Japanese stepdaughter and had lived in Africa for many years. 'I don't simply see the world from my Catholic perspective but I'm quite familiar with the Jewish and Muslim religions. (…) I hope that my students feel that there's someone who

---

1   Although it remains an intergovernmental rather than an EU process, the European Commission is now a partner in the Bologna Process (Wachter 2004). Specific areas of concern include the harmonization of institutional structures; the development of a comparable grading and credit-transfer system; encouraging the mobility of students, teachers, and researchers; co-operation on quality assurance; and the European dimension of higher education (see European Commission 2009).

can look beyond any narrow nationalist thinking, without neglecting my Swabian origin'. Also, Mr. Meier rejected the attitude of many Germans to address ethnic minority people as 'foreigners' and thought this to be a cliché that harms students' sensitivity.

Unlike at Tannberg, where some teachers constructed an exclusionary concept of Europe, there was ample evidence that staff in Goethe Gymnasium tried to promote an inclusive multiethnic concept of Europe (i.e., a multicultural notion of Europeanness) and attempted to integrate all students into the school community. For example, the school prospectus showed that, when racial discrimination in Germany boiled over in the 1990s into a series of violent attacks by young neo-Nazi skinheads, the school management organized a series of theme days against hostility. Students covered the outer walls of the school building with national flags from around the world. The school organized a parent brunch twice a year to bond the different school communities together and fostered the relationships between parents, students and teachers. The teachers I spoke to maintained that, as far as they could, they tried to integrate ethnic minority students into their lessons. For example, Miss Adler, the head of geography, strongly argued in favour of a multicultural/international dimension:

DF: How do you include ethnic minority students and address their particular needs in your lessons?

MS. ADLER: Well, first of all I ask where they come from and let them talk about their country of origin. I have a lot of Turkish, Italian and Spanish children in all my classes and we once developed a questionnaire and went to the market hall and specifically asked Italian, Spanish and Turkish traders about the products they sell, you know, products like olives, goat cheese and so on and the kids could learn a lot from that and could see that this is part of Germany's diversity. Also, erm, when we talk about volcanoes in Italy or agriculture in Mediterranean countries students are directly addressed. Mediterranean countries are very similar in their structure and that gives me the flexibility to talk about tourism in Greece or Turkey and then say that it is similar in Spain. (…) I always try to include an international and European dimension in my lessons cos national thinking is a thing of the past.

European and multicultural values also figured prominently in the curriculum of subjects such as geography and history at Goethe (see also Appendix 4). For example, in geography, three out of four teaching units in Year 6 (ages 11 to 12) were spent on Europe with students studying the location of Germany in central Europe, the continent of Europe, and European integration. The entire Year 8 (ages 13 to 14) dealt with global and multicultural geographical issues including India and China, Japan, the United States, and the Muslim world. In history, for half of Year 7 (ages 12 to 13) and the entire Year 8 (ages 14 to 15), the curriculum taught students about medieval Europe, absolutism in Europe, and the Greeks and

Romans. Only some of the Year 10 teaching units explicitly dealt with German national agendas including World War II and National Socialism. However, unlike in the two English schools as we shall see in Chapters 6 and 7, the curriculum did not celebrate national history and the two World Wars. Goethe Gymnasium delivered the mandatory curriculum but in its own unique way, through the promotion of European *and* multicultural agendas.

Cultural Tolerance and Social Integration

Arguably, the fact that Goethe Gymnasium mediated ethno-religious and cultural differences through notions of tolerance, liberalism and a strong sense of community helped students to learn more about other cultures and to make contact with students from different backgrounds. Nearly all 15-year-olds said that, on the whole, they felt 'comfortable and safe' in Germany. A number of reasons emerged in the discussions I had with a group of four Turkish boys. The reasons they gave for their 'comfort' were revealing. They consisted of the familiarity with the local area, a degree of adaptation to the German way of life, the generally good life in Germany which was associated with social class, contacts and friendships with other people, civil rights and the view that Germany is a free country. These reasons were well expressed in the following extract:

DF: How comfortable would you say you generally feel in Germany?

ZAFER: I like it here cos you can live a very good life here as a foreigner, also cos there are many others but, erm, yes.

YENER: I feel very comfortable here. I've adapted and I couldn't, well, Turkey is my origin but in Turkey I couldn't live like I live here, particularly cos I've got everything here.

SEVILIN: Here, you've got many chances to climb up in society as a foreigner, I think.

IREM: I couldn't imagine life elsewhere. I'm talking about Stuttgart, not Germany. I'm familiar with the area. I grew up here. Loads of people know me although I'm in Turkey six weeks during the summer. And when I'm there I think "just imagine another six weeks; that would already be too much".

ZAFER: You just have your rights here and in other countries, I think, that's not the case. You won't be suppressed much as a minority here, when you have another religion. It's just a free country with a good welfare system.

Although the four Turkish boys were aware of their advantaged backgrounds, they were unable to put themselves into the position of the socially deprived students described in the previous chapter. Ali maintained that 'Germany is relatively safe although you can't be totally safe everywhere today cos of terrorism'. Similarly, Nadine drew on the notion of terrorism arguing that 'a lot's been done for security but you can't do much if someone plans an attack no matter how strong the security measures are'. Clearly, these statements were influenced by the memories of the September 11 terrorist attacks on the United States and the Madrid train bombings in March 2004, which took place two weeks before these interviews. The fact that none of the respondents referred to the presence of ethnic minority communities was suggestive of the importance of social class over ethnicity. Social class becomes a unifying factor here which contributes to the societal well-being of these 15-year-old youth.

Besides socio-economic background, parental encouragement and educational motivation seemed to have contributed to students' sense of belonging. Several interviewees mentioned that their parents cared a great deal about their education. Parental support was not dependent on ethnicity or gender. For example, Andreas argued that 'my mum always looks that I am studying, she controls me'. Fatima, a Turkish girl maintained that 'my parents want me to do A-levels, to study at university and to have a good job. And they support me; they're willing to spend money as long as it's for school' and Ali, a Turkish boy, argued that 'they give me everything; I have everything, everything I want; tutors and so on, books. My parents demand a lot from me'. Both Fatima's and Ali's remarks show a liberal, open-minded and supportive attitude on the part of these Turkish parents who did not favour boys over girls with regard to education. Cornelia reveals the academic-mindedness and caring nature of her parents:

DF: What do your parents do to make you feel comfortable in school?

CORNELIA: They totally support me. I mean, when I come home from school I can just put down my things and eat. My mum cooks before she goes to work and leaves the food in Tupperware for me and then I know what to do. That's my mum. Erm, things are just easier that way. (...) My uncle gives me private tuition in maths and physics. My parents support me with that and allow me to revise with him on the dining table for an hour while they go somewhere else. We have an open living and dining room, and then they can't watch TV and go somewhere else to let me have my private lessons and, yes, my uncle is very supportive. There are no problems at all. They all support me a lot.

The culturally tolerant atmosphere at Goethe Gymnasium also contributed to students' well-being. For example, Ali argued that 'there are loads of different nationalities [29 nationalities], I feel comfortable here. This school doesn't make much of a difference between "foreigners" and Germans' and Zafer added that 'the school simply makes me feel part of the community and it doesn't matter from which country you come from'. Other school efforts that were mentioned by the 15-year-olds included trips, group discussions and patience on the part of teachers. In particular, Nadine mentioned that 'teachers take their time to explain things because they know that there are different people here'. Here, Nadine referred to the multicultural nature of the school arguing that some students might need more time than others. She also mentioned the beautiful architecture of the building and the fact that all her friends are in this school too. 'During break times I'm together with my friends and the atmosphere is just great. That's what I like about this school, being together with friends and having fun'. These views stand in stark contrast to what we have seen at Tannberg Hauptschule where some teachers see ethnic minority students, and the Turkish students in particular, as the 'Other'.

Students' stronger sense of integration at Goethe Gymnasium was also expressed in their cross-ethnic friendships. There were no reports of ethnic tensions and all I saw was that students formed groups along gender lines so that there were boys-only and girls-only tables in the classrooms. Although many 15-year-olds had interethnic friendships, there was a slight tendency amongst Turkish youth to form non-German friendship groups which, according to Zafer, was the result of 'all foreigners [being] somewhat equal in their behaviour, just the way they live, they're different from Germans I think, cos they live in a different country and lead a different life'.[2] Nevertheless, Nerhim's best friend was German and the other three girls had German friends too:

DF: Could you tell me a bit about your friends?

SEMRA: Well, my friends are predominantly non-Turks but foreigners from Greece, Italy and Croatia. I've also got German friends but prefer foreigners.

NILGÜN: Turks, Germans, Greeks too; fairly mixed I'd say but that doesn't really matter. I get on very well with Germans too.

NERHIM: I've many friends from different backgrounds, but my best friend is German. That's no problem. I mean, I get on well with everybody in principle. I have no problems whatsoever and that's why I've so many different friends.

ZEYNEP: Well, I've different friends from different countries too. I've never had any problems and stuff.

SEMRA: I think it's stupid when you've got problems with Germans. I mean, we're in Germany but I've no problems with the Germans.

---

2   During the course of the interview, however, Zafer further differentiated between his Italian and Turkish friends who have a different temperament, behaviour, language and religion.

Similarly, as a result of the school's culturally tolerant atmosphere, the ethnic majority students I interviewed had mixed friendships and typically argued that personality was more important than ethnicity when choosing friends. Arguably, socio-economic background and the lower number of minority ethnic students compared with Tannberg Hauptschule might have also impacted friendship patterns. However, given that ethnic majority and Turkish youth in both Tannberg Hauptschule and Goethe Gymnasium had mixed friendships, this seems to be more a result of the school ethos and the more inclusive interpretation of combining multiculturalism and Europe. For example, Kai argued that 'I don't choose friends according to nationality; it's important what the character of a person is like' and Jonas added that 'I don't mind which nationality they have. I've to get on with them'. The openness and tolerance of Sophie and Nadine, which may have been reinforced through the school's teaching of mutual respect and intercultural tolerance, allowed the girls to gain an insight into the (home) culture of some of their classmates and boyfriends. During our conversations, both girls maintained that, despite some religious differences, their friends had very similar characters:

NADINE: I've a Turkish friend and at their home I always have to be very polite. But they give you so much, when I go there, they offer you so many things, whatever you want. That's just so nice. But you've to be polite and respect all the different traditions. That's simple; or, I have a Greek friend too and when I go to his place, they have lots of holy pictures on the wall and talk in Greek and stuff, erm. Then I sometimes ask what this and that means, and learn a lot. That's good.

SOPHIE: My boyfriend is Italian, a proud Italian. And that's how I got to know the Italian cuisine and mentality. But I've lots of Turkish friends too. My best friend is Spanish and I've lots of Croatian friends too. But it also has to do with the area I live in. There are lots of foreigners; but I don't have a problem with that cos I don't pick my friends according to nationality, looks or language, but other personal criteria.

However, while being careful not to generalize from a few personal experiences to an entire group, other ethnic majority interviewees argued that there were certain character and cultural differences between Germans and migrant minorities. For example, Lena refused to make any general comments about Turkish and German youth saying that 'there's a certain difference depending on how they live their culture and religion. I don't think that you would see a Turkish girl wearing a headscarf in a nightclub kissing a bloke. It all depends how they've been brought up and how much their parents have adapted'. Lena was not only aware of the factors impacting on an individual's character and behaviour (e.g., parental level of integration, education, values), but also distinguished between what I would call the 'traditional Turk', whom she described as wearing a headscarf, and the 'westernized liberal Turk'. The latter was more the type of Turkish student I encountered at Goethe Gymnasium as none of the girls wore the hijab and all dressed in a very western way wearing jeans and trainers. Only one Turkish boy (Zafer), who described himself as a German Turk, signalled his Turkishness by wearing red jumpers and a necklace in the shape of the moon star on the Turkish flag.

In contrast, the ethnic majority students who took part in the mixed-sex focus group were less cautious about generalizing from their personal experiences to an entire ethnic group and talked about the differences between Germans and Turks. Without engaging with the first half of my question, Lisa contrasted what she perceived as the strict Turkish mentality with the more easy-going character of Germans:

> DF: To what extent have you noticed any similarities and differences between you and your friends?
>
> LISA: I mean the biggest difference is to the Turks cos they mix up everything; their religion and mentality and so on. They're really strict and we're more easy-going and that's why we mix more with more easy-going nationalities. I mean it's all fine when you're friends with a Turk in school. But when I go to her place, her friends look at me in a strange way and stuff and I've to be very careful what I say and do and I just feel a bit uncomfortable then.
>
> KAI: That's what I noticed too. I was at my Turkish friends' places too and many things are different there.
>
> LISA: I mean, I constantly have the feeling that I do something wrong.
>
> VANESSA: That's got to do with their tradition and stuff. Turkish girls are not supposed to have boyfriends and sex before marriage and I find that a bit exaggerated nowadays in Germany. (…) When I'm at a place of a friend from another country, the parents are often unable to speak German and then my friend has to translate for her mother what I said and so.

However, despite these alleged socio-cultural and ethnic differences, this group of students still formed friendships with the Turkish community both inside and outside the school. There were few signs of any ethnic tensions within the school community. Both ethnic majority and Turkish minority students reported only isolated discriminatory incidents. For instance, Sema argued that 'I've recently heard from my teacher that Turks always have cleaning jobs and that's really hurt me; and then the headscarf is the next problem'. Sema's remarks not only revealed the ways in which some teachers positioned Turkish youth as inferior to Germans but also alluded to the German debate about whether or not headscarves should be allowed in public institutions. Both Maximilian and Alexander maintained that there were some teachers at the school who disliked other nationalities and gave better marks to Germans. Generally however, the dynamics between teachers and students, as well as amongst students, were far from being conflictual and Goethe Gymnasium's liberal and progressive approach earned them considerable local media coverage as a model for overcoming ethnic differences and raising intercultural tolerance.

By contrast, a number of Turkish interviewees felt subject to discrimination and prejudice outside Goethe Gymnasium, much of which revolved around verbal abuse (e.g., foreigners, potato, sexist remarks) and cultural insensitivities (e.g., wearing of headscarves, gender roles in the Turkish society). Some of the cultural insensitivities students encountered outside school are exemplified in the following quotation:

DF: Have you ever experienced any form of discrimination or prejudice?

PELIN: Well, people often ask me why I don't wear a headscarf. That's annoying; I then think "what kind of impression do you have of us". I find that really stupid, these court shows on TV and so; they picture Turkish men beating their women and that's really getting on my nerves that they show this on the telly. I mean, that just doesn't reflect reality any more.

NURHAN: Yes, that's not true. I'd say the Turks are as modern as you are. They can just do whatever they want to and it's up to the individual whether or not they want to wear a headscarf; everybody can decide that alone. (…)

AYSEGÜL: People ask me whether my mum wears a headscarf and whether I need to pray now and other stuff and that's just annoying.

MELIK: They ask things like whether the Koran allows me to masturbate and whether we'd force women to marry us. I mean, there are certain things we're not allowed to do, like sex before marriage, but then we just don't do that. (…)

ISMET: What's also very rude is when they say "eat döners"; for example, some are making fun of the Turks and then they go and eat a döner. I find that rude; then they should go for Italian food.

The above extract highlights the stereotypes these Turkish students are confronted with in German society. Pelin argued that the alleged suppression of Turkish women 'doesn't reflect reality any more', thus indicating her awareness of the changing role of women in the Turkish society. Other incidents of discrimination and prejudice were reported by Zafer and Irem, two Turkish boys. Zafer argued that 'I walked around with a black friend of mine, twice; we got checked by the police once and on another occasion they arrested us on the spot just like that', thus alluding to a potential institutional racism in the German police force.[3] Irem described an incident of verbal abuse saying that 'I was once in a park and there was an elderly German man and I just looked at him, just looked at him, and then he already started to curse saying 'shit foreigners' and things like that. Why does he want to put us all in one pot'? Irem's experiences were examples of the racist sorts of incidents reported in Germany.

Some of the ethnic majority students at Goethe also provided accounts of prejudicial experiences they had had outside school. However, contrary to the accounts of the group of Turkish students, their discriminatory experiences were linked to issues of social class and gender rather than ethnicity. In particular, Felix and Lisa were aware of their advantaged background (e.g., better clothes, better school):

DF: Have you ever experienced any form of prejudice or discrimination?

VANESSA: Well, it sometimes happens that they say "you shit Germans".

KAI: Or potatoes.

FELIX: Depends on the clothes too, cos you're dressed better if you've more money; well, Germans do that and then they [Turks] scold us cos Turks are sometimes dressed differently or so and then they just look at your clothes. (…)

LISA: They behave very badly. Young people, mostly boys, girls are different and they accept things. Girls are more approachable and sociable but the boys just wanna talk to their own kind and are really bad sometimes.

DF: Who do you mean by "they" and what do they do?

LISA: Well, foreigners, mostly Turks and Italians. Boys that come on to us are mostly Turks; they walk around the streets and make "ssh, ssh". And then they can't say normal things, they say "oh, look at her ass" and so and laugh. And the way they look and they're so stupid sometimes. I mean there are also intelligent Turks and so; but the others they go to a Hauptschule.

In addition to low-level ethnic conflict and discrimination within Goethe Gymnasium, students' willingness to adapt to the German way of life was further

---

3   Archer (2003) argued that irrespective of the social class of the neighbourhood in question, Muslim students encountered similar discrimination and prejudice. She highlights three ways in which her interviewees responded: violence, counter-racism and ignorance. There is little evidence from the data I collected as to whether the Turkish students at Goethe adopted any of these strategies.

indicative of their level of integration in this school. A large number of both ethnic majority and Turkish 15-year-olds felt that integration and multiculturalism were compatible and that migrant communities should integrate into the German society *while* also maintaining their culture, customs and traditions. This meant learning the German language and practising intercultural tolerance and mutual respect. For example, the group of German girls considered knowledge of the German language as a key for successful integration. 'They should master the German language. I know so many "foreigners" who can't speak a word of German. If I go to a country then I should first learn the language so that I can communicate and integrate and don't just go there. They should perhaps take a German language course'. Similarly, the group of German boys referred to the need for ethnic minority communities to integrate and adapt in order to prevent parallel societies:

> DF: To what extent should people who come to Germany from other countries give up part of their culture, customs and traditions to fit in?

> MAXIMILIAN: I don't think they should give up their culture but should integrate into the German society, not that we have a group of Germans and a group of Turks who cannot get on with each other.

> ALEXANDER: They should be able to adapt to a certain extent. The religion, there are mosques here in Germany too which is ok.

> LEON: In Turkey, there are quite a few Germans and there's not a single church and I find that quite unfair. But if there's no demand then it doesn't make much sense to have a vicar without a parish.

> TIM: They should accept us cos we also accept them.

> MAXIMILIAN: A black person, for instance, says here in Germany that he's German which is right. He's adapted and so and that's good.

> ALEXANDER: And when the Turks come to Germany they should learn German.

> LEON: They should at least have a good command of the German language.

Some of the Turkish interviewees also argued that 'one should adapt the language, that's what we have to master above all'. However, there were also those who argued that they would not give up parts of their culture, customs and traditions (e.g., 'I'm strictly against that, no matter what the Germans think; we've our rules and I'd never deny my culture'), and others who thought that 'a foreigner who comes to Germany, especially from Turkey, has to give up a few things in order to live here. For example, the headscarf; no matter how religious you are, it's just impossible to wear a headscarf here'. For most interviewees, however, there was no contradiction between integrating into the German society and retaining their culture, customs and traditions.

(Inter)National Politics and National-European Identities

The most important political issues for 15-year-olds at Goethe Gymnasium included national socio-economic topics (e.g., unemployment, apprenticeship places, health reform, immigration, the ageing German population, and education) as well as international topics (e.g., pollution, terrorism, US elections, Iraq war, poverty in Africa, human rights). The difference between ethnic majority and Turkish minority students was that the latter emphasized human rights and civic rights to a greater extent. However, there were no indications that Turkish students referred to the EU membership debate or any other Turkish political issues.[4] Apart from Ali, all three interviewees in the following quotation referred to the high unemployment rate which, at the time of the interview in March 2004, was 10.9 per cent of the German working population:

DF: What do you see as the most important political issues nowadays?

YENER: Unemployment, the pension system as such and what my future will be like. That's the most important for me. My future and, yes, war and human rights; but a job and all the financial stuff is a bit more important. (...)

ALI: Erm, for me, politics is very interesting; for example, the USA when they went to war with Iraq and that they were there before that too. I questioned my dad a lot. I am very interested in the EU and the USA at the moment. [...]

CORNELIA: I'd first of all say unemployment and immigration policy but global topics are important for me too. And, erm, family and education and so, I'd say all the social topics are more important for me, I'd say. (...)

MAXIMILIAN: Unemployment. Above all, that we get more jobs and that jobs do not move to China, for example. We're so strong economically and should help smaller countries like Nigeria or so; children are starving to death there.

While some students said that in history and politics lessons they learned about political parties, the structure of the German Parliament, the election system and Europe, others called for even more topical and international political issues in

---

4   Three main reasons emerged from the student interview data as to why Turkish and ethnic majority 15-year-olds were relatively knowledgeable about national and international political issues: media, parents and the school.

school. For example, the group of German girls claimed that 'we've talked a lot about the headscarf, but not enough about international things. Teachers should discuss more things and explain the backgrounds. I've only heard that from my parents and, well, in the news'. Similarly, the mixed-group of Turkish students maintained that 'we should be educated about what's going on in the outside world now and not just historical facts. We've some who say that those things that are happening right now are more important'. Arguably, the demands of some of these students would be better met if history and politics teachers included a 'current affairs lesson' in their weekly schedule.

Although a majority of ethnic majority and Turkish minority students seemed to be interested in politics and showed an awareness of both national and international issues, their political knowledge about Europe and the EU still appeared to be somewhat patchy at times (but was much better than in Tannberg Hauptschule), despite the school's emphasis on Europeanness. For example, the group of German boys knew about the existence of the EU structural fund meant to help poorer countries, and were also aware of the cultural and climatological differences in Europe. Samuel thought that 'the EU represents the opinion of Europe (…) and when a country wants to join, it has to fulfil some criteria but I'm not sure what things exactly'. Despite knowing that 'some criteria' must be fulfilled by countries who want to join the EU, Samuel falls short of naming any of the Maastricht and Copenhagen criteria.[5] In the following discussions, both Semra and Andreas pointed to the expansion of the EU but were not exactly sure how many and which countries will join:

DF: What do you know about Europe and the EU?

SEMRA: Erm, Europe was founded after World War II; that's what I've learned in History. Initially it was only Western Europe and then Eastern Europe became part of it too. EU means the European Union. I think there are twelve countries or perhaps more. [...]

ANDREAS: In a few weeks, new countries will join the EU, it's getting bigger and bigger which is good and bad. I think that the idea of a European Union hasn't really worked as it should have in the fifteen countries and now even more will join. And in a few years, some more will join again. The borders are open and it's called the EU but they don't really belong to it. The new members slow down the integration process.

---

5   One of the 1993 Copenhagen criteria provides for the implementation of the objectives of economic and monetary union. Central and eastern European countries that joined the EU in 2004 and 2007 as well as any future candidates will not be able to opt out of the euro. One of the 1992 Maastricht criteria says that the general government deficit may not exceed 3 per cent of the gross domestic product, or should be falling substantially or only be temporarily above.

Nevertheless, the sample of students at Goethe Gymnasium had by far the highest score of students in all four schools when asked to locate ten countries correctly on a geographical map of Europe (Britain, Germany, Spain, Finland, Italy, Turkey, Portugal, Poland, France, Ukraine). Arguably, the fact that the average scores were higher in both Tannberg Hauptschule (62.6 per cent) and Goethe Gymnasium (77.3 per cent) compared with the two English schools is a result of the schools' emphasis on Europe rather than German values as well as Germany's generally pro-European approach, which we have seen in Chapter 2. Nine out of ten students at Goethe Gymnasium located five countries correctly on the map, with boys doing better than girls. Although German students had a slightly higher average score than their Turkish peers, the fact that this was not statistically significant was an indication of Turkish students' familiarity with Europe and the knowledge they had gained from being educated at a Gymnasium.

The concept of 'multicultural Europeanness' promoted at Goethe Gymnasium also shaped students' discussions about the extent to which we should be governed by European institutions. Unlike in the other three schools, where young people preferred national governments, a majority of 15-year-olds argued for more European integration at Goethe Gymnasium (e.g., 'national laws would be subordinated to the European Constitution'). Nerhim, a Turkish girl, alluded to the notion of a European family, which Sir Winston Churchill powerfully described in his September 1946 speech at Zürich University arguing that, under and within the United Nations, the concept of a European family in the form of a United States of Europe should be created. The following passage highlights the generally pro-European discourses of these students:[6]

> NERHIM: Well, I find the EU, the unification of all these countries, a good thing. It's just the same within a family; for example, when you have a problem then you discuss that amongst four or five people and so; and I find it good that Europe is doing the same generally speaking. (…) Europe is like a family; they gather and debate what could be improved and that's really good.

> LENA: I think that this would result in a state where one has the power, is rich, and I find that a good idea.

> ANNA: If we get thrown into one party, it has to be the same everywhere. It would resolve some problems.

Other examples which were suggestive of the ways in which ethnic majority and Turkish youth related to national and European issues emerged from the

---

6   These findings were corroborated by the fact that in the survey, a majority of 15-year-olds thought that global political issues (e.g., peacekeeping, terrorism, the Third World, equal opportunities, pollution) should be dealt with by European institutions whereas national political issues (e.g., family, employment) should be dealt with in Berlin.

discussions I had with Melik and the group of four Turkish boys. Melik, a Turkish boy, argued that if there was further European integration, 'the language would have to be the same too', thus alluding to the status of English as a lingua franca for Europe. When asked about Germany's relationship with Europe, the Turkish boys argued from a German perspective that Germany is at the heart of Europe and an important and powerful country:

DF: How would you describe Germany's relationship with Europe and the EU?

ZAFER: Well, I'd say Germany is a very powerful country; one of the big countries. You can see that with the European Central Bank which is in Frankfurt. It's just in the middle of Europe.

YENER: Germany is the driving force in Europe and the EU was founded by Germany and the European Central Bank in Germany. They've close political ties with other European countries, like France.

SEVILIN: I think that if Hitler hadn't existed, Germany would today lead Europe and so. They had a few historical problems but I think they'd lead Europe, although it would still be called Europe. Germany would have the say, but now they have to be cautious and hold back. Germany is at the heart of Europe and without Germany today's Europe wouldn't be what it is.

Germany's geographically central location in Europe as well as the country's strong commitment to Europe were also some of the main reasons why a majority of interviewees felt that Germany should feel closer to Europe than America. Several interviewees distanced themselves from the policies of the Bush administration to argue that Germany should feel closer to Europe. For example, the group of ethnic majority boys employed a discourse of 'us' (Europeans) and 'them' (Americans), claiming that 'they've gone to war mainly because of the oil in Iraq. The first thing they took control of was the oilfields; there are other problems in Africa and so. They didn't justify the Iraq war with terrorism'. What is interesting in this statement is the boys' awareness of other problems in Africa that the United States does not seem to care about as well as the association of the US-led Iraq invasion in 2003 with mainly economic interests. Girls also referred to notions of pride, ignorance and influence:

DF: To what extent do you think that Germany should get closer to Europe or the United States of America?

SEMRA: Why USA?

ZEYNEP: Exactly. Germany is in the EU; America is another continent.

NERHIM: They're really proud of themselves and think "oh, we're Americans, we don't want anything else. We only speak our language, only speak English and the others, the rest of the world doesn't interest us". And it could happen that students in lessons – friends who go to America and my teacher told me that – even ask whether or not Germany still has a king. I really find this country a bit backward, sorry. But they do influence the Germans when it comes to movies and clothes for example. I mean, I also wear those kinds of clothes from the States cos I like it.

ZEYNEP: The USA has already enough influence on Germany. That is enough. I mean, when Germany got even closer to the States, that wouldn't be good. (…)

NILGÜN: Germany needs to have close ties with Europe; Germany must get on well with all EU countries for political reasons and stuff. USA is a superpower but Germany doesn't need them cos Europe's getting bigger and bigger and the US smaller and smaller as a superpower; on the other side is China and the EU.

Nilgün's remarks that the days of America as a superpower might be numbered were similar to the argumentation of the French historian and demographer Emmanuel Todd (2004) who predicted the fall of the United States as the sole superpower. Todd, who had already predicted the demise of the Soviet Union, anticipates that American hegemony would wane and an enhanced role would emerge for what he calls 'Eurasia'.

The Goethe Gymnasium school's interpretation of 'Europeanness' to include multiculturalism encouraged the Turkish students to relate positively to Europe, to construct a European political identity, in contrast to the findings at Tannberg where students were not happy to talk about supranational entities as separate (European/ global) identities. Many students I interviewed at Goethe engaged in a discussion about Europe rather than just listing concepts that came to their mind when they heard the word Europe. For example, 15-year-olds typically referred to the EU, the euro and the eastern enlargement in 2004 as well as different languages and culture when defining Europe. Leo argued that 'I think about the expansion, and I also cast my mind back to Columbus. Europe used to be the centre of the world; many things started here', thus alluding to the Industrial Revolution in eighteenth-century England as well as the 'discovery' of America by Christopher Columbus in 1492. The male and female ethnic majority students referred to Europe as a 'union of countries that has come closer together since the launch of the euro', thus showing an awareness of the ever-increasing process of European integration. A group of Turkish girls compared and contrasted the current political structure of Europe with that of America, thus referring to the decade-long debate amongst policy-makers and politicians about the future (final) structure of Europe:[7]

---

7   Some construe the idea of a more political Europe or even of a 'United States of Europe' as a strategy for the continent (e.g., Verhofstadt 2006). Others are keen to emphasize

DF: What comes to your mind when you hear the word "Europe"?

SEMRA: Well, Europe consists of countries that have got together, a community with the same currency. But you can't say that that's a giant country cos there are different languages and you can't say that Europe is one culture. The people are kind of similar but there are nevertheless other cultures and France isn't like Germany and it's different in England. Europe just has the same currency but not the same language and culture.

NILGÜN: For me, Europe is more geographical. It's also more simple that you can move from one country to another. There's the euro, but I don't really like it. I mean, people think that all Europeans are the same but, in reality, there are quite different cultures. I've got relatives in France and when we crossed the border it looked quite different. It's not one country.

SEVILIN: You can't change the cultures, only the laws. I don't think there'll ever be something like a United States of Europe. That's somehow not possible. Maybe it's just a term cos in America each state has its own laws too but the language and culture is the same, and that's not the case in Europe.

ZEYNEP: They all see themselves as Americans.

Despite engaging in European political discourses, most 15-year-olds made identification with Europe dependent on stays abroad (e.g., 'I only know Germany; if I was living in Spain for a few years, then I'd more say that I'm European cos I'd be familiar with different countries'), parental influence (e.g., 'my parents experienced a lot and tell me a lot about other countries and cultures; Europe plays an important role for me too cos I'm interested in getting to know these other countries'), and the school curriculum (e.g., 'we learn a lot of European languages here in school and talking in Italian, English and French to other people makes me feel partly European'). The young people I talked to felt positive about Europe:

DF: To what extent do you see yourself as European?

ALI: Erm, of course I'm European. Europe is very big and is getting bigger and bigger. And when Turkey joins the EU it'll be even bigger. Europe is getting more and more important to me cos of Turkey. [...]

---

that they had merely joined an internal market and that they are not willing to go beyond a 'common market de luxe' (see Emmanouilidis 2009b). As a result, there is a lack of orientation regarding the question of Europe's future. Emmanouilidis (2008) has argued in favour of a 'differentiated Europe' where a European federal state is neither advisable nor realistic.

SAMUEL: Europe, the EU, plays an important role in my life. When I go abroad it's just so simple. There are hardly any border controls and it's just getting easier and easier. The countries are not on their own anymore and are together; and there are no borders anymore, very open. [...]

MARIAM: I feel European because of the euro. The euro impacts on your life. I mean, in the newspaper they always talk about the euro, Eurozone, Europe and so and I've noticed that the countries are getting closer and closer and not every country has its own policy. And the economy has grown together too. And you can travel to other countries without any problems at the borders.

Several ethnic majority students employed the image of a chain of identities arguing that Stuttgart, Germany and Europe were all interlinked and thus sites for identity formation. In particular, the group of German boys thought that 'yes, we live in Europe; Stuttgart and Germany are part of Europe so I also feel partly European. But the Italians, English are all Europeans too. So, if I said I was *only* European [rather than European German or German European] then people might think I'm Polish or so'. However, there was no evidence in the data that young people felt European-*only* or that they privileged Europeanness over national identities.

Instead, while Europe was *part* of young people's identities at Goethe, a majority of Turkish students I interviewed emphasized their German identities over and above Turkishness. They based their national identification on notions of birth and residence. Zeynep, a Turkish girl, thought that 'I'd say more German than Turkish. My dad works here, I plan to study here after school and work here as well' and Nilgün, another Turkish girl, also prioritized her German identity saying that 'I was born here and that's why I feel more German'. In the following quotation from a discussion with the group four Turkish boys, Sevelin felt alienated from Turkey (which he viewed as a holiday destination) as a result of being born in Germany; Yener saw a new Turkish German subculture emerging from the Turkish influence from his parents and the German influence on the streets; and Irem referred to a possible loss of identity and the emergence of a single German identity amongst third- and fourth-generation Turkish Muslims in Germany:

DF: Where do you feel you belong to?

ZAFER: Stuttgart.

YENER: Me too.

SEVILIN: For me, this is my home and when I go on holiday to Turkey, I mean, I go there as a tourist although it's my country of origin. And when I go to the village my parents come from, they call me "the relative from Germany" and Stuttgart has become my home. And I don't think that I'd feel part of any other city.

IREM: In Turkey, I wouldn't feel as comfortable as here although my parents come from there. But I was born here and live here. (…)

YENER: I'd say I'm German but the problem perhaps is to have the Turkish influence of my parents at home, cos they grew up in Turkey, and the German culture on the streets; that together is really a new culture for me and the foreigners are perhaps a new culture here. (…)

IREM: I mean it's already difficult for my parents to pass on all the Turkish culture to me and when I pass it on to my children it will be even less and at some point nothing might be left. And eventually, the generation after us or so will say "we're Germans" just like the black people in America say they're Americans.

In contrast, many of the ethnic majority students at Goethe celebrated regional Swabian identities and formed a chain of identities, arguing that Stuttgart, Baden-Württemberg and Germany were all integrated spheres; 'they belong together, Stuttgart is part of Baden-Württemberg and Baden-Württemberg is part of Germany and Germany is situated in Europe; it's all kind of together'.[8] Risse (2004) refers to these interacting, or complementary, identities as 'nested' like Russian dolls, 'cross-cutting' or folded into each other like a 'marble cake'. The group of four German boys preferred the closer, and thus more familiar, local and regional citizenship levels over the German national level:

DF: Where do you feel you belong to?

MAXIMILIAN: Here. I've never lived anywhere else. I think that I'm a citizen of Stuttgart.

ALEXANDER: Me too. I feel part of Stuttgart too. But I also see myself as a Swabian and, of course, as a German; but I do think I'm Swabian.

LEON: Exactly. That's more direct.

TIM: Yes, that's what I think too.

JONAS: Well, I feel more as a Stuttgarter than Swabian or German.

DF: Why?

---

8 Other areas in Germany also have strong regional identities, notably Bavaria and Berlin. One would thus expect to find similar results among ethnic majority and migrant minorities in other parts of the country.

MAXIMILIAN: Well, I've been living here for fifteen years now, all my friends are here and I was born here too.

ALEXANDER: I feel at home here cos I've always been living in Stuttgart. That's the smallest unit and then Baden-Württemberg. But Stuttgart is the closest.

Similarly, the group of German girls (while also feeling partly European) privileged local and regional identities while problematizing the notion of a German national identity, arguing that 'the only point when I'd feel German is when I speak the German language, my mother tongue. I wouldn't say I'm proud of my country which has to do with the past. If you said "you're proud of being German" you'd be considered a right-wing nationalist or racist because of the past'. As we have seen in Chapter 2, successive German Governments mediated the concept of nationhood through the dominant European agenda and that Europe became a focal point for the organization of the German educational system. As a result of Germany's ambivalent relationship with its past, some ethnic majority youth, such as the group of German girls, privileged local and regional identities but the majority seemed to employ national-European identities.

There were exceptions. Cornelia, for example, developed an identity that had more in common with a global citizenship identity. In the following quotation, Cornelia, an ethnic majority German girl with dreadlocks, was very keen on learning about other cultures, arguing that she felt part of the world because of her well-travelled and knowledgeable parents:

CORNELIA: I'd say I feel part of the world. (...) That's maybe cos my parents lived in Africa for eight years and my dad has travelled a lot due to his job; right now he is working in London. He tells me a lot and I just think we only have this one world; I know that sounds a bit silly but we should make the best out of it. I don't mind at all whether I'm talking to a German, Australian or Turk or whatever. The main thing is that you get on well with everybody and share similar interests, and you just have to make the best out of this world. If people insist on their opinion and it's not good for the world, or the running of the world, then we just have to do something about it. Well and, as I said, we only have this one world and I feel I'm part of it and care about it.

In contrast, the Turkish interviewees, all of whom were born in Stuttgart, did not identify with the regional Baden-Württemberg level (which is similar to what we saw in Tannberg Hauptschule) or the global level. For example, the boys and girls in the mixed-sex Turkish group referred to blood (e.g., ancestors) and family (e.g., home) to distance themselves from Swabia as a political and ethnic identity. Melik remarks in the following excerpt that he feels like a Turkish Stuttgarter, a German-European Turk, or a Turkish German, suggesting the multidimensional and hybrid nature of young people's identities at Goethe:

DF: To what extent do you see yourself as Swabian or German?

MELIK: I feel as a Turkish Stuttgarter so to speak, a German-European Turk or a Turkish German, but not Swabian. I don't know the Swabian culture and, I think, I'd have to be German for that with my ancestors being Swabians too.

NURHAN: You'd have to experience the culture at home but we can only see our Turkish culture and, I mean, I wouldn't want to lose that. I don't really know the Swabian way of life. Sometimes, teachers make Swabian jokes and stuff.

ISMET: (imitating the Swabian dialect) Gel.

NURHAN: We don't really know much Swabian stuff.

ISMET: I'd like to add that I don't see myself as a Swabian either, more as a Stuttgarter. It's also easier to get to know the German culture, just here generally by living here, but the Swabian culture is more at home and I'm not around that. Sometimes I don't really know whether something is particularly Swabian.

NURHAN: Perhaps Stuttgart is the Swabian world and it appears to me like a German world but maybe I don't fully grasp the contrast; I should go to Berlin or so for a while and see what the differences are.

Time and again, Turkish students such as Nurhan also spoke of being afraid of losing their Turkish identity as a result of integrating (or assimilating) into German society. Their Europeanized German identities had become so prevalent in the lives of these Turkish boys and girls that they felt their Turkishness was marginalized.

Not surprisingly, therefore, there was little difference regarding the ways in which both groups of students conceptualized Germany, thus indicating the degree of integration on the part of Turkish youth. The survey revealed that both ethnic majority and Turkish minority youth associated cultural symbols (e.g., language) and Europe (e.g., part of Europe) most strongly with Germany. Unlike students in Tannberg Hauptschule who gave the concept of multiculturalism (e.g., multicultural country) a low priority, it came third in the hierarchy of associations with Germany amongst students at Goethe Gymnasium.[9] This may have been a result of the school's liberal interpretation of Europe and the promotion of multicultural alongside European values.

---

9   The item on the questionnaire asked students to rate from 1 (not at all) to 5 (very strongly) thirteen concepts regarding association with Germany. These were: part of Europe; multicultural country; language; flag; cars; football; celebrities; large families; white people; the euro; Christian country; power; and weather.

The extent to which the school politics of a multicultural Europe shaped the discourses and identities of students was also highlighted in the discussion I conducted with a group of male and female students. Vanessa's comments highlighted the extent to which national values and characteristics were submerged in Germany. In an environment where nationhood is mediated through European and multicultural agendas, students like Vanessa appeared to struggle to talk about typically German things:

DF: What do you associate with Germany?

MAXIMILIAN: Very good and high.

ALEXANDER: In sport too. Michael Schumacher is the best German. The best of all; we can be proud of him.

LISA: The German language.

MARIE: Yes, and the German flag.

VANESSA: In Germany there are so many other cultures, it's so multicultural that there's nothing typically German any more. I mean, people say that the Americans eat fast food and the Chinese have slanty eyes, and others call us Krauts and long noses. I don't know what's typically German, maybe blond hair and blue eyes.

LISA: There are not that many Germans who have blond hair and blue eyes.

ALEXANDER: Other countries don't have a Chancellor, and I also think about the reunification.

Synthesis of German Case Studies

To sum up, the liberal and inclusive interpretation of Europe in Goethe Gymnasium appeared to allow young people to position themselves within both national and international (e.g., European) political discourses and also enabled students to relate to the concept of Europe as a political identity in addition to local, regional or national identities. On the whole, following the national pattern, the two German schools promoted Europeanness rather than German identities, albeit with different emphases. The teachers I interviewed at Goethe Gymnasium seemed to ally the concept of Europe with multiculturalism whereas, at Tannberg, education was more Eurocentric with some teachers getting close to being Muslimophobic. Because the European dimension was privileged over and above national and multicultural agendas, young people in both schools had relatively high levels of knowledge about Europe and the EU, particularly at Goethe Gymnasium, where students' privileged backgrounds allowed them to take part in school exchanges and to travel across Europe (as opposed to their predominantly working-class peers at Tannberg). Despite some of the teachers' comments, there were few xenophobic attitudes amongst the groups of youth. Some Turkish students, particularly at Tannberg, were positioned as 'foreigners' and 'others' by their German classmates and, consequently, employed Turkish German identities. In contrast, in a liberal school environment like Goethe Gymnasium they engaged in national discourses and also thought of Europe as part of where they belonged. While the ethnic majority students I talked to in Tannberg Hauptschule mainly employed Swabian German identities, they prioritized German European identities at Goethe Gymnasium. This suggests that, as a result of their schooling, community experience, and socio-economic background, young people in the two schools developed very different forms of identities, for instance with regard to European and ethnic identifications.

Adopting a similar analytical approach, we now turn our focus to another European country: England. Because of England's links with the Commonwealth, the emphasis on Britishness, and the earlier development of multicultural and anti-racist approaches, the relationship with Europe is very different from Germany. Schools developed rather different policy approaches, which I found to be associated with distinct results in the shape and development of young people's political identities.

PART II
England

Chapter 5
Sustaining National Identities in England

This chapter focuses on three main phases to describe the construction of Britishness. Firstly, the period of immigration and 'deracialization of schooling' (1948-1979), during which time educational policies were by and large not framed in a 'racially explicit' way (Troyna and Williams 1986). Secondly, I describe the racialization of education and concurrent emergence of the New Right under the Conservative government of Margaret Thatcher (1979-1988). Finally, I examine the simultaneous development of citizenship education, the growth of European political and educational issues, and the rise of Muslimophobia in the wake of the attacks on the US, the US-British War on Iraq, and the London train bombings (1988-2009).[1] A renewed debate in the most recent period over the compatibility of Britishness and Muslim identity further complicates the relationship between national, European and multicultural agendas, and sets England apart from Germany. In particular, three major crises have heightened the tensions between Muslims and non-Muslims in England: the Rushdie affair of the late 1980s, the September 11 attacks in the United States, and the July 2005 London bombings. The rise of Muslimophobia in schools, and in society at large, has become one issue common to European countries in the first decade of the twenty-first century. (Turkish) Muslim populations often face enormous conflict and marginalization, for instance, in terms of employment and education. The following analysis highlights the political and educational turning points in each of these periods of British political history, and in so doing, indicates how the school system has been shaped by shifting political priorities, and how the rise of Muslimophobia has played out in England.

Immigration and the Deracialization of Education: 1948-1979

On 22 June 1948 the troopship Empire Windrush arrived at Tilbury, bringing 492 work-seeking Jamaicans to England (Cashmore 1989). Post-Windrush immigration waves from the Caribbean and, subsequently, from the Indian subcontinent mainly

---

1   As previously noted, the data collection for the empirical part of this book took place in 2004, and the macro-political events between 2005-2009 are thus not shaping school policies or youth identities in this study. However, events after 2004 are relevant for our understanding of broader European and transatlantic discussions. Chapters 2 and 5 therefore serve both as a context for the school case studies and the broader debates raised by this book.

brought people to England from former colonies, often with different religions and phenotypes (Philipps 1999, Klein 1993). Unlike Germany, England not only has a long tradition of race and immigration policies (see Table 5.1), but the debates prompted by immigration have also been different from post-war Germany where migrant workers did not have German citizenship. This section shows that the concept of Britishness was protected and reinforced in this period through immigration policies and educational initiatives alike. National identity was sustained through monoculturalism, with the then Department of Education and Science doing little to respond to demands from within and beyond the education sector for a policy commitment to tackling diversity. At the same time, England's relationship with Europe was deeply ambivalent and reluctant, making it unlikely that schools were affected by the European political agenda during this period.

In 1948, the British Nationality Act created Citizen of UK and Colonies (CUKC) status in response to the creation of separate citizenships by newly independent Commonwealth countries. CUKCs and Commonwealth citizens all had the right to enter, settle, and work in Britain. Solomos (1992: 10) observed that although the law allowed for 'the vast majority of British subjects from the colonies and independent Commonwealth countries (...) to enter and settle in the UK', the state was more concerned with encouraging 'the use of migrant labour from Europe' because the Government perceived coloured British citizens from the colonies as a problem. To resolve labour shortages in certain sectors of the economy, the British Government sent Ministry of Labour officials to camps for displaced persons or political refugees in mainland Europe to recruit manual workers, mainly from Poland, Germany and the Ukraine. Those recruited workers who came to England became European Volunteer Workers, a scheme similar to the contract migrant labour system set up by European countries. The relatively liberal attitude towards the arrival of European workers contrasted sharply with the fears expressed about the social and racial problems seen to be related to the arrival of 'coloured' colonial workers who were nevertheless British subjects (Solomos 1992, 1993). The political debate about immigration thus focused on the supposed social problems of having too many black migrants, and the question of how they could be stopped from entering given their legal rights in the 1948 British Nationality Act.[2] Harris (1988: 53) argued that the debates about coloured immigration reinforced a racialized construction of Britishness which excluded or included people on the grounds of race defined by colour:

> When individuals (...) spoke of maintaining the English way of life, they were
> not simply referring to economic or regional folk patterns, but explicitly to the

---

2   Carter, Harris and Joshi (1987) argued that the period between 1948 and the 1962 Commonwealth Immigrants Acts involved the state in complex political and ideological racialization of immigration policy including the need to control coloured immigration. The 1953 Aliens Order increased restrictions on non-Commonwealth immigration by introducing work permits.

preservation of the "racial character of the English people". We have developing here a process of subjectification grounded in a racialized construction of the British subject which excludes or includes people on the basis of race/skin colour.

While citizens of any Commonwealth nation could move to Britain and settle down without formalities until 1962, the 1962 Commonwealth Immigrants Act restricted permanent residence in Britain to people who already held British passports and the dependants of people already resident in Britain. Solomos (1992: 12) regarded the 1958 race riots in Nottingham and Notting Hill as an 'important watershed in the development of racialized politics in Britain', arguing that the reluctance to restrict coloured immigration in earlier years resulted from a concern about whether legislation excluding black people could be implemented without causing embarrassment to Britain's position as head of the Commonwealth and Colonies.[3] Nonetheless, subsequent legislation, including the 1968 Commonwealth Immigrants Act, called for maintaining immigration controls in an even stricter form (see Hiro 1991). The 1968 Act limited Citizens of UK and Colonies (CUKC) entry rights to those with ancestry or birth in the United Kingdom, and was aimed at excluding United Kingdom passport holders of Asian descent from East Africa (Kenya and Uganda). This is just one example of the ways in which the policies of the Conservative and Labour Parties converged between 1962 and 1968 in favour of stricter immigration controls (Solomos 1992, 1993).

The political debate about immigration was pushed beyond strict controls towards notions of repatriation by the Conservative Enoch Powell's 'rivers of blood' speech in Birmingham in 1968, following inner-city riots in Brixton and Handsworth. Powell called for repatriation as the only effective solution to the social problem of coloured immigration. At that time, a new wave of migration from the Indian subcontinent started, a wave that would continue throughout the 1970s and 1980s (Philipps 1999). The 1969 Immigration Appeals Act, according to Solomos (1992: 19), 'institutionalized a process of deportation for those breaking conditions attached to entry' and 'legitimized restrictions on the right of entry of those who were legally entitled to settle in Britain through the obligation that dependents seeking settlement in Britain had to be in possession of an entry certificate'. The 1971 Immigration Act by the Conservative government then replaced previous legislation but guaranteed safeguards to Commonwealth citizens already settled in Britain. While Commonwealth citizens entering under a voucher system could settle in Britain under the previous law, after the 1971 Act

---

3   The 1962 Act differentiated between Citizens of UK and Colonies (CUKC) and citizens of independent Commonwealth countries. All holders of Commonwealth passports were subject to immigration control except those who were (a) born in the UK; (b) held UK passports issued by the UK Government; or (c) persons included in the passport of one of the persons excluded from immigration control under (a) or (b). Other Commonwealth citizens had to obtain an employment voucher to be able to enter Britain.

they could enter only on the basis of work permits. This act allowed the potential for millions of white Commonwealth citizens to settle in Britain while denying this right to almost all non-white Commonwealth citizens.

The period between 1962 and 1971 thus saw the introduction of three major pieces of immigration legislation aimed largely at excluding black immigrants (Commonwealth Immigrants Act 1962, Commonwealth Immigration Act 1968, Immigration Act 1971). Although the policies themselves did not explicitly refer to racial differences or racial categorization, many of them were broadly seen as exclusionary on grounds of race. Indeed, this was true of many immigration policies passed by the UK since World War II. The full set of immigration policies between 1948 and the present, summarized in Table 5.1 (and explained further in the remainder of this chapter), constitute examples of what Troyna and Williams (1986) called, 'discursive deracialization', wherein persons speak purposely to their audiences about racial matters, while avoiding the overt deployment of racial descriptions, evaluations and prescriptions.

In addition to Caribbean and Indian immigrants, Turkish Cypriots and mainland Turks also migrated to England during the years following World War II. Unlike in Germany where a rather homogenous group of Turks migrated for economic reasons, in England, the Turks form a rather heterogeneous minority who emigrated for political reasons. In the 2001 Census, 47,149 individuals stated on their forms that they were of Turkish ethnicity and 13,556 that they were Turkish Cypriots, but many others would simply have ticked options such as 'White Other' without specifying any further details, so no accurate or comprehensive data are available. It has been estimated, however, that there are 80,000 Turkish people living in Britain, of whom 60,000 live in London. In addition, there are an estimated 120,000 Turkish Cypriots. In the 1950s and 1960s, when the National Organization of Cypriot Fighters was fighting for union with Greece, many male Turkish Cypriots fled their increasingly politically unstable island to seek refuge in England (Sonyel 1988). The Cypriots chose England due to colonial ties and the high levels of employment in post-war England (King and Bridal 1982). The wave of migration from mainland Turkey, on the other hand, gained momentum after the military coup by General Evren in 1980 (Mehmet Ali 2001, Issa 2005). These Turkish Muslims (as well as the Cypriots) came from different parts of the country. Küçükcan (1999) argued that the northern part of Turkey was an important sending region, as well as Central Anatolia and the south-eastern part of Turkey. Finally, in the late 1980s and early 1990s, many Kurds arrived to England as refugees. As a result of the diversity of the Turkish migration in England, many young Turkish Cypriots are second-generation immigrants, whereas most mainland Turkish people were born in Turkey (and thus are first-generation immigrants). However, given the similar discourses I found during data analysis between these subgroups, I decided to treat them mostly as a single category when reporting findings, unless explicitly stated otherwise.

Table 5.1 Immigration policies and race relations legislation in England

Year	Legislation
1948	British Nationality Act
1953	Aliens Order
1962	Commonwealth Immigrants Act
1964	British Nationality Act
1965	Race Relations Act
1968	Commonwealth Immigration Act
1968	Race Relations Act
1969	Immigration Appeals Act
1971	Immigration Act
1976	Race Relations Act
1980-5	Statements of Changes in Immigration Rules
1981	British Nationality Act
1985-7	Amendments to the Immigration Rules
1988	Immigration Act
1990	Statement of Changes in Immigration Rules
1993	Asylum and Immigration Appeals Act
1996	Asylum and Immigration Act
1997	Special Immigration Appeals Commission Act
1999	Immigration and Asylum Act
2000	Race Relations (Amendment) Act
2002	Nationality, Immigration and Asylum Act
2003	Race Relations (Amendment) Regulations
2004	Asylum and Immigration (Treatment of Claimants, etc.) Act
2006	Immigration, Asylum and Nationality Act
2007	UK Borders Act
2008	Criminal Justice and Immigration Act
2009	Borders, Citizenship and Immigration Act

Source: Author's compilation of legislation from the Office of Public Sector Information (http://www.opsi.gov.uk/legislation/uk).

British national identity and notions of citizenship were not only challenged by the arrival of Turkish and other migrants, but also by a simultaneous process of European integration which slowly began to affect policy-makers and politicians in England during this period. However, unlike the German Government who employed the concept of Europe as an identity after the Second World War, according to Katzenstein (1997: 31-32), the Europeanization of British national identity was undercut by:

> the traditional identity of being a global power and a victor of World War II (…); the special partnership with the United States (…) reflected in Britain's adamant opposition to developing a common security and foreign policy within the EU (…); [and] the traditional British role of playing off one European state against another from a position of splendid isolation.

The British Government, according to Geddes (1999), made three fundamental miscalculations about Europe in the 1950s, when it refused to join the European Coal and Steel Community. Firstly, the government held the view that supranational integration was foredoomed and that Europe's federalizing tendencies would soon flounder on the rocks of member states' national concerns. Secondly, Britain believed that the problems of the post-war era could be met by establishing a free trade area (EFTA),[4] and that supranational integration was unnecessary. Thirdly, Britain was discouraged by other leaders, notably the French President, to embark on or continue its European integration course. Charles de Gaulle, who came to power in France in 1958, was suspicious of Britain because he saw it as a potential rival to French leadership in Europe and too closely linked with the United States. When Britain finally opted to join the EEC/EC, De Gaulle vetoed Britain's application for membership twice.

By 1961, Harold Macmillan, the then British Prime Minister, realized that Britain needed to find a new place in the world since 'the old white dominions were increasingly autonomous, the Indian Empire had become independent fourteen years previously' and 'the [African] territories of the Empire were prepared for independence' (Woodard 1998: 12). Economic concerns also impelled the bid to membership since EFTA was not successful compared with the EEC. At the time, Britain was lagging behind the EC in all economic indicators and Macmillan increasingly feared exclusion both from European markets and from consultation in European policy (May 1999). President de Gaulle resigned in France in 1969 and was replaced by Georges Pompidou, a supporter of British EC membership, opening the way for the Conservative Prime Minister Edward Heath to lead Britain into the EC in January 1973. Harold Wilson led the Labour government to call a referendum in support of Europe, which resulted in a victory for continued EC membership by a margin of two to one in 1973 (Woodard 1998). However, the Labour party was soon divided again over EC membership and opposed EC membership by the early 1980s, together with Enoch Powell, one of the most influential political right-wingers in post-war Britain and member of the Conservative party. Britain thus spent the first decade of membership arguing about the terms of accession. In addition, Britain began seeking a budget rebate since, by the end of the 1970s, the country was the second largest contributor to the EC budget even though it had the third-lowest gross domestic product per capita of the then nine member states (Geddes 1999: 35).

Despite these discussions at the macro-political level and the slowly emerging European dimension in England, the school system saw few changes in response to Europe during this period. At the same time, the British school system did not pass

---

4   The 1959 Stockholm Convention established EFTA with seven members including Austria, Britain, Switzerland, Sweden, Portugal, Norway and Denmark. Two years before that, the Treaty of Rome had already established the European Economic Community (EEC) and Euratom with six founder members including Germany, France, Italy and the three Benelux countries.

any major new educational initiatives responding to Commonwealth immigration, despite its growing importance. From the early 1950s to 1965, education in England was largely assimilation-based (similar to the concept of 'foreigner pedagogy' in Germany, which was designed to help children with German language deficits whilst also preparing them for possible return to their country of origin). British policy took for granted that all ethnic minority people and their cultures were inferior, and that their values and beliefs were of secondary importance when compared with those held by British groups. The main educational problem of ethnic minority groups was their underachievement. The knowledge they brought to school was considered to be inadequate, and as a result, testing increased during the 1960s to 'prove' the educational inferiority of ethnic minority children (see the discussions in Mullard 1982). Politicians blamed family instability and the disadvantages associated with cultural level of the home for school failure.

During the 1960s, there were two policy developments addressing the issues raised by increasing diversity. Firstly, the government opened language centres for the provision of English as a Second Language to those children whose mother tongue was not English (Troyna 1992). Secondly, since the presence of a high proportion of ethnic minority children in one class was thought to slow down the general routine of working and hamper the progress of the whole class, the then Education Secretary, Sir Edward Boyle, informed the House of Commons in 1963 that no one school should have more than about one-third of ethnic minority students. In 1965 the local education authorities were therefore advised to arrange for the dispersal of ethnic minority children over a greater number of schools (also known as 'bussing') in order to avoid undue concentration in any particular school (see Mullard 1982). Like in Germany, these assimilation-focused policies show England's reluctance to accept the consequences of migration-related diversity.

In the mid-1960s, partly due to the underachievement and continuing influx of migrants, the educational approach to ethnic minority students shifted and the concept of Britishness appeared to be constructed in more pluralistic terms, recognizing other cultures. Education was thus integration-based from 1965 to the early 1970s (Troyna 1992). For Roy Jenkins, then Home Secretary, integration referred not to 'a flattening process of assimilation' but to 'equal opportunity accompanied by cultural diversity in an atmosphere of mutual tolerance' (Runnymede Trust 2000). During these years dispersal policies were officially abandoned. The new focus was the perception that ethnic minority children were likely to have a poor self-image, or low self-esteem (see Milner 1975). As a result, some schools attempted to change ethnic minority students' self-image through the introduction of Black studies in the curriculum. By 1975, criticism about monoculturalism was given institutional backing in the report 'A Language for Life' (Bullock 1975).[5] The result, according to Troyna (1992), was a fusion of

---

5 The 'Bullock Report' also suggested that bilingualism be appreciated in schools. 'When bilingualism in Britain is discussed, it is seldom if ever with reference to the inner-city populations, yet over half the immigrants in our schools have a mother tongue which

integrationist and cultural pluralist convictions that led the concept of multicultural education to reshape the school agenda. The Green Paper 'Education in Schools: a consultative document', asserted that 'our society is a multicultural, multiracial one and the curriculum should reflect a sympathetic understanding of the different cultures and races that now make up our society' (Department of Education and Science 1977: 4).

To sum up, we have seen that during this period (1948-1979) there were few 'racially explicit' policies in England apart from the dispersal policy known as 'bussing'. Education was viewed as a means of assimilating and integrating minority ethnic groups into British society. Whilst the assimilation-based approach (1950s to 1965) emphasized national British/English culture and values, the integration-based approach (1965 to mid-1970s) attempted to integrate cultural and ethnic difference within the concept of Britishness. However, policy-makers and politicians adopted a rather reluctant approach to European integration. The slowly emerging European dimension appeared to have no major implications on England's school system during this period.

The New Right and the Racialization of Schooling: 1979-1988

The return of a Conservative government in 1979 under the leadership of Margaret Thatcher brought a shift in the British relationship between national, European and multicultural agendas. There were two competing trends in this period. On the one hand, the rhetoric and action of Conservative governments after 1979 were geared to the notion of a British 'way of life' that was threatened by 'outsiders' (Barker 1981). The resulting conflictual relationship between national and multicultural agendas culminated in the 1988 Education Reform Act, introducing the National Curriculum. These nationalistic sentiments were also the reason why the European agenda continued to receive little attention during this period. On the other hand, paradoxically, a number of educational initiatives during this period sought to address the increasing cultural and ethnic diversity in schools. Troyna and Williams (1986) maintained that educational policies which focused explicitly on the 'racial' nature of society figured prominently on the political agenda in the early 1980s – a process they called 'discursive racialization'. These educational policies reflected a 'growing awareness of and indignation at racial injustice', and employed the strategy of 'racial evaluation and prescription [which] is directed at refuting racism and eliminating racialist practices' (Reeves 1983: 175). Below I consider each facet in turn.

The Conservative government in 1979 was intent on re-establishing a concept of British nationhood. The 1981 British Nationality Act (see Table 5.1) abolished the status of Citizens of UK and Colonies (CUKC) of the 1948 British Nationality

---

is not English (…). These children are genuine bilinguals, but this fact is often ignored or unrecognized by the schools (Bullock 1975: 293-94).

Act, and replaced it with three separate citizenships. Firstly, the 1981 Act established British Citizenship for those CUKC citizens who had a close relation with the United Kingdom, the Channel Islands and the Isle of Man (i.e., those who possessed the right of abode). Secondly, the Act created British Dependent Territories Citizenship (BDTC) for people connected with the British overseas territories at the time. And thirdly, the Act instituted British Overseas Citizenship (BOC), for those CUKCs that were not eligible for British Citizen status or BDTC status. Solomos (1992: 22) argued that the BOC status 'effectively exclude[ed] British citizens of (mostly) Asian origin from the right of abode in the UK'. In a sense, according to Macdonald (1983: 69), the 1981 Act 'enshrines the existing racially discriminatory provisions of immigration law under the new clothing of British citizenship and the right of abode'.

The passing of the 1981 Nationality Act and the increasing use of internal controls over ethnic minority people in all spheres of life reinforced a two-tier citizenship for ethnic majority and ethnic minority people which made its way into education. 'Black' workers, Troyna and Williams (1986) argued, continued to occupy unskilled and semi-skilled jobs vacated by the white indigenous workers at the time of economic expansion. But because these workers were locked in declining industries in decaying inner-city areas, they were also particularly vulnerable to redundancy and prolonged unemployment, and their children attended the most problematic schools. As a result, people living in these inner-city areas experienced 'discursive racialization' most directly, especially children in schools (Troyna and Williams 1986). The ideological perception and conception of these ethnic minority students as 'alien', as threats to established socio-cultural mores and as unfair competitors for increasingly scarce resources, constituted elements of a new racism. This contrasted sharply with the government's avowed educational goals of equality of opportunity, multiculturalism and anti-racism which prevailed throughout the 1980s. The presence of ethnic minority students in inner-city areas that had suffered most from the recession in the early 1980s (when for instance unemployment rose from 5.3 per cent in August 1979 to 11.9 per cent in 1984), placed a new stress on schools to respond to racial inequalities resulting from political and economic developments.

The growing tensions between notions of nation, citizenship, national belonging and concepts of race were succinctly addressed in Paul Gilroy's (1987) book *There Ain't No Black in the Union Jack*, a title derived from a National Front slogan. For Gilroy, racism had the capacity to link discourses of xenophobia, Englishness, Britishness, militarism and gender difference into a complex system that gave race its meaning. Gilroy (1987: 55) argued that racism specifies who may legitimately belong to the national community, pointing out that:

> Nationhood is not an empty receptacle which can be simply and spontaneously filled with alternative concepts according to the dictates of political pragmatism. The ideological theme of national belonging may be malleable to some extent but its links with the discourses of race and the organizational realities of these

groups are not arbitrary. They are confined by historical and political factors which limit the extent to which nationalism becomes socialist at the moment that its litany is repeated by socialists.

The 1980s also saw a shift from 'deracialized' views of the English society as being politically and culturally homogenous to notions of cultural pluralism, maintaining that the English society consisted of different groups that were culturally distinctive and separate under the political authority of a neutral state. This model encapsulated a new government focus on the notion of cultural diversity, emphasizing that English society consisted of different groups that were culturally distinctive and separate. 'The conditions which give rise to this model' were, according to Gibson (1976: 7), 'the continuing academic failure of students from a certain ethnic minority group whose school performance continues to lag behind national norms'. The aim of the new educational approach was to improve academic performance in order to provide equality of opportunity, and the strategy was the provision of a culturally relevant curriculum. As the logic went, a pluralist England should have a positive commitment to difference and to preservation of group culture, traditions and history. Only the political authority of the state was equally binding on all groups; cultural assimilation was not expected. For some, this new emphasis on cultural pluralism meant the pursuit of a policy of total cultural segregation; for others, it meant a policy of revised integration based upon a more equitable distribution of power (see Mullard 1982).[6] Overall there was a shift from notions of cultural superiority and tolerance to a recognition and accommodation of diversity with schools actively developing multicultural and anti-racist initiatives.

As the above debate suggests, the 1980s saw schools take a central role in a major public policy debate about multiculturalism in England. The Swann Report *Education for All* (Department of Education and Science 1985: 36), of which there is no equivalent in other European countries, characterizes multiculturalism as enabling 'all ethnic groups, both minority and majority, to participate fully in shaping society (...) whilst also allowing and where necessary assisting the ethnic minority communities in maintaining their distinct ethnic identities within a framework of commonly accepted values'. Arguably, today's debate over how to promote cultural diversity and social cohesion at the same time (to which we shall return later in the book) can be traced back to this policy document which for the

---

6 At the government level, the Green Paper 'Education and Schools' (Department of Education and Science 1977) was regarded as the harbinger of this change from integration to cultural pluralism (see Carrington and Short 1989). It argued that the curriculum should reflect a sympathetic understanding of different cultures and races. The 'Rampton Report' called for a systematic review of the curriculum in every school, irrespective of its ethnic composition, and stressed the need to combat curricular ethnocentrism (Department of Education and Science 1981).

first time alluded to a sense of civic unity and national identity through community cohesion whilst also advocating ethnic identities.

In addition to promoting a new role for multiculturalism in schools, the Swann Report (Department of Education and Science 1985) also identified a number of variables affecting the achievement of migrant children since the 1960s. Firstly, analysts showed that school performance closely correlated with socio-economic status, and that socially disadvantaged migrant communities were disadvantaged in these terms. Secondly, the report pointed to racism and prejudice, both within and outside schools, as major causes of educational problems. Thirdly, the number of teachers with a migration background was seen to be too small to meet the needs of ethnically diverse school populations. Fourthly, migrant students' lower command of English was a barrier to academic success. And finally, school curricula were seen as more exclusive than inclusive, and thus viewed as not appropriate to the needs of migrant communities.

In response to the finding on migrant students' lower command of English, the Swann Report (Department of Education and Science 1985) suggested that English as a second language should be included as part of a programme of language education for all children, not in separate language centres or separate units within schools. All local education authorities were further told to expect their schools to produce clear policy statements on education for all, and monitor their practical implementation. Pluralism was to be reflected in curricula and examinations.

However, the lofty government goals for multicultural education did not go far enough, according to some analysts. Sarup (1986) argued that despite such good intentions, multicultural educational approaches in England were based on notions of assimilation during this time. Mullard (1982), Troyna (1992) and May (1994) similarly argued that 'multicultural education was simply the latest and most liberal variant of the assimilationist perspective; the differences [between assimilation, integration and cultural pluralism] tended to be in degree rather than kind' (Troyna 1992: 71). For these scholars, the new multicultural models failed to address the larger power and racial inequalities within schools and society at large. These critiques then led to yet another educational response.

Anti-racist education, which developed alongside multicultural education, addressed and embraced the growing cultural and religious diversity in schools. However, unlike the more liberal multiculturalists which called for minority ethnic groups to be able to maintain their linguistic and cultural heritage, anti-racists were far more radical and called on black people to defend themselves against racist laws and stand up for racial justice. Anti-racist educators not only asked schools to recognize the heritage of migrant children and promote mother-tongue teaching but also called on schools to remove discrimination from the curriculum and instead teach about equality and social justice. Troyna (1992) further examined why and how the anti-racist educational approach emerged alongside the multicultural approach, and distilled the contributory factors into three categories. Firstly, local black community groups drew attention to the way racism in education delimited the academic progress of their children. Secondly, 'the racialization of policies in local government settings', which 'was influenced greatly by a need to attract black electoral support' (Troyna 1992: 77), led officers and councillors to listen to the criticisms by black parents about the educational opportunities offered to their children. Lastly, there was general agreement among policy-makers and educators that the schooling system should assume a crucial role in preventing the recurrence of the 1981 urban race riots by promoting equality of opportunity and combating racism.

My read of these events leads me to conclude that the 1981 urban race riots partly contributed to this shift in political and educational ideology towards anti-racist education. In 1981, half-way through Thatcher's first term in office, violence erupted in South London and further rioting broke out in London, Liverpool and Manchester. The problems of English cities and the difficulties of policing multiethnic communities became major focuses of national attention. The Scarman Report *The Brixton Disorders* (Scarman 1981: 2.35) criticized the problems of 'racial' disadvantage and urban deprivation, arguing that:

> Overall they [ethnic minority communities] suffer from the same deprivation as the "host community" (i.e., the majority population), but much more acutely. Their lives are led largely in the poorer and more deprived areas of our great cities. Unemployment and poor housing bear upon them heavily, and the educational system has not adjusted itself satisfactorily to their needs. Their difficulties have been intensified by the sense they have of a concealed discrimination against them.

These conflicts and violence put race and ethnicity on the school agenda, sparking a trend whereby many schools and local education authorities developed official policies on their work in multicultural and anti-racist education. However, without any national, mandatory multicultural and anti-racist school policies, such initiatives were often limited to multiethnic inner-city areas (Taylor 1995). National pressure finally came in the form of the Education Support Grants (ESG)[7] policy (Department of Education and Science 1987), which boosted efforts for local education authorities to develop their multicultural resources, funded schools in developing specific curricular themes (e.g., Indian and Caribbean literature), and supported the organization of whole-school events including study tours to Asian and African countries. ESG-funding, as Taylor (1995) argued, helped to support 'artists in residence' programmes, giving both teachers and students the chance to work with visitors whose cultures provided new knowledge as well as a vehicle for the social development of students. The idea was that, for example, 'Black visitors to schools (…) can give white students a new understanding of [historical

---

7   The ESG programme raised awareness, developed knowledge, provided resources and introduced multicultural concerns to relatively monocultural schools. 120 ESG projects were funded in Britain between 1985 and 1990. By 1987, two-thirds of all local education authority had a multicultural policy statement (see Tomlinson and Craft 1995).

events like] the African-Caribbean-European slave trade triangle' (Taylor 1995: 109). The active engagement of schools in multicultural and anti-racist initiatives in the 1980s thus challenged Thatcher's monocultural approach to Britishness.

In 1988, Thatcher's administration introduced a National Curriculum as part of the Education Reform Act, but not surprisingly, multicultural and anti-racist education received little attention in the curriculum (Department of Education and Science 1988) under Thatcher. Instead, the legislation largely removed the concept of multiculturalism from the National Curriculum (see the debates in Sarup 1991, Troyna 1994, Moore 1997),[8] highlighting the nationalistic sentiments of policy-makers and politicians of the time (see for example Hardy and Vieler-Porter 1990). Hardy and Vieler-Porter (1990: 173) criticized how the National Curriculum and regulations governing religious education and school assemblies sought to use education to reconstruct a national identity based on a narrowly-defined notion of Englishness. Citing Whitty and Menter (1989), they argued that the influence of New Right racism could be detected in the 1988 Act in a number of ways:

> The very emphasis on *National* in the National Curriculum, the centrality of a notion of national testing with all the cultural and linguistic bias which that implies, the failure to recognize languages other than Welsh and English as students' first language, and the omission (...) of any reference to the 1985 Swann report.

The image of the British nation was a crucial and early part of the Conservative government under Thatcher, and as a result, race-related fears were used to legitimate the government's 1988 Education Reform Act (Hardy and Vieler-Porter 1990). Specifically, Hardy and Vieler-Porter argued that the 1988 Act provided 'a popular education within an ideological framework which is individualistic, competitive and racist' (Hardy and Vieler-Porter 1990: 177). They provide evidence for this argument with extensive analysis of the discourse of leading conservative politicians of the time. For example, in Thatcher's 1979 interview on World in Action, she stated that 'people are really rather afraid that the country might be rather swamped by people with a different culture' (...) and went on to say that 'we are a British nation with British characteristics'.

The individual, in this period in England, was narrowly conceptualized as a consumer, divorced from traditional attributes of class, religion or language. In this climate which placed individual and family above community and society,

---

8 Key changes included national tests of student achievement, a system of local management of schools with school funding of schools contingent on a student admission formula, a compulsory National Curriculum for all students in state schools from ages 5 to 16 (specified by subject in more prescriptive detail than most other countries), open school enrolment with parents able to send their child to the school of their choice, and parental right to vote that their children's schools opt out of existing local education authority control (see Convey and Merritt 2000).

schools and local education authorities found it difficult to deliver social justice. Therefore, as Blair and Arnot (1993) observed, the black communities and the anti-racist educational movement had little impact on the structuring of the new curriculum. At the same time, they gave it a somewhat hostile reception, claiming it contained new assimilationist notions and lacked a multicultural dimension. As the new curriculum indicates, the language of educational debate had changed to include an emphasis on value for public money, a consumerist approach entailing parental power and the accountability of schools and teachers. As Whitty (1989) maintained, the 1988 Education Reform Act gave market forces precedence within whole areas of policy which had previously been subject to detailed governmental regulation and planning. For example, the law increased the powers of governors, as well as the influence of parents and members of the local business community on governing bodies. In addition, the law allowed parents to send their children to the school of their choice. These changes represented a new brand of conservative thinking in the 1980s and 1990s, a New Right which Whitty (1989, 2008) identified as having 'neo-liberal' and 'neo-conservative' approaches to education and curriculum development. Thatcherism, according to Whitty, linked the neo-conservative emphasis on tradition, authority, national identity, and patriotism (as opposed to multiculturalism), with an espousal of neo-liberal free market economics and their application to the education system. Thatcher's drive for an essentially market-based and centralized education system has continued to this day through Conservative (1979-1997) and New Labour policies (since 1997), according to Whitty (2008).[9] The conservative trend has included targeted attempts to tackle disadvantage, emphases on school improvement by setting attainment standards, and the idea that school diversity and parental choice will result in higher standards.

Debates during this period also addressed multiculturalism, multicultural and anti-racist education, and the compatibility of the national and multicultural political and educational agendas. However, the European dimension continued to receive little attention in England and, unlike multicultural education, did not specifically appear amongst the themes and dimensions of the 1988 National Curriculum. At the national level, a consensus regarding membership in the European Community (EC) only began emerging amongst English politicians after the budget issue had been resolved in 1984 at the Fontainebleau summit. At the time, Margaret Thatcher advocated a single market within which people, goods, services and capital could move freely (Woodard 1998). However, Thatcher's positive attitude towards Europe did not endure, and indeed became particularly hostile towards the idea

---

9   Demaine (2005) offers a slightly different take arguing that rather than leaving education to the market, New Labour has focused on the needs of those most likely to be failed by the notion of equal opportunity in a quasi-market. Still different, Hills and Stewart (2005) maintain that while New Labour has made 'genuine progress in reducing disadvantage, especially among families with children', Britain still remains a very unequal society.

of strengthening European institutions. Germany and her partners (e.g., France) asserted that attainment of the single market necessitated increased powers for supranational institutions such as the Parliament in Strasbourg, in order to ensure that decision-making efficiency and a measure of democratic accountability followed the transfer of authority to the European level. But the English thought the single market could be achieved without any institutional reforms (see May 1999). A few years later, when the EC member states began working on the details of a common currency, Thatcher firmly set herself against any further integrative processes. It was not until John Major took office, and signed the Maastricht Treaty (despite deep division over Europe within his party), that England grew closer to the EU. A small and determined band of Eurosceptics subsequently defied the government repeatedly by calling for a referendum on Maastricht. But these emerging EU-level interactions with England were unlikely to affect schools until the 1988 Resolution by the European Council of Ministers of Education, which began to suggest hints of change were possible in England (Council of Ministers of Education 1988). In contrast, as we have seen in Chapter 2, by the late 1980s, the European agenda had largely taken over the issue of 'identity' and schooling in Germany.

Citizenship, the New European Agenda and Muslimophobia: 1988-2009

Since the late 1980s, notions of Britishness and with it the concept of citizenship have been increasingly challenged by Europeanization, and devolution of policy-making powers (e.g., education) to Scotland and Wales in the late 1990s. The development of citizenship education has thus become a key means of promoting national pride and identification. This final section of the chapter describes how the relationship between national, European and multicultural agendas in this period became increasingly more complex, creating an ever more confusing set of agendas for schools to mediate.

Unlike Germany and other European countries, England has no tradition of citizenship education (Kerr 1999) and public attention has only been drawn to the issue since the introduction of 'education for citizenship' in the 1988 National Curriculum.[10] The intention of introducing citizenship was to ensure that all students would receive some 'education for citizenship'. However, with widespread confusion over the demands of the National Curriculum, education for citizenship was generally ignored and did not greatly influence citizenship education in schools (Derricott 2000). It was not until New Labour came to power in May 1997 that the

---

10 See Heater (1990), Brennan (1981) as well as Brindle and Arnot (2001) for a historical account of the development of citizenship education in England. Brindle and Arnot (2001: 26), for instance, argue that early initiatives to encourage education for citizenship had 'little impact on the schools; and with no statutory framework for a curriculum, schools [in England] were highly resistant to change'.

status and profile of citizenship education in England began to grow. Soon after New Labour came to power, the then Education Secretary David Blunkett established the Citizenship Education Advisory Group under the chairmanship of Professor Sir Bernard Crick 'to provide advice on effective education for citizenship in schools [and] to include the nature and practices of participation in democracy; the duties, responsibilities and rights of individuals as citizens and the value to individuals and society of community activity' (Qualifications and Curriculum Authority 1998: 4). The 1998 Crick Report *Education for Citizenship and the Teaching of Democracy in Schools* recommended that citizenship be mandatory in secondary schools and optional in primary schools. There was definite emphasis on 'active' citizenship in the Crick Report and reference to the changing constitutional context in which citizenship education was being introduced. The Report argued that by the end of compulsory schooling students should 'know about the changing constitution of the UK including the relationship between the two houses of Parliament, the changing role of the monarchy, shifting relationships between England, Scotland, Wales and Northern Ireland and Britain's relationship with the European Union and the Commonwealth' (Qualifications and Curriculum Authority 1998: 51).

According to Osler and Starkey (2001: 292), the Crick Report presented British citizenship as inclusive of national and regional differences between England, Scotland, Wales and Northern Ireland. However, the report characterized visible ethnic minorities as 'other' when it discussed cultural diversity. For example, it said that 'minorities must learn and respect the laws, codes and conventions as much as the majority – not merely because it is useful to do so, but because this process helps foster common citizenship' (Qualifications and Curriculum Authority 1998: 18). As this quote shows, the report assumed that visible ethnic minorities needed to change somehow in order for England to have a common citizenship. This put new demands on schools and their approaches to socializing ethnic minorities, as well as their approach to teaching citizenship.

In response to the Crick Report, the government introduced citizenship education in September 2002 as a new statutory subject for students aged between 11 and 16 in the National Curriculum. In line with these requirements, schools are now asked to develop students' citizenship skills in highly specified ways, as evidenced by the following quote (Qualifications and Curriculum Authority 2000: 4):

> Citizenship gives pupils the knowledge, skills and understanding to play an effective role in society at local, national and international levels. It helps them to become informed, thoughtful and responsible citizens who are aware of their duties and rights. It promotes their spiritual, moral, social and cultural development, making them more self-confident and responsible both in and beyond the classroom. It encourages pupils to play a helpful part in the life of their schools, neighbourhoods, communities and the wider world. It also teaches them about our economy and democratic institutions and values; encourages

respect for different national, religious and ethnic identities; and develops pupils'
ability to take part in discussions.

Under the new policy, schools have been expected to cover topics summarized under
three curriculum strands. Firstly, 'political literacy' is described as requiring schools
to teach about the 'institutions, issues, problems and practices of our democracy'
and as encouraging students to make themselves effective in public life 'through
skills and values as well as knowledge (Qualifications and Curriculum Authority
2000: 4). Secondly, 'community involvement' is defined as teaching pupils 'how
to become helpfully involved in the life and concerns of their neighbourhood and
communities' and as pupils 'learning through community service'. Thirdly, 'social
and moral responsibility' is described as students learning 'self-confidence and
socially and morally responsible behaviour, both in and beyond the classroom,
towards those in authority and towards each other'. Schools are required not only
to encourage students to respect authority but also to develop a more democratic
ethos, to empower students through the development of their critical capacities, to
encourage them to become more actively involved with decision-making, and to
consider the distribution and use of power within society.

The London train bombings happened in July 2005, immediately following
my fieldwork, and prompted further changes to citizenship education. Following
the bombings, then Education Secretary Alan Johnson commissioned a review
of how English schools taught citizenship and diversity. The resulting review by
Sir Keith Ajegbo, *Diversity and Citizenship in the Curriculum Research Review*,
argued there was still not enough emphasis on British identity and history in
British schools (Department for Education and Skills 2007a). The report argues
that a new citizenship strand should be developed that includes political literacy,
community involvement, and social and moral responsibility. The extent to which
this will impact schools and the environment in which students develop their
political identies remains to be seen. Since September 2008, based on the Ajegbo
Review, a fourth strand, 'Identities and diversity: living together in the UK'[11]
brings together critical thinking about ethnicity, religion and race; an explicit link
to political issues and values; and the use of contemporary history in teachers'
pedagogy to illuminate thinking about contemporary issues relating to citizenship.
This includes the multiple identities that may be held by groups and communities
in a diverse society, and the ways in which these identities are affected by changes
in society. Students should learn about how migration has shaped communities;
common and shared identities and what unifies groups and communities; how

---

11 Instead of strands, following a comprehensive reform of the secondary school
curriculum, these are now referred to as key concepts underpinning the study of citizenship
(democracy and justice, rights and responsibilities, identities and diversity) and key
processes which are the skills students need to learn to make progress (critical thinking and
enquiry, advocacy and representation, taking informed and responsible action).

poverty affects life chances; and how life in England has been shaped by political, social, economic and cultural changes.

The notion of an inclusive understanding of citizenship education, and the challenge of developing approaches to citizenship education that meet the needs of a multicultural Europe, have been discussed extensively by Osler (1994, 1995, 1999) as well as Osler and Starkey (2001, 2003). Osler suggests that 'citizenship education is seen across Europe as playing a central role in strengthening democracy and in challenging racism as an antidemocratic force' (1999: 13). Arguing in favour of multiple identities, the author underlines that there is a need within both the ethnic majority population and the ethnic minority groups to recognize diversity and a range of identities. She thus characterizes an appropriate citizenship education as one which encourages the development of 'an inclusive rather than an exclusive understanding of national identity and citizenship' and 'promote[s] an understanding of the rights and responsibilities of democratic citizenship [that is] not dependent on ethnic affiliation or identification but recognis[es] and support[s] diversity both within and between societies' (Osler 1994: 40).

The extent to which effective practice in citizenship education developed in English schools during this period has been measured and evaluated in the 'Citizenship Education Longitudinal Study', conducted by the National Foundation for Educational Research (NFER). The study tracks over 10,000 of the first young people to receive continuous entitlement to citizenship education from age 11 to 18 (2001 to 2009), with the aim of assessing the short-term and long-term effects of citizenship education on students' knowledge, skills and attitudes. The first cross-sectional survey found that prior to September 2002 'almost two-thirds (65 per cent) of school leaders had an existing agreed strategy for teaching citizenship education' and this theme 'was most commonly taught, as reported by 90 per cent of school leaders, through citizenship-related modules in [Personal, Social and Health Education]' (Kerr et al. 2003: 102). Other common delivery patterns included the use of extra-curricular activities and tutorials, and a cross-curricular approach with citizenship-related topics taught through geography, history, English and religious education. Three-quarters of schools (75 per cent) had already appointed a co-ordinator for citizenship education.

In a more recent report from the study, Kerr et al. (2004) identified four school approaches to citizenship in England. 'Minimalist schools' still seemed to be at a planning stage, given that in this cluster there was a dearth of strategies for using extra-curricular activities as a vehicle for its delivery or recognizing achievement in citizenship education. 'Focused schools' had schemes in place to recognize achievement but the need remained to develop opportunities for active citizenship in the school and wider communities. 'Implicit schools' were not yet focusing explicitly on citizenship in the curriculum but they provided opportunities for active citizenship (and thus had the potential to become progressing schools, according to Kerr et al.). 'Progressing schools' had made the most progress with regard to implementing citizenship education in the curriculum as well as in the school and wider communities. These last schools had an ethos that was mostly participatory and supportive of the aims of citizenship education, offered and used extra-curricular activities for citizenship education, and drew on varied delivery methods. The 84 surveyed schools fell into the categories about equally, with 25 per cent in each category. In 2006, the proportion of progressing and implicit schools was unchanged whereas the proportion of minimalist schools decreased and the proportion of focused schools increased (see Ireland et al. 2006). The authors also noted an increase in the use of dedicated timeslots, and an increase in teacher and student awareness.

The most recent report, which focuses on young people's civic participation, argues that young people (age 16-17) exhibit relatively strong community attachment, with greater attachment to closer, more familiar communities. In other words, they are more attached to their local neighbourhood and town than to their country or Europe. Overall, young people's attitudes have shifted from when they were in Year 7 (age 12-13) to when they are in Year 11 in that they feel less attached to all communities except the school (see also Benton et al. 2008).[12] The authors further observe that civic participation is affected by ethnicity and socio-economic background – with the most positive attitudes found amongst middle-class Asian girls and the most negative ones among working-class ethnic majority and Afro-Caribbean boys. Although the period of the study does not overlap precisely with my own fieldwork, the findings link in important ways with my school discussions. As will become evident later, I found similar results regarding students' identification with closer, more familiar communities.

Arguably, despite a comprehensive review of the secondary school curriculum in this period, the citizenship education curriculum guidelines still leave the ideas of European citizenship and supranational identity somewhat underdeveloped. This despite recommendations from the European Council of Ministers of Education in its Green Paper on the European Dimension in Education (1993: 6). The result is a disconnect which shows Britain's continuing ambivalence toward EU-level policies:

> Education systems should educate for citizenship; and here Europe is not a dimension which replaces others, but one that enhances them (…). Education for citizenship should include experiencing the European dimension (…) and socialization in a European context (…) because this enables each citizen to play a part on the European stage (…) Teachers should develop a European perspective alongside national and regional allegiances.

---

12   An updated typology of school approaches in the fifth annual report of the Citizenship Education Longitudinal Study reveals that there are four main types of delivery of citizenship education: curriculum driven citizenship, student efficacy driven citizenship, participation driven citizenship, and citizenship-rich driven citizenship (for more details on these four main models, see Kerr et al. 2007). Methods of delivery include dedicated discrete timetable slots (one-third of schools) and part of Personal, Social and Health Education (two-thirds of schools).

Nevertheless, some schools in England have developed a European agenda, such as the Anglo European School in Essex. More commonly, however, the European dimension is now subsumed under a 'global dimension' as one of seven cross-curricular dimensions – the others being creativity and critical thinking, technology and media, enterprise, community participation, cultural diversity and identity, and healthy lifestyles (Qualifications and Curriculum Authority 2009). The implementation of this new global dimension was based on a guidance paper, commissioned shortly after the end of my fieldwork in 2005 by the then Department for Education and Skills, 'Developing the Global Dimension in the School Curriculum' (Department for Education and Skills 2005). This document outlines aspects of global citizenship such as social justice, conflict resolution, diversity, human rights, sustainable development, interdependence and values and perceptions. Unlike in other European countries, a separate body of literature has developed around global citizenship education in England (e.g., Osler and Vincent 2002, Osler and Starkey 2003, Graves 2002, Marshall 2007). The introductory notes to the programmes of study for each subject provide a signpost for schools when embedding a global dimension across the curriculum. For example, in history, students are asked to develop their own identity through an understanding of history at personal, local, national and global level. Unlike in other European countries (see Faas forthcoming) these chains of identities hardly include the European level.

Compared with national, multicultural (and most recently also global) issues, the government has given little specific advice and curriculum guidance on precisely what content and form the European dimension should assume, thus indicating a rather lukewarm British approach to the European agenda (see Tulasiewicz 1993). Unlike Germany, England has devoted most of her energy to emphasizing national competitiveness rather than partnership with the EU. 'Since approaches to the European dimension are less constrained by examination syllabus prescriptions (…) there are noticeable differences from the traditional parts of the curriculum. It consists of much out-of-school activity [such as exchanges and visits] involving contacts with personnel other than teachers' (Tulasiewicz 1993: 246). A discrete European dimension, according to Tulasiewicz and Brock (2000), would consist of European knowledge; European skills including travel, hosting, guiding and communication to enable youth to plan and execute activities together in a region they share as Europeans; and European attitudes, which would enable young people to develop a European political identity.

In 2000, prior to the secondary curriculum review, Convey and Merritt argued that, although the programmes of study in some National Curriculum subjects included a European dimension (notably geography, history, art, music and modern foreign languages), 'there is still no specific statement that such a dimension must be included'. The authors go on to argue that 'of course an *awareness* of Europe goes beyond *knowing* about Europe' (Convey and Merritt 2000: 396, original emphasis). The authors looked at a range of subjects suitable for developing a European dimension such as modern foreign language teaching and observed that, at the time, the learning of one foreign language was compulsory from ages 11 to 16 (key stages 3-4) and that a second language was optional in English secondary schools. Tulasiewicz (1993: 254) optimistically concluded that 'no doubt modern foreign languages will thrive'.

However, the 2002 Government Green Paper 'Extending Opportunities, Raising Standards' (Department for Education and Skills 2002) suggested that the compulsory foreign language in the National Curriculum at key stage 4 (ages 14 to 16) be dropped. This despite the European Commission's recommendation that all students should master at least two European languages in addition to their own by the end of their compulsory education (European Commission 2001a).[13] In response to these plans, the Nuffield Languages team (2002) argued that three years of language learning at secondary level would be a step backwards in the National Curriculum. Nonetheless, modern foreign language learning in English schools ceased to be compulsory beyond the age of 14 in September 2004. At the same time, it became a non-mandatory subject (i.e., an entitlement) at key stage 2 (ages 7 to 11). Although the recent *Languages Review* by Lord Ron Dearing (Department for Education and Skills 2007b) did not necessarily recommend that students should be required to study a modern foreign language at key stage 4, it recommended strengthening the incentives for schools and youth themselves to continue with languages after 14 and that languages should be compulsory between seven and 14 (key stages 2 and 3). A mandatory foreign language at key stage 2 was indeed reinforced in the *Independent Review of the Primary Curriculum* by Sir Jim Rose (Department for Children, Schools and Families 2009) and will become a statutory requirement of the National Curriculum from 2011. However, England is not just unique in Europe for subsuming the European dimension under the umbrella of a global dimension but also for specifying that the mandatory modern foreign language can be either 'a working language of the European Union' such as French, German, Spanish *or* 'any major spoken world language' such as Mandarin, Japanese, Urdu or Arabic. While it could be argued that this undermines the development of a European political identity (and perhaps strengthens the idea of a globally-orientated citizenship), it could also be argued that this rather innovative approach takes account of the particular non-European migration background of many ethnic minority students in England and implements the EU criteria of promoting communication in the mother tongue and communication in foreign languages (see Council of the European Union 2006).

Concurrent with a growing, albeit modest, awareness of a European dimension in education, the New Labour government under Tony Blair (1997-2007) adopted a more Europhile political approach compared with the preceding Conservative governments. Not only did New Labour sign up to incorporate the Social Chapter

---

13   The Green Paper 'Extending Opportunities, Raising Standards' suggested that 'whilst not making it a compulsory part of the National Curriculum, we will give each child an entitlement to learn a language at primary level by 2010' (DfES 2002: 4). This was repeated in the 2005 Government White Paper '14-19 Education and Skills' (DfES 2005).

into the Maastricht Treaty,[14] it also approved the draft European Constitution (which was subsequently put on hold in June 2005 following rejections in referenda in the Netherlands and France) and, most recently, the Treaty of Lisbon under the premiership of Gordon Brown (since 2007). Arguably, however, the Brown administration is more Eurosceptic than its predecessor. Evidence of this includes the fact that Prime Minister Brown thought it more important to attend a question-and-answer session with a House of Commons Committee on 13 December 2007 instead of signing the reform treaty at the same time as every other of the 26 EU leaders did. He did eventually put his name to the treaty four hours after the official ceremony and behind closed doors. In opposition, the Conservative Party, with the support of a majority of the English population, ruled out membership of the euro and thus established itself as the main anti-Europe party. In the 2009 European elections, the United Kingdom Independence Party (UKIP), whose main election platform advocates Britain's withdrawal from the EU, beat the governing Labour Party into third place to secure 13 European Members of Parliament with 16 per cent of the national vote. Arguably, these political developments underline the dilemma the New Labour governments under Blair and Brown have faced in retrieving notions of Britishness and responding to continental calls for further European integration.

This debate about notions of Britishness/Englishness, and their compatibility with European and multicultural agendas, came to the fore in the first decade of the twenty-first century. One of the aims of the Commission on the Future of Multiethnic Britain, chaired by Lord Bhikhu Parekh, was to redefine what it means to be British and whether it was possible to reimagine Britain as a nation, or post-nation, in a multicultural way. It was precisely this section on the future of Britishness that sparked most controversy. The Parekh Report (see Runnymede Trust 2000) argued that devolution to Scotland, Wales and Northern Ireland undermined the notion of Britishness by its consequent questions about English, Scottish and Welsh identities. For first-generation immigrants, Britishness has been a reminder of colonization and empire, and to that extent was not attractive. The report (Runnymede Trust 2000: 38) also argued that for British-born generations, the concept of Englishness often seems inappropriate, since:

> To be English, as the term is in practice used, is to be white. Britishness is not ideal, but at least it appears acceptable, particularly when suitably qualified – Black British, Indian British, British Muslim and so forth. However, there is one major and so far insuperable barrier. Britishness, as much as Englishness, has systematic, largely unspoken, racial connotations. Whiteness nowhere

---

14   The Social Chapter became an agreement between the then eleven EU member states. Under Article 2 of Maastricht's Social Chapter, the Council of Ministers can issue directives, adopted by qualified majority voting, on improvement of the working environment, health and safety, working conditions, equality between men and women and occupational integration.

features as an explicit condition of being British, but it is widely understood that Englishness, and therefore by extension Britishness, is racially coded.

New Labour's approach, which I would call 'multicultural Britishness' (i.e., a combination of notions of multiculturalism and social inclusion), has presented a major shift in thinking about the concept of nationhood. Unlike the Conservative governments which largely excluded ethnic minority communities from the idea of nationhood, the New Labour administration promoted race equality, and the 2000 Race Relations Amendment Act represented the first race relations legislation for 25 years (see Table 5.1). From 2002 on, all public authorities – including schools, colleges and local education authorities – have a duty to promote race equality by eliminating racial discrimination, promoting equality of opportunity, and working toward good 'race relations'. The Race Relations Amendment Act also laid out specific duties for schools, including the implementation of a written policy on race equality, the monitoring of recruitment and progression of ethnic minority staff and students, and an assessment of the impact of new and current policies on ethnic minority staff, students and other service users.[15] In addition, it called for a system for monitoring grievance, discipline, appraisal, staff development, and termination procedures by ethnicity.

The Nationality, Immigration and Asylum Act of 2002 also engaged with the debates surrounding race equality, social inclusion and citizenship in multicultural Britain, and thus reasserted the concept of nationhood. The legislation requires residents seeking British citizenship to be tested to show 'a sufficient knowledge of English, Welsh or Scottish Gaelic', to have 'a sufficient knowledge about life in the United Kingdom' and to take a citizenship oath and a pledge at a civic ceremony (Home Office 2002). In September 2002, the year preceding this study, the government established an independent advisory group, chaired by Sir Bernard Crick, to advise the Home Secretary on the method, conduct and implementation of a 'Life in the United Kingdom' test, also known as Britishness or citizenship test. The resulting report *The New and the Old* (Home Office 2003) made a number of recommendations for new migrants to Britain. Firstly, prospective citizens should be assessed on their progress in English, and required to move from one English for Speakers of Other Languages level to another, with the minimum movement being from 'no English' to a 'sufficient level to take up unskilled employment'. Secondly, applicants would have to learn English and citizenship in parallel. Thirdly, the report called for a 'Life in the United Kingdom' handbook, which would include a short introduction to Britain's history and society, and be given

---

15   The Race Relations Amendment Act has been further amended by the Race Relations (Amendment) Regulations in 2003, which transposed the two European Commission directives (Council of the European Union 2000a, b). However, since the Employment directive does not go beyond the sphere of employment, it fails to offer the same levels of protections afforded under present race relations legislation in England.

to all those applying for naturalization as well as other legal migrants with work permits. The report rejected an exclusive notion of Britishness, arguing that:

> To be British does not mean assimilation into a common culture so that original identities are lost. Assimilation to such a degree has not, after all, happened for most people in Wales and Scotland, nor historically for Irish and Jewish immigrant communities. (...) To be British seems to us to mean that we respect the laws, the elected parliamentary and democratic political structures, traditional values of mutual tolerance, respect for equal rights and mutual concern; and that we give our allegiance to the state in return for its protection.

Another government document from the same time period, the Cantle Report (Cantle 2001: 10) similarly argues for a 'greater sense of citizenship' informed by 'common elements of "nationhood" [including] the use of the English language' (Cantle 2001: 19). At the same time, this other report stresses that 'we are never going to turn the clock back to what was perceived to be a dominant or monoculturalist view of nationality' (Cantle 2001: 18). The Cantle Report's lead author has elsewhere pleaded 'let's not just throw out the concept of multiculturalism; let's update it and move it to a more sophisticated and developed approach' (Cantle 2006: 91). The report was published following the inquiry into civil unrest and 'rioting' between ethnic majority and Asian Muslim youth in several northern English towns during the summer of 2001.[16] It thus argued that migrants in Bradford, Oldham and Burnley were leading 'parallel lives', and called for the 'urgent need' to promote community cohesion based on a greater knowledge of and respect for the various cultures in Britain. The report intertwined notions of community cohesion, citizenship and national identity, and has generally brought discourses of community cohesion and assimilatory aspects of 'integration' to the fore. These civic integrationist (or even assimilationist) tendencies have since competed and, according to Meer and Modood (2009), sought to 'rebalance' the recognition of diversity in previous policies.

The government's latest strategy for race equality and community cohesion, 'Improving Opportunity, Strengthening Society' (Home Office 2005), and its follow-up, 'One year On – A progress Summary' (Department for Communities and Local Government 2006: 1-2), reiterate the two key aims of 'achieving equality between different races; and developing a better sense of community

---

16   Other post-riot reports (i.e., Ritchie 2001, Clarke 2001, Ouseley 2001) led commentators to critique Muslim distinctiveness in particular and multiculturalism in general. For example, Cesari (2004: 23-24) maintains that 'whether in the areas of housing, employment, schooling or social services, the [Cantle] report describes an England segregated according to the twin categories of race and religion'. The notion of 'parallel lives' and Britain 'sleepwalking to segregation' was reinforced in 2005, following the London attacks, by the then Chair of the Commission for Racial Equality, Trevor Philipps, who called for a more integrated society (see also Finney and Simpson 2009).

cohesion by helping people from different backgrounds to have a stronger sense of "togetherness"'.[17] This includes, for example, 'raising the achievement of groups at risk of underperforming i.e. African-Caribbean, Gypsy Traveller, Bangladeshi, Pakistani, Turkish and Somali pupils' which is meant to contribute to a cohesive community in which 'there is a common vision and a sense of belonging; the diversity of people's different backgrounds and circumstances is appreciated and valued; those from different backgrounds have similar life opportunities' (Department for Communities and Local Government 2006: 7). Indeed, the most recent comment from the government-sponsored Commission on Integration and Cohesion (2007: 5), explicitly distinguishes integration from assimilation:

> Very many of the definitions of cohesion and integration offered in the response to the Commission on Integration and Cohesion consultation spontaneously include a level of concern to distinguish integration from *assimilation*, stressing the importance for true cohesion of accepting – and celebrating – difference. Individual and group *identities* should not be endangered by the process of integration, but rather they should be enriched within both the incoming groups and the host nation. Cohesion implies a society in which differences of culture, race and faith are recognized and accommodated within an overall sense of identity, rather than a single identity, based on a uniform similarity.

Since September 2007, schools have been under a new duty to promote community cohesion which is reflected in the secondary curriculum review. First, according to the Department for Children, Schools and Families, 'the curriculum for all maintained schools should promote the spiritual, moral, cultural, mental and physical development of pupils at the school and of society, and prepare pupils at the school for the opportunities, responsibilities and experiences of later life'. Second, 'schools have a duty to eliminate unlawful racial discrimination and to promote equality of opportunity and good relations between people of different groups (Department for Children, Schools and Families 2007: 2). The new citizenship programme of study explicitly offers opportunities for schools to address their statutory duty to promote community cohesion as part of the new 'fourth strand' on identities and diversity. By community cohesion, the Department for Children, Schools and Families (2007: 4) means 'working towards a society in which there is a common vision and sense of belonging by all communities; a society in which the diversity of people's backgrounds and circumstances is appreciated and valued;

---

17   The UK Borders Act (2007) provided the UK Border Agency with new powers to tackle illegal working; the Criminal Justice and Immigration Act (2008) introduced a special immigration status for those believed to have been involved in terrorism and other serious crimes; and the Borders, Citizenship and Immigration Act (2009) requires a residential status of eight years (up from six years) before being eligible for naturalization. It also introduces a voluntary community service for migrants which can reduce the length of the naturalization process by up to two years.

a society in which similar life opportunities are available to all'. Schools thus need to emphasize what different groups of students hold in common.

Table 5.2 not only indicates the increasing processes of hybridization in the form of four 'mixed'categories which Parekh (2000), Hall (1991, 1992) and Modood (1992, 2000) referred to, but also underscores the increasingly multiethnic nature of the population of England. At the time of the most recent census in 2001, ethnic minority groups formed 9.1 per cent of the population, compared with just 6.2 per cent in 1991:

Table 5.2 The ethnicity of residents in England in 1991 and 2001

Ethnic groups	Residents in 1991	Percentages in 1991	Residents in 2001	Percentages in 2001
Total	47,055,204	100.0	49,138,831	100.0
White	44,144,339	93.8	44,679,361	90.9
All ethnic minority groups	2,910,865	6.2	4,459,470	9.1
Indian	823,821	1.8	1,028,546	2.1
Pakistani	449,646	1.0	706,539	1.4
Bangladeshi	157,881	0.3	275,394	0.6
Chinese	141,661	0.3	220,681	0.4
Other Asian	189,253	0.4	237,810	0.5
Black Caribbean	495.682	1.0	561,246	1.1
Black African	206,918	0.4	475,938	1.0
Other Black	172,282	0.4	95,324	0.2
White and Black Caribbean	n/a	n/a	231,424	0.5
White and Asian	n/a	n/a	184,014	0.4
White and Black African	n/a	n/a	76,498	0.2
Other Mixed	n/a	n/a	151,437	0.3
Other ethnic groups	273,721	0.6	214,619	0.4

Note: The four 'mixed' categories were only introduced in the 2001 census. As a result of the eastern enlargement of the EU in 2004, there are now also an estimated 600,000 Poles in England (Federation of Poles in Great Britain) and smaller numbers of Slovakians and Czechs. Exact numbers will only become available in the 2011 census.
Source: Office for National Statistics (http://www.ons.gov.uk/census/index.html).

Of particular relevance for the empirical analysis in the subsequent two chapters is the 200,000-strong Turkish community in England which, unlike in other European countries, consists of three main groups: mainland Turks, Turkish Cypriots and Kurds. The Turkish community has faced enormous conflict and marginalization in the English society. Mainland Turks, Turkish Cypriots and Kurds have mostly worked in, or owned, shops such as coffee houses and kebab stores, thus making employment opportunities more restricted and less appealing because of the low wages and long hours characteristic of these shops (Enneli 2002). In addition, Avni and Koumbarji (1994) report that in the London Borough of Hackney, around 80 per cent of mainland Turks live in council housing, and 20 per cent of Turkish Cypriots are owner occupiers. In 2000, neighbouring Haringey was classified as the 37th most deprived area in England out of 354, with 30 per cent of residents living in council houses, and less than half of the residents being owner occupiers. This indicates that the Turkish community in England, particularly the mainland Turks and Kurds, is marginalized in economically deprived areas in north London, the location of my study's two English schools.

Most if not all of these Turks are also Muslim, and since 1988, Muslims have increasingly been characterized as 'dangerous individuals' with a capacity for violence and terrorism as well as 'culturally dangerous' in ways that threaten the British way of life.[18] The fear of Muslims has led to a debate over the relationship between the national (i.e., Britishness) and multicultural agendas (i.e., Islamic culture). Unlike in earlier periods (e.g., the 1981 social unrest among Afro-Caribbeans in England), the emphasis of multiculturalism debates shifted from phenotype to religion. Islamophobia, or Muslimophobia, as Archer (2003) maintains, started in 1988 with the publication of the book 'The Satanic Verses' by British Indian author Salman Rushdie, and led to a steady and discernible increase in public concerns over fundamentalist Islam throughout the 1990s. The discourse of Muslimophobia in England was further fuelled by concerns about social unrest amongst the Muslim groups following media reports of the street riots in Oldham and Bradford in 2001, and the London bombings in July 2005. This has led to increased questioning not only of the concept of multiculturalism, but of Muslim loyalties in particular, often on the assumption that Muslims are not willing to integrate into society or adopt its political values.

These socio-political events have reinvigorated debates about multiculturalism and national identity and propelled British Muslims to the centre of public discourse, while also impacting representations and stereotypes of Muslim students. Muslim boys have been singled out as educational 'problems' who form part of an 'underclass', and Muslim boys suffer the highest rates of racism in school (Archer 2003: 36). The rise of anti-Muslim prejudice also led the Department for Education and Skills to publish guidance for schools and, two years later, the National Association of Schoolmasters Union of Women Teachers (2003: 5), the largest trade union for teachers, published the document 'Islamophobia: advice for schools and colleges' (updated following the 2005 London bombings) recommending that:

---

18   For example, in 1993, the Conservative Party MP Winston Churchill expressed his fears that within the next 50 years the 'British way of life' would be destroyed and 'the muezzin will be calling Allah's faithful to the High Street mosque' (cited in Bhavnani and Phoenix 1994: 172). Such fears follow in the rhetorical footsteps of Conservatives such as Enoch Powell and Margaret Thatcher.

Schools and colleges should identify practical ways in which they intend to counter Islamophobia and anti-Muslim prejudice and racism. Practical opportunities might include the use of assemblies; citizenship lessons; tutorial time; parental meetings and home-school agreements; and counselling and advice facilities for students and staff. (…) Islamophobia is an issue for all schools and colleges, regardless of the number of Muslim students/students or staff within the establishment. Schools and colleges should communicate clearly to all students, parents, staff and the wider community its rejection of racism and other forms of bigotry including Islamophobia and anti-Muslim prejudice and racism.

This new emphasis on religion has prompted one of the latest educational debates in England, the desire for state-funded faith-based schools. There are currently over 4,700 state-funded Church of England schools, over 2,100 Catholic schools, 35 Jewish schools, and 28 Methodist schools. In contrast, there are only 10 Muslim public schools (a further 130 Muslim schools are non-state funded). Thus, campaigns for faith schooling in the state sector are indicative of 'a modern society which is widely perceived as increasingly secular but is paradoxically increasingly multi-faith' (Skinner 2002: 172). The Government White Paper 'Schools: Achieving Success' (Department for Education and Skills 2001) sets out new responsibilities of local education authorities and the procedures to be followed to this end. Paragraph 5.30 explicitly states the government's position that 'faith schools have a significant history as part of the state education system, and play an important role in its diversity. […] We wish to welcome faith schools, with their distinctive ethos and character, into the maintained sector where there is clear local agreement'.

The reasons behind this growing desire for Muslim schools include a desire to incorporate more faith-based principles into an integrated education system so that the 'whole person' can be educated in an Islamic environment (see Hewer 2001), and a preference for single-sex schooling (e.g., Dawkins 2006). In addition, there is a call to respond to a lack of specialist training in the Islamic religious sciences in conjunction with general education so that young people might 'be educated to serve their communities as potential religious leaders' (Hewer 2001: 518). Advocates also want to see more aspects of Islamic culture embedded within school curricula that are otherwise normally couched within an ethnocentric Christian-European tradition (e.g., Douglass and Shaikh 2004). And finally, many believe that greater accommodation of difference will help address the low achievement among Pakistanis and Bangladeshis, especially boys, and prevent further marginalization (see Haque 2000).

At the time of my fieldwork, there were over 300,000 Muslim students in English schools. Ethnic minority students made up 15.3 per cent of the total student population (13.8 per cent in secondary schools), as summarized in Table 5.3:

Table 5.3 The ethnicity of students in English schools in 2004/05

Ethnic groups	Total number of students 2004/05	Percentages of students 2004/05
Total	6,597,200	100.0
White	5,587,500	84.7
All ethnic minority groups	1,009,700	15.3
Indian	155,800	2.4
Pakistani	188,700	2.9
Bangladeshi	76,700	1.2
Chinese	23,900	0.4
Other Asian	52,100	0.8
Black Caribbean	94,400	1.4
Black African	133,200	2.0
Other Black	28,600	0.4
White and Black Caribbean	68,500	1.0
White and Asian	38,500	0.6
White and Black African	19,300	0.3
Other Mixed	66,000	1.0
Other ethnic groups	64,000	0.9

Source: Based on data from the Department of Education and Skills (2005).

To sum up this discussion of national identity and education in England, I have argued that the concept of Britishness has been mediated through the promotion of multicultural values in English schools, creating a new identity that I call 'multicultural Britishness'. At the same time, national identity and citizenship have been challenged by post-war Commonwealth immigration and by increasing processes of European integration, which have also brought new immigration from Eastern Europe following EU enlargement in 2004. As a result of increasing migration to England, including post-war Commonwealth migration and recent intra-European migration, 'immigrant' has for many people become synonymous with 'coloured immigrant', thereby intertwining issues of migration, race and multiculturalism. Successive English governments have emphasized the concept of British nationhood[19] and as a result schools have tended to emphasize national identity over and above supranational agendas. This chapter has set the context for my empirical study of youth in two London schools, which have interpreted the macro-political context in different ways. Unlike Germany's strong promotion of European values, England has had a more politically contentious relationship with the EU. Note, however, that the fieldwork was carried out amidst ongoing debates about the 2004 European elections and a 'rebalancing' of (Meer and Modood 2009)

---

19   This was reinforced in 2009 when the naturalization process was extended from six to eight years of residence.

or 'retreat' from (Joppke 2004) multiculturalism. Let us now turn to Millroad and Darwin School in London.

Chapter 6

Ethnic Conflict in Millroad School

Millroad School, a predominantly working-class comprehensive school, is located in the east of an inner-city, multiethnic London borough surrounded by small shops and cafes, most of which are owned by the local Turkish community. Sixty per cent of Millroad pupils are eligible for free school meals, and only 23 per cent attain five or more A* to Cs in the General Certificate of Secondary Education (GCSE) examinations.[1] This borough is characterized by high diversity within the ethnic minority population, an active political community, and a history of concern for race equality. Millroad School had 1,204 students on roll during the academic year 2003/04, the year before the study. The majority of students (968, or 80.4 per cent) come from ethnic minority communities, with African Caribbeans forming the largest group (367 students), followed by Turks (320 students). Exclusion rates are high amongst Turkish and African Caribbean students (6.6 and 9.3 per cent, respectively), and relatively low for ethnic majority and Asian students (5.5 and 6.2 per cent, respectively). The overall exclusion rate per academic year is around 8 per cent (98 out of 1,204 students). Also, Asian students attain an average of 4 GCSEs at grades A*-C, while Turkish achieve just 1.9 on average, African Caribbean attain 1.6, and the working-class ethnic majority students attain 1.0.[2]

Unlike in Germany, the regional government in London does not have direct control of the school system and curriculum, and there is far more room for local education authorities and schools within the local area to develop rather different approaches to national, European and multicultural issues. At key stage 3 (ages 11-14) students study English, mathematics, science, art, music, citizenship, physical education, drama, technology, information technology, world studies (a combination of history, geography and religious education) as well as personal, social and health education and modern languages. Millroad School offers introductory language courses in French, Turkish, Spanish and German for its Year 7 students and encourages students to learn two languages, generally French and Turkish, from Year 8 onwards. The school has applied for Language College Status and is developing visits and links with other countries including France and Turkey. At key stage 4 (ages 15-16) all students have an individual study programme drawn from the following range of examination courses: English

---

1   In the British grading system, grade A* is the highest and F the lowest grade (a fail grade). The benchmark for monitoring how well a school is doing has been the percentage of students achieving five or more A* to Cs.

2   In general, ethnic majority students in working-class schools in Europe have lower achievement levels.

language and literature, French, German, mathematics, science, Turkish, Spanish, technology, art, information systems, business, drama, media studies, geography, music, history and sociology. Religious education, information technology and physical education are compulsory for Year 10 and 11 students. Students are also offered vocational experiences, including the opportunity for work experience within the EU.

In recent years, the catchment area of the school has been at the centre of violent outbreaks between Turkish and Kurdish heroin gangs. Benedictus (2005) observes that, in 2002, local war broke out which involved around 40 Turkish and Kurdish men fighting a street battle with sticks, knives and guns. This led to the murder of a 43-year-old Kurdish carpenter, which prompted widespread cries for change. Besides the violence within these Turkish groups, Mehmet Ali (2001) argues that local fights between African Caribbean and Turkish youth gangs have caused great concern. Some older brothers and sisters, she maintains, have contacts with the Turkish and Kurdish mafias or the Caribbean Yardies (i.e., young and often unemployed Jamaican males aged 18-35). These conflicts have spilled over into Millroad School and resulted in ethnic divisions between the African Caribbean and Turkish communities.

Millroad School mediated national identity through a politics of diversity and, in so doing, reasserted the concept of cultural pluralism that prevailed in the 1970s and early 1980s. The school established an extra-curricular Turkish enrichment class to enable students to read, write and speak in Turkish and was working on the publication of a Turkish newspaper at the time of fieldwork. The school also offered Turkish as a GCSE subject. The Excellence in Cities programme (a targeted attempt by the New Labour government to tackle disadvantage) also introduced new ways of providing curriculum support. For example, Turkish-speaking students are exempt from their normal school curriculum for six lessons per week while working with a Turkish Cypriot learning mentor. These efforts at maintaining home cultures were undoubtedly important. But Millroad's approaches to multiculturalism were ultimately problematic. As my evidence shows, a school which celebrates diversity without fostering a common bond between the diverse groups of students (as Millroad did), encourages young people to retreat into their ethnic identities.

Working with Cultural Diversity

Millroad School attempted to bring together national and citizenship agendas with their existing multicultural approach to ethnicity. The teachers I interviewed argued that the school aimed to create multicultural, global, critical and well-informed citizens. For example, Mr. Green, the head of history, maintained that a citizen is 'not just someone with political rights, someone who's a member of a particular society, but actually the whole idea of a world citizen, you're actually part of a diverse global community and you have rights and obligations'. In addition, the citizenship co-ordinator thought that teachers should make use of the potential of having diverse classes, arguing that 'when you've got a particular cultural or ethnic group, you can actually get those people to do the teaching of the other kids about their experiences or their particular culture. They do the teaching; you use the particular groups rather than you doing it'.

'Personal, social and health education (PSHE) and citizenship', as the subject is called at Millroad, was delivered in three ways, including official curriculum, a range of out-of-hour activities (e.g., involvement in an active citizenship network project with the aim of producing short films about the work of a local community group or charity), and theme days. For example, during my fieldwork, Year 9 had recently had a theatre company looking at sexual health. According to Mr. Wilson, the citizenship co-ordinator, Millroad School used to have one hour a week of personal, social and health education with the idea of fusing the national citizenship agenda to it. But, he said, 'this year, they've put it into the 25-minute morning registration and assembly period; so in that 25-minute period you should have three mornings a week at least a 15-minute activity that addresses some aspect of the citizenship and PSHE curricula. I find it very unsatisfactory but that's the setup at the moment'. The school's approach to citizenship was thus 'minimalist', given that citizenship was not examined (Kerr et al. 2004, see the classification and discussions in the previous chapter).

Despite spending little time on citizenship, Millroad School dedicated a lot of time to celebrating its ethnic and cultural diversity, as the following excerpt from the school prospectus reveals:

> We recognize that the social, cultural and linguistic diversity in our community is an important resource and an aspect of our ethos we seek to promote and celebrate. We give our students opportunities to take responsibility and develop citizenship within the school community and beyond. (…) An important part of our work is giving our young people the knowledge and personal strength to be good citizens in a multicultural world which is fast changing. (…) Everything we do is geared to our two central aims: to raise standards and expectations, and to develop the school campus as a distinctive pioneering learning environment for students and the community – in short to make it a magnet for the community.

During fieldwork, I observed a Turkish Kurdish Celebration Week. Students were asked to discuss their identities in terms of culture and language during lessons; students were taught to greet each other with *merhaba* (hello) when arriving for tutor time; and when students answered the register they were asked to say *burda* (here) to show that they were present. Also, when leaving the registration session, they said *güle güle* (goodbye). The aim during this week was for all students to learn key words in Turkish to further their understanding of Turkish as a world language. In addition, there were many ethnic pictures in the school building including wall displays of Islamic patterns painted by students, quotations from famous ethnic minority leaders such as Atatürk or Mandela, and slogans such as

'I care', 'Let's work together' in various community languages. The multicultural ethos was thus very visible at Millroad.

The teacher interviews provided further evidence that Millroad School emphasized diversity and difference over and above national citizenship and community cohesion. The discussion with Mr. Taylor, the head of geography, indicated that the school was aware of its sizeable Turkish community (27 per cent) and their particular needs:

> DF: How do you include the different ethnic communities in the school and address their particular needs in the teaching of geography?
>
> MR. TAYLOR: Yeah, we have particularly a lot of students whose second language is English. I mean a lot of them speak very very little English and one of the Year 8 classes I teach on environmental issues, we're looking at the problem of litter around the school and make it an environmental and how it can be solved. So they're starting to do bilingual posters in Turkish and English like "put your litter in the bin" or mottos like "put the litter in the bin or the headmaster will beat you in" or something, yeah. And it's in Turkish and English so I encourage other students in the class and make it a bilingual motif to get through, encourage lots of work that relates to where they're from. (…) We have theme days in the school and opportunities for them to show the ethnic and cultural diversity of the school, of our students in the school.

The principal, Mr. Moore, also mentioned a number of specific strategies for including ethnic minority students in the Millroad School community. Firstly, 'with the ethnic minority achievement team, when new arrivals come into the school with limited English, they have a special induction reception programme, and they work with a particular teacher and then they're fed into the curriculum'. Secondly, 'we are looking at two supplementary schools, one for Turkish-Kurdish students on a Saturday morning, and one for Afro-Caribbean students, boys in particular (…) to target the needs of particular groups a lot more precisely'. Thirdly, we 'keep data on students that shows ethnic background and so, I could tell you now how our kids have achieved last year'.

While Millroad School emphasized cultural pluralism, the European agenda seemed to be a relatively low priority at the school. Although the Modern Foreign Languages Department displayed a number of posters with the different languages the school teaches (i.e., French, German, Turkish, Spanish) and posters regarding the eastern enlargement of the EU, Mr. Green, the head of history, maintained that the multicultural agenda is the dominant one in Millroad School and favoured over a European educational dimension:

> DF: Like geography and citizenship, history should include a European dimension. What do you make of that?

MR. GREEN: I think history should include a world dimension. I mean, I think that actually – there's been a debate in history, with the development of the National Curriculum, about the extent to which it should be British history. When the National Curriculum was first introduced, there was an attempt to introduce a greater element of Britishness. This was resisted by history teachers. However, it's still the case that the National Curriculum has a much stronger bias in terms of British history. I don't think there are a great deal of opportunities for a specifically European dimension. Does that bother me? Not so much that there aren't opportunities for a European dimension because I'm interested in African history, for example, we look at African civilization. I'd be interested at developing a unit based around Islamic civilizations, I'd be fascinated to be able to do something around Turkish history. I think that the history that we do in the school, we need to try and relate it to the students we have in the school and their cultural backgrounds.

Nevertheless, some teachers in this sample did see a need to educate students about Europe. The head of geography, for instance, was keen to stress that 'I'm actually developing a change in the schemes of work that we teach and the structure I've had, (…) it needs a European dimension' but so far 'well, we've [only] touched on Europe'. The challenge for Millroad School thus appears to be how to combine the politics of diversity with the new European agenda and this is perhaps best expressed by Mr. Taylor, the head of geography who argued that 'the curriculum is in a developing stage; changes are necessary because of the changes in the European Union'. At the time of fieldwork, the geography syllabus only had one European teaching unit in Year 8 (Italy: a European country) while highlighting the importance of an international perspective with units on Japan and Brazil in addition to local and national issues (see Appendix 4).

On the other hand, the teachers were very aware of divisions between the African Caribbean and Turkish communities. For example, Mr. Moore, the school principal, observed that 'there are issues around how young Turkish people as first-generation immigrants come to terms with western society; many of the Turkish community live entirely in a Turkish environment. (…) They have no experience of living with Afro-Caribbean people, so there is a lot of racism in that community'. Here, Mr. Moore emphasized that the origins of this peer group conflict lay outside the school rather than being the result of the promotion of a politics of cultural diversity.[3] Mr. Moore hoped that mixing staff and students and promoting intercultural awareness could tackle the divisions between African Caribbean and Turkish students:

---

3 Unlike in the two German schools, the diversity of the school population is reflected in the composition of its staff with 28 ethnic majority teachers and 60 ethnic minority teachers, nine of whom are of Turkish origin. For example, Year 10 Turkish students have a Turkish Cypriot learning mentor for six lessons per week.

DF: How are you going to address this division between the Afro-Caribbean and the Turkish-Kurdish communities?

MR. MOORE: That's a very good point; we've had a number of incidents in the school and we need to do a lot more proactively to mix students. And actually some of the students are saying "but look at the staff! They are very ethnically mixed but they don't mix with each other either!" and we've done a workshop with staff about this and looked at how we work together and one of the things that has come out of this, and some teachers don't yet have the confidence to do this, but you are absolutely right to spot that and it happens a lot but in some areas it's being challenged and what we're increasingly looking to do and we need to support staff on this is mix the groups more and every class should have a seating plan and the seating plan should be determined by the teacher. Now what actually happens is often the teacher allows the kids to kind of determine it. (…) Lots of our African-Caribbean kids don't know the names of the Turkish kids, lots of the Turkish kids refer to them almost as a group and this goes back to citizenship, you've got individual students who are breaking the mould who are actually challenging that and saying, you know, I'm friends with him, you know, we can't be like this, so you've got to work at it on several fronts but it's about dialogue in the end.

However, given that the root of the conflict appears to be outside Millroad School, attempting to disseminate 'good practice' from within the school into the local community seemed an ambitious agenda. Since the dynamics between groups of students were strongly affected by community relations and the local economy, it remains to be seen whether such school efforts reduce the divisions. But what is evident here from Mr. Moore's argument is that the school was aware of the conflict and took the issue very seriously by directly attempting to 'work with' ethnic conflict.

Ethnic Conflict and Racialized Discourses

Despite the school's pro-multicultural policy and teaching units that were developed to address the needs of ethnic minority students, there were violent gang fights and Turkish students were often mocked for their ethnicity and nationality. This resulted in a strong sense of ethnic solidarity amongst the sample of Turkish students. When I observed some of the lessons, I noticed that students sat along ethnic lines in almost all classrooms, with some tables of only African Caribbean students and other tables with only Turkish Kurdish students. And while ethnic majority interviewees[4] mostly had mixed friendship groups, the Turkish students

---

4   In this working-class context, the terms 'majority' and 'minority' are in reality inverted (due to the smaller number of white students) which is important to understand the

had few cross-ethnic friendships and formed groups along ethnic lines. This was demonstrated in my discussions with mainland Turkish (Halil, Baris) and Turkish Cypriot (Sarila) students:

DF: Could you tell me a little bit about your friends?

BARIS: They're all Turkish.

HALIL: They come from where I come from.

BARIS: Same place we come from. Only she's [Sarila] got black friends.

SARILA: I've got mixed friends. I've got lots of different friends really.

HALIL: Kosovo [laughs]

SARILA: It depends like there's different things of friends, there's like close friends most of my close friends are either Turkish or Cypriot.

BARIS: Can I ask you about your black friends?

SARILA: I have lots of different friends, [HALIL: They come from different backgrounds] I don't know, but like the closest ones are Turkish Cypriot.

BARIS: Why's you friends with black people though?

SARILA: Because I have mixed race cousins and I was-

BARIS: Cos black people, I hate them.

SARILA: I was brought up with them, ok, I know their dad, chat to them and everything.

BARIS: Black is different. Black people are dickheads, that's it.

Baris' racist remarks exemplify the peer group conflict in Millroad School between the Turkish community and African Caribbean students. When asked about the reasons for these tensions, many Turkish interviewees referred to cultural and religious differences. For example, some argued that English and black people had no respect for others. 'They don't go kissing their nan's hand', he said. Respect,

---

ethnic dynamics and power struggles. However, for the sake of keeping with the terminology in other chapters, I will continue to refer to white British students (who account for only 19.6 per cent) as ethnic majority.

Baris argued, meant showing someone, especially elder family members, that you care and he felt that ethnic majority and African Caribbean people were short of these family bonds.

Ethnic solidarity amongst the sample of Turkish students, particularly mainland Turks, was also based upon common Muslim religion, language, culture and physical appearance. Tarik, for example, used these criteria to differentiate between his Turkish and non-Turkish classmates:

> TARIK: I've got one English friend in this school, and he finds it funny, like, because Turkish people are kind of hairy and they got hairy faces and everything, cos I have got a hairy face, they're like ["stupid" accent] "oh, why have you got a hairy face, why are you doing that, why don't you shave" and stuff, and I'm like [annoyed voice] "there's no need, cos I'm Turkish you know what I mean, it's not my fault if my hair comes out", and then they're like "how comes we don't have it, we don't have it like" and that's what I'm trying to say, that we don't really match. Like my Turkish friends, they don't say nothing, they find it normal cos they got hair on their faces as well.

> DF: Are there any other differences or similarities?

> TARIK: Yeah, the way I speak, they find it funny cos I use a lot of slang language, and when I speak they don't really understand. And what they don't really like about me is when I speak to other Turkish people in Turkish, they get annoyed, they get really annoyed, cos they don't understand and they're like "you're in a British country, why are you talking Turkish for?" and that really annoys me.

Ethnic majority classmates made fun of Tarik's more masculine, Mediterranean look exemplified by his amount of facial and body hair. However, for English peers, Tarik also contributed to this conflict by speaking Turkish and showed little understanding why classmates of other backgrounds might get annoyed when he speaks Turkish rather than English. Ethnic majority students perceived the language barrier, as one English boy pointed out, as hampering the integration of Turkish students into the school community. For example, 'most of the Caribbean people, when they came to this country was speaking English so that made it easier for them. I think the Turkish community, because it's the newest, kept its language and that's in this school particularly it's been quite, erm, quite insular'.

This argument was taken even further in the discussion I had with a group of four Turkish boys. Drawing on a theme of 'us' (Turkish people) and 'them' (English people), the boys argued that they were positioned as Turkish Muslims by their ethnic majority peers which made it hard for them to develop a British identity:

> DF: How comfortable would you say you feel in England?

MUHAMMAD: Not that comfortable. Like some like, erm, last I've heard of people like, they've got their own places, some people, some, er, racist English people come there and go, that, "leave our country alone, go back to your country" go to places there, and there's lots of them, and they've been, like they've gone into places and get you "leave our country, this ain't your country", most of them.

ONAN: "This is our place", "you don't belong here" and stuff like that.

DF: And then how did you react?

KHAN: Cuss them back!

YILDIRAN: Yeah, that's what we do really if anyone says anything to us, we say to them.

ONAN: [speaking Turkish]

YILDIRAN: And then it gets into gang fights.

KHAN: Like, you see a couple of them come in, you call your mates, then they call their mates until one of them gets down.

The discussion highlights that, in addition to the separation between African Caribbean and Turkish students, there is also conflict between the smaller number of ethnic majority and Turkish students who appeared to construct a narrow identity that excludes Turkish students from the concept of nationhood. The group of Turkish girls added that 'you're sort of uncomfortable about how people see you, if they see you as a stereotypical (Turkish) person like, if you say you're Turkish, they will say you would know they're sort of thinking of you in a different way'.

The teachers also seemed to have fuelled some of these racialized discourses and differentiated in a negative way between the various cultures and groups of students inside Millroad. This strongly resembles Mac an Ghaill's (1988) accounts of racist stereotyping when he found that Asian males were seen by their teachers as students of 'high ability' whereas African Caribbean males were perceived as having 'low ability' and discipline problems.[5] Twenty years later, the students I interviewed felt that teachers were still working with some of these stereotypical

5   See also Gogolin (2002) who writes about the monolingual and monocultural orientation of teachers in Holland, Germany, Belgium and the Netherlands, with implications for the 'othering' of those who do not belong to the ethnic majority. Sleeter (1993) talks about a colour-blindness of teachers in their talk about schooling. Devine (2005) who analysed Irish teachers' views on diversity noticed both classed and racialized discourses.

images. Arguably, the ways in which teachers differentiated between different cultures and students may have contributed to the conflict in this school as well as Turkish and African Caribbeans' fight over which group controls the school territory:

> DF: To what extent do you think that all students are part of the school community?

> BARIS: I don't.

> SARILA: No, I don't either.

> HALIL: No, no, you know.

> BARIS: They [referring to teachers] treat every culture different ways. Like when they see black people, they're like "there's no point wasting your time", or with Turkish people, "there's no point wasting your time". That's how they see it.

> SARILA: It's all about stereotypes.

> BARIS: They just think about first time, they just see they just what they hear about you, that's what they think about you. […]

> DF: Why do you think are people treated unequally here?

> SARILA: Racism. Basically.

> BARIS: Because of us they [African Caribbeans] can't control the school. They piss us off.

> DF: What do you do to control the school?

> HALIL: Control them. […] Violence is a good way. They mess us around, we beat them up. Stare at them they stare back at you, knock them out.

Baris and Halil referred to violence and aggression in striving to retain control over Millroad School. Baris provided a shocking account of how he physically abused fellow black students in the school to exercise his authority as a male Turkish person. This was confirmed by a group of ethnic majority boys, arguing that 'the Turks kind of rule this school (…) if there's ever a fight, they bring every single Turkish person they know, then they'll just make it a gang fight'. This shows how the ethnic solidarity amongst the Turkish students, which is a result of the hostile climate in the school, was used in this struggle for power which reinforces the ethnic divisions amongst the school populations (see also Devine and Kelly 2006). Since the Turkish students were disadvantaged both socio-economically and ethnically, this exercise of control within the boundaries of Millroad School was probably their only chance to create a sense of superiority. Using violence and racism thus enabled them to reverse the hierarchy of race.

However, the African Caribbean students on the whole did not accept the self-acclaimed authority of the group of Turkish students (boys) inside Millroad School and challenged them in a variety of ways. The most common form of retaliation was verbal abuse. For example, African Caribbean students drew on the double meaning of the word 'turkey' to mock and ridicule the Turkish interviewees:

DF: Have you experienced any form of prejudice or discrimination?

YILDIRAN: Well yeah, they did actually. They said I'm a "F…ing Turk", which hurts me, it's in a way, like, "you're a Turk, you're not with us, you're not same, you're not same person, you're just odd", you know?

MUHAMMAD: Some people sometimes take the piss by like saying, you know the turkey, they say like "I'm going to go and buy a turkey and cook it".

YILDIRAN: Oh yeah-

MUHAMMAD: - and they're taking the piss like that.

YILDIRAN: Yeah, at Christmas. They-

MUHAMMAD: they go, they go, we're going to buy a turkey-

YILDIRAN: They pee you off! They go "I wanna go and get a turkey and eat it".

MUHAMMAD: And I then I get really pissed.

YILDIRAN: And this in Turkey, its actually it what you eat at Christmas,

MUHAMMAD: And that's what most of them, like, when it is Christmas, they go we're going to get a turkey and eat it tonight, and that pisses me off sometimes, that really pisses me off but I have to take it.

The use of the word 'turkey' has several different connotations here beyond the common bird. Firstly, it refers to notions of festivity and Christianity as a turkey is usually eaten at Thanksgiving in the United States and during Christmas in England. The image of the bird has a symbolic or even hierarchical meaning as Yildiran said that 'they [e.g., white, Christian] wanna go and get a turkey [e.g., non-white, Muslim]'. Secondly, a turkey can also be a stupid or silly person, which further puts the Turkish students in an inferior position. The fact that the country is named after the bird thus makes it particularly difficult for these students to defend their nationality and ethnicity by cussing members of other ethnicities.

Such wordplays and their different connotations were also discussed by Cohen (1988), who argued that ethnic majority working-class youth linguistically constructed black students as 'jungle bunnies' from the 1960s on, linking racist myths (Blacks come from the jungle) with sexual fantasies (Blacks breed like rabbits) to reinforce a racist misrecognition (Blacks are animals). For Cohen, the jungle addressed in this insult is not just an imaginary place of black origins associated with the colonial past, but also the place of moral panic associated with a life in which white youth find themselves positioned alongside their black peers as 'animals and savages'. For both the African Caribbean students cited by Cohen (1988) and the Turkish students at Millroad, these negative connotations reinforced their ethnic solidarity and exclusion from the concept of nationhood and, as a result, made it extremely difficult for Turkish youth to identify as British.[6]

While the discussion has so far focused on the two main groups at Millroad, African Caribbean (30 per cent) and Turkish students (27 per cent), it is also important to note how the ethnic majority students (who accounted for only 20 per cent) responded to the hostile climate at Millroad. For example, the group of four ethnic majority boys also felt unsafe and uncomfortable in the school because of the divisions between the African Caribbean and Turkish community. They were torn between engaging in the verbal abuse and racism of the two main groups, and acknowledging the marginalization and stereotyping of African Caribbean and Turkish students:

JOHN: I don't feel very comfortable at all.

BILL: I think we ain't got enough rights because all these foreign people come into our country, they're getting all the rights and we aren't getting the rights, so they get all the shops and everything, what do we get? They got all our money, they get all the cars, all we get is a house based in a little thugged-out area. If they really cared about England then they would put us somewhere, just say put us in a place where all nice people are and then put a place where like all the thugs are.

DAVE: Well that's just causing segregation.

BILL: Well, it's not really. I was watching Crimewatch the other day, yeah? And they said all these immigrant people coming over through tunnels and all sorts

---

6   These racialized discourses might well be linked with a lack of awareness among working-class youth of acceptable forms of discourse and masculine behaviour more broadly (see, for instance, Mac an Ghaill 1994, Sewell 2000, Archer 2008).

yeah? And then police take them to the immigration, and immigration just say "yeah you can stay here". So if anything, if they keep saying "Tony Blair's done whatever about our ... we don't want immigrants over here", why don't you just kick them back to their country? Take them back to their country.

JOHN: I do feel sorry for some of them though, cos some of them are genuine, like, being tortured or something terrible has happened to them and then people just stereotype them because of what the other people from their culture would do.

While Bill felt threatened that England might be swamped by 'all these foreign people' who get shops and everything, and thus employed a theme of 'us' (English, our country) and 'them' (foreigners) when talking about ethnic minority communities, John felt that it is not fair to stereotype people and send those who have been tortured back to their country of origin.[7] However, because of the struggle for dominance between the African Caribbean and Turkish peers, they felt that their 'white ethnicity' was more of an advantage outside school, where they formed the majority. 'If you're like black or Turkish it's more of an advantage inside school, cos you seem to have more power and authority'. In other words, inside the school, Turkish and African Caribbean youth fought over who controlled Millroad whereas the ethnic majority students felt more at the top outside the school. The teachers reinforced this hierarchical perception by doing a lot of work, including weekend trips, to bond the Turkish and African Caribbean communities together. This left the small group of ethnic majority students in a disadvantaged position as the teachers appeared to be more concerned with the larger African Caribbean and Turkish communities. The ethnic majority students thus did not have the numerical capacity to engage in the struggle for control over the school.

Underlining this point, a number of Turkish interviewees indicated that their ethnic background was more of an advantage inside Millroad School. The following excerpts from interviews with two Turkish girls highlight the two different worlds these students live in. On the one hand, they find safety in, and solidarity with, their large number of Turkish peers *inside* the school, leading to few cross-ethnic friendships. On the other hand, in the London community, where they are in the minority, Olcay and Sefika are being positioned as the 'other', which made it very hard for them to blend into the larger society:

---

7   The contrasts between male and female voices are fully discussed by Carol Gilligan (1982). In this excerpt, John referred to principles of justice arguing that 'it's not fair on other like, the good ones but, if most of them are in the wrong then I think it's the correct'. In contrast, girls often put themselves into the position of other people. Harriet argued that she does not feel 'comfortable and safe' in England when she thinks about 'all the people that's being murdered and raped'.

DF: To what extent do you feel that your ethnic background is an advantage or disadvantage both inside and outside the school?

OLCAY: In a way it's an advantage, cos there are a lot of Turkish people in our school, and it's like easier to blend in with them, cos when we talk Turkish and everything, it's an advantage in a way. But I don't really see a disadvantage of being Turkish, there's no disadvantage. [...]

SEFIKA: I think my Turkish thing, yeah, is, er, like ... outside yeah, it's like a disadvantage, but in this school yeah, it's like an advantage cos there's all different things yeah, all different countries and religions together, yeah.

DF: Why's it a disadvantage outside the school?

SEFIKA: It's you know, cos people outside, yeah, and, for example, me being Turkish, I don't know yeah, me being outside and someone just comes up to me and says this and this and aaah, I don't really know.

Although the ethnic majority students I interviewed were not involved in any gang fights or physical abuse, they nevertheless employed racialized discourses to position themselves, particularly in relation to their Turkish peers. For example, Lucy saw herself, and the English people in general, in a racially and culturally superior position who would 'inflict some of our culture on them [Turkish people]', an image resembling England's past as a dominant global power during the age of imperialism:

DF: How problematic do you think is it to be different in England?

ELLIE: It's quite hard innit, cos, all the time you just get - [drowned out by Holly]

HOLLY: But if you want to, it doesn't really make any difference. Because if you like, see that you can change, not change yourself, but kind of, if you're different it depends in what way you mean different.

ELLIE: It can be a good thing because you can bring new stuff to the community.

HOLLY: No but at the end [drowned out by Lucy]

LUCY: Yeah. But what's it brought to us? Kebabs? That's all they brought to us. Kebabs. They ain't brought nothing extra to the English community. But if we went to Turkey, like, they'd like inflict some of our culture, we'd inflict some

of our culture on them and they'd be like "oh wow". I bet they don't even have
Playstation 2 over there.

KATIE: [whispers] Fish and chips.

As this quote illustrates, phenotype is largely silenced as an issue in all the accounts
provided by students. Instead, cultural superiority (e.g., Playstation 2) emerges as
a theme. The racially charged atmosphere at Millroad, which is dissimilar from
the other schools in this study, also disillusions Gilroy's (2004: 131) hope for the
future of inner-city youth and the 'spontaneous tolerance and openness evident
in the underworld of Britain's convivial culture'. There is little evidence here of
the sort of 'convivial multiculturalism' Gilroy (2004, 2005) describes, little to
indicate the 'processes of cohabitation and interaction that have made multiculture
an ordinary feature of social life in Britain's urban areas and in postcolonial cities
elsewhere'. Conviviality, for Gilroy, means the everydayness of living with
and through human difference, which eventually renders race insignificant and
inessential. In contrast, the divisive peer cultures at Millroad make the boundaries
of race, culture, identity and ethnicity appear somewhat impermeable. There is
thus still some way to go, at Millroad School at least, toward Gilroy's postcolonial
world without racial difference and prejudice.

Since ethnic majority students were in the minority in Millroad School,
they mostly had ethnically diverse friendship groups. Contacts with the Turkish
community were limited as the ethnic majority youth did not see Turkish youth
as fitting in culturally, because they spoke a different language, had a different
religion and looked different. However, several ethnic majority interviewees were
aware of the diversity of the Turkish community at Millroad and in the borough
at large and did not see them as one homogeneous community. Paul, for instance,
argued that 'I think there's some Turkish people who relate to us, cos they've sort
of settled in with the English culture, but there's like a big group of Turkish people
that don't really fit in with the English culture and all their family's Turkish and
speak Turkish and then they just sort of have Turkish friends cos it's easier'. Here,
Paul differentiates between second-generation Turkish Cypriots who are relatively
integrated into the English/British culture and first-generation mainland Turks.[8]
This conflictual context helped shape students' political identities and made it
difficult for the group of Turkish students to be integrated and to identify with
England/Britain, let alone Europe.

---

8   Enneli et al. (2005) also found that Turkish Cypriots were less disadvantaged in
housing, employment and education compared with mainland Turks, but that the Turkish
community as a whole faced enormous conflict and marginalization in the English society.

Political Knowledge and National(istic) Identities

Both ethnic majority and Turkish minority students in this school struggled to talk about Europe in political terms. For example, the group of ethnic majority girls did not appear to know much about the expansion of the EU, despite the fact that our discussion took place days before the historic referendum on a European Constitution in May 2004. Their discourse very much focused on the disagreement between France and England regarding the Iraq war:

> DF: What do you know about Europe, about the European Union?
>
> ELLIE: [laughing] Nothing!
>
> KATIE: Nothing.
>
> DF: What is happening at the moment in Europe?
>
> ELLIE: Erm, there's a lot of disagreement about the Iraq war, whether it should have happened and stuff. Because, um, England was very go for it, and I know France was very very against it and I think that's I dunno which other countries, but I think there were quite a lot more that were saying we shouldn't do it, and the English government, even though most of the people in England didn't want it to happen, decided to go ahead with it anyway.
>
> LUCY: I don't watch the news.
>
> DF: In the UK, they are now talking about this European Constitution; they want a referendum for that. Have you heard of that recently?
>
> KATIE: Like, I read a lot of newspapers and I watch some news, but I've never heard of that. Well, they may not, you know, advertise it as much as they should do. None of us here heard that; so that must mean that they're not doing as much as they can to make people know that it's expanding.

The girls were not aware of the debate about a European Constitution at the time, and Katie pointed towards what she perceived as a low media representation of European issues in England. Other ethnic majority interviewees, such as Robert, claimed that the marginalization of European agendas in England led to his poor knowledge about Europe and its institutions. 'The European Parliament is never like televised, we don't know what they actually, if Parliament [Westminster] passes a bill we'll know about it, I don't know what goes on in the European Parliament'. Similarly, Turkish respondents had difficulties to make sense of how Europe and the EU work in political terms:

DF: What do you know about the European Union or Europe?

BARIS: European Union, what's that?

SARILA: Well, nobody knows nothing about it basically.

BARIS: What's the European Union?

SARILA: You think I know?

BARIS: I heard about it, but I don't know what it is.

SARILA: Me neither.

HALIL: Is it the power?

BARIS: I'm asking you.

SARILA: I don't really know, no.

HALIL: Cos the Union-

BARIS: The Union's a bunch of people that decides something, but I don't know.

HALIL: It's the only power.

Other 15-year-olds, such as Olcay, referred to the Turkish EU membership bid when asked what they knew about Europe in political terms. Europe was seen through a Turkish national (i.e., familiar) lens. Those who argued against membership typically said that Turkey's laws and morals do not meet European standards and that the country is very poor with a great deal of homeless people. Respondents also pointed towards the financial costs, saying that membership would mean 'improving their [Turkey's] economic conditions at the expense of the rest [of the EU countries]'. Those students who wanted Turkey to join the EU pointed towards the social changes that have taken place in Turkey or the fact that a large number of Turkish people already live in Europe.

The concept of Europe as a political identity did not easily fit with young people's English or Turkish identities at Millroad. Turkish interviewees were acutely aware of their 'otherness', emphasizing their different religion, different phenotype and limited power. The group of four Turkish boys also construed the notion of Europe in monocultural terms, arguing that Europeans are essentially white Christian people:

YILDIRAN: Let's say I go to India or something, or I don't know, I'm just giving Egypt or America or any other Canada, Canada or something then I would say "ah, I'm coming from Europe", basically that's about "I'm coming from Europe" but I'm not like, you know European or anything.

MUHAMMAD: I wouldn't even say Europe, you can't say I'm European.

DF: Why not?

MUHAMMAD: Unless your races country is a European country as well ... like where you're from, whether your first country is in Europe cos basically we're used to seeing white people, white people as European, so basically-

YILDIRAN: English people.

MUHAMMAD: I would say I live in Europe but I'm not European.

ONAN: Yeah same, because you're not living all around Europe, you're just living in one place, one country.

KHAN: Erm, the thing is that if you was Europe, yeah, you'd like understand that, you know, I come from Europe, cos you know yeah, but I can't say I'm European cos I'm not Christian.

MUHAMMAD: I don't say I'm Christian, I say I believe in Christianity but I don't say I'm Christian, that's the same as saying I'm from Europe but I'm not European.

The notion of 'being European' did not sit comfortably with any of the Turkish boys in this group, most notably Muhammad, for whom identification with Europe is based on the concept of race rather than residence. The use of the word 'race' is particularly interesting here as it underlines that the students were aware of the racial differences in society. The explicit use of the concept of race as a means of distancing themselves from white Christians might be linked to the school dynamics and the ethnic/racial conflict there; it was not used by any of the students in Darwin School, as we shall see later.

Like the Turkish students, the ethnic majority students I spoke to positioned themselves outside the notion of Europe by drawing on a modified version of the theme of 'us' (English) and 'them' (continental Europeans):

JOEY: Don't really see ourselves as part of Europe. It's more like all the countries that are joined together and we're just sort of the odd one out that drives on the left and has the pound.

EDDIE: Yeah, because we're sort of separated, we're an island off Europe. We're not, yet, because I don't see myself as part of Europe really. We're off Europe, just off Europe.

KELLY: Yeah, it's like they always say British and then they say European. Like, when you say European, for me I think of places like, erm, erm, countries like … like I can't think of, like-

EDDIE: Switzerland and France. And like places further down.

JOEY: Probably Germany actually.

KELLY: Yeah. And it's like, cos it's right [indistinct] island, but in a way, and we are different in similar ways, like you know.

JOEY: Especially now because we're sort of less tied to Europe and more tied to America, we're sort of very westernized.

Discussions often centred around British insularity as well as her general otherness amongst the group of 27 EU countries. Being 'the odd one out that drives on the left and has the pound' as well as being 'an island off Europe' makes it difficult for the new generation to identify with Britain as part of Europe. The group of ethnic majority girls pointed towards official documents, including forms and questionnaires, in which a differentiation has been made between Britain *and* Europe (see Shennan 1991). Also, the group argued that it is context-dependent whether or not they identify themselves as European:

DF: To what extent would you think of yourself as Europeans?

ELLIE: If you were saying, you know, are you African or American or European, then I'd see myself as European but if you're talking, you know, in a more detailed thing, then I wouldn't say I was European, I'd say I was English or British.

DF: Why's that?

ELLIE: Cos it feels more specific. If I say like, if you say you're European that could come from any place really in Europe.

KATIE: And also, when you do questionnaires or you have to fill out a form, it always asks you if you are white-UK or white-European, well we are supposed to be Europe is supposed to be part of the United Kingdom as well. So you wouldn't class yourself as European in ways like that because you've got like, if they want Europe to be with the United Kingdom, France and they should put like, white-European should be in with like the white-UK, the white-UK should be in with the white-European. But if like Amy said, you were talking about American, African, European, you'd class yourself European.

ELLIE: Yeah, I think there seems to be a lot of stuff, like on a form that separates the UK from Europe and, er, yeah, so. So you don't really you think of yourself from the UK, you don't, I never think I'm from Europe cos Europe just feels like the place on the continent, it doesn't feel like the UK.

The concept of the national further came to the fore when students discussed the extent to which Britain should be governed by European institutions. Interviewees almost unanimously agreed that they preferred national governments rather than a European government. For example, the group of Turkish girls thought that a supranational government would be 'hard to control' and that people would not have much of a choice to go to another European country if they did not like the rules and the laws. The ethnic majority male and female students I interviewed were afraid that English people could not make much of a difference and would not have much of a say if decisions were only made at a supranational European level:

DF: To what extent do you think we should be governed by EU institutions?

EDDIE: No.

PAUL: No, I don't think we should, cos otherwise no one has a say, it's like, what difference can we make. Nothing!

AMY: Cos it basically be like England, Germany and France and Spain, cos bigger countries'd be making the laws and littler countries would just like have to abide by them. And they probably won't have their say in what's going to happen and stuff.

JOEY: And I think you have to be like, the, you have to have individual governments for each country, cos each government has to adapt to the, to that actual country cos all the countries are different like, they've got different people, er, whatever. So I don't think, I don't think that would work.

While Amy justified her anti-European discourse arguing that larger member states, such as England, Germany and France, might overrule smaller countries, Joey added that one government could not represent so many different countries and people. Other ethnic majority students in the sample provided a detailed account of England's geo-political relationship with Europe. For example, the group of boys and girls emphasized that their country has been out of touch with other EU member states, employing the image of 'a black sheep'. The group justified their use of the 'black sheep image' saying that 'we've followed the Americans and then taken some wrong decisions', alluding to England's participation in the US-led Iraq war in 2003. 'And now', the group of boys and girls felt, 'it's going to be very hard to get back into Europe'.

The group of five Turkish girls also mainly engaged with national political issues and did not perceive supranational political topics to be relevant to their lives:

DF: What do you see as the most important political issues today?

HARIKA: I'm not into politics, so that's just, I hear about it, but I don't really, you know, get myself into it.

NAGIHAN: I think it's with Turkey, Turkey is a separate country and Cyprus is a separate country. But half of Cyprus is Greek.

TULIP: I think that Cyprus should get into Turkey I reckon, and Cyprus is shut up! That's what I think.

JIHAN: I don't think so.

SERAP: I don't think so.

NAGIHAN: No, because if the Turkish side goes to Turkey yeah, then the Greek side will take over the Turkish side as well yeah, and in the first place-

TULIP: Not cos, imagine someone asks me, "where do you come from?", I say Cyprus, sometimes they think I'm Greek. But I'm not Greek!

NAGIHAN: Yeah, but you say you're from the Turkish part innit?

TULIP: Yeah, but that's too long to say that.

Four main reasons emerged from the data as to why these Turkish 15-year-olds were relatively knowledgeable about national Turkish political issues: parents, media (television), visits to the country, and Saturday school. Most Turkish interviewees in Millroad School reported that they watch Turkish or Turkish Cypriot television channels telling them about the current political situation in the country, and that their parents passed on a lot of information to them. In contrast, the school itself was hardly mentioned as a source for political information. Most Turkish respondents agreed that 'they don't really teach us anything' about politics. The group of ethnic majority boys powerfully argued in favour of more politically-orientated citizenship lessons and less teaching about issues they thought they were already familiar with such as drugs, guns and sex:

DF: What sorts of political things does the school teach you about?

JOHN: The school doesn't teach us nothing like that.

BILL: Not like that.

DAVE: It doesn't teach you like citizenship things, like how you should act, what you should do.

KEN: Well they're say they're going to and then they don't.

BILL: They don't.

DAVE: It's like PSHE, we don't do nothing, they tell you about drugs and that's it.

KEN: Drugs and guns.

JOHN: And sex.

BILL: Basically that took an hour a week of our education away from us. We could've learnt something better than that.

JOHN: We knew about them stuff as well.

In general, how students identified appeared to be deeply affected by the ethnic experience in their school. The celebration of diversity over and above national identity and community cohesion in a context where students' conflict is ethnic or racial was associated with young people retreating into their ethnic identities (i.e., Englishness or Turkishness). This process of '(re)-ethnicization' due to perceived personal or group discrimination is vividly described by Skrobanek (2009). He argues that, as a form of reaction to negative experiences of personal and collective integration, members of ethnic groups identify more strongly with their ethnic community and have a higher risk of intra-group-specific ethnic behaviour. Focusing on 289 young people of Turkish origin in vocational-track German schools (*Hauptschule*), and drawing mainly on social psychological research where the re-ethnicization theory has been more prominent (e.g., Wakenhut, Martini and Forsterhofer 1998, Berry et al. 2006a, 2006b, Birmann and Trickett 2001,

Jetten et al. 2001), Skrobanek (2009) found that nearly 90 per cent of the youth he interviewed felt strongly or very strongly connected to their own group whereas about a quarter show a tendency towards (re)-ethnicization. He also noted that young people with a higher level of education (such as in Goethe Gymnasium and Darwin School) exhibit a lesser tendency towards (re)-ethnicization than those with a lower level. This led him to conclude that, in general, when young people with an ethnic background perceive personal or group discrimination, they are likely to retreat into their own group or to be more oriented to group-specific properties such as language. Discrimination, he maintains, lowers the permeability of group boundaries (i.e., restricts access to feel part of other groups or communities such as Britain) and, in turn, strengthens ethnic identity. Whilst this was not the case at Tannberg Hauptschule in Stuttgart, where the relationships between youth were congenial, it could be observed among both ethnic majority and Turkish minority students at Millroad.

Many mainland Turkish respondents deployed concepts of birth and pride to identify with their ethnic background, arguing that 'I feel I belong to Turkey, but, because of the economy of Turkey, it forces us to come to England' and 'your background's there [in Turkey] and all your grandparents, and, grandmas have been living there, so you have to follow'. In contrast, the sample of Turkish Cypriot students, in addition to their ethnic identity, drew on the concept of residence to partially also identify with the national British citizenship level. For example, the group of five Turkish (Cypriot) girls argued about whether you can be both Turkish and English/British at the same time. Harika and Jihan seemed to have developed hybrid identities although the discussion shows that they, too, privilege their Turkishness:

DF: So you would say you feel you belong to both Turkey and England?

HARIKA: Yeah.

TULIP: No, I don't think so.

JIHAN: But still isn't it, cos you were born here, yeah, and you been living here, yeah, and you go over to like Turkey and Cyprus once in your life, yeah, you don't know nothing yeah.

TULIP: But if you're someone and your parents are Turkish, that's what you are.

NAGIHAN: No, I'm Turkish but-

JIHAN: I didn't say you're not, but-

HARIKA: But you shouldn't say "oh, I've got nothing to do with England".

TULIP: No, you can like my step-parents are English that's it, you can't say you're English or half-English.

JIHAN: Or you can say – you were born there, innit?

HARIKA: No but when someone asks you you're not going to say "I'm English", it's just that you're going to be able when something happens, when there's a war, when there's a football match, let's say, you should, and let's say England's playing against Brazil or something then you would have to support England but when England's playing against Turkey you can support Turkey cos that's your race.

When I probed further, the Turkish Cypriot girls provided a fascinating account of how they differentiated between the regional English and national British citizenship levels. The notion of 'being English' was linked to concepts of birth, race and 'whiteness' while the notion of 'being British' was associated with the concept of residence and was also thought of as a wider and more inclusive term. In other words, 'British is like everybody', you can become a British citizen by law:

DF: Could you tell me the difference between being English and British?

HARIKA: If you're English, well, your parents are English; your generation is English and so on. But if you're British you can have a race but then change, but because you're then living here you can become a citizen or something so, you can say you're a British citizen, I'm a British citizen, but you can't really say I'm English. So when someone asks me "what are you", I'm like "Turkish, but I'm a British citizen" or something.

DF: What makes the difference between English and British?

HARIKA: British is like everybody.

NAGIHAN: Yeah.

TULIP: Where the law, erm, sort of, erm, gives you the right to be British and so on [HARIKA: Yeah] and you know be a citizen-

HARIKA: And that's [indistinct] everyone.

TULIP: -and when the law really can't decide on how you're going to be English cos you're you have to be born as English basically-

JIHAN: Yeah.

TULIP: But British you can become British.

While the Turkish British hybrid identity emerged as an option for second-generation Turkish Cypriot students, the first-generation mainland Turks I interviewed were not able to differentiate between being English and British.[9] Some ethnic majority students also privileged national(istic) identities and saw themselves as English rather than British, a term they associated with the concept of blood and birth. For example, the group of boys differentiated between the generic term 'British' and more particular constructs such as 'English' or 'Scottish':

DAVE: English is more like … specific.

BILL: Yeah, Britain's just like I mean … for example, you could come over to this country, be here for a certain amount of years and you'd "become" British. But English like, you have to be born here, raised here [KEN murmurs agreement], be like one of us. So British is just a crap word, it's just a load of crap really.

KEN: British is like the official name for it, and English is like what the actual people are like.

JOHN: It's like, if you're from Scotland, people don't say "Oh, I'm British", they'll say "I'm Scottish". [murmurs of agreement]

JOHN: Cos most people when they hear "Oh, I'm from the United Kingdom", they think "England", that's what most people think, well that's pretty much what most people think, they don't think "ah, he could be from Wales, I dunno", they just think England straight away. Whereas if you say "I'm Scottish", they don't know it's in the United Kingdom, like if you're in America or something like that.

Emma was less one-sided and took a more distant approach attempting to put herself into the position of other people, such as the press, to differentiate between concepts of Englishness and Britishness. 'English to me always sounds kind of a bit, very white, very kind of racist in some ways. It's the kind of thing that the right-wing press say. Um, I think Britain has more kind of diverse and stuff connotations than English … I think English would be like a race, whereas British would be like a kind of culture'. We have seen earlier in this chapter how some of

---

9   See also Enneli, Modood and Bradley (2005) who argued that young Turks were ambivalent about what it means to be British and reluctant to adopt that identity. 68 per cent of females and 75 per cent of males in their study chose only ethno-religious identities for themselves. 84 per cent of the young people who were not born in Britain did not think of themselves as British. They thus suggest a relationship between being born in Britain and identifying with Britain.

the ethnic majority students I interviewed referred to the concept of Englishness as a racial category and established a hierarchy placing themselves in a superior position compared to their Turkish peers for example. Englishness, for some of these ethnic majority students, is thus a nationalistic identity that excludes minority ethnic peers from the concept of nationhood.

However, it is important to differentiate within the sample of ethnic majority students at Millroad. Not all of them celebrated Englishness and 'wanted to go and get a turkey and eat it'. Some first and foremost identified with school, family and friends:

> DF: Where do you feel you belong to?

> PAUL: At the moment it's the school community, that's the most important. Cos that's where we're around most of the time … the London community or the English community doesn't really matter at the moment.

> AMY: Yeah, it's like family, school, friends. It's not the bigger picture for me.

> DF: Why are family, school and friends so important for you?

> JOEY: Well, they do more for you in a personal way. The others are just a label, but that's, that's actually you see what's going on.

> KELLY: Yeah, and you feel the benefits and like you can actually do something within our family and friends and school, but, because of our age, and maybe other reasons, we cannot do anything, voice our opinions about anything else, apart from what's around us, what we see and feel and hear every day.

> JOEY: I think it also makes you feel part of a community if you know a lot about it, like, sort of feel a bit Australian cos my mum tells me about stuff, and I've only been there a couple of times.

This discussion underlines that familiar communities (family, friends and school) were preferred by some ethnic majority respondents over more distant communities (London, England, Britain). This reflects the latest report of the Citizenship Education Longitudinal study (Benton et al. 2008), which argued that young people show greater attachment to closer communities, such as their local neighbourhood and town and particularly the school, than to their country or Europe. Also, as Kelly and Joey put it, within the familiar communities, the voices of young people are heard better than at the national or supranational level where 'we don't really have that many rights in the decision making or anything'. Joey added that knowledge and travel experiences might be further reasons why 'the bigger picture' is not that relevant for 15-year-olds in Millroad School.

However, the processes of identity formation are not only affected by knowledge and travel experience but, may also reflect the parental socio-economic background. The background survey showed that more than one third of students (34.6 per cent) have skilled and unskilled manual parents. Only around 15 per cent of students said they have professional middle-class or routine non-manual parents. Before I move on to compare and contrast these findings with a sample of ethnic majority and Turkish youth in a predominantly middle-class London comprehensive (Darwin School), I shall summarize what we have learnt about the political identities of different groups of young people in this racially charged and rather divisive school environment.

Summary

We have seen that Millroad School mediated national agendas through the politics of cultural and ethnic diversity while offering only limited acknowledgement of the processes of Europeanization. The Turkish respondents, particularly the sample of first-generation mainland Turks, faced substantial conflict. They were subject to verbal and physical abuse, including gang fights with the African Caribbean community, and engaged in a struggle for power and control of the school. As a result of these peer group conflicts, which appeared to originate in the wider local community, Turkish students formed a group based on ties of ethnic solidarity, including common religion, language, culture and physical appearance. In this highly racialized and divisive school environment, most Turkish minority and ethnic majority students frequently drew on the theme of 'us' and 'them'. The mainland Turks strongly identified with their ethnic background and most ethnic majority respondents identified with England. Only the Turkish Cypriot youth appear to have developed more hybrid Turkish British identities, possibly because they had experienced the British culture to a certain extent in Cyprus prior to migrating to England. The ethnic majority students, who were in the minority in this school, adopted a hostile approach to diversity, positioned their Turkish classmates as 'others', and in many cases, celebrated their Englishness.

It would have been fascinating to interview some of the African Caribbean students to find out how they negotiated their political identities in this environment and thus to understand the culture of the school more fully. Arguably, African Caribbeans were positioned as 'others' as well but, unlike the Turkish students, they were English-speaking 'others' and mainly Christians. Future research must look more closely at this issue, as it was beyond the scope of this study.

Chapter 7

Political Integration in Darwin School

This final empirical chapter analyses the responses of ethnic majority and Turkish minority youth in Darwin, a school located in a predominantly middle-class area in the same London borough as Millroad School. Darwin School interpreted and acted on the national privileging of Britishness over and above multicultural and European agendas in different ways. Unlike Millroad, Darwin is one of the highest-performing comprehensive schools in London in terms of GCSE results (71 per cent of five or more A* to C in the General Certificate of Secondary Education annual examinations). This predominantly middle-class school strongly emphasizes academic performance. Just 27 per cent of Darwin's students are from ethnic minority backgrounds, with Turkish and Turkish Cypriot students making up just 2 per cent of the student population (33 students). The school celebrated commonalty rather than cultural and ethnic difference. In this liberal and inclusive environment, Turkish youth could relate better to their ethnic majority peers. Social class became one of the unifying factors, giving students an advantaged position within the British society.

As noted above, Darwin School is located in the same Inner London borough as Millroad School; however, Darwin is in the western part of this borough, which is more affluent than the area surrounding Millroad. The Turkish community is virtually invisible in the streets, and the village-like atmosphere of the area boasts a selection of trendy bars and restaurants. Walking along the broad streets of the school's catchment area with their grand houses and Edwardian architecture immediately gives an impression of the socio-economic privilege of many residents. This local community is a favourite location for actors, writers and musicians, and people in the media and entertainment world. In addition, a youth project in this area provides a variety of extra-curricular activities and training for young people, including after-school homework club, pottery classes, basketball and football coaching. There were virtually no signs or reports of any ethnic tensions or conflict in this area during the period of my fieldwork.

Darwin School opened in 1983 as a mixed neighbourhood comprehensive and has a total of 1,507 students. Around 16 per cent of the students (250 pupils) have English as an additional language although there are few at the most basic level compared to about 25 per cent of students in Millroad School. The largest ethnic minority groups are African Caribbean (10.3 per cent) and Asian (6.9 per cent). Attainment differed between the various groups of students, with ethnic majority students achieving on par with the Asian students, while the African Caribbean and

Turkish students underachieved.[1] African Caribbean (17.4 per cent) and Turkish students (15 per cent) have the highest temporary exclusion rates whereas these are very low for Asian (2.9 per cent) and ethnic majority students (1.8 per cent). Boys were more often excluded than girls.

To achieve academic excellence, Darwin School aims to provide each student with a broad, balanced and coherent curriculum in accordance with the National Curriculum. The school was granted Technology College Status in 1997.[2] In key stage 3 (ages 11-14), students have a common curriculum comprising English, mathematics, integrated science, a modern foreign language, physical education, design technology including food and textiles, creative arts comprising art and design, dance, drama and music, geography, history and religious education, information communication technology, and personal and social/citizenship education. All students study French, German or Spanish in Years 7 and 8, with a second language for the more able linguists added in Year 9. In key stage 4 (ages 14-16), students begin a programme of eight subject courses. Students are expected to study each area of the curriculum until age 16. Although Darwin School has organized a large number of exchange visits and school trips to France, Germany and Spain, it does not have any European school partnerships like Goethe Gymnasium in Stuttgart. This chapter provides evidence that in a school which mediates the relationship between national, multicultural and European agendas through the lens of integration, and where the peer cultures are less fraught, 15-year-olds develop ethno-national (e.g., Turkish British) identities, regardless of their ethnicity.

The Politics of Integration

The ethos of Darwin School and indeed its curriculum suggested that young people were encouraged to think of themselves as liberal democratic British citizens living in a global multiethnic international community. These messages were transmitted for example through citizenship lessons. Citizenship was both a cross-curricular theme and part of 'Personal, Social and Health Education' (PSHE-Citizenship). The citizenship co-ordinator added that 'some schools have just called it "citizenship" and put social and personal into it, but we haven't done that. I don't think that's a good idea because there is more to a person than just

---

1   These results are similar to Goethe Gymnasium in Stuttgart where the ethnic majority students also received the highest average grade (2.6) and the ethnic minority students were generally lower-achieving, with Turkish youth underperforming by as much as half a grade (3.1).

2   Technology College is a term used in the UK for a specialist school that focuses on design and technology, mathematics and science. The Specialist Schools Programme in the UK also includes for instance designated language colleges. Despite their special status, these schools must nevertheless deliver a wide and balanced range of subjects.

being a citizen. (…) You have a sort of like personal dimension to your being'. Unlike at Millroad, PSHE-Citizenship was taught one hour per week. Mr. Davis, the citizenship co-ordinator, argued that 'two would be even better but then you'd have to make it into an examined subject at GCSE. You couldn't do two hours a week without examination in Year 10'. At the time of fieldwork, Kerr et al. (2004) would have probably classified the school's approach to citizenship as 'progressing' because staff had already renamed PSHE into PSHE-Citizenship and began to teach a revised syllabus (see Chapter 5 for an explanation of Kerr's full typology).

Darwin's citizenship curriculum sought to shape students' beliefs about action in their local, national and global communities.[3] Five units dealt with the values of liberal democracy, including human rights and discrimination, and freedom of speech. The citizenship co-ordinator expressed this notion of a liberal democratic citizen:

> DF: What sort of citizen does the citizenship curriculum aim to create?
>
> MR. DAVIS: Well "create" is quite a powerful word cos that would suggest you have an ideal type in mind. I suppose the basic ideology if that's the word you want to use, or framework, would probably be the type of citizen that supports and continues sort of liberal democracy. So you wouldn't want to create a citizen who was intolerant, bigoted, narrow-minded, ultranationalist; you'd wanna create a citizen that sort of understands and sees democracy as sort of a viable, valuable system but liberal democracy, this kind of liberal values in its broadest sense. But basically I think you want to create a reflective, thinking person, that's the sort of aim and idea not a person who you can, you know, programme, a more open and free person I suppose. Someone who's aware of their responsibilities, aware of their rights, aware of their duties, and aware of the kind of political situation that exists in this country, and the wider world.

Some of the other teachers I interviewed also felt that the educational aim should be to create 'questioning, curious and informed citizens' although, as the deputy principal (Ms. Williams) pointed out, this strategy could lead to difficulties. For example 'the whole Iraq war caused a massive, very impressive reaction amongst [parts of] our school community, and some really were enquiring and questioning citizens there, who were questioning the government's decisions'. Ms. Williams maintained that:

---

3   PSHE-Citizenship teaching units include: the working of the school community, children's rights, bullying, vandalism, drugs, healthy eating, democracy and local politics, disability issues as well as prejudice and discrimination at key stage 3; and human rights issues, careers and drugs education as well as study skills at key stage 4.

Our aim is to make sure we have students who understand the community that they are living in, and are able to engage with that community in a positive way; and to understand that individuals can make a difference, can achieve real outcomes, and it's actually trying to help students to see that they can play that [active] role.

Ms. Williams further argued that the National Curriculum 'should be driving forward the idea of living within a multiracial, multiethnic community and working with other people within that community. (…) It's important to understand the differences but it's most important to understand the similarities. [Darwin] School does not celebrate any faith, we don't celebrate difference; we celebrate similarity'. The ethos of Darwin School seemed to emphasize common ground and cohesion rather than diversity and difference, and one unifying and integrative factor was teachers' belief in the values of a liberal democratic British society. The school prospectus further highlighted the notion of political incorporation and an inclusive British national identity:

The school strives to be a high-performing inclusive community school, fully committed to active citizenship and academic excellence. We value all who learn and work here; promoting a strong sense of community within and beyond the school. (…) Bilingualism is actively encouraged and supported and opportunities offered to be examined in community languages. (…) All students are of equal concern and the school promotes self-discipline and empathy for others, both within the school and the wider community. (…) The teacher cannot be neutral towards those values which underpin liberal democracy. Values such as freedom of speech and discussion, respect for truth and reasoning, the peaceful resolution of conflicts, are the means whereby indoctrination is combated and prevented.

Despite this inclusive approach, or perhaps because of it, Darwin School made little effort to integrate students on the basis of common European membership. The supranational European context was largely absent from Darwin's citizenship curriculum, and did not appear in other subjects typically used to promote a European dimension, such as geography and history (see Appendix 4). For example, only one geography teaching unit in Year 8 dealt with Europe. The remainder of the curriculum was structured around local, national and global issues (e.g., international disparities, Brazil, Australia, UK climate, vine farm, Lincolnshire); and the history curriculum centred on the two World Wars as well as British national history. The deputy principal not only acknowledged that the notion of Europe 'is an area we don't address explicitly in citizenship', but she also said that Darwin School has done little teaching about Europe:

DF: How important do you think a European dimension or agenda is in the curriculum here at [Darwin School]?

MS. WILLIAMS: It's not. We haven't done it. We don't do it. I think we address it inexplicitly, through some of our curriculum, but we certainly haven't taken it on board, I think, in terms of citizenship, there are bits that we do very well, there are bits we have yet to develop and one of the areas we have to develop is the whole idea of Europe, and the whole idea of looking at the European community, looking at the European Parliament, we don't, to my knowledge, teach that to our students. The citizenship curriculum has only been developed this year and we need to include that [a European dimension] within it. One of the things I'm quite keen to do is, obviously, we've got the election coming up on the 10th June (2004) and I'm quite keen we actually do something within the school around that. I am going to be using external events to try and kick-start that within school. We don't do that explicitly and I think we should. We're going to have a referendum in the UK about the issues, and I think that our students need to be able to understand what the issues are.

The other teachers I interviewed also said that the curriculum should include more of a European dimension. Mr. Davis, the citizenship co-ordinator, provided a summary of the difficulties of implementing a European curricular dimension, arguing that 'the trouble is that this country [England] has got quite a proud history, and with history as a major subject, history tends to be national history, you know what I mean, and if it's international it's to do with wars'. Mr. Davis perceived citizenship as an ideal subject for promoting European values. But when asked about the European topics he actually teaches, he said that 'we don't sort of, well, I suppose look towards the European Common Market'. The main reason for this educational imbalance, he argued, is 'the tension in this country between Europeanization and Americanization. I think a lot of them [students] would feel more American than European because of the language, TV programmes and music'. Miss Williams, the deputy principal, also acknowledged that the school has focused more on an inclusive multiethnic national agenda, arguing that 'I think we're very good on the multicultural, multiethnic identity and, because of that, probably in terms of the national. That's probably fairly implicit in terms of what we're doing with the students but I would argue with the European dimension, we are less strong'.

Some researchers (e.g., Dolby 2001) have emphasized popular culture as a location for identity formation. My study shows some evidence of this. I observed for instance several Italian boys in the German schools wearing their national colour 'blue' to indicate their identification with Italy. Another Turkish boy (who saw himself as a Turkish German) displayed and lived his Turkishness by wearing a red jumper and a necklace in the shape of the moon star on the Turkish national flag.

However, as Dolby also argues, aspects such as the macro-political context or the school itself can also impact on young people's identities. One of the citizenship teachers in my study, Mr. Davis, characterized his students in a way that indicated his understanding of their identities as drawing from multiple sources as Dolby describes, including fashion, peer group cultures, media and sexual imageries:

> MR. DAVIS: I think that young people's identities are quite fluid, I mean they're actually finding identities, I mean, a person of 12 for example, you know, do they think about identity? They're thinking about "Who are my friends?", "What group am I in at school?" erm, you know, "Do I like girls, do they like me?", it's all these things that go through young people's heads. (…) Their identities may be sort of shaped by fashion, so we've got kids in this school who are what they call "grunge" [they wear torn trousers and have messy hair], kids who are called "gothic", kids who are skinheads. And there are kids that are sort of skateboarders, and they wear different clothes, and to them, that is their identity, they actually feel – it's not gang mentality but it is teenage identity, it's different from what we think as sort of cultural or political identity, I think at a young age. (…) In PSHE-Citizenship we would talk about things like hatred in society, intolerance as opposed to tolerance, and acceptance, and in that sense, you would hope to encourage a flowering of ones individuality. I prefer to use the term individuality rather than identity.

Miss Smith, the head of geography, who had by chance taught in both Millroad and Darwin School, summed up the different positions of students and teachers to national, multicultural and European agendas by saying 'we have kids here [in Darwin School] who have really travelled, who have been to places that I've never been to, that have actually quite a good conceptual understanding of what these places are like and "otherness" and that kind of thing, and that's different [than Millroad School]'. From this perspective, parental influence including socio-economic background and ethnicity can be seen to be important factors in the construction of young people's political identities.

Congenial Relations and Social Integration

The concept of ethnicity seemed to play only a subordinate role in relations between youth, possibly as a result of the school's emphasis on community cohesion as well as the more similar socio-economic background of students. Instead of the divisive peer cultures we saw at Millroad, mixed student friendship groups built around trust, personality and good character were suggestive of a higher level of interaction:

> DF: Could you tell me a bit about your friends, where they come from and so on?

> AKASMA: I've got Turkish, I've got English, I've got Indian, I've got mixed friends.

GÜLAY: Well, a friend is a friend, it doesn't if they agrees with you, what you say, and doesn't go and cheer you up to everyone what you say, promises you-

ELVAN: Yeah, not two-faced.

GÜLAY: And cheerful and you now.

ELVAN: Why does it only have to be Turkish innit?

GÜLAY: You're my friend.

ELVAN: I know.

AKASMA: Well I don't look for a friend, oh she's Indian, or I keep away, I just don't mind, a friend is a friend, like she said, you know, when they've got the right character, when they've got the right personality than that's a friend.

FAIRUZA: Agree.

Arguably, the limited number of Turkish students in Darwin School (2.2 per cent) may have prevented the students from achieving the level of ethnic solidarity we saw at Millroad (26.6 per cent Turkish students). Some 15-year-olds at Darwin said that they met some Turkish friends outside school in a local youth club. And despite the mixed nature of Turkish students' friendship groups at school, some Turkish students (particularly the boys) said that they had more Turkish than other friends because 'you can relate to your own country much more and with other people you've got to build up the bond between you, but with someone in your own country, the bond's already there'. Nevertheless, even Osman and Mehmet (who made the previous comment) had African Caribbean and ethnic majority friends at school. These cross-ethnic friendships and apparent level of inclusion at school may be a result of the students' socio-economically advantaged status and the ethnic composition of Darwin School. But the school's approach to including all students into the school community likely played a role as well.

The ethnic majority students I interviewed also had mixed friendship groups, although some reported having fewer friends from ethnic minority backgrounds because of the school's ethnic composition and the fact that some of these friendships had already formed in primary school. The notion that middle-class 15-year-olds did not base their choice of friends on ethnicity was also evident in the following discussion:

MATTHEW: Er, it's completely mixed I think.

WILLIAM: A lot of my friends are like Greek, Russian, Middle East.

RICHARD: Turkish.

JAMES: [name] is Russian, but you wouldn't really think he's-

RICHARD: I mean, most of the people I'm friends with out of school are British or Greek or something like that. But, there isn't, there isn't much difference because ever it is not like because that someone is Asian or black or Greek or whatever that you're not friends with them.

MATTHEW: I don't think it really makes a difference where they're from-

RICHARD: It's just who you get along with. And also, it's sort of, it's also about who lives in your area because you're not just going to say "oh-" because it's easier to be friends with people in your area because you can speak to them.

JAMES: Yeah. (…) There are obviously people that, and there are people they just don't fit in at all I mean, fit in is quite a harsh way of saying it. But there are people who are like loners really.

HENRY: Yeah, like [name of an ethnic majority boy], I felt sorry for him, but he's not a particularly nice person, he's actually homosexual.

James' remark about people who do not fit in, which is then further explained by Henry, underlines this notion of ethnic neutrality in students' discourses, while bringing to light other ways students discriminate in choosing friends. The idea of fitting into society and not being loners or outsiders was not used with regard to ethnic minority communities (as it was so often the case in Millroad School), but instead with regard to homosexuals, another societal minority. Generally, the parental advice given to both ethnic majority and Turkish minority interviewees at Darwin School was not to be friends 'with people who are, you know, that does drug-dealing or smoking'. Owen, for instance, said that his parents had never made any comments about the darker skin colour of his Indian friend. 'We never said anything about the fact that he was, quite Indian I suppose, when I was five or six or whatever, and it probably makes a difference how I turned out'. The fact that ethno-racial background was not an issue for Owen's parents led him to argue that it was not going to be an issue for him either.

The school's emphasis on similarity and the smaller numbers of minority young people in the school population likely contributed to the lower importance of ethnicity in friendship groups, and the lower level of ethnic conflict at Darwin. But class is a potentially important aspect as well, and specifically what Reay et al. (2008: 240) referred to as 'the socially inclusive middle class as opposed to Gidden's (2000) [idea of the] socially exclusive middle class'.[4] The 'socially inclusive middle-class' student and family actively embraces diversity and is open to difference, something which Hage (1998: 128) termed the 'ethnic surplus value' in which the white middle classes see themselves as further enriched through the consumption of ethno-cultural diversity. From this perspective, diversity and inter-ethnic friendships become a source of social and cultural capital and thus form part of young people's increasingly important civic and intercultural competences. Many of Reay et al.'s (2008: 243) middle-class families felt passionate about the need to produce tolerant children and thus decided to send their children to inner-city comprehensive schools, like Darwin School, 'providing multicultural experiences that home life cannot'. However, while Reay's parents valued the 'ethnic other', many parents feared the 'working-class other' (Reay 2008, Reay et al. 2007). I do not have enough evidence to conclusively determine the extent to which this commitment to diversity and valuing the 'other' played a role amongst the middle-class students and parents at Darwin School. My sample was also different from Reay's in the sense that, in 2004, Darwin School was one of the higher-performing comprehensive schools in London in terms of GCSE results, while Reay et al.'s study focused on families sending their children to schools with average or below average GCSE results. Nevertheless, it might well be the case that several of my interviewees at Darwin corresponded to Reay's 'socially inclusive middle class' thereby contributing to the higher levels of interaction between ethnic majority and migrant minority students.

The degree of social comfort provides another example suggesting a higher overall level of social integration among 15-year-olds at Darwin School. In only a few cases did (Turkish) students argue that 'Turkey's more safe' because there are fewer 'drug users and mad people and drunk people there'. Neither did Turkish students on the whole see Outer London as safer than Inner London because of racism in inner-city boroughs. Generally, these students saw England as a safe place:

> SAFAK: I feel really safe, because, there are like you have police around, you have people who care around, you know, I mean, you do get bad people but you get them everywhere. I mean, you can't go to a place where there isn't someone who's done something bad in their life. Everyone's done something bad, whether its something little like lie, tell the smallest lie, or something like kill a person. But I feel safe here, cos this is where I've grown up and I know everything and I know people, and you know, I just know who to keep out of the

---

4 See also the discussions in Butler and Robson (2003) and Ball (2003) for the UK context and Ehrenreich (1997) and Brantlinger (2003) in the United States. They all talk about the excluding and exclusive white middle classes and a fearful retreat of the white middle classes from the public sector in the context of increasing globalization, individualization and privatization in the twenty-first century. Reay et al's (2008) middle classes depart from these 'norms'.

way from and stuff, but yeah, I feel really safe, because the majority of people are good people. (…)

ZOE: I do feel quite comfortable, generally just like walking about and stuff, but I was going on the train the other day and I wasn't scared, but a part of me, cos you know the Madrid thing recently (11 March 2004), part of me thought "I hope nothing happens" because I think you just do generally after that, and it obviously didn't. But I think a lot of things are happening, like a lot of terrorism and stuff all over the world, that you eventually think it's going to be here sometime, so, but hopefully we're a little bit more prepared, like medical ways and all those things they've been doing, like if there's chemical explosions they've been trying to re-enact how it would be.

Ian added that 'I feel kind of safe around [area of London], because there is like loads of people around, there's loads of shops that are open and it's like quite a rich area'. However, living in a socio-economically advantaged and allegedly safe area can also bring certain risks with it although, as Ian put it, 'it's more of that kind of mugging, than it is like crime like car stealing or shooting'. It is quite possible that the reason so many Turkish and ethnic majority interviewees in Darwin School felt safe was because they have never had to live in socially deprived areas with high unemployment and crime rates, such as the eastern part of this London borough where Millroad School is located.

Arguably, then, the data seems to suggest a higher level of social integration in this school due to the generally more advantaged socio-economic situation of its students. And indeed, ample references were made by both ethnic majority and Turkish minority 15-year-olds to their socio-economic background. For example, Owen was aware of his relatively privileged status, mentioned the word 'class', and described himself as 'not exactly rich but compared to a lot of people I'm very well off':

OWEN: I'm relatively independent. I mean, my parents ask me how my school day was and they provide me with equipment and things like that, and sometimes they provide me with help, but when you get to sort of GCSE, your education is starting to eclipse your parents, in a way, unless they specialized in that subject, so it's sort of difficult for my parents to actually, you know, give me help in the particular subjects. But I suppose, in a way, I'm a relatively privileged student, I mean I wouldn't say that I was actually upper-class, I mean, compared to some of the students who go to this school, I'm relatively like, not exactly rich, but compared to a lot of people I'm very well off. I mean my parents they provide me with a computer with which to do my work on and we have internet at my house.

But class was not the only factor, the school played a role as well. Unlike at Millroad, where there were mixed feelings regarding the school's efforts to make students feel 'comfortable', both Turkish minority and ethnic majority students at Darwin School felt that teachers supported them with their education as much as possible, and treated everybody fairly. As Zoe put it, 'we're all just treated equally generally. (…) If a white person was being naughty then they'd get shouted at, but so would a black person in the same way as a white person would be shouted at. It's not like unfairly dealt with'. This opinion was shared by Turkish 15-year-olds arguing that 'they [teachers] treat me the same as they'll treat the next person and it's all like really fair and everyone's just getting along. In contrast with Millroad School, only the group of male and female Turkish students discussed an incident of verbal abuse:

DF: Have you ever experienced any form of discrimination or prejudice?

KEMAL: Yeah.

AFET: No.

DF: What was that?

KEMAL: Erm, I remember in school someone shouted something like "Turkish dickhead" or something.

NEYLAN: They wrote it all over the walls, like about Kurdish people, but that's not Turkish, that's Kurdish. I'm not Kurdish.

AFET: He's Turkish, he's got a Turkish accent.

[muttering in Turkish]

DF: What did they write?

ADEM: They'll just say stupid things like go and eat some turkey or things like that.

NEYLAN: Don't tell them that you're Turkish then.

AFET: But that's just wrong!

Similarly, ethnic majority interviewees only reported a few isolated incidents of name-calling (e.g., gingerbread, gay). Interestingly, nearly all these statements were made by girls and not boys, with ethnic majority girls claiming that they were given 'some attitude' by African Caribbean girls in the school. For instance, Jennifer said that 'people always say to white people "Oh, don't be racist to black people", but I find that most racism comes from black people or from people from other cultures to white people'. The attitude ethnic majority girls perceived from some African Caribbean girls at Darwin seemed to have influenced their identities. For example, during a discussion I had with a group of five ethnic majority girls, three of them mentioned that 'there's a thing where you're named like a wigga or something'. Since the term 'wigga' can be defined as an ethnic majority person trying to be or acting 'black', this suggests that some ethnic majority respondents were seen as trying to copy African Caribbean girls.

Several Turkish 15-year-olds talked about trying to adapt to the English lifestyle. This could partly be the result of Darwin School's agenda of promoting an inclusive national identity and thus integrating students into the school community. But it might also have to do with the messages Turkish youth were getting from the media, parents, friends and macro-political discourses directed toward migrants in general.

DF: To what extent should people who come to England from other countries, like Turkey, give up part of their culture, traditions to fit in?

OSMAN: They should just be themselves. Do what they want.

ZEKI: Act how they are.

MEHMET: I think they should adapt to the English lifestyle, whether they like it or not, you know, they've got to live here, they got to why be different, when you can be the same, you know?

OSMAN: I think it ain't about like, when you say adapt, it's basically fitting into other people's places and I don't think you've got to fit into other peoples [someone whispers: culture], yeah, to be accepted, they should accept you for being yourself.

MEHMET: Yeah, but, I dunno, if you come from Iran, yeah, you don't know, you don't go around doing the thing, you know, wearing the turban yeah.

OSMAN: Why not, it's your culture though?

MEHMET: It's your culture but why make life hard for yourself? Why give people a reason to, er, be prejudiced against you?

OSMAN: Yeah but, I wouldn't change, if I was a strong Muslim, and I had to wear like the hats that they wear and things like that, the clothes, I wouldn't change my clothes for other people. They look at me, they look at me, that's my culture.

While Osman (and Zeki) adopted a more traditional approach and appeared to struggle to adapt to the English way of life, Mehmet argued in favour of the school's principle of emphasizing similarity and cohesion rather than difference. By 'adapt[ing] to this lifestyle', Mehmet not only meant learning the English language but also dressing in a more westernized way. The importance of popular culture, such as clothing, for the construction of young people's identities is further highlighted by Nadine Dolby (2001), who argues that identities manifest themselves and are reinforced through attachments to aspects of popular culture or 'taste'. By dressing in a particular way or listening to popular music (e.g., Britpop), young people live identities that are highly dynamic and hybridized. Regarding dress in particular, the ethnic majority male and female students did not agree that ethnic minority people could fit into society while keeping some of their culture, customs and traditions:

DF: To what extent should minority ethnic people give up part of their customs and traditions to fit in?

CHARLES: I don't think people should really have to give up what they've lived like to fit in.

OLIVIA: It may not be to fit in, they might, say yeah, in schools or may get bullied or something for what they're dressing like.

CHARLES: Oh, right, yeah I see what you mean.

OLIVIA: They might have to change that just to-

CHARLES: Yeah, but that is that's still fitting in.

ADAM: I think you can fit in at the same time as keeping some of your traditions.

CHARLES: Yeah, because most people keep their traditions at home, like the food they eat, the clothes they wear-

CHARLOTTE: Yeah, [indistinct] at home I think.

CHARLES: -the language they speak. Things like that.

ADAM: It shouldn't be definitely what you should do, it should be what you want to do.

CHARLES: Well, yeah, what you want to do.

ADAM: It's hard enough to come to a new country, get into their traditions, so if you're up for it you should do it.

Adam pulled together the opposite views of Charles and Olivia by proposing that 'you can fit in at the same time as keeping some of your traditions'. Thereafter, Charles modified his arguments saying that ethnic food, clothing and languages could be maintained at home but not necessarily in society at large. Although I did not analyse my data in terms of how students viewed this public-private maintenance of traditions, it is nevertheless an important distinction and one that characterizes for instance debates in France, where ethno-cultural identities are not officially recognized in the public sphere but considered part of the private sphere (for more on this, see Raveaud 2008).

Ethno-National Political Discourses and Identities

The promotion of national agendas in a school which emphasized similarity was associated with weak identification with Europe for both ethnic majority and Turkish minority youth. Despite the mild pro-European approach under New Labour, the processes of Europeanization have received little attention in the development of citizenship education, with British curricula instead promoting the idea of 'multicultural Britishness'.[5] Consequently, many ethnic majority interviewees struggled to talk about Europe:

DF: What sorts of things do you know about Europe and the European Union?

ANNE: Not much!

VICTORIA: It's really difficult,-

ANNE: I don't know anything.

VICTORIA: -totally out of my depth.

ELIZABETH: It's quite confusing cos it changes so much, that people-

ANNE: The euro.

SOPHIE: There's places part of it [indistinct]

ELIZABETH: Oh, isn't there a referendum or coming up for something or other?

---

5   This is explicitly reasserted in the revised secondary curriculum from 2008.

VICTORIA: A what? What's that?

ELIZABETH: I dunno. I just heard it, walking through my house and the news was on somewhere, this whole thing about-

VICTORIA: What's a referendum?

ELIZABETH: I don't know.

ANNE: I know about the euro because I was in Ireland when it was going through.

VICTORIA: They don't have it in Ireland.

Arguably, students' partial and confused political understanding of Europe was related to the limited coverage of European issues in the British mass media and the failure of schools to promote a discrete European dimension in the National Curriculum (for a discussion of this last point, see Tulasiewicz 1993, Convey and Merritt 2000). Similar reasons can be deployed to justify the difficulties Turkish 15-year-olds had to engage in European political discourses. Some Darwin students referred to 'power', 'opposition to America' and 'community of countries' when asked about the EU. Typically, however, Turkish interviewees neither knew the purpose of the EU, nor understood how European institutions generally work, as this excerpt highlights:

DF: What do you know about the European Union or Europe actually?

ADEM: It happened after World War II; France and Germany, they like made an agreement, and then loads of other countries joined or something.

NEYLAN: What happens when you're in the EU anyway?

AFET: Nothing, you're just

ADEM: No, you get to, the United Nations.

NEYLAN: What do you get?

ADEM: You get into the United Nations.

NEYLAN: So what, who cares? Why can't the whole world be in it? That's not fair.

ADEM: Cos they're not.

[one of them speaks indecipherably]

NEYLAN: It's just stupid!

There were only two main sources from which 15-year-olds received their political information: parents and the media, particularly television. Turkish students reported that they watched both Turkish and British television channels. They did not, however, mention 'visits to the country' and 'Saturday school' as information sources, underscoring the fact that this group of Turkish students was more westernized particularly when compared to Millroad School (as described in Chapter 6). In contrast, respondents hardly mentioned the school itself as a source for political information, commenting only that they learned about the two World Wars, human rights, discrimination and prejudice in some history and geography lessons.

In contrast, both Turkish minority and ethnic majority students frequently drew on national political discourses when talking about England's role in Europe and within the wider world. In the following excerpts, both Mustafa and Mehmet (Turkish Cypriots) talked about monetary issues while Safak (Turkish Cypriot) focused on England's geo-political relation with Europe:

> MEHMET: Britain should be in the EU but I don't think they should change the currencies, cos that would affect Britain dramatically, you know, because the British pound is, you know, really valuable and if this happened, yeah, the economy of Britain's going to drop, so it's not going to be good for us. [...]

> MUSTAFA: Yeah, I think they're more distant cos, erm, like firstly they wanted to keep the pound here. Everyone wants to keep the pound. But if we did actually take like, the euro, our economy would be stronger, and it would help other countries as well because it would make our economy work because we'll have a stronger force, because the whole of Europe is our working force. [...]

> SAFAK: I think they're kind of part of it, but in a way they're not they're just kind of "are" with Europe as in, because, they're like, they're in the EU and stuff, and you know, Britain is in the continent of Europe, so they should be involved with their own continent instead of going off somewhere else.

Mehmet appeared to be arguing from a British viewpoint saying that 'it's not going to be good for *us*' to adopt the euro. Mustafa's statement further reveals the transition from a non-British Turkish perspective (e.g. *they*'re more distant, *they* wanted to keep the pound here) to a British perspective (e.g. if *we* did, actually, take, like, the euro, *our* economy would be stronger). These shifting viewpoints reflect the struggle some of these students faced in balancing their identities, and it shows the impact of English society and way of life on their identities. Their position allowed both first- and second-generation Turkish students in the sample to employ national British discourses leading to their comments on the role of England in Europe.

Similarly, ethnic majority students were less confused than their peers at Millroad when talking about national political agendas in relation to Europe. Students frequently referred to notions of insularity, separateness and detachment, and also mentioned England's special relationship with the United States:

DF: How would you describe England's relationship with Europe?

RICHARD: Detached a bit.

MATTHEW: Yeah it is. We go and side off with the United States and stuff and beg from them, and all of the other countries think it's a bad idea and they tell us that but nobody ever pays attention.

WILLIAM: Yeah, I'd say we're kind of split between Europe and America.

JAMES: I don't think we're that split just cos we have a different currency. [...]

JENNIFER: I don't think when I think of Europe I don't really think we're part of it. I don't know why. I just look at it.

ELIZABETH: In a way I think we're more similar to America because of the language, because like we don't speak French or German. [...]

CHARLOTTE: England is a really small part of Europe, and it's not attached.

OLIVIA: Yeah, we're separate.

CHARLES: An island off it, we've always been separated from its sort of affairs, and British pride is quite strong, I suppose, really.

Charles alluded to the level of national pride in England, suggesting that it was 'quite strong', possibly stronger than elsewhere in Europe. Linguistic and political reasons were also mentioned for why England might be more similar to America and thus less attached to Europe. And William referred to what could be called England's 'sitting-on-the-fence' politics, wherein policy-makers and politicians have long been undecided whether to deepen their ties with Europe or America. The special partnership with the United States was portrayed by these students as one of several factors undermining the Europeanization of British national identity (discussed in Chapter 5).[6] Arguably, the above quotation exemplifies the extent to which student discourses and political identifications are affected by the national political context in England.

Students' political discourses and identifications were also shaped by current international developments during the period of the study. For example, the fact that a large majority of both ethnic majority and Turkish minority interviewees in Darwin School argued that England should get closer to Europe must be seen in relation to the unilateralist policies of the Bush administration (2000-2008) and the Iraq war, which was condemned by most European countries (and indeed by most interviewees at Darwin at the time of fieldwork in mid-2004).[7] Students in England mainly justified their responses to questions about Europe by referring to political reasons (e.g., 'America is already very powerful'; 'Blair is just going along with Bush'), whereas only a small minority of interviewees deployed geographical reasons (e.g., Britain is part of Europe). In mid-2004, the image students had of the United States was a negative one:

> DF: To what extent do you think that England should get closer to the United States or closer to Europe?

> SIBEL: Closer to Europe and not closer to Bush, because I think that, erm, after what Bush has done to Iraq that Bush could do that to his own country, and to his family and friends, and that erm, my own thought is that London, well, England, is just helping Bush as Blair's a bit frightened of Bush, or Bush can actually, I dunno, threaten him or something.

Sibel did not respond to the specific question of whether England should get closer to the United States or Europe, but instead quickly began describing Bush as the personification of America and responsible for attacking Iraq. There were a number of respondents who supported closer ties with Europe, however, alluding to the notion of power in reference to the United States. For example, William argued that 'if Britain is friends with the US, it's only two people, I mean it's hard to get big disagreements whereas with Europe there's lots of less powerful countries that all have to agree together to actually get something done cos they're not as powerful as the US'; and Mehmet maintained that 'if they're going to get

---

6   In his 2008 Lord Mayor's Banquet Speech, Prime Minister Gordon Brown explained this special bond yet again by stating that 'Winston Churchill described the joint inheritance of Britain and America as not just a shared history but a shared belief in the great principles of freedom, and the rights of man – of what Barack Obama described in his election night speech as the enduring power of our ideals: democracy, liberty, opportunity and unyielding hope'.

7   Only Britain and Spain actively supported the US-led invasion of Iraq in 2003 amidst fierce opposition of both other European countries, notably France and Germany, and the UN Security Council.

closer to one side, it should be the EU because America's already a really powerful dominance, and they don't need any extra support'. Ian linked notions of politics and power with identity:

DF: Should England get closer to Europe or the United States of America?

IAN: I guess if England did get closer to Europe, I guess people in England would feel European rather than just English or British, but if we, I think it would be good if we got closer to Europe.

DF: Why?

IAN: Because then, well, it'd just like, I dunno, like with [mumbles] laws and stuff would be the like, the same and stuff, and we'd be like, well, one big country really. Like all of us just joined up.

Yet, there were also those few (mainly Turkish) 15-year-olds who argued that England *should* get closer to America. For example, Mustafa argued that Britain's economy was more similar to that of the United States, and Osman added that it was Britain's drive for power that eventually resulted in closer ties with the United States saying that 'if Britain had the choice they'd go to America 'cos Britain really likes to be in power'.

Another major issue this study examined is the relationships between Turkishness and/or Britishness and students' identification with Europe. As a result of England's lukewarm approach to Europe, young people struggled to imagine the notion of Europe as part of their identities. The group of ethnic majority boys not only referred to the boundaries of the continent of Europe but also cited European history when defining Europe. Ethnic majority students also referred to the 'starry flag', 'travelling', 'holidays' and 'Euro Disney' in Paris when defining Europe. Turkish interviewees talked about similar aspects and also elaborated on their country's EU membership debate. However, while Turkish students in Millroad School employed a theme of 'us' (Turkish people) and 'them' (European people) and thus put a distance between themselves and Europe, mainland Turkish and Turkish Cypriot students in Darwin School identified with Europe so long as the notion of Europe included Turkey. Typically, respondents argued that 'if Turkey was in the European Union, then I would see myself as more of a European' and 'I see myself wherever Turkey belongs in Asia or whatever'. A number of Turkish Cypriot interviewees, such as Mustafa and Safak, referred to British insularity and separateness from Europe arguing that 'I am European 'cos I'm in Europe, and I'm in Britain which is in Europe and part of the European society; but I don't see myself as a European because Britain has its own kind of bubble, separate from Europe'. Here, Mustafa and Safak positioned themselves in ways that fit with the British national discourse. Their familiarity with national sociopolitical debates and perspectives alongside feelings for their country of origin are indicative of young people's hybridized Turkish British identities – identities that are new, fluid and discursively produced including ethnic and/or political categories.

In another interview, Mustafa fully analysed England's position within Europe, alluding to the referenda on the single currency and the constitution and evaluating the consequences of a 'no' vote for England.[8] His explanations could just as easily have come from one of the ethnic majority students, because it was so similar:

> DF: To what extent would you see yourself as European?

> MUSTAFA: I don't really see myself as European, because, erm, I don't know, I just, erm, I'm not sure because I'd sort of be like failing my argument now if I said that I don't see myself as European because if I was born in Europe I'd see myself as European, but I'm not born there so I guess I call myself British, cos I was born here and, like growing up here, since day one. That's it.

> DF: That's interesting that you are saying that, because you were born in England, and England has been part of the EU for decades, and now you were just saying "I'm not born in Europe"?

> MUSTAFA: But the thing is, I don't see England being a strong … I know they're quite strong in Europe, but I guess like I think like Europe's sort of latching onto England, and I think England's more distant from Europe, even though they're quite strong contenders in the European Union. Now if you've seen the news, they're actually thinking to vote not to be key contenders in the European Union, so they'll be more of the people that's on the marginal lines of Europe, instead of the core players of the [EU], like Germany or France.

Ethnic majority students at Darwin referred to Britain's separateness in similar ways and struggled to position themselves within a European discourse. In the following discussion, the students who took part in the mixed-sex focus group agreed that Europe is a rather irrelevant, distant community with which they have few connections. These students defined Europe as a geographical zone and too broad a category to identify with:

> DF: What role would you say Europe plays in your life?

> ADAM: Nothing.

> CHARLES: Nothing, whatsoever.

> CLARA and OLIVIA: [murmur agreement]

---

8   Both referenda were put on hold in June 2005, then in the case of the constitution replaced by the Treaty of Lisbon (Council of the European Union 2007).

ADAM: Wouldn't really like it to play much of a role either.

CHARLES: It's got nothing to do with me, it's a bit irrelevant.

CHARLOTTE: You wouldn't say you were French cos that's in Europe.

ADAM: It's just a zone.

CHARLES: You wouldn't say "hello, I'm European".

DF: Why wouldn't you say that?

ADAM: Cos you're an individual from many different places, in Europe.

CHARLES: European is too broad a generalization to class anyone as, whereas British obviously is much smaller, has less minorities, less groups to put yourself in, so it's easier to say "Yes I am British", but even in England, even in London, few people would say "yes I'm British", they'd say "I'm from London", "I'm from Essex", "I'm from Kent", or, "I'm from Oaks", cos people like to give themselves the smallest community to put themselves within, so they can feel more special.

The tension between Englishness (or Britishness) and Europeanness is played out here. The girls felt that saying you are from England is 'kind of more personal, a more detailed answer of where you actually come from' whereas saying you are European could mean many different things. The divisive idea of 'us' (English) and 'them' (continental Europeans) used by ethnic majority youth at Millroad was not overtly used at Darwin, although they still talked about British insularity and distance from continental Europe. Instead, identification with Europe was more conditional and context-dependent (e.g., 'if Turkey was in the European Union, then I would see myself as more of a European'; 'if we had the euro, we might see ourselves more as Europeans'). Arguably, the fact that 15-year-olds at Darwin appeared to be more receptive to the notion of Europe than their counterparts at Millroad may also have had to do with Millroad students' greater (socio-economic) ability to travel within Europe.[9]

Despite the overall rejection of Europe, some 15-year-olds, such as Ian and Owen, deployed a very pro-European tone. Ian commented that Europe was important and that he felt part of it. He criticized England's stance towards the common currency by saying that 'England have just gone kind of different to the

9   There is further evidence from the quantitative data that young people at Darwin, particularly ethnic majority girls, identified more strongly with Europe while considering their ethno-religious identities to be less important compared with their peers at Millroad (45 per cent European, 80 per cent ethnic identity, 70 per cent religious identity).

rest of Europe; well most of Europe have gone with the euro, apart from England and I think we should'. Owen argued that:

> The European Parliament is a good thing, that's definitely a good thing. I mean, if we embrace things like that, and the EU constitution, then I think it will make for a better world actually (...) and as I said, I feel a European citizen, but there's only so far I can go, unless the leaders of this country make a jump to, like, unite the whole of Europe.

Both ethnic majority and Turkish minority 15-year-olds showed a higher level of social integration in terms of inter-group friendships as well as multidimensional ethnic and political identities compared with their peers at Millroad, which allowed them to develop ethno-national (e.g., Turkish British, English British) identities. Second-generation Turkish Cypriots, and to a lesser degree first-generation mainland Turks, identified with both Britain and their country of origin. The Turkish Cypriot identity played at least an equal part in how young people saw their political identities:

> DF: What role would you say does your Turkish Cypriot background play in your life today?

> SAFAK: Well, it plays a big part cos that's my origin, but I'm not too, like, I don't think of it as a big big part where everything I do is revolved around that. I think cos, you know, I don't live there and I don't know people - I do know some people but they're not like the people I know here, that I like, all my friends are here, and my close family's here, so obviously I care more about them than I do distant family who I only see once a year. But it does, it plays a big part as to who I am, because of the way, cos that's just who I am, cos I am Turkish-Cypriot, but I don't think I don't make my whole life go around that. I kind of just, I just try to stay in-between and care about both things just as much, like, just as equally, but obviously that's harder cos I do a lot of things here, like watch British TV, that makes me learn more about England and London, than I do about Turkish, because, well, I watch Turkish TV less.

Safak tried to balance her various identities by attempting to stay 'in-between' and care about both societies. She tried hard to keep herself equally well-informed about the two countries by watching television but she found it difficult 'to care about both things'.[10] Also, Safak directly referred to notions of proximity and distance, arguing that she cares more about her close friends and family in England than about distant family members in the Turkish part of Cyprus whom she only

---

10   See Butterfield (2004) for a similar discussion of identity struggles among second-generation West Indians in New York. She also argues that schooling is an important factor for identity formation.

sees once a year. Some of the difficulties Safak had negotiating 'two cultures' have also been highlighted by identity researchers such as Caglar (1997), who viewed hybridized identities as potentially problematic because they involve 'dual cultural membership' and 'dual loyalties'. Tizard and Phoenix (2002: 225), by contrast, in a study of 58 youth of mixed black and white parentage from a range of social backgrounds, explored their identities, cultural orientations, feelings about black and white people and expectations of racism. They found that 'the majority of our sample seemed very confident in their identity as both black and white'. Drawing on the insights offered by post-structuralist theory, Tizard and Phoenix describe how their respondents depart from binary oppositions of black *or* white (Turkish *or* British) and instead emphasized that it is possible to be both black *and* white (Turkish *and* British). Clearly, the concept of identity involves complex processes of negotiation; identities cannot easily be formed, as the discussion with Safak exemplified.

At Darwin School, a hybridized Turkish British identity, which we saw emerging only tentatively amongst a few Turkish Cypriots at Millroad School, was not only clearly expressed by second-generation Turkish Cypriots like Safak, but also by first-generation mainland Turks such as Toker. However, Darwin students still saw their ethnic background as more important to them than being British:

DF: Where do you feel you belong to?

TOKER: I think I'm part of Turkey, still. I think I'm part of Britain as well, cos I've got a British passport.

DF: Can you explain that a bit more?

TOKER: I say Turkey cos I was born there and I lived there for 7 years, so, that's why I think Turkey. Half of my life was there. Dunno, about Britain, cos I've got, cos I think I dunno!

DF: What are the differences between Turkey and Britain?

TOKER: The difference is England's more rich, and Turkey's poor, but I think Turkey is a much better place to live in.

DF: Why?

TOKER: Erm, I dunno, erm, people are more friendly and I like the places, erm, cities.

The ethnic majority students I interviewed also had multidimensional identities revolving around familiar communities such as family, school and friends, as well as London and England. As William put it, 'I think more locally but as we get older, wider things [e.g., Europe, world] will become more important as they affect us more'. The ethnic majority students additionally provided a very useful explanation as to how they saw these familiar or close identities as interlinked and why they are all partly relevant to their identities.

> ADAM: School's kind of a duty that a child has to fulfil, erm, I was born in London, which happens to be in England [they laugh], therefore I'm a citizen of London and England, and my school, which is in London, so therefore they're all kind of interlinked.

> CHARLOTTE: If you don't, If you weren't in London, you wouldn't be able to go to [name of the school], if you weren't in Britain you wouldn't be able to live in London, because you can't because London's in Britain.

> DF: To what extent would you say all these things are equally important?

> ALL: Yeah.

> CHARLES: Cos you're a community inside a community inside a community.

However, these chains of multiple identities did not include supranational levels; rarely did the students I interviewed argue that Britain is part of the EU, and therefore important to their identities. In contrast, we saw that both ethnic majority and Turkish minority students in the two German schools frequently drew on the geo-political argument that Germany is part of the EU, making them feel somewhat European. And while some 15-year-olds at Darwin School, such as the members of the mixed-sex discussion group, felt they belonged to England, others associated more with Britain. For example, Zoe argued that 'I think I am part of Britain. It doesn't really bother me that I especially belong to England, it's just Britain as a whole because we've got a British passport and everything'.

In contrast, both first-generation mainland Turks and second-generation Turkish Cypriot students generally preferred the term British, which was perceived as a more inclusive multicultural category, rather than English, which was associated with race, birth and blood (e.g., English ancestors, English parents):

> DF: Could you tell me the difference between being English and being British?

> SAFAK: Well, being English is just like being, like having English parents and, you know, just having, being whatever, however far you can trace it back, it's always been from here, whether it's been from medieval times or Tudor times or whatever, it's always been from here, cos that's when you're actually English, but British Britain's a multicultural place, cos you know it's Scottish, English,

Welsh and stuff, and erm, if you, because it's such a multicultural place there are other cultures here that come, and cos I'm from here.

Other interviewees, particularly Turkish students, could not explain the difference between 'being English' and 'being British' to any great extent and even some of the ethnic majority students struggled to make sense of these two concepts. In the following passage, Elizabeth explains how difficult it was to identify with Britain because there was no British sports team.[11] The girls had a confused and often vague conceptualization of English, British and the United Kingdom, and it was not at all clear what they associated with each of these terms:

DF: Could you tell me the difference between being English and being British?

ANNE: There isn't a difference. Is there?

VICTORIA: British is belonging to a larger thing.

SOPHIE: You're not British if you come from Wales!

VICTORIA: Yes you are! British is Wales, Scotland and England [murmurs of agreement]

SOPHIE: Is that Britain? Oh yeah. That's Britain. But English is just England.

JENNIFER: Yeah, British is like a lot wider area, I suppose, and to be English is just from England.

ELIZABETH: The thing is with British is that none of the sports and stuff are "British" team, they're all kind of "England", "Scotland", blah, so it's kind of hard to feel kind of part-

JENNIFER: But British is the same as United Kingdom then.

ELIZABETH: But it's hard to feel kind of proud of United Kingdom, because they never represent it [someone murmurs] yeah they don't do anything!

The notion that familiar communities (e.g., home, school, friends, London) were more important when negotiating political identities than distant societies (e.g., Europe, world) was evident when I asked about the extent to which Turkish minority

---

11 According to the quantitative data, cultural symbols (i.e., football, monarchy, flag) were more strongly associated with 'being English' and England than monocultural concepts (i.e., Christian country, white people), which may have to do with the promotion of an inclusive multiethnic national identity ('multicultural Britishness') at Darwin School.

and ethnic majority students saw themselves as Londoners. Most interviewees felt that they belonged to London and Owen explained why he felt part of the English capital:

DF: How do you feel about your local community here in London?

OWEN: Well, I like, I like living in London, partly because, you feel connected with everyone else. I mean, I live in Greater London and I go into like the city, like inner-city London, quite a lot, and it's, er, it's, although it's not like a friendly community, it's not a bad community. I mean, I've never experienced someone being incredibly horrible to me in London, I've experienced people being kind in London. And I like the way, erm … here there's a whole load of cultures in London, and I like, I like being part of that. That's why I'd rather say I was part of London than the rest of the UK. Because it's like, it's multicultural in London. I mean, this school is like, sort of, a good representation of that I think. And, if I go to another part of the UK where it's, like, very predominantly white, it doesn't actually feel right to me, and that's because I've been brought up in London. But I suppose I feel more comfortable with a mixture of different cultures and religions and skin colours, than a place where it's like all-white, or like all-white with only a few, like people from different races.

Owen based his local identification on 'friendly people' in London who have never done him any harm and the fact that London was a multiethnic and multifaith city. Owen's identification with the school community becomes evident in his qualifying statement that the school was 'a good representation' of multicultural London.

Summary

To sum up, in this primarily middle-class school in London, which celebrated similarity and promoted academic excellence and inclusivity, young people appeared to have developed ethno-national (i.e., Turkish British, English/British) identities. Young people understood their identities around familiar communities (e.g., London) instead of distant membership groups (e.g., Europe). Darwin School's promotion of national agendas over and above supranational and multicultural agendas was associated with 15-year-olds struggling to talk about Europe in political terms and often developing confused discourses around European political issues. Many Turkish youth in the study positioned themselves within British national discourses, suggesting they may have been more integrated with Britain compared with their peers at Millroad. While the high level of ethnic and racial conflict at Millroad was associated with ethnic majority students privileging Englishness and Turkish minority respondents privileging Turkishness, ethnicity appeared to play less of a role in the lives of 15-year-olds at Darwin. This finding was evident in Darwin students' and teachers' conceptualizations of Britishness. It was also evident in the more congenial peer cultures at Darwin, which likely contributed to Darwin students' hybridized ethno-national identities (Turkish British, for example).

The identities young people expressed in this research were more complex than those usually found in more quantitative studies. For example, a recent study by Heath and Roberts (2008: 8) found that in England, Scotland and Wales 'a majority of residents have dual identities and there does not appear from these data to be a continuing decline in British identity or a continuing rise in exclusive national identities'. They further argued that, although ethnic minorities tend to feel a strong sense of belonging to their own ethnic groups, their study shows clear evidence of 'dual' rather than 'exclusive' identities. While my study does show that both ethnic majority and minority ethnic youth mostly have multiple identities (except for young people at Millroad School), these are more complex than simply 'dual' identities. Instead, youth in this study of schools in Germany and England appeared to have forged identities involving not only national and regional affiliations, but also local and supranational attachments and, in several cases, non-political identities such as family, school and peer groups. I also found 'newer' identities such as popular culture. I return to this final point later.

Although the two London comprehensives were in the same national framework, the resulting identities to which students subscribed were rather different. The two schools had different approaches to the macro-level British context, with Millroad School celebrating cultural and religious diversity, and Darwin School emphasizing social cohesion around Britishness. The result appears to have been a sense of conflict and division at Millroad, where teachers ended up investing a great deal of time to try and bond the conflicting Turkish and African Caribbean communities together while doing relatively little to integrate the smaller number of ethnic majority students. On the other hand, Darwin School had a more multicultural agenda embedded in a civic conception of the nation (an approach that could be called 'multicultural Britishness'). This approach was associated with lower levels of ethnic conflict at Darwin, whereas Millroad School had much more ethnic conflict spilling over from the local community. I shall now move on to summarize and interpret the main findings of these case studies, and discuss some of the theoretical and empirical implications by situating the underlying themes in this study into a wider European and transatlantic context.

Chapter 8
Inclusive Citizenship and Social Cohesion

This study of youth political identities in different European countries is a highly topical and fascinating one given the considerable demographic, economic, political and socio-cultural change currently taking place in Europe. At the same time, the study makes important contributions to the immigration, citizenship, identity and ethnicity research literature on both sides of the Atlantic, and incorporates the views of educationalists and sociologists as well as political scientists. The study is the first of its kind to bring together between-country and within-country differences in youth identity formations. By analysing the perspectives of ethnic majority and Turkish minority youth, the study intertwines the potential effects of national, European and multicultural political agendas, rather than looking at each dimension separately. Finally, the study unravels a wide range of factors shaping contemporary youth identity negotiation, including social class, ethnic relations, and school-level factors. In so doing, I offer new insights into the particular role of school dynamics in shaping youth identities, including school ethos, peer cultures and school-level policy approaches. The findings of the study suggest that national citizenship agendas and identities involve complex ethnic negotiations, circumscribed by the presence or absence of European dimensions. I argue that these findings point to the need for policy-makers, politicians and educators alike not only to rethink concepts such as the nation-state and Europe along more inclusive multiethnic and multifaith lines, but also to revisit the challenge of balancing diversity and social cohesion. In this way, governments might begin to promote more inclusive citizenship and educational policies that are based on what works best on the ground in multiethnic schooling contexts across Europe.

This final chapter of the book closely reviews the study's contribution to scholarship on the negotiation of political identities, honing in and summarizing my evidence regarding school policy approaches, youth political identities, school dynamics, and a theoretical model for conceptualizing youth political identities. In particular, I compare and contrast the various school policy approaches and assess their impact on the different forms of hybrid identities (sometimes emphasizing the ethnic and other times the political dimension of hybridity) alongside other important factors shaping interethnic relationships and identities such as socio-economic background. I then broaden the discussion to situate my findings within the transatlantic scholarship on immigrant integration, critically examining dominant theoretical explanations for the integration of immigrants and their children, and considering how my findings on political identity formation offer new insights for the European and American literatures. I especially point toward the need to study the complexity of contemporary identities and to consider identity as a marker for social integration. Finally, the last section of the chapter reviews some of the wider theoretical and political implications arising from the study.

The Negotiation of Political Identities

Nations in Europe differ considerably in their responses toward European integration and migration-related diversity. This is reflected for instance in the ease (or not) with which immigrants can apply for and receive permanent residence and citizenship status. Currently, Switzerland (12 years), Greece (10 years) and Austria (10 years) are among the most difficult countries to obtain citizenship whereas Ireland (5 years), the Netherlands (5 years) and France (5 years) have relatively fewer barriers. Based on the literature and evidence from this study, countries can broadly be grouped into at least four categories reflecting their legacies and current approaches to diversity and European integration. Firstly, there are 'old migration societies' like Germany who have traditionally developed a more monocultural but Europhile vision. Secondly, there are 'old migration societies' like Britain who have historically been more multicultural and Eurosceptic. Thirdly, there are 'new migration societies' such as Greece who have embarked on a more monocultural but Europhile road. Fourthly, there are 'new migration societies' such as Ireland with an arguably more multicultural outlook but some scepticism toward EU institutions.[1] This shows, in part, that the 'anti-multiculturalists' in Europe tend to be more pro-European whereas the 'multiculturalists' struggle to ally these two concepts. This has important implications for education policy. In this book, I have demonstrated these implications for England and Germany, and further discussed the considerable variations of these macro-level approaches at school levels.

Germany has taken considerably more time than England to develop deliberate processes of integration, despite its strong welfare system model. As described in Chapter 2, Germany's opposition to long-term immigrant residents is related to its predominant understanding of society as monocultural, despite a growing number of non-German immigrants. The growth of post-war immigration overshadowed the attempts by policy-makers and politicians to reconceptualize the shattered national identity in European terms. England, by contrast, recruited labourers based on who initially had the right to reside permanently in the host country, as described in Chapter 5. This difference in recruitment is crucial to consider in examining the different approaches to migration in these two 'old migrant receiving' countries. Although both countries initially developed assimilationist educational approaches (i.e., 'foreigner pedagogy' in Germany; assimilation and integration in England), the integrationist approach in England attempted to recognize, albeit to a limited extent, cultural and ethnic differences within the concept of Britishness. On the

---

1   Ireland, for instance, has twice rejected EU treaties in referenda (Treaty of Nice in June 2001 and the Treaty of Lisbon in June 2008) whereas the Greek saying goes that they are European and Europeans are in fact Greek.

other hand, the German educational approach in the 1960s and 1970s, also known as 'foreigner pedagogy' (*Ausländerpädagogik*), was viewed as the key means of assimilating migrant children into a monocultural conception of Germany. Germany was reluctant to reconceptualize her national identity as multicultural, perhaps as a result of the fact that policy-makers and politicians had just shifted the country's national agenda towards European integration.

The result has been that Germany, a founding member of the European integration project, has used schools and the curriculum to construct a Europeanized national identity since the 1980s and 1990s. England, by contrast, has experienced Europe very differently, seeing little reason to reconceptualize her national identity in European terms, and thus seeing little effect of the processes of Europeanization on schools. Instead, the politics of Europe, initiated by Germany and France, have been undercut in England by the special relationship with the United States, the geographical detachment from continental Europe, and England's post-war role in the Commonwealth (see Katzenstein 1997). Consequently, England engaged little with the European project until the 1960s, when Prime Minister Macmillan realized that his country needed to change its strategy as the Empire was rapidly falling apart. However, it has been extremely difficult for politicians to promote a sense of European identity in England where the level of national pride has been much higher than in Germany (because of the fact that England had won the War). Unlike Germany, England's relationship with Europe has been largely based on economic reasons, and governments have faced the dilemma of having to engage with an entity they have felt only loosely attached to and that has been led, for most of the time, by joint Franco-German initiatives.

The result, as this study shows, is that the different historical engagements with national identity, cultural diversity and European integration have had enormous implications for the kinds of identities students can access in school in these two countries. For example, as early as 1978, Germany made attempts to include a European dimension in schools, whereas the European dimension has received little attention in England and is conceptualized as part of a broader global educational dimension. The following sections summarize in greater detail the school-level findings, and their connections with the broader policy agendas just described.

School Policy Approaches

Residues of these macro-level policy approaches enacted since World War II can still be found in schools today, and this study shows the ways in which they influence the construction of young people's identities. In Germany, Tannberg Hauptschule, located in a predominantly working-class inner-city area in Stuttgart, mediated national and citizenship agendas through a dominantly European and arguably, at times, a Eurocentric approach. The teachers tried their best to deliver the mandatory curriculum set by the regional Ministry of Education. This curriculum, as we have seen, privileged European agendas over and above national and multicultural agendas in subjects like geography and history. As a result, at a school like Tannberg, with 62 per cent minority ethnic students, the teachers appeared to do little to address the cultural and ethnic diversity of the large ethnic minority population, while Millroad School in London had a similarly large number of working-class minority ethnic students, but took a more pluralist approach. Teachers at Goethe Gymnasium, located in a predominantly middle-class area in Stuttgart (comparable to the location of Darwin School), also drew little on regional policy debates around multiculturalism. However, both the principal and the head of religious education there had a deeply ambivalent relationship towards German national identity and referred more frequently to Germany's Europeanized identity. This submerged national identity was reflected in the school's approach of 'multicultural Europeanness', which emphasized the common bond of Europe, but at the same time encouraged individuals to keep their ethnic identities (a contrast with Darwin School which seemed to ally the concept of Britishness with multiculturalism). This divergence between Tannberg and Goethe underscores the fact that although the German school system was under the direct control of the regional government, schools and teachers could and did interpret and deliver the mandatory curriculum in different ways.

In contrast, as a result of the English Government's policy approach, Europe was a relatively low priority in the two London schools. Millroad School, located in a predominantly working-class environment in Inner London (that was not dissimilar to that of Tannberg Hauptschule), offered only limited exposure to the processes of Europeanization. It mediated national identity through the politics of cultural diversity and, in so doing, reasserted the concept of cultural pluralism. Millroad made citizenship education a low priority and instead celebrated its cultural and ethnic diversity through events such as Turkish Kurdish Celebration Weeks. This is a very different scenario from what we saw in Tannberg Hauptschule in Stuttgart which, following the national pattern, promoted strong European agendas to create social cohesion. On the other hand, Darwin School, located in a middle-class area in the same Inner London borough as Millroad, celebrated similarity rather than diversity. This common ground was not based on Europe, but instead rested on the idea that the school should encourage its students to think of themselves as liberal democratic British citizens living in a global multi-ethnic international community. In so doing, this school was much closer to New Labour's model of 'multicultural Britishness' and, like Goethe Gymnasium, allied the concept of multiculturalism with social inclusion. Darwin further displayed a far greater emphasis on citizenship education, which actively promoted the values of a liberal democratic, multicultural British society, and was both a cross-curricular theme and part of Personal, Social and Health Education. However, like Millroad, Darwin School reflected the prioritization of national (and multicultural) agendas over and above European agendas, underscoring the overall lack of a European dimension in the two London schools. Based on the ethnic composition and discussions I had with teachers, it would have been much more of a challenge to promote a European dimension in a school like Millroad, where the majority of young people originated from non-European countries, compared with Darwin, where 72 per cent of students were British.

Table 8.1 summarizes, from a comparative research point of view, the different governmental and school policy approaches in Germany and England:

Table 8.1 Governmental and school policy approaches in Germany and England

	Germany		England	
Government level	Very strong European dimension Weak multicultural agendas Submerged national identity		Weak European dimension Awareness of multicultural agendas Very strong national agendas	
School level	**Tannberg Hauptschule**	**Goethe Gymnasium**	**Millroad School**	**Darwin School**
Population	320 students 18% Turkish	564 students 5% Turkish	1,204 students 26% Turkish	1,507 students 2% Turkish
	Second-generation mainland Turkish students only	Second-generation mainland Turkish students only	First- and second generation Turkish, Turkish Cypriots	First- and second generation Turkish, Turkish Cypriots
Location	Working-class inner-city	Middle-class inner-city	Working-class inner-city	Middle-class inner-city
Achievement	Lower	Higher	Lower	Higher
Curriculum topics	39.5% national 34.5% European 26.0% diversity	39.5% national 34.5% European 26.0% diversity	50.5% national 12.5% European 37.0% diversity	50.5% national 12.5% European 37.0% diversity
School approach	**Eurocentric Education**	**Multicultural Europeanness**	**Celebrating Diversity**	**Multicultural Britishness**

Note: The curriculum topics represent the percentage of total teaching units in history and geography addressing national, European and migration-related issues. N = 23 teaching units in history and 31 teaching units in geography, for a total of 56 teaching units in the two English schools (41 history, 44 geography in the two German schools).

Given these different school environments, demography, and policy approaches, the students in these four schools experienced quite contradictory and different messages about national, European and multicultural agendas. The different governmental and school policy approaches to these three agendas set the context for the responses of ethnic majority and Turkish minority youth, and were major factors affecting identity negotiations. Below, I reassess the data on young people's political identities.

Youth Political Identities

The concept of hybridity, defined in the opening chapter of this book as the emergence of new and fluid identities including ethnic and/or political categories, worked differently in these four school settings and was affected by a wide range of factors. These varied factors include school policy approaches, the school dynamics between students and teachers as well as amongst students (peer cultures), socio-economic background, and the history of migration. In the two working-class schools, many ethnic majority and Turkish minority youth, and especially the male students at Tannberg, privileged the ethnic dimension of their hybrid identities (e.g., 'being Swabian'). At Millroad School in London, where we saw the strongest ethnic conflict and divisive peer cultures, both groups of students almost exclusively emphasized their ethnic belonging (i.e., their Turkishness or Englishness). In this ethnically-charged school environment, the concept of hybridity appeared not to have been operationalized to any great extent. In contrast, in the two middle-class schools, a majority of students emphasized the political dimension (e.g., 'being British') of hybridity, although some Darwinian students in the study, and first-generation mainland Turks in particular, still privileged their ethnicity. This echoes Butterfield's (2004) findings among Afro-Caribbeans in New York that revealed how a working-class sample of youth developed far stronger ethnic identities compared to middle-class respondents. My finding that some 15-year-olds (at Millroad) retreat into their own ethnic groups also supports Skrobanek's (2009) re-ethnicization theory arguing that discrimination lowers the permeability of group boundaries and thus results in young people forming strong groups along lines of ethnic solidarity.

A methodological caveat is in order here because it was not possible within the scope of this study to determine the relative importance of each of the individual factors affecting young people's identities. In order to get a fuller picture of the school culture and dynamics, it would have been necessary to look at *all* the groups of youth within one school. However, this research did not tap the ways in which African Caribbean youth in the two English schools (30 per cent at Millroad and 10 per cent at Darwin) and, similarly, how Italian youth in the two German schools (10 per cent at Tannberg and 6 per cent at Goethe) forged their political identities and how they interacted with and positioned their ethnic majority and Turkish minority classmates. My informal observations indicated that African Caribbean youth at Millroad were also positioned as 'others' and subject to racism (e.g., 'black people are dickheads, I hate them'). They were perhaps in a slightly more advantaged position compared to their Turkish peers because their Christian religion and English language made it easier for them to relate positively to their ethnic majority classmates, with whom they formed stronger relationships. But the methodology of the study did not allow me to determine this with certainty, though the informal discussions did suggest that ethnic majority respondents tended to have more African Caribbean friends than Turkish friends.

Overall, the empirical evidence in this study suggests that the governmental approach to national, European and multicultural educational agendas, as well as the different prioritization of European agendas in Germany and England, are important factors in explaining the *between-country* differences of young people's identity formations.[2] The interview data described throughout the book shows this finding, and here I also provide additional data from a test of young people's ability to locate countries on a map of Europe. This test showed that although the data do not directly measure what 15-year-olds knew about Germany or England, young people in the two German schools generally revealed a higher level of knowledge about Europe than their counterparts in the two English secondary schools. For example, as shown in Table 8.2, young people in both Tannberg Hauptschule and Goethe Gymnasium scored significantly higher than their counterparts in the two English schools when asked to locate ten European countries correctly on a geo-political map of Europe.

Table 8.2 Young people's correct location of countries on a map of Europe

	Germany (per cent)	England (per cent)	Tannberg (per cent)	Goethe (per cent)	Millroad (per cent)	Darwin (per cent)
Britain	85.6	85.1	76.8	93.5**	81.3	89.1
Germany	89.6	51.0**	85.3	93.5	37.4	65.3**
Spain	86.1	52.4**	78.9	92.5*	38.3	67.3**
Finland	25.7	8.7**	15.8	34.6**	4.7	12.9*
Italy	94.1	64.4**	89.5	98.1*	54.2	75.2**
Turkey	66.8	33.2**	58.9	73.8	33.6	32.7
Portugal	81.2	37.5**	74.7	86.9	28.0	47.5**
Poland	58.9	14.4**	48.4	68.2*	11.2	17.8*
France	85.6	56.7**	75.8	94.4**	43.0	71.3**
Ukraine	30.2	10.6**	22.1	37.4*	12.1	8.9*
Average	73.3	41.4**	62.6	77.3	34.4	48.9

Note: * Significance below 0.05; ** Significance below 0.01.
Source: Reproduced from *Journal of Youth Studies*.

Over 80 per cent of students in the German sample correctly identified the location of six western-central European countries. In contrast, only one country (Britain) was correctly identified by eight out of ten students in the English sample. Students located Eastern European countries (Poland and Ukraine) and Turkey least of all.

---

2   See Castles and Miller (2003) for an explanation of between-country differences in integration.

On average, 62.6 per cent of countries were correctly identified by students at Tannberg Hauptschule versus 77.3 per cent at Goethe Gymnasium, showing much higher averages than England, where 34.4 per cent of countries were correctly located by students at Millroad and 48.9 per cent at Darwin. Comparing the within-country results, we additionally see that students in the more middle-class schools (Goethe and Darwin) were also significantly better at locating European countries than students in the working-class schools (Tannberg and Millroad).

Young people in the two German schools, particularly at Goethe, also had a wider range of opinions when talking about Europe. Unlike Tannberg students, Goethe students were able to engage in a discussion about Europe rather than just listing basic concepts that came to their mind when they heard the word Europe (e.g., the euro, united countries). These more Europe-aware students referred, for example, to the geographical differences within Europe, the need for greater European integration, and the origins of the EU. In contrast, students' knowledge about European issues was much more limited in the two English schools, particularly at Millroad. Although many respondents knew about the possibility of Turkish EU membership and also felt comfortable talking about the relationship between England and Europe, some (e.g., ethnic majority girls at Millroad School) blamed the low media representation in England for not knowing more about Europe while others (e.g., ethnic majority boys at Millroad School) criticized the school for focusing too much on local issues. Although knowledge is not necessarily the basis of young people's political identities, the evidence in this study suggests that it could well have affected their identity formation processes, especially with regard to the construction of a supranational European identity which was higher in countries and institutions that actively promoted such an identity through their curricula and school policies and ethos (e.g., Germany's Goethe Gymnasium).

Summary of School Dynamics

The school dynamics, including ethos, peer cultures, and curricula, were amongst the most important factors in accounting for the *within-country* differences of young people's identity formations in this study.[3] In Tannberg Hauptschule, the Turkish respondents were subject to verbal abuse and discrimination because of their cultural and religious 'otherness'. Some of the ethnic majority students saw their Turkish classmates as 'foreigners' and thus sent a strong message to them that they were different (e.g., Muslims, non-Europeans) and not part of mainstream society. Some of the teachers also revealed a degree of cultural insensitivity toward Turkish students and, on occasion, were getting close to being Islamophobic (e.g., the Muslim sauce incident, or privileging the cross over the hijab) and saw Turkish minority students outside the European framework. These Eurocentric approaches at Tannberg made it quite difficult for Turkish 15-year-olds to relate positively

---

3   See Crul and Vermeulen (2003, 2006) for an institutional approach explaining between-country differences in integration.

to Germany, let alone Europe. However, as a result of being born in Germany, they seemed to be able to mediate such socio-ethnic marginalization through cross-ethnic friendships and saw themselves as 'Turkish German' or 'Turkish Stuttgarter'. The Turkish youth in turn positioned their ethnic majority classmates as 'potatoes', which appeared to be a means by which the Turkish students could fight back against the oppressive remarks of their peers and teachers. The ethnic majority interviewees, too, showed a hybrid (Swabian German) rather than a singular political identity.

At Goethe Gymnasium, by contrast, the peer group and teacher-student dynamics were less divisive, and I observed very little ethnic conflict. Both ethnic majority and Turkish minority students in the study showed a higher level of overall integration in the school, as observed through cross-ethnic friendships. Observations and interviews did reveal a slight tendency amongst Turkish 15-year-olds to form non-German (mixed European) friendship groups because the Turkish youth seemed to feel somewhat closer to the other non-German ethnic minority groups with whom they shared their migrant children status. However, there were no obvious signs of any ethnic tensions within the school community, an outcome I attribute partly to the school's approach to integrating students on the basis of common European values. Some Turkish youth explicitly mentioned that 'this school doesn't make much of a difference between "foreigners" and Germans' and were able to mediate any socio-cultural and ethnic differences through notions of tolerance, liberalism and a strong sense of community. Outside the school, the Turkish youth did report experiencing similar sorts of racist incidents as their peers at Tannberg, and felt that they were seen as 'foreigners'. Unlike at Tannberg, however, their privileged backgrounds created better opportunities for them within and beyond school (e.g., jobs, travelling) and, consequently, they felt comfortable in German society and saw themselves as German European.

Millroad School in London demonstrated the strongest ethnic conflict. Community conflict in the school neighbourhood was associated with violent gang fights and the more frequent mocking of Turkish students for reasons of ethnicity and nationality. The divisive peer cultures were further evident in the tendency amongst Turkish youth at Millroad to form ethnic friendship groups, and the fact that students sat along ethnic lines in classrooms. Peers saw the Turkish respondents as religiously, linguistically and culturally different, as 'Others', which made the Turks feel very uncomfortable. Indeed, the level of aggression between African Caribbean and Turkish youth over control of school territory was such that some Turkish 15-year-olds threatened and physically abused African Caribbean youth who, in turn, reasserted their power by playing with the word 'turkey'. In their struggle for power and control, both groups, which were roughly equal in size (30 per cent of the student body), retreated into their own ethnic groups. In this conflictual setting, the Turkish youth saw themselves as 'Turkish-only'. The ethnic majority youth, who were in the minority (19 per cent), were left marginalized by these power struggles between the two main groups at Millroad, and teachers found themselves all too often focusing on reducing the divisions between Turkish and African Caribbean students. The hostile climate led some ethnic majority 15-year-olds to engage in verbal abuse and racism against the two ethnic minority groups and push for 'English-only' in the school.

Like in Germany, British schools had far less tension between ethnic groups in middle-class localities. But while Europe became a unifying factor for students at Goethe Gymnasium in Stuttgart, Darwin School in London tried to integrate its students on the basis of being British citizens living in a multiethnic community. In both Goethe Gymnasium and Darwin School the relationships between the various school communities were relatively congenial and students were able to develop cross-ethnic friendships. Ethnic majority and Turkish minority Darwinians claimed that they never felt marginalized because of their race or class background. Instead, there were some incidents where students were seen as homosexual and it almost seemed as though the ethnic dynamics we saw in the other three schools had been replaced by sexual dynamics at Darwin School. However, there were also isolated incidents where ethnic majority girls in the study were trying to copy African Caribbean girls whom they saw as role models. Overall however, ethnic majority and Turkish minority youth felt relatively comfortable talking to each other, which was associated with the development of ethno-national (i.e., Turkish British or English British) identities. These findings underscore that multidimensional political identities are far more common than singular identities, both amongst ethnic majority and ethnic minority youth.

Some readers might wonder about the extent to which within-country differences in political identities stemmed from school policy approaches compared with social class differences among students. Let me drive home the point that I do believe this study shows that socio-economic background matters as well, and is intertwined with other factors shaping young people's identities. As argued in this book, my study shows for instance a privileging of the ethnic dimension in working-class localities and a more political dimension of hybridity in middle-class localities. It was the middle-class localities that appeared to respond to their multiethnic student populations by promoting inclusive citizenship models and, in so doing, allied the concept of diversity with social cohesion – what I called 'multicultural Britishness' in Darwin School and 'multicultural Europeanness' in Goethe Gymnasium. However, neither of the more working-class schools promoted such inclusive policy approaches. While this suggests that class is a strong explanation for the differences observed, the fact that Turkish students' socio-economic backgrounds were similar across all four schools suggests that the differences observed may have also had a lot to do with how schools responded to government policy. As indicated at the outset of this book, Turkish 15-year-olds in both Goethe Gymnasium and Darwin School had parents with similar backgrounds that were 'less middle class' than the ethnic majority youth in both localities. At Goethe Gymnasium, 28.6 per cent of Turkish 15-year-olds had skilled and unskilled parents while 33.3 per cent had professional middle-class and routine non-manual parents. Similarly, 23.5 per cent of Turkish students at Darwin School had skilled and unskilled parents while 11.8 per cent had professional middle-class and routine non-manual parents. In contrast, ethnic majority youth had 69.2 per cent and 67.9 per cent professional middle-class and routine non-manual parents at Goethe and Darwin respectively. Not only were Turkish student backgrounds similar across all four schools, but students also mixed well in both working- and middle-class localities in Germany. This further undermines the view that social class is the main factor in shaping relationships across ethnic lines and instead points toward the importance of different policy approaches taken by the schools.

Chains and Triangles of Identities

Ethnic majority students in the two German and English schools formed what I call a 'chain of identities', integrating local, regional and (supra)national spheres. In particular, ethnic majority youth in the two German schools forged their political identities by linking the local Stuttgart, regional Baden-Württemberg (or Swabian), national German, and supranational European citizenship levels. However, as a result of the different prioritization of European agendas at German and English government levels, these chains of identities generally did not include supranational levels in all countries, as shown by the case of ethnic majority students in the two English secondary schools. Ethnic minority Turkish 15-year-olds, by contrast, developed different forms of hybrid identities. One of the most notable differences between ethnic majority and Turkish minority youth was that majority-group students, in both Germany and England, generally also had a regional identity (i.e., Swabian or English) whereas virtually none of the Turkish respondents saw themselves as Swabian or English.

Put differently, Turkish 15-year-olds broke the chain by linking, for example, the local with the supranational levels (e.g., Stuttgart European identities) or the local with the national levels (e.g., Turkish Stuttgarter identities). This suggests that Turkish students in the four schools positioned themselves within what I call a 'triangle of identities'. In such a triangle, it is possible to combine all the different political identities (e.g., local, regional, national, supranational) without seeing one sphere as being integrated within the other. In fact, unlike many ethnic majority youth, most Turkish interviewees perceived the regional and national identities as competing and provided astonishingly detailed accounts of why they saw themselves as British but not English or German but not Swabian. In both the German and English sample, the Turkish 15-year-olds perceived the regional identity as an ethnic identity based on descent, meaning that you have to be born Swabian or English in order to draw on these identities (and they are thus unavailable to Turks).

Unlike Pakistani and Bangladeshi communities in Europe, and men in particular, who tend to define their identities along religious lines (Archer 2003), Muslimness does not figure prominently in the multidimensional hybrid identities of young

Turks in either Germany or England.[4] Archer's (2003) Pakistani and Bangladeshi Muslim boys primarily identified in terms of their Muslim identity – which she called 'un-hybrid' identities – whereas girls constructed distinctly hybrid British Muslim identities. In contrast, both male and female Turkish youth in my study held many different forms of hybrid identities. For example, at Tannberg Hauptschule and Goethe Gymnasium, some male students argued that their country of origin was more important than Germany while female Turkish students claimed that Germany was more important to them than Turkey. This gender dimension might have to do with their different roles in the relatively patriarchal Turkish society where women traditionally have a more domestic role and men carry on their family honour and identity. Unlike youth in Archer's research, hardly any of the Turkish youth in this study explicitly identified themselves as Muslim. This may partly be a result of the fact that Islam in Turkish communities is more liberal in interpreting religious dictum. It may also be that, for my Turkish 15-year-olds, 'being Turkish' already included a sense of religious belonging, or they might not have wanted to emphasize their Muslim identity to me as a Christian researcher. It could further have to do with the different ways in which the interview questions were put to the young people. While Archer (2003) asked whether students were more proud of being Pakistani or Muslim and, in a rather closed way, whether 'being Muslim' was important to them, I tended to ask, in a broader and more open-ended way, where they felt they belonged to or how possible it was to be both Turkish and British.[5]

Table 8.3 summarizes, from a comparative research point of view, the ways in which ethnic majority and Turkish minority youth understood their identities.

This comparative analysis of youth identities found that the four schools had quite different approaches to addressing diversity, and to addressing issues of citizenship and Europe in their curricula. These different school policy approaches were associated with national political differences in historical relations with Europe, national identity, and responses to migration-related diversity. Alongside a number of other factors, these school approaches impacted on the identity formation of geographically and socio-economically different groups of young people and led to the emergence of different identities across ethnic majority and minority lines, across schools. The politics of diversity and the promotion of

---

4   Other studies tell a different story. For example, Brettfeld and Wetzels (2007) found strong religious ties amongst a majority of the Muslim population (87.3 per cent), 15-year-olds (86.5 per cent) and Muslim students (76.7 per cent). They clustered religiosity into four categories: (a) minimally religious (17.5 per cent); (b) orthodox religious (21.9 per cent); (c) fundamental religious (39.6 per cent); and (d) traditional conservative (21 per cent). Haug, Müssig and Stichs' (2009) survey showed that religiosity is particularly evident among Muslims of Turkish and African origin (Sunnis) whereas Muslims of Iranian descent (Shiites) consider themselves less religious.

5   Brettfeld and Wetzels (2007) as well as Haug, Müssig and Stichs (2009) also framed questions around religiosity.

cultural pluralism only worked as a cohesive device with positive ramifications for identity development in contexts where it is was allied with inclusion (as shown in Goethe Gymnasium and Darwin School). However, celebrating diversity or promoting ethnocentric (Eurocentric) views appeared to not only undermine social cohesion and lead to young people retreating into their own ethnic groups, but also seemed to drive the various school communities further apart. The result was nationalistic (or Eurocentric) views and *more* rather than less conflict. Thus, we can conclude that assimilation-based approaches on the one hand and cultural pluralist policies on the other are both ineffective means of bonding together ethnic majority and minority communities, in schools and society at large. Instead, as these case studies show, what works best on the ground are integration policies that incorporate diversity and allow *all* people to forge new identities that are recognized and valued at school and government level.

Table 8.3 The political identities of ethnic majority and Turkish minority youth

	Tannberg Hauptschule	**Goethe Gymnasium**	**Millroad School**	**Darwin School**
School policy	Eurocentric Education	Multicultural Europeanness	Celebrating Diversity	Multicultural Britishness
Peer cultures	Divisive/ congenial: some conflicts	Congenial: very little conflict	Divisive: substantial conflict	Congenial: very little conflict
Youth identities	**Ethno-national and local**	**National-European**	**National(istic)**	**Ethno-national**
	Ethnic majority: Swabian German	*Ethnic majority*: Swabian European	*Ethnic majority*: Englishness	*Ethnic majority*: English/British
	Turkish minority: Turkish German/ Stuttgarter	*Turkish minority*: Stuttgart or German-European	*Turkish minority*: Turkishness	*Turkish minority*: Turkish British

These empirical discussions are based on four schools in two countries. However, the findings have implications for discussions far beyond Stuttgart and London. This study raises broader European and transatlantic issues around the political and educational challenges of incorporating migrants and their children, as well as issues around theorizing and investigating these similar challenges in different country contexts. This is why I now expand my findings to include a discussion and synthesis of some of the European and American literatures, showing how the present study has insights to offer the broader literature on immigrant integration, identity and schooling.

The Second Generation in Europe and the United States

Cross-national youth research on immigrant incorporation and the second generation is also becoming more popular in countries beyond Europe, notably the United States, albeit with a focus on educational outcomes rather than identity. Despite some similarities around the need to respond to increasing migration-related diversity, there are noticeable transatlantic differences both with regard to theoretical conceptualizations of multiculturalism and empirical research. Despite the different ethnic and racial make-up of European and American societies, policy-makers, educators and academics on both sides of the Atlantic have been simultaneously scratching their heads over how to include ethnic minority communities and how to reconceptualize national identities and schooling approaches in more inclusive multiethnic ways. Drawing on the empirical evidence in this book, I engage with some of the major American and European theoretical and political struggles arising from migration. I argue that the insights gained from fieldwork in London and Stuttgart schools relate not only to these local contexts, but also to the larger problem of inclusive citizenship and schooling that multiethnic cities face. My study of political identities among youth thus offers some insights into how to address these issues in other European and international contexts.

Questions of integration in Europe and the United States differ significantly in that the United States continues to focus mainly on race, ethnicity, and language while there has been a shift in Europe from phenotype to the religious dimension of multiculturalism. Most observers attribute this in part to the terrorist attacks in Madrid (2004) and London (2005), and the tensions between national majorities and Muslim minorities in England (2001), France (2005) and Denmark (2005). There are an estimated 15 million Muslims in Europe today, about 4 per cent of the European population (Savage 2004), and a larger number than the combined populations of Finland, Denmark and Ireland. Religion thus dominates second-generation integration debates in Europe.

In contrast, race, ethnicity and language remain at the fore of academic and political debates over immigration in the United States. This is exemplified for example, by the heated discussions over Proposition 227 and the referendum in June 1998 in California, which was designed to end bilingual education (Spanish and English) in that state (see Olsen 2009, Nieto and Bode 2007). The view has been that a bilingual education policy would undermine social cohesion just like the presence of large Muslim communities in Europe has been viewed as challenging national identities. Despite the different emphases on religion in Europe and language and ethnicity in the United States, there is a unifying element in this debate in that in both contexts those that undermine social cohesion and are perceived as a threat to society – Mexicans or Latinos in the United States and Muslims of different origins in Europe – are constructed as 'Other'.[6] Huntington (2004) controversially asserts that Mexicans are the single biggest threat to American identity. Zolberg and Woon (1999: 5) point out that Islam is like Spanish. Both 'are metonyms for the dangers that those most opposed to immigration perceive as looming ahead: loss of cultural identity, accompanied by disintegrative separatism or communal conflict'. These 'are emblematic of larger issues of inclusion and exclusion, which in the last instance are about identity' of the hosts and of the immigrants (Zolberg and Woon 1999: 28). European identity, they argue, remains embedded in Christian tradition in relation to which a highly diversified Muslim population in Europe constitute a visible 'Other' (see Triandafyllidou 2010, Mandel 2008). In the United States, the English language emerged early on as a socially cohesive element balancing religious, racial and ethnic diversity, making Spanish-speaking immigrants into the threatening 'other', and leading to such rejections of diversity as California's June 1998 passage of Proposition 227 outlawing bilingual education in the state.

Bilingual education in the United States emerged out of the civil rights movement of the 1960s, and the Civil Rights Act of 1964 in particular, which advocated equal protection, constitutional rights applied to language, and educational access for the undocumented. By 1972, California had voted in its first bilingual education law promoting mother-tongue teaching, followed by the Bilingual Bicultural Education Act of 1976 which required school districts to offer bilingual education programmes to each student. However, by the mid-1980s, the Latino population had risen sharply and anti-immigrant sentiment took over the debate (Olsen 2009). This led to the demise of bilingual education in California and a departure from the social programmes and civil rights of the 1970s and 1980s. Bilingual education was portrayed as being responsible for Latino school failure and framed in the politics of recognition. Most recently, there are signs of a new paradigm of bilingual and cross-cultural competences for all through curriculum redevelopments and a feeling that two languages are better than one. This albeit slow paradigm shift away from affirmative action programmes toward inclusivity is important also for debates in Europe where intercultural or multicultural education has often been framed as being more important for ethnic minority than majority students (e.g., Tomlinson 1990, Damanakis 2005). Yet, countries differ widely in their approach to language teaching. For example, Sweden and the Netherlands require 120 hours

---

6   I am not arguing here that Muslims do not play an important societal role in the United States but rather that they have not been constructed as the 'Other' partly because of their smaller numbers and partly because of their middle-class professional backgrounds and higher educational level compared to more working-class Muslim labour migrants in Europe who also originate from more rural areas in Turkey, Pakistan or the Maghreb.

professional development per annum dedicated language use and how to operate in multilingual, multiethnic classroom compared to just three hours in the United States (see also Gándara and Rumberger 2009). Reframing bilingual education policies in the United States and promoting multilingual language programmes that include the heritage and host language of the second generation could thus be another fruitful policy strategy for bonding together increasingly diverse groups of people in societies, in addition to revising school-level approaches (see also Gogolin and Neumann 2009).

Another major difference between Europe and the United States in the field of immigrant incorporation and the second generation revolves around diversity and cohesion. In Europe, as we have seen, there is a contested conceptual differentiation between multiculturalism and interculturalism. European theorists like Tariq Modood (1997, 2005a, 2005b, 2007) highlight that there are many different multiculturalisms and multiple ways in which the state can respond to culturally diverse societies. He defines multiculturalism as the political accommodation of minorities formed by immigration to Western countries from outside the West, and includes notions of democratic citizenship, individual rights and ethno-religious diversity. This focus on ethno-religious diversity (as opposed to linguistic diversity in the United States) is central to Modood's concept. Modood (2007) critiques North American theorist Will Kymlicka's liberal multiculturalism or societal-culture based multiculturalism (1989, 1995, 1998, 2001) because of its focus on group rights as well as cultural and political needs. Modood argues that Kymlicka's theory centres on language and is meant to protect and empower ethno-cultural groups, but his theory has a 'secularist bias' (i.e., state neutrality about language is impossible but state neutrality about religion is possible). In contrast, Modood maintains that states are multilingual, multi-religious and multicultural. Placing religious groups, and especially Muslims, outside multiculturalism as a policy idea, he maintains, might work in the United States and Canada, but makes multiculturalism irrelevant in Europe. The evidence from my study leads me to agree with Modood that multiculturalism is a form of integration informing actual policies and should not be demonized and narrowly defined in pluralistic terms, as many governments have done. Central to this is the idea that the state should promote cultural diversity *and* social cohesion (instead of being neutral) and that integration is a two-way process requiring adjustments from members of the national majority and minority communities. When policy takes this approach, the result is the formation of hybrid identities that we have seen in the case studies in this book. At least two of the schools – Goethe Gymnasium in Stuttgart and Darwin School in London – have allied multiculturalism and integration and thus promoted an inclusive form of citizenship either at the national (Darwin) or European (Goethe) level.

While Modood (2007) adds a cohesive, or integrative, element to multiculturalism – which Meer and Modood (2009) have called a 'civic rebalancing' of multiculturalism – a great deal of the American education literature focuses on cultural and structural explanations for assimilation, including 'new assimilation theory' (Alba and Nee 2003) and 'segmented assimilation theory' (Portes and Zhou 1993).[7] The obvious difference is that European theorists like Modood start from the ethnic minority perspective and rethink multiculturalism to include a cohesive element, whereas American scholars like Alba start from the opposite end and rethink the one-way assimilation approach into the host society and culture along more flexible, pluralistic lines. Both theoretical paradigms, however, emphasize a two-way process of assimilation or integration that requires some adaptation (to language and cultural elements) on the part of migrants and hosts, and a rethinking of national identity. Alba and Nee's (2003) approach departs from 'old assimilation theory' of middle-class White Anglo-Saxon Protestant identities (e.g., Warner and Srole 1945) and instead emphasizes that assimilation does not preclude retaining elements of ethnic culture. Reacting to the Chicago School's definition of assimilation as 'a diverse mainstream society in which people of different ethnic/racial origins and cultural heritages evolve a common culture that enables them to sustain a common national existence' (Alba and Nee 2003: 10), Alba and Nee (2003: 47) reconceptualize assimilation as an intergenerational process 'affected not just by the social, financial and human capital of immigrant families but also by the ways individuals use these resources within and apart from the existing structure of ethnic networks and institutions'.

Alba and Nee (2003) differentiate between three boundary-related processes in their new assimilation theory. Firstly, they identify boundary crossing, which implies that someone moves from one boundary to another without any real change to the boundary itself. This is also viewed as a 'bright boundary' (Alba 2005) with no ambiguity in the location of individuals with respect to it. Secondly, they identify boundary blurring, which implies that the social profile of a boundary has become less distinct and the clarity of the social distinction involved has become clouded. Assimilation of this type involves hybrid, or hyphenated, stages that allow individuals to feel as members of both the ethnic minority and the majority. Thirdly, they define boundary shifting as the relocation of a boundary so that populations once situated on one side are now included on the other. This transforms former outsiders into insiders. Alba and Nee (2003) maintain that the first two processes are currently relevant to second-generation migrants in the United States.[8] This is certainly also the case among the Turkish communities in this study, not only in

---

7 A third, less prominent, type of assimilation is 'straight-line assimilation' or 'bumpy-line assimilation' (Gans 1973) or 'old assimilation theory' (Warner and Srole 1945), based on the idea that assimilation unfolds over generations.

8 See Alba (2005) for a discussion of bright versus blurred boundaries with regard to citizenship in Germany (primarily ius sanguinis, i.e. bright boundary) and the United States (ius soli, i.e. blurred boundary); and religion where the boundary for Catholic Mexicans in the United States is blurred compared to the situation of Muslims in Europe. The bright versus blurred distinction thus reveals a meaningful difference between Europe and the United States.

the mainly working-class German and English schools, but in the more middle-class localities as well.

In contrast, 'segmented assimilation theory' argues that migrants assimilate into different sectors of society. One path, according to Portes and Zhou (1993) is acculturation and eventual integration into the white middle-class. The other leads in the opposite direction to poverty and assimilation into the underclass. Segmented, or downward, assimilation is theorized as being reinforced through phenotype, location and the absence of mobility ladders. Portes and Rumbaut (2001) verified the fundamental tenets of the theory in a major study into the second generation in San Diego and Miami. Drawing on twelve stories of different migrant families (from Mexico, Cuba, Nicaragua, Colombia, the Dominican Republic, Haiti, Jamaica, Trinidad, the Philippines, China, Laos, Cambodia, and Vietnam), the authors found that for some immigrants, such as refugees from Vietnam, Laos or Cambodia, the assimilation process is much easier because society chooses to welcome them and provide active governmental support and assistance. On the other hand, the unprivileged groups, generally non-white immigrants, are at risk of becoming a 'new rainbow underclass' that will join 'the masses of the dispossessed, compounding the spectacle of inequality and despair in America's inner cities' (Portes and Rumbaut 2001: 45) despite shifting to English as the preferred means of expression.

Segregation of migrant groups and socio-economically weaker sections of the ethnic majority community in particular inner-city areas is instrumental to segmented assimilation theory, and this is stronger in the United States than in Europe (see for example Thomson and Crul 2007, OECD 2008). The OECD Thematic Review on Migrant Education, for instance, highlights that migrant children in the United States (but also Greece, Canada, Austria and Belgium) are far more unevenly distributed and concentrated in specific areas and schools when compared with many European countries including Ireland, Spain, Italy, Portugal, the Netherlands and Germany. Alba (2005) therefore criticizes that segmented assimilation theory is less helpful in Europe than his notion of bright boundaries (or boundary crossing). My study does show some evidence for segmented assimilation theory, as in contexts of conflict such as Millroad School, 're-ethnicization' (Skrobanek 2009) prevents segments of the school society from assimilating or integrating into the mainstream and young people instead retreat into their ethnic identities with fewer chances of success. This process I observed is not so dissimilar from segmented assimilation (Portes, Fernández-Kelly and Haller 2005).

In the language of American scholars, there is no uniform assimilation path in either England or Germany (and probably also not in the rest of Europe) just like there is not the level of poverty and segregation to validate 'segmented assimilation'. Another problem with assimilation theories is their underlying ethnic majority perspective. As an alternative, it might be worth considering some of the European-developed theories, such as the notion of an integrative or 'civic' multiculturalism in the United States. Multiculturalism is no less a loaded and contested term than assimilation but variants of multiculturalism – such as 'inclusive multiculturalism' where schools promote diversity and cohesion or 'pluralistic multiculturalism' where schools only celebrate or promote diversity – are more likely to be found across Europe *and* the United States.

Segmented assimilation theory and transnationalism theories (see Bauböck 1994, Çaglar 2007, Smith 2007, Wessendorf 2007) are also problematized by Vivian Louie (2004, 2006: 539), who argues that her 'Dominican respondents were evaluating their [educational] outcomes against those of peers in the Dominican Republic and of co- and panethnic members in the United States [while her] Chinese respondents relied on a multi-layered ethnic filter, as they compared themselves to co- and panethnics across different segments of United States society'. The pessimism of Louie's Chinese sample regarding educational experiences was linked with an absence of parental homeland comparisons whereas her Dominican respondents drew strongly from a transnational perspective. A limitation of segmented assimilation theory, she argues, is the notion that individuals draw on a single frame of reference to assess their educational performance in the United States. In reality, however, contemporary migrant youth have multiple frames of reference that can inform their understandings, including the parental homeland (see also Levitt and Waters 2002). 'A key theme', Louie (2009: 542) observes, 'is that ties to the homeland offer a way for the second generation to cope with the ways in which their groups are viewed and often marginalized in the United States' – a process that has been termed 're-ethnicization' in some of the European literature (see Skrobanek 2009). In contexts of lack of opportunity combined with conflict and discrimination, migrants may develop stronger ethnic identities and attachments to their homeland, which was clearly illustrated in Millroad School, where we saw that Turkish minority youth retreated into their own community and privileged Turkishness.

This brings me to a third and final theme on the factors affecting second-generation integration, and identity formation and schooling in particular. There has been a plethora of research in the United States in recent years (some of which adopts a transatlantic perspective) that considers educational performance and inequalities – not identities – as a marker for successful integration (e.g., Holdaway, Crul and Roberts 2009, Alba and Silberman 2009, Crul and Holdaway 2009, Zirkel 2008, Pong and Hao 2007).[9] Europe, by contrast, has seen an 'avalanche' around the concept of identity. According to Bauman (2001), identity has become a prism through which other life aspects are examined in our globalizing world that offers a range of identities to choose from. Where North American scholars

---

9 A similar body of research is of course also found in Europe including Heath and Brinbaum (2007) who looked at seven European countries and the United States. They found that the educational disadvantage of migrant children from Europe is explained by the educational position of the parents but that some non-European immigrant groups continue to be disadvantaged even after controlling for parental background (see also Gillborn and Mirza 2000).

have investigated identity, the focus has been largely on ethnic and racial identities rather than political (or citizenship) identities and the connections between political and ethnic identities in schools and society (e.g., Alba 1990, Waters 1990, 1999, Kasinitz, Mollenkopf and Waters 2004, Kasinitz et al. 2008). Arguably, this underscores that race and ethnicity are still more powerful concepts in the mindset of North American scholars compared to European researchers, and points to a need for more research into how identity processes shape integration.

These studies do provide some hint that second-generation migrants do not just have multidimensional ethnic *and* racial identities but also political identities. But these other identities are often left unexplored. For example, Kasinitz et al. (2008) observed a 'New Yorican' ethno-local identity but all too often 'asked about ethnic and racial identity' only. Alternative identities, such as school, friends and family, were almost completely untouched by the study. Given the complexities of ethnic, political and 'new' alternative identities found among ethnic majority and Turkish minority youth in London and Stuttgart, I would expect to find more nuanced political identities in the lives of young people in the United States as well – be it in New York, Miami or San Diego. To their credit, class, gender, and an American national identity were occasionally referenced in these studies but de-emphasized in the overall findings. This American identity research tradition, and the limited study of the interface between ethnic and political identities, particularly among educationalists and sociologists, requires further unpacking.

The American literature points to socio-economic background, and how it intersects with ethnicity, as being important for identity formation. For instance, Waters (1999) found in her study of second-generation West Indian (Afro-Caribbean) youth in New York that identities are affected by class status, race and gender. She outlines three paths of identity development: identifying as African Americans, identifying as ethnic or hyphenated Americans, and adopting or keeping an immigrant identity. West Indians who identified as African American tended to be from disadvantaged socio-economic backgrounds whereas middle-class youth were more likely to identify as West Indian Americans. Boys, she argued, felt more racial solidarity with African Americans and girls felt less independent than their male counterparts due to parental control. Lee (2004: 317) comments that 'Waters' study helps us to understand how race, ethnicity and class interact to shape the black second generations' identities and assimilation processes'. Butterfield (2004), who questions Waters' threefold typology, further illustrates how ethnicity and class intersect. Her working-class Afro-Caribbean youth, who mainly reside in Brooklyn, developed a strong ethnic identity whereas her middle-class sample, who lived in Queens, placed less emphasis on the ethnic aspect of their hybrid identities.[10] Lee (2004: 333), by contrast, found that 'working-class Korean Americans appeared to be shedding their ethnic identity more quickly and willingly than their middle-class counterparts', because they grew up with fewer ties to the Korean community and felt closer to other working-class minorities. However, although it addresses class (which my study does as well), the literature is rather silent on the political identities of these young people, including local, regional, national and global identities.

On the other hand, although the North American and European scholarship identifies a range of factors shaping educational attainment, the role of schools in the process of adaptation and identity negotiation is similarly limited, although a few studies address the issue. For instance, a study of schooling and diversity in Portugal employing segmented assimilation theory (Marques, Valente Rosa and Lopes Martins 2007) concludes that downward assimilation is less likely in Europe due to the stronger welfare state, with the exception of southern European countries, which have weaker welfare states (see also Green, Preston and Germen Janmaat 2006). This study argues that ethnic minority groups that do not have sufficient social and cultural capital to do well in education struggle to integrate into the Portuguese education system, and the authors maintain that the incapacity of the school system to reduce the educational disadvantages of migrant children can be interpreted as a sign of 'a weak state' (Marques, Valente Rosa and Lopes Martins 2007). The importance of government policy and the role of schools is further underlined by Holdaway and Alba (2009) and Fraga and Els (2009) who argue that, besides socio-economic positioning, racial discrimination, family cultures, and aspirations, the formation and implementation of policy at the school (or state) level affects educational attainment. This results in Indians and Chinese outperforming the ethnic majority population in the United States, and is also linked with Afro-Caribbeans and Mexicans in particular lagging behind.[11] On the other hand, the Chinese tend to be educated in prestigious public schools whereas the Dominicans see Catholic schools as a way of avoiding bad neighbourhood schools and the West Indians and Mexicans remain in weaker public schools with conflict levels similar to the ones we saw at Millroad School in London (see also Louie and Holdaway 2009). While these studies underline the role of schools, they

---

10   Drawing on the same decade-long Immigrant Second Generation in Metropolitan New York Study, Warikoo (2004) observed a new type of ethnic identity what she calls 'cosmopolitan identity' among her sample of Indo-Caribbeans. She also found that none of her respondents simply identified as American but had developed hybrid multidimensional identities. Yet, here too, political and alternative identities remain largely unexplored.

11   This is similar to the achievement gaps in England and other European countries. In England, for instance, Chinese and Indians outperform the ethnic majority population whereas (male) Afro-Caribbeans as well as migrant students of Pakistani, Bangladeshi and Turkish descent – all of whom are Muslims – struggle and are also disadvantaged in housing and the labour market (e.g., Enneli, Modood and Bradley 2005, Modood, Berthoud and Lakey 1997).

do not address identity as a key marker for inclusion and reveal little about how integration levels and identity negotiations can differ within a country – let alone a city – as a result of different mediation of education policies.

Studies have also shown that the ethnic makeup of schools' administration and teaching force can matter for the achievement of ethnic minority students. Gibson and Hidalgo (2009) found that inclusive teaching staffs had a positive impact on educational outcomes and integration of migrant students. Gibson and Hidalgo's study of highly mobile migrant farmworkers in the United States found that 'the advisors create spaces of belonging within a larger educational context in which migrant students all too frequently experience alienation and marginalization' (Gibson and Hidalgo 2009: 702). The authors argued for the need to ensure that migrant youth have role models with whom they can identify in schools and who can connect them with the resources needed for success in school. My own study indicated that schools like Tannberg Hauptschule (62.4 per cent ethnic minority students compared with 2.9 per cent ethnic minority teachers) and Goethe Gymnasium (24 per cent ethnic minority students and 0.6 per cent ethnic minority teachers) in Stuttgart highlight the discrepancies in Germany between a multicultural student population and a largely monocultural teacher population. This invisibility of role models is arguably counterproductive to the notion of intercultural education and does little to facilitate the integration of the second generation. The situation was somewhat different in England, at least in Millroad School (80.4 per cent ethnic minority students compared with 68.2 per cent ethnic minority teachers), whereas Darwin School (27.8 per cent ethnic minority students and 5.2 per cent ethnic minority teachers) was more similar to the German schools in terms of student-teacher backgrounds. Clearly, having a multiethnic staff does not automatically lead to higher levels of integration, particularly not if staff members privilege ethnic and cultural identities over commonalty, as was the case in Millroad School in London. However, it could represent one means to ensure integration is seen as a two-way process.

Unlike American scholarship, some recent European literature has begun to more explicitly address the role of schooling in shaping interaction and civic identity formation among the second generation. Most notably, Sunier (2009: 1556) carried out a study of Dutch and British schools and concluded that schools 'are crucial sites where principles of national civil incorporation are transmitted to pupils'. Although the schools Sunier discussed resembled each other in terms of neighbourhood, ethnic composition and policies adopted by the school board, Sunier found that each had its own way of managing ethnic and religious diversity, as well as migration. Sunier draws on a larger project of four schools in Berlin, Paris, Rotterdam and London (see Schiffauer et al. 2004) and employs the concept of 'civil enculturation', which he conceptualizes as a trajectory that transforms individuals into citizens. 'Once individuals in any given nation-state go through a process of discursive assimilation or civil enculturation, they may be expected to acquire specific competences that enable them to meet the civic requirements and conventions of that particular state' (Sunier 2009: 1557). Civil cultures, he argues, are mainly received through explicit and implicit curricula at school.[12] This raises questions about the ways in which schools reflect society. Sunier (2009) and Schiffauer et al. (2004) provide convincing findings but I find their study to be limited since it includes just one school per country (which the authors acknowledge). This represents a major caveat, especially in light of this book's discussions of four secondary schools in London and Stuttgart, which clearly showed that schools *within* a country mediate the national political culture in rather different ways and, as a result, often have different ethos (i.e., approaches to mediating policies, for example ethnocentric or inclusive) and curricular interpretations. Sunier (2009) and Schiffauer et al's (2004) work, important as it is, thus misses a crucial point, which this book has addressed.

Only recently has transatlantic research on immigrant incorporation and the second generation begun to move away from a focus on migrants themselves and the social and cultural capital they bring with them to studies of the national context (e.g., Bloemraad 2006, Crul and Vermeulen 2003, Heckmann and Schnapper 2003) and institutional factors (e.g., Schiffauer et al. 2004, Pong and Hao 2007, Holdaway, Crul and Roberts 2009). However, most of these studies continue to focus on the structure of the educational systems and the educational inequalities and performance outcomes of different ethnic groups. This approach downplays the importance of identity as a marker for integration and the role of school dynamics such as peer cultures, ethos and curriculum interpretations in the process of identity development.

This book not only set out to address this empirical gap in the transatlantic research literature, but also reconceptualizes the way we think about contemporary identity formation, and tries to unravel the complex factors shaping these identity negotiations. In contrast to a great deal of the American scholarship, I did not approach my ethnic majority and Turkish minority youth in England and Germany by asking about their ethnic and racial or religious identities per se but, much more openly, about their identities in general and the communities they felt they belonged to. In contrast to a great deal of European research, I also looked beyond the outcomes (i.e., attainment levels) education systems produce and the factors involved in that, to ways in which schools within a country and between countries respond to government policies. As Holdaway, Crul and Roberts argue (2009: 1395), 'national policy on a particular issue may be subject to substantial variation in its implementation at the level of local education authority and again at the level of the individual school'.

In sum, I have argued in this section that Europe and the United States have responded differently to the challenges arising from migration-related cultural

---

12   For a comparative curriculum analysis of history, geography and citizenship education in Greece, England and Germany, see Faas forthcoming.

and ethnic diversity, both at a theoretical and empirical level. There is, however, considerable cross-fertilization with European scholars drawing on US-developed concepts and American scholars turning more towards cross-national research frameworks. The main contributions of my study to the transatlantic debates decribed in this section first include evidence that moves discussions of second-generation integration beyond an emphasis on educational attainment toward identity as a key concept for social inclusion. Secondly, I have provided evidence that 'othering' processes are still intact both at school level and in societies at large but can be addressed by developing inclusive governmental and school policy approaches. Thirdly, my research on schools in two countries has shown that researchers and policy-makers should not be deterred from common challenges of how to balance cultural diversity and social cohesion because of conceptual differences (around multiculturalism, interculturalism and assimilation); despite their different pathways, these ideas converge around the need to rethink the nation-state and other social entities along more multiethnic lines whilst asking migrants and their children to adapt to their new environments. Finally, I have presented evidence to further promote comparative research that unravels the complexity of factors affecting integration and identity development within and between countries. I now discuss in greater detail the implications of the main findings from this comparative study and relate them to theory and policy.

Implications for Theory and Policy

The main theoretical implication of this book is the need for researchers to rethink the notion of identity and to explore the interconnections between ethnic and political identities. As mentioned at the beginning, previous studies focused on either white and ethnic minority identities or citizenship identities, thus underplaying the ways in which the two intersect. This is especially the case in the United States where there has been a plethora of research into ethnic and racial identities, but relatively little acknowledgement of political and alternative identities such as popular culture, animal rights, vegetarianism, anti-war movement and environmentalism (see for instance Dolby 2001, Heath, Martin and Elgenius 2007). These 'newer', or alternative, identities were also not the main focus of this book but the very open-ended nature of my questions nevertheless allowed young people to voice such identities, if they thought of them as important. One example is Zafer, a Turkish boy at Goethe Gymnasium, who signalled his Turkishness by wearing red jumpers and a necklace in the shape of the moon star on the Turkish flag. Another example comes from the case of several Italian boys in the German schools who wore blue shirts to signal identification with the 'azzuri' football team.

When I discussed post-structuralist approaches to identity earlier on, we saw that Nayak (2001: 183), for instance, argued that 'post-structuralist analyses investigate the multiple interconnections between race, gender, sexuality and social class'. However, my data suggests that the dynamics between youth are not simply ethnic dynamics but also political dynamics involving categories of citizenship such as British or European citizenship. Both ethnic majority and Turkish minority youth had no singular identity but employed hybrid Turkish British/German, Swabian German and German European identities as a result of a complex interplay of governmental policies, their schooling and community experience, social class positioning and culture, ethnicity and migration history, and likely other factors not yet entertained in this study.

Although not explicitly examined in this book given that most of my respondents were fifteen, age may nevertheless have some impact on identity construction as well. There is a good deal of research in Europe, mostly among developmental psychologists such as Barrett (1996, 2001), and Barrett and Short (1992), who argue that a shift in young people's self-categorizations takes place between the ages of six and ten.[13] Their research found that by ten years of age, youth tended to categorize themselves as Europeans as well as English, and they had thus acquired, in addition to their national identity, a supranational European identity. This shift was associated by Barrett and his collaborators with an increase in geographical knowledge of Europe (see also Savvides and Faas, forthcoming, for a comparison of 15-year-olds at Darwin School with 17-year-olds at the European School at Culham in England). I did find some evidence in my study that points toward an age-related dimension in identity development. At Millroad School in London, a group of four ethnic majority boys felt that racialized discourses and ethnic tensions increased with age. 'When you're like in years 5 and 6, you don't see colour. Like you'll just, in year 5, you'll just speak to anyone, whereas like as people get older, it's like they gradually got into their groups'. This suggests the need to include age in the theoretical model for researching youth identities below.

It is also important for our understanding of identity development to consider how terms such as 'being German', 'being Turkish' or 'being European' have both political and ethnic connotations, referring to categories of citizenship and ethnic or even religious origin. The concept of citizenship also relates differently to both political and ethnic dimensions. For example, Germany has prioritized the principle of 'ius sanguinis' (citizenship by birth/ethnic origin) whereas England has favoured the 'ius soli' approach (citizenship by territoriality, see Brubaker 1992). Since many 15-year-olds in this study produced different forms of hybrid identities by placing varying emphasis on ethnic and political aspects of identity, I offer a new theoretical model that takes account of these realities by including both ethnic and political dimensions and other factors affecting contemporary identity negotiations. These are summarized in Figure 8.1.

---

13 Sociologists and educators have recently also weighed into these debates and noticed underdeveloped supranational identities at primary school age compared with adolescents (e.g., Papoulia-Tzelpi, Hegstrup and Ross 2005).

Figure 8.1 Theoretical framework for the analysis of youth identities

The diagram may have general relevance and could well help future comparative identity studies in Europe and beyond. The scheme is particularly useful in the current challenge of responding to migration-related diversity in Europe and the United States as it considers the socio-economic, ethno-religious and cultural diversity of populations within Europe and beyond, both among ethnic majority and ethnic minority communities. The discussions throughout this book suggest that main factors (e.g., school policy approaches, socio-economic positioning) and subsidiary factors (e.g., ethnicity, generation, age) shape identity negotiations, and I have argued that the within-country differences in political identities among students have mainly to do with different school-level policy approaches. In addition, the findings of the study reveal that it is more important to be aware of how these factors are intertwined rather than statistically proving or disproving one or the other.

Inclusive Citizenship and Social Cohesion

Let me return now to my discussion about US-developed theories, including segmented assimilation and new assimilation theory, and elaborate on some of the differences from the multicultural perspective found in some of the European research. These theoretical debates are useful for our empirical research into the ways in which inclusive citizenship and school policy approaches impact on integration and identity formation. I agree with Thomson and Crul (2007) that the concept of segmented assimilation suffers on empirical grounds, both in European schools and societies at large as the theory is very much dependent on particular structural features of American society including higher levels of segregation. Having said that, migrants should neither be expected to eventually assimilate into mainstream society nor should this become an espoused political strategy, because as we have seen in Tannberg Hauptschule, such an ethnocentric assimilation-based approach prevented the group of young Turks from identifying with Europe as a political identity. The political and educational challenge that needs to be addressed is therefore not one of how best to assimilate newcomers into the majority context (or different segments of the majority society), but how to include them and mobilize their linguistic and cultural capital to promote inclusive citizenship models and cohesive school policy approaches, as we have seen both at Goethe Gymnasium ('multicultural Europeanness') and Darwin School ('multicultural Britishness').

On the other hand, this study provides no empirical evidence that the promotion of multiculturalism, or cultural pluralism, in schools and society at large is beneficial for either ethnic minorities or the ethnic majorities. Quite the contrary, the case of Millroad School demonstrated that ethnic conflicts in the area surrounding the school spilled over into the school and resulted in ethnic divisions between the African Caribbean and Turkish communities who 're-ethnicized' and strongly emphasized their ethnic identities. However, the school conflict was not necessarily reduced by mediating national agendas through the politics of cultural diversity. Although the school principal tried to promote intercultural awareness and organized special events to bond the conflicting communities together, it appeared to be too ambitious an agenda to try and disseminate 'good practice' from within the school into the local community.

There is evidence that the politics of multiculturalism produces higher levels of integration when allied with social cohesion – an approach I call 'inclusive or integrative multiculturalism'. In this study, this approach allowed young people to engage with the British/German or European identities on offer. We have seen that both Goethe Gymnasium and Darwin School adopted such approaches, with the former integrating students into a multiethnic concept of Europe by promoting multicultural and European agendas whereas the latter school integrated students into a multiethnic concept of Britishness by promoting cultural diversity and social cohesion.[14] The main policy implication is therefore not to promote cultural diversity or assimilationist approaches, but to combine the two – as has been the case in both Goethe Gymnasium and Darwin School – and promote inclusive multiethnic and multi-religious models of citizenship at national and European levels to address the issue of marginalized communities. There is considerable potential for political concepts such as 'multicultural Britishness' or 'multicultural Europeanness' to be a common ground for both ethnic majority and ethnic minority youth to negotiate their political identities. This is underscored by the fact that a regional identity (i.e., 'being English' or 'being Swabian') was not accessible for Turkish minority youth and the same was the case for a global identity which was even more unfamiliar than a European identity to nearly all 15-year-olds – only Cornelia at Goethe Gymnasium saw herself as having a global identity. In sum, both the politics of multiculturalism and the politics of Europe can become an integrative and cohesive device if thought of in multiethnic ways.[15] This, as we have seen, allows 15-year-olds to negotiate new hybrid identities by drawing on both their ethnic and cultural identities and the identities of the societies they now live in.

In many ways, these empirical findings and policy implications provide evidence for Modood's (2007) defence of multiculturalism as a public policy approach and his reasoning that multiculturalism and integration are not diametrically-opposed concepts and must be brought together to inform one another. Schools and governments who follow this approach find it easier to bond together their culturally diverse populations with positive implications for their political identity negotiations. Schools that embark on an ethnocentric (or Eurocentric) approach – given the leeway teachers and school management have to mediate governmental policies – run the risk of alienating ethnic minority communities while those schools which simply celebrate cultural and religious diversity might reinforce ethnic tensions and conflicts. Such findings also send a note of caution to all those educators and policy-makers who are currently returning to more integrationist or even assimilationist approaches in Europe and, at the same time, they provide a much-needed European-developed theoretical and empirically-grounded framework for analysing issues of integration and identity negotiation. Alba's (2005) boundary-related concept, as we have seen, has some value in the European context but it is couched in an assimilatory ethnic majority framework whereas the notion of 'inclusive citizenship' (multicultural citizenship at national or supranational level) is couched in a more pluralistic – yet socially cohesive – ethnic minority perspective.

---

14   Koopmans et al. (2005) agree that there is a need to balance diversity and cohesion, and that too much cultural pluralism can lead to parallel societies.

15   See Nieto and Bode (2007) for a discussion of the positive impacts of multicultural education.

Linked with this issue of balancing diversity and cohesion, and worth mentioning in the current context of Turkish EU accession, is the potential of a multiethnic multifaith concept of Europe for the identity formation of marginalized Muslim communities in Europe. The notion of 'multicultural Europeanness', as we have seen in Goethe Gymnasium, was associated with Turkish youth engaging with Europe as a political identity and expressing national-European identities. If however, Europe is conceptualized as an exclusionary monocultural Christian concept, as was the case in Tannberg Hauptschule, then Turkish students struggle to connect with a European identity. Politicians and educators in Europe are therefore presented with the challenge of constructing and promoting an inclusive, multi-religious model of Europe – one which addresses the issue of marginalized Muslim communities and promotes multicultural and traditional European values. As this study shows, ethnic minority youth seemed to be able to gain from the opportunities associated with the European knowledge economy if Europe was reconceptualized in multiethnic terms. This might not only help prevent Eurocentric education but could also help Turkish and other young people forge a loyalty to Europe.[16] Further studies into the Turkish community at different stages during EU membership negotiations would be welcome. As Turkey gets politically closer to Europe and prepares for accession, young people's political identities are likely to be affected. There is already good evidence in my data that some Turkish 15-year-olds make their European identification dependent on their country of origin joining the EU.

To sum up, this book set out to explore the ways in which processes of European integration, globalization and migration are intertwined and challenge national identities, and how young people understand their identities in light of these different policy agendas. One of the main findings was that school-level actors mediated national government policies and that these school approaches made different identities available to students. The forms these identities took in the various school and country contexts depended on a variety of factors including socio-economic background and school policy approaches (although it was not possible to determine which of these mattered the most). The finding that students crossed ethnic lines in friendship groups at both Tannberg Hauptschule and Goethe Gymnasium in Germany, together with the generally similar socio-economic background of the sample of Turkish students across all research sites, suggests that the *school approach* mattered a great deal for integration outcomes like interethnic friendships and identity negotiations.

This study has further raised important questions about what sorts of political and educational approaches work best to bond together diverse groups of people whilst at the same time promoting maintenance of their cultural and linguistic heritage. The book provides conclusive evidence that when policy-makers and

---

16   Similarly, the concept of the nation-state could be rethought along multiethnic multifaith lines, as is the case in England, and thus become a playing field where social cohesion and cultural diversity are promoted simultaneously.

educators bring together notions of multiculturalism and integration, ethnic minority students feel more included in schools. At the same time, the study shows how celebrating diversity or promoting assimilation-based approaches can be unhelpful for attaining social cohesion and connecting young people to a common identity. If anything, such exclusionary approaches lead to re-ethnicization and even reinforce ethnic tensions. Overall, the case studies in this book shed light on the theoretical and empirical commonalities and differences raised by the study of immigrant integration, and illuminate new avenues for policy-making and European and transatlantic debates on immigrant incorporation and the emergence of new forms of political identities.

Appendix 1 – Interviewees

Tannberg Hauptschule in Stuttgart (Student focus groups)

Name (Pseudonym)	Sex	Age	Ethnicity	Education
Serpil	F	15	Turkish	Vocational
Azize	F	16	Turkish	Vocational
Sema	F	16	Turkish	Vocational
Zerrin	F	15	Turkish	Vocational
Bülent	M	15	Turkish	Vocational
Cengis	M	15	Turkish	Vocational
Haka	M	15	Turkish	Vocational
Zeheb	M	15	Turkish	Vocational
Tamer	M	16	Turkish	Vocational
Yeliz	F	15	Turkish	Vocational
Umay	F	15	Turkish	Vocational
Ugur	M	15	Turkish	Vocational
Cari	F	15	Turkish	Vocational
Julia	F	15	German	Vocational
Verena	F	16	German	Vocational
Andrea	F	15	German	Vocational
Manuela	F	16	German	Vocational
Jan	M	15	German	Vocational
Dominik	M	16	German	Vocational
Florian	M	15	German	Vocational
Michael	M	15	German	Vocational
Benjamin	M	16	German	Vocational
Tobias	M	15	German	Vocational
Jessica	F	16	German	Vocational
Franziska	F	15	German	Vocational
Sebastian	M	15	German	Vocational

All Turkish-origin students are second-generation, i.e. born in Germany. Those older than 15 usually repeated a school year at some point.

Goethe Gymnasium in Stuttgart (Student focus groups)

Name (Pseudonym)	Sex	Age	Ethnicity	Education
Zeynep	F	16	Turkish	University track
Semra	F	16	Turkish	University track
Nilgün	F	16	Turkish	University track
Nerhim	F	16	Turkish	University track
Zafer	M	16	Turkish	University track
Yener	M	15	Turkish	University track
Sevelin	M	15	Turkish	University track
Irem	M	16	Turkish	University track
Pelin	F	15	Turkish	University track
Nurhan	F	15	Turkish	University track
Aysegül	F	15	Turkish	University track
Melik	M	15	Turkish	University track
Ismet	M	15	Turkish	University track
Sarah	F	16	German	University track
Anna	F	15	German	University track
Lena	F	16	German	University track
Sophie	F	15	German	University track
Maxmilian	M	15	German	University track
Alexander	M	15	German	University track
Leon	M	15	German	University track
Tim	M	15	German	University track
Jonas	M	15	German	University track
Lisa	F	15	German	University track
Marie	F	16	German	University track
Vanessa	F	15	German	University track
Felix	M	15	German	University track
Kai	M	16	German	University track

All Turkish-origin students are second-generation, i.e. born in Germany. Those older than 15 usually repeated a school year at some point.

Millroad School in London (Student focus groups)

Name (Pseudonym)	Sex	Age	Ethnicity	Education
Harika	F	15	Turkish Cypriot	Low achieving
Jihan	F	15	Turkish Cypriot	Low achieving
Nagihan	F	15	Turkish Cypriot	Low achieving
Tulip	F	15	Turkish Cypriot	Low achieving
Serap	F	15	Turkish	Low achieving
Yildiran	M	15	Turkish	Low achieving
Muhammad	M	15	Turkish	Low achieving
Khan	M	15	Turkish	Low achieving
Onan	M	15	Turkish Cypriot	Low achieving
Halil	M	15	Turkish	Low achieving
Baris	M	15	Turkish	Low achieving
Sarila	F	15	Turkish Cypriot	Low achieving
Karli	F	15	Turkish Cypriot	Low achieving
Hollie	F	14	British	Low achieving
Ellie	F	14	British	Low achieving
Lucy	F	14	British	Low achieving
Katie	F	14	British	Low achieving
Bill	M	15	British	Low achieving
Ken	M	15	British	Low achieving
Dave	M	15	British	Low achieving
John	M	15	British	Low achieving
Amie	F	14	British	Low achieving
Eddie	M	14	British	Low achieving
Joe	M	14	British	Low achieving
Paul	M	14	British	Low achieving
Kelly	F	14	British	Low achieving

All mainland Turkish students are first-generation migrants, i.e. born in Turkey whereas all Turkish Cypriot students are second-generation, i.e. born in England.

Darwin School in London (Student focus groups)

Name (Pseudonym)	Sex	Age	Ethnicity	Education
Akasma	F	14	Turkish	High achieving
Gülay	F	14	Turkish	High achieving
Elvan	F	14	Turkish	High achieving
Fairuza	F	14	Turkish	High achieving
Mehmet	M	15	Turkish Cypriot	High achieving
Zeki	M	15	Turkish	High achieving
Osman	M	15	Turkish	High achieving
Erol	M	14	Turkish	High achieving
Adem	M	14	Turkish	High achieving
Afet	F	14	Turkish Cypriot	High achieving
Kemal	M	15	Turkish	High achieving
Neylan	F	15	Turkish Cypriot	High achieving
Elizabeth	F	15	British	High achieving
Victoria	F	14	British	High achieving
Anne	F	15	British	High achieving
Sophie	F	15	British	High achieving
Jennifer	F	15	British	High achieving
Richard	M	15	British	High achieving
James	M	15	British	High achieving
William	M	15	British	High achieving
Henry	M	15	British	High achieving
Matthew	M	14	British	High achieving
Adam	M	15	British	High achieving
Charlotte	F	15	British	High achieving
Charles	M	14	British	High achieving
Olivia	F	15	British	High achieving

All mainland Turkish students are first-generation migrants, i.e. born in Turkey whereas all Turkish Cypriot students are second-generation, i.e. born in England.

Student interviews in the four schools

Name (Pseudonym)	Sex	Age	Ethnicity	School
Sema	F	16	Turkish	Tannberg
Cari	F	15	Turkish	Tannberg
Bülent	M	15	Turkish	Tannberg
Tamer	M	16	Turkish	Tannberg
Andrea	F	15	German	Tannberg
Iris	F	16	German	Tannberg
Ralf	M	16	German	Tannberg
Peter	M	15	German	Tannberg
Fatima	F	16	Turkish	Goethe
Mariam	F	16	Turkish	Goethe
Zafer	M	15	Turkish	Goethe
Ali	M	15	Turkish	Goethe
Nadine	F	15	German	Goethe
Cornelia	F	16	German	Goethe
Andreas	M	15	German	Goethe
Samuel	M	16	German	Goethe
Sefika	F	15	Turkish	Millroad
Olcay	F	15	Turkish Cypriot	Millroad
Tarik	M	15	Turkish	Millroad
Erkan	M	15	Turkish	Millroad
Emma	F	15	British	Millroad
Harriet	F	16	British	Millroad
Stephen	M	15	British	Millroad
Robert	M	15	British	Millroad
Safak	F	14	Turkish Cypriot	Darwin
Sibel	F	15	Turkish	Darwin
Toker	M	15	Turkish	Darwin
Mustafa	M	15	Turkish Cypriot	Darwin
Zoe	F	15	British	Darwin
Katie	F	15	British	Darwin
Owen	M	15	British	Darwin
Ian	M	15	British	Darwin

All mainland Turkish students are first-generation migrants, i.c. born in Turkey whereas all Turkish Cypriot students are second-generation, i.e. born in England.

Teacher interviewees in the four schools

Name (Pseudonym)	Position	School	Date interviewed
Mr. Müller	Deputy Principal	Tannberg	April 2, 2004
Mr. Koch	Citizenship Co-ordinator	Tannberg	February 13, 2004
Ms. Brandt	Geography Co-ordinator	Tannberg	February 20, 2004
Ms. Klein	RE Co-ordinator	Tannberg	February 18, 2004
Ms. Fischer	Principal	Goethe	March 1, 2004
Mr. Meier	Citizenship Co-ordinator	Goethe	April 1, 2004
Ms. Adler	Geography Co-ordinator	Goethe	April 5, 2004
Ms. Weber	RE Co-ordinator	Goethe	April 2, 2004
Mr. Moore	Principal	Millroad	March 17, 2004
Mr. Wilson	Citizenship Co-ordinator	Millroad	March 18, 2004
Mr. Taylor	Geography Co-ordinator	Millroad	March 17, 2004
Mr. Green	History Co-ordinator	Millroad	April 22, 2004
Ms. Williams	Deputy Principal	Darwin	May 12, 2004
Mr. Davis	Citizenship Co-ordinator	Darwin	April 30, 2004
Ms. Smith	Geography Co-ordinator	Darwin	May 4, 2004
Ms. Brown	RE Co-ordinator	Darwin	April 28, 2004

Appendix 2 – Student Questionnaire

This questionnaire is designed to help me gain an understanding of your views about England and Europe. To help me get the best results, I would really appreciate it if you could **answer all questions** as best as you can. All your responses will be confidential.

ABOUT YOU

1. What sex are you? Please circle one.

   Male   Female

2. Please tick which category best describes your ethnic origin or descent.

White British/Irish	
Other White	
Turkish	
Indian	
Pakistani	
Bangladeshi	
Chinese	
Other Asian	
Black Caribbean	
Black African	
Other Black	
White and Black Caribbean	
White and Asian	
White and Black African	
Other Mixed	
Other (please state)	

3. What is your father's job title?

_____

4. What is your mother's job title?

_____

ABOUT CITIZENSHIP

5. What do you associate with the word *citizenship*?
   Circle as many items as appropriate.

Family	Skin colour	Education	Religion
Student/Pupil	Europe	Age	London
England	Boy/Girl	Britain	Ethnic origin/descent

6. How strongly do you associate the word *citizen* with the following things?
   Circle one number for each row (from 1 = not at all to 5 = very strongly).

   A citizen is someone who …

	Not at all				Very strongly
belongs to a community	1	2	3	4	5
votes in elections	1	2	3	4	5
lives in a country	1	2	3	4	5
has responsibilities	1	2	3	4	5
is over eighteen years old	1	2	3	4	5
has rights	1	2	3	4	5
is born in a country	1	2	3	4	5
has a passport	1	2	3	4	5
understands politics	1	2	3	4	5
obeys the law	1	2	3	4	5
is a national of a country	1	2	3	4	5
takes part in discussions	1	2	3	4	5
has parents who are citizens	1	2	3	4	5
other things (please state)	1	2	3	4	5

   _____

7. What country are you a citizen of? Please write down your answer.

   _____

8. Please number the following in order of importance (1, 2, 3, 4, 5), starting with 1 as the term which is most important to you.

Britain	
Europe	
London	
Region	
World	

9. What country are your parents citizens of? Please write down your answer.

_____

ABOUT ENGLAND

10. How strongly do you associate the word *England* with the following things? Please circle one number for each row (from 1 = not at all to 5 = very strongly).

	Not at all				Very strongly
Monarchy/Royal family	1	2	3	4	5
White people	1	2	3	4	5
English language	1	2	3	4	5
Weather	1	2	3	4	5
Celebrities	1	2	3	4	5
Power	1	2	3	4	5
Christian country	1	2	3	4	5
Saint George's flag	1	2	3	4	5
The euro	1	2	3	4	5
Football	1	2	3	4	5
Part of Europe	1	2	3	4	5
Multicultural country	1	2	3	4	5
Large families	1	2	3	4	5
Other (please state)	1	2	3	4	5

_____

11. Please circle one of the following. I see myself as …

British   English   Scottish   Welsh   a Londoner   None of these

Please write down some reasons for your answer.

_____

12. How much are the following issues covered in school?
    Please answer by circling one number for each row
    (from 1 = never to 5 = very often).

	Never				Very often
London	1	2	3	4	5
Europe	1	2	3	4	5
Britain	1	2	3	4	5
England	1	2	3	4	5
Global issues	1	2	3	4	5

ABOUT EUROPE

13. Do you see yourself as *European*? Please circle one.

Yes   No

Please write down some reasons for your answer.

_____

14. How strongly do you associate the word *Europe* with the following things?
    Circle one number for each row (from 1 = not at all to 5 = very strongly).

	Not at all				Very strongly
United countries (EU)	1	2	3	4	5
White people	1	2	3	4	5
Continent	1	2	3	4	5
Football	1	2	3	4	5
Christian culture	1	2	3	4	5
Wealthy countries	1	2	3	4	5
Power	1	2	3	4	5
Common currency (euro)	1	2	3	4	5
Open-minded (e.g. sex)	1	2	3	4	5
Strong family bonds	1	2	3	4	5
Advanced countries	1	2	3	4	5
Large families	1	2	3	4	5
Holidays	1	2	3	4	5
Common policies	1	2	3	4	5
Other (please state)	1	2	3	4	5

_____

15. From the following list, please circle the countries which you think are in Europe.

France	Bulgaria	Israel	Morocco
Tunisia	Netherlands	Italy	Malta
Slovenia	Russia	Portugal	Lithuania
Turkey	Finland	Germany	Croatia
Britain	Norway	Denmark	Spain
Poland	Estonia	Greece	Ukraine

16. Would you ever want to work and live in another European country? Please circle one.

Yes   No

If Yes, please write down the names of two European countries you would prefer to work and live in.

1. _____   2. _____

17. Should the following political issues be dealt with by the European Union (EU) or the national (British) government? Please tick one box for each row.

	European Union	British Government
Terrorism		
Immigration		
Education		
Justice		
Employment		
Equal opportunities		
Pollution		
Third World		
Peacekeeping		
Family		

18. How much would you like sitting next to the following people in class?
    Please circle one number for each row (from 1 = not at all to 5 = very much).

	Not at all				**Very much**
American	1	2	3	4	5
English	1	2	3	4	5
Indian	1	2	3	4	5
Turkish	1	2	3	4	5
Arab	1	2	3	4	5
Scottish	1	2	3	4	5
Chinese	1	2	3	4	5
African	1	2	3	4	5
Russian	1	2	3	4	5
Pakistani	1	2	3	4	5
Welsh	1	2	3	4	5
German	1	2	3	4	5
Bangladeshi	1	2	3	4	5
Italian	1	2	3	4	5
Irish	1	2	3	4	5
Polish	1	2	3	4	5

19. Please find and write on the map the letter for each country:

A = Britain	C = Spain	E = Italy	G = Portugal	I = France
B = Germany	D = Finland	F = Turkey	H = Poland	J = Ukraine

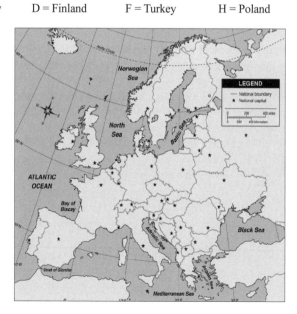

CULTURAL DIVERSITY

20. (a) Is your ethnic background important to you? Please circle one.

Yes   No

(b) Please describe your ethnic background.

_____

(c) Please explain what your ethnic background means to you.

_____

21. How strongly do you agree with the following statements?
    Please circle one number for each row (from 1 = not at all to 5 = very strongly).

	Not at all				Very strongly
Knowledge of other cultures and religions is as important as knowing about your own.	1	2	3	4	5
Minority ethnic communities should give up part of their customs to fit into English society.	1	2	3	4	5
England is a Christian country.	1	2	3	4	5
All students are part of the school community.	1	2	3	4	5
Students should get additional holidays to celebrate their cultural festivals.	1	2	3	4	5
Being white is an advantage in schools.	1	2	3	4	5
I have been discriminated against by other people for my ethnic background.	1	2	3	4	5
Teachers should share my ethnic background.	1	2	3	4	5
Muslim countries, like Turkey, should be allowed to join the European Union.	1	2	3	4	5
I value multicultural education.	1	2	3	4	5
Being different is problematic in England.	1	2	3	4	5
Religious symbols, like headscarf and cross, should be banned from schools.	1	2	3	4	5
I feel comfortable living in the English society.	1	2	3	4	5

22. Do you think that all students are treated equally in this school?
    Please circle one.

Yes   No

Please write down some reasons for your answer.

_____

23. (a) Do you have friends from other ethnic groups? Please circle one.

Yes   No

(b) If Yes, which ethnic group(s) do your friends belong to?

Please tick as many boxes as appropriate.

White British/Irish	
Other White	
Turkish	
Indian	
Pakistani	
Bangladeshi	
Chinese	
Other Asian	
Black Caribbean	
Black African	
Other Black	
White and Black Caribbean	
White and Asian	
White and Black African	
Other Mixed	
Other (please state)	

24. (a) Is your religious background important to you? Please circle one.

Yes   No

(b) What is your religion?

_____

(c) Please explain what your religion means to you.

_____

25. What should schools teach you about?

Please number the following in order of importance (1, 2, 3, 4), starting with 1 as the most important topic.

British culture	
European culture	
Cultural differences in the world	
Different religions	

Thank you!

Appendix 3 – Interview Guides

Interview guide for student focus groups

Biographical details

1.   Please introduce yourself.
2.   How long have you lived here?
3.   Could you tell me a bit about your family's background, your home?
4.   What is your religion?/what is your country of origin?/
         what language do you speak at home?
5.   When did your family migrate to England?

Positioning

6.   How would you describe a *citizen*?
7.   What are you a citizen of?
8.   What do you associate with *England*?
9.   Could you tell me the difference between *being English* and *being British*?
10.   When you hear the word *Europe*, what comes to your mind?
11.   To what extent do you think you are European?
12.   How possible is it to be English/British and European at the same time?

Integration

13.   Do you have friends from other ethnic backgrounds? Please tell me about them.
14.   Have you experienced any form of discrimination or prejudice?
15.   What is living in the English society like; how comfortable do you feel?
16.   To what extent should minority ethnic people give up part of their customs
        and traditions to fit in?
17.   How problematic is it to *be different* in England?
18.   To what extent do you think that *all* students are part of the school community?
19.   To what extent is *being white* an advantage or disadvantage?

Politics

20.   What do you see as the most important political issues today?
21.   What sorts of things does the school teach you about?
22.   What do you know about the European Union?
23.   How would you describe England's relationship with the EU?
24.   To what extent should England link to Europe and/or the USA?
25.   To what extent should we be governed by European Union institutions?
26.   How do you feel about expanding the EU to include Muslim countries (like Turkey)?

The guide for the individual student interviews was structured similarly except that some of the questions were framed more personally to build up student profiles.

Interview guide for (deputy) school principals

1.	What are the main educational concerns for your school?
2.	What resources does the school have to promote citizenship education and European awareness?
3.	How much support do you get from parents?
4.	How would you define the term *citizen*?
5.	How is citizenship taught at this school?
6.	What sort of citizen does the school aim to create?
7.	What kind of national identity would you say the curriculum should promote?
8.	How important do you think citizenship education is for the identity formation of your students?
9.	How important do you think a European dimension in the curriculum is?
10.	To what extent do you think that a European educational dimension is compatible with a national and multicultural dimension?
11.	One of the goals of the European dimension is to 'strengthen in young people a sense of European identity'. To what extent do you think you are achieving this?
12.	Could you tell me about the European profile of the school in terms of classroom projects or extra-curricular activities linked with Europe?
13.	How does the school educate its students about other cultures and religions?
14.	What has been done in this school to include minority ethnic students into the school community?
15.	How do you feel about religious symbols in state schools, such as Muslim headscarves, Jewish skullcaps and Christian crosses?
16.	How do you know the school is getting the balance between European, national and multicultural values right?
17.	Is there anything you would like to add to our discussion?

Interview guide for curriculum co-ordinators

1.	How would you define the term *citizen*?
2.	How is (citizenship, geography, religion) taught at this school?
3.	Could you describe your own involvement in the provision and teaching of (citizenship education, geography, religious education) at this school?
4.	What sort of citizen does the (citizenship education, geography, religious education curriculum) aim to create?
5.	What do you think about the overall attention given to (citizenship education, geography, religious education) in the curriculum?
6.	(Citizenship education, geography, religious education) should include experiencing the European dimension. What do you make of that?
7.	How does the (citizenship education, geography, religious education) programme encourage your students to develop a range of identities?
8.	How important do you think (citizenship education, geography, religious education) is for the identity formation of your students?
9.	How suitable do you feel (citizenship education, geography, religious education) is for the promotion of different educational dimensions?
10.	What do you do to make (citizenship education, geography, religious education) an interesting and relevant subject for all your students?
11.	What resources do you draw upon to teach (citizenship education, geography, religious education)?
12.	How do you include your minority ethnic students and address their particular needs in the teaching of (citizenship education, geography, religious education)?
13.	How often or actively do you teach potentially controversial topics such as citizenship legislation in relation to minority ethnic communities?
14.	How do you think that the provision of (citizenship education, geography, religious education) at this school could be improved?
15.	To what extent do you think that the (citizenship education, geography, religious education programme) is getting the balance between European, national and multicultural values right?
16.	Is there anything you would like to add to our discussion?

Appendix 4 – Curricula

Citizenship, geography and history curricula at Tannberg Hauptschule

---

Citizenship:

Year 6 (age 11-12)
The living space of youth (e.g., family, school, friendship groups, 'foreigners' in Germany)
Local political decisions (e.g., tasks of the municipality, mayor and district council)

Year 7 (age 12-13)
Newspaper and television as information sources (e.g., freedom of the press)
Youth and the state under the rule of law (e.g., sense of justice)
The federal state of Baden-Württemberg (e.g., the political system including elections)

Year 8 (age 13-14)
Germany as a parliamentary democracy (e.g., political parties, power distribution in a democracy)
The European Union (e.g., significance of European unification, EU institutions, youth in Europe)
Measures to ensure peace (e.g., tasks of the German armed forces, peace maintenance)
Family in our time (e.g., role of the family, state protection of families, state help)

Year 9 (age 14-15)
Political participation and democratic culture in Germany (e.g., political debates)
Extremism and violence in political debates (e.g., extremist parties and organisations)
International politics (e.g., instruments of international politics, conflict regions)

Geography:

Year 5 (age 10-11)
Orientation on earth (e.g., shape, continents, oceans, day and night, working with maps)
Local orientation (e.g., local weather and climate, the regional area of Baden-Württemberg)
Local agriculture (e.g., agricultural changes, ecosystems, marketing, local farm production)
Mountains in south-western Germany (e.g., the Black Forest, the Swabian Alb, topography)
The city as a living environment (e.g., structure and functions of a city, Stuttgart)

Year 6 (age 11-12)
Orientation in Germany (e.g., topographical overview of Germany, federal states, Berlin capital)
Coal mining changes the landscape (e.g., mining fields in Germany, types of coal, resources)
Ocean and coastline (e.g., protecting the coastlines, National Park Wattenmeer, harbour cities)
The Alps: a high-mountain range (e.g., transport, an endangered living environment, glaciers)

Year 7 (age 12-13)
Europe at a glance (e.g., political structure, Eurotunnel, topographical orientation)
France: our neighbour (e.g., world city Paris, city partnerships, agricultural products, topography)
Northern Europe (e.g., Gulf Stream, glacial features, Atlantic fishing, North Sea oil, topography)
Great Britain (e.g., physical geography, Industrial Revolution, Lowlands and Highlands)
Mediterranean countries (e.g., mass tourism, agriculture, living and working, cultural traditions)
The changing map of Europe (e.g., state-building, a new EU member state, reasons for change)

Year 8 (age 13-14)
Global climate and vegetation zones (e.g., overview and structure of areas)
Polar regions (e.g., polar day and night, Eskimos, changing Antarctica, resources, climate changes)
Dry zones (e.g., desert, types of deserts, changing deserts, Sahel zone, desertification)
Tropical rainforests (e.g., importance for global climate, shifting cultivation, deforestation)
Living in one world (e.g., life in the Third World, developing countries, international aid projects)

Year 9 (age 14-15)
The European Union (e.g., member states, environmental protection, disparities in Europe)
The United States of America (e.g., national parks, Silicon Valley, belts, New York, ghettoes)
In-depth study of one country (e.g., Japan, Russia, China or Australia, geographical aspects)

History:

Year 6 (age 11-12)
Local historical artefacts (e.g., monuments, local festivals, archaeological procedures, museums)
Egypt: an early high culture (e.g., the significance of the Nile, calendar, pharaoh, technology)
The Greeks (e.g., democracy, Olympic Games, art and science, alphabet, Athens under Pericles)
The Roman Empire (e.g., the Romans in south-western Germany, Roman cities and names)
Europe and Charles the Great (e.g., Charles the Great, Frankenreich German King Henry I)

Year 7 (age 12-13)
Medieval Age (e.g., aristocracy, city and citizens, rural life and economic forms, feudal system)
Kingdom, aristocracy and church (e.g., Otto the Great, Concordat of Worms, Investiture fight)
The Staufer Emperors (e.g., Emperor Barbarossa, the time of Frederic I, the Staufer Emperors)
The New Age (e.g., printing, Columbus discovers America, destruction of Indian high cultures)
Reformation and the Thirty Year War (e.g., Luther's theses, Augsburg religious freedom)

Year 8 (age 13-14)
Absolutism (e.g., Ludwig XIV, absolutism in south-western Germany, life of the population)
American Independence and French Revolution (e.g. human rights, storming of the Bastille)
Napoleon and Congress of Vienna (e.g., Napoleon and Europe, German unification movements)
The German empire under Bismarck (e.g., founding of the German Reich, politics of Bismarck)
Industrialization (e.g., technical and scientific inventions, sociological changes, mass production)

Year 9 (age 14-15)
World War One (e.g., reasons, timeline, the year 1917, armistice, October revolution in Russia)
The Weimar Republic (e.g., Versailles Treaty, economic crisis, the rise of the Nazi Party, Hitler)
World War II (e.g., declaration of war on Poland, USA, Holocaust, timeline, Bonhoeffer)
Germany: from division to unity (e.g., post-war Germany, Berlin Wall, Nato, reunification)
European unification (e.g., German-French relations, economic and political European integration)

Source: Adapted from Schemes of Work (Tannberg Hauptschule, translated from German).

Citizenship, geography and history curricula at Goethe Gymnasium

Citizenship:

Year 10 (age 15-16)
The individual in society (e.g., the significance of family, the individual in different groups)
Democracy in Germany (e.g., democracy in the municipality, tasks of political parties)
The individual and the law (e.g., compulsory military service, court proceedings)
Economy and working world (e.g., consumers and markets, employers and employees)

Year 11 (age 16-17)
Society and welfare state in Germany (e.g., structure of German society)
Economic politics and system (e.g., social market economy, structural policy)
European unification and Germany (e.g., unification process, EU political decisions)

Year 12 (age 17-18)
Sovereignty of the people (e.g., political participation in the development of an informed opinion)
Political decision-making processes (e.g., the legislation process, control of the government)
The German democratic system (e.g., federal structure, parliament and government)

Year 13 (age 18-19)
Peace and security policy in Europe (e.g., peace maintenance through treaties, armed forces)
Overcoming of disparities for peace in the world (e.g., north-south conflict)

Geography:

Year 5 (age 10-11)
Orientation on earth (e.g., shape, continents, oceans, day and night, working with maps)
Local orientation (e.g., local weather and climate, the regional area of Baden-Württemberg)
Landscapes in Baden-Württemberg (e.g., the Black Forest, the Swabian Alb, topography)
Cities and industrial areas in Baden-Württemberg (e.g., structure and functions of a city, Stuttgart)

Year 6 (age 11-12)
Orientation in Central Europe (e.g., topography, Germany's location in Europe, political system)
Areas of Germany (e.g., economic areas Rhine Valley, coastal areas, Berlin, agricultural zones)
The continent of Europe (e.g., Alps, North Europe, West Europe (Britain, France), South Europe)
European integration (e.g., unity and diversity, common projects and goals (Eurotunnel), migration)

Year 7 (age 12-13)
The tropics (e.g., humid tropics (rainforests), sub-humid tropics (desertification), population)
Tropical-subtropical dry zones (e.g., desert areas, nomads and oases, agricultural systems, life)
Polar regions (e.g., polar day and night, Arctic and Antarctica, resources, climate changes)
Global climate and vegetation zones (e.g., seasons, atmospheric circulation, zonal orientation)

Year 8 (age 13-14)
India and China (e.g., population, agriculture, caste system, monsoon, Beijing, urbanisation)
Japan (e.g., topography, traditional and modern forms of living, economic power, natural disasters)
USA (e.g., changing agriculture and industry, the North American city, national parks)
Russia and its neighbours (e.g., topography, population, Moscow, problem areas, industrialization)
Culture zones (e.g., the Muslim and oriental world, the oriental city, characteristics and change)

Year 11 (age 16-17)
Human life on earth (e.g., the earth's crust, atmosphere, soils, protecting the earth's atmosphere)
Socio-economic processes in Europe (e.g., industry and service sector, EU agricultural areas)
Socio-economic processes in developing countries (e.g., economic and societal structures, Asia)
World economy and world trade (e.g., structure of world trade, import and export, terms of trade)

History:

Year 7 (age 12-13)
Past and present: introduction to History (e.g., local historical artefacts, life conditions in the past)
Early human beings (e.g., Holocene hunters and gatherers, tools, clothing, settlement, changes)
Egyptian high culture (e.g., characteristics, calendar, pharaoh, pyramids, other early high cultures)
The Greeks (e.g., democracy, Olympic Games, Alexander and Hellenism, the Attic polis)
The Roman Empire (e.g., republic and expansion, emperors and Romanisation, Augustus, life)

Year 8 (age 13-14)
The beginnings of Medieval Europe (e.g., the Carolingians, Christian heritage, Charles the Great)
Life forms in Medieval Europe (e.g., king and emperor, the Staufer Emperors, rural forms of life)
Changes in Medieval Europe (e.g., crusades and the conquest of Jerusalem, Islam and Europe)
Forming of a new era (e.g., technology and science, discoveries and colonies, Reformation, pest)
Absolutism in Europe (e.g., Europe during Enlightenment, Ludwig XIV, Prussia and absolutism)

Year 9 (age 14-15)
American Revolution (e.g., the struggle for independence, USA as the first democracy, settlement)
French Revolution (e.g., 1789 storming of the Bastille, Napoleon and Europe, Jacobeans)
Industrial Revolution (e.g., beginning in England, industrialization of Europe, social issues)
19th Century Germany (e.g., Congress of Vienna, unification movements, 1871 German empire)
Imperialism and World War I (e.g., European imperialism, reasons and consequences of WWI)

Year 10 (age 15-16)
USA and Soviet Union and their importance for Europe (e.g., October Revolution)
The Weimar Republic (e.g., society in the 1920s, democracy, end of the Republic, radicalisation)
National Socialism (e.g., Third Reich, fascism in Europe, persecution of Jews, reasons of WWII)
Germany after World War II (e.g., anti-Hitler coalition, occupation zones, East and West Germany)
Toward Reunification (e.g., Cold War, Adenauer, German Democratic Republic, Reunification)
International problems in their historical dimension (e.g., Germany and her neighbours, crises)

Source: Adapted from Schemes of Work (Goethe Gymnasium, translated from German).

Citizenship, geography and history curricula at Millroad School

Citizenship:

Year 7 (age 11-12)
Bullying and prejudice (e.g., types of stereotyping, discrimination, how to challenge racism)
Taking responsibility (e.g., democratic participation, school council elections, what is citizenship?)
Britain: a diverse society (e.g., national statistics, Commission for Racial Equality, MacPherson)

Year 8 (age 12-13)
Local democracy (e.g., local council, school council, polling cards)
Debating a global issue (e.g., Martin Luther King, Holocaust, asylum seekers)
Crime (e.g., Safer Schools Partnership, consequences, action on drugs, theft, bullying)

Year 9 (age 13-14)
Governments and voting (e.g., Downing Street, Welsh Assembly, Scottish Parliament, your MP)
Human rights (e.g., why voting today, why women had to struggle for the vote in Britain)
Promoting interracial tolerance (e.g., Holocaust Day, Martin Luther King)
Sex, relationships and drugs (e.g., HIV Aids, contraception, risks of alcohol, Boots Drug Store)

Year 10/11 (age 14-16)
Taking part (e.g., planning a community event, Eid, Ramadan, Remembrance Day)
Relationships (e.g., sex education, feelings, separation and divorce, marriage and family life)
Europe: who decides? (e.g., referendum on single currency, should we have on language)
Consumer Rights and Responsibilities (e.g., workplace, consumer education, trading standards)

Geography:

Year 7 (age 11-12)
Hazards (e.g., how volcanoes and earthquakes happen, the Indian earthquake)
Map skills (e.g., grid references, map symbols, how to measure distance, how to describe routes)
Settlement (e.g., early settlements, benefits and problems of settlement growth, land use in towns)
Transport (e.g., developments in transport, the Eurotunnel, traffic in urban areas)

Year 8 (age 12-13)
The United Kingdom (e.g., what is the UK, physical and human features, migration)
Economic activities (e.g., primary industries, types of farming, how has farming changed)
Weather and climate (e.g., what is Britain's weather, forecasts, local features affecting wind)
Italy: a European country (e.g., main physical and human features)

Year 9 (age 13-14)
Development (e.g., too many people?, indicators of development, how the rich can help the poor)
Japan: a developed country (e.g., physical features, sources of energy, industry, changes)
Brazil: a developing country (e.g., main physical and human features)

Year 10/11 (age 14-16)
Climate, environment and people (e.g., polar region, tropics, US and UK wetlands, ecosystems)
People and places (e.g., developed (London, Tokyo) and developing (Bombay, Nairobi) cities)
People, work and development (e.g., British north-south divide, exploitation, Europe, poverty)
Water landforms and people (e.g., Colorado River, Grand Canyon, hydrosphere, Oxbow lakes)

History:

Year 7 (age 11-12)
Medieval Realms (e.g., Battle of Hastings, how William gained control of England, King John)
From Henry to Elizabeth (e.g., the Christian churches, life in Elizabethan England)

Year 8 (age 12-13)
Black peoples of the Americas (e.g., abolition of slavery, American Civil War, triangular trade)
The English Civil War (e.g., the execution of Charles I, Oliver Cromwell)
The French Revolution (e.g., liberty, equality, fraternity, Bastille Day, Napoleon)

Year 9 (age 13-14)
The First World War (e.g., long-term reasons, assessing the First World War)
Hitler and the Holocaust (e.g., persecution of Jews, dilemmas in Nazi Germany, resistance)
Changes in the 20th Century (e.g., the changing role of women, the origins and role of the UN)

Year 10/11 (age 14-16)
Germany 1919-1945 (e.g., the rise of the Nazi Party, youth and propaganda, the Holocaust)
Medicine (e.g., 1350-1750, 1750-1900, 20th century changes in medical knowledge and treatment)
South Africa (e.g., society after World War II, apartheid in action)

Source: Adapted from Schemes of Work (Millroad School).

Citizenship, geography and history curricula at Darwin School

Citizenship:

Year 7 (age 11-12)
Children's rights (e.g., student rights at school, UN Convention, children and work)
Bullying (e.g., why bullying happens, strategies for dealing with bullying)
Vandalism (e.g., vandalism affects us all, anti-social behaviour and its consequences)

Year 8 (age 12-13)
Running a community (e.g., elections, voting, Westminster government, local government, laws)
Drugs education I (e.g., drugs laws in the UK, legal and illegal drugs, risks of alcohol, addiction)
Health education I (e.g., healthy eating, exercise, health problems, smoking, alcohol, depression)

Year 9 (age 13-14)
Human rights and discrimination (e.g., UN declaration, discrimination in the media, racism)
Drugs education II (e.g., drugs laws in the UK, legal and illegal drugs, risks of alcohol, addiction)
Health education II (e.g., healthy eating, immunization, personal hygiene and healthcare)

Year 10/11 (age 14-16)
Freedom of speech and censorship (e.g., attitudes to censorship, censorship of advertising, speech)
Torture and amnesty (e.g., definitions and nature of torture, Amnesty International)
Careers and higher education (e.g., applications and interview skills, post-16 education, guide)

Geography:

Year 7 (age 11-12)
Down Under (e.g., where and what is Australia?, climate and vegetation, tourism, Sydney)
Making or breaking the land (e.g., changing coastlines, coastal deposition, coastal erosion: Dorset)
Hot and bothered (e.g., climate of the UK, temperatures round school, ecosystem, Coldfall Woods)
Settlement (e.g., early settlements, London, how Warkworth developed, the growth of Tokyo)

Year 8 (age 12-13)
Disaster strikes (e.g., natural hazards, volcanoes, the Kobe earthquake, tectonic activity)
Running out? (e.g., types of energy, renewable and non-renewable resources, energy conservation)
Italy: an EU country (e.g., role of the EU, population distribution, Valle d'Aosta, skiing, industry)
The land shall provide (e.g., food production, types of farming around the world, agribusiness)

Year 9 (age 13-14)
Only one earth (e.g., sustainable development, Amazon Rainforest, Antarctica, global warming)
Development and tourism (e.g., measuring development, benefits and problems of tourism)
Brazil: a developing country (e.g., cities of SE Brazil, how independent and developed is Brazil)
Living in cities (e.g., North American city, mega cities (Cairo, Calcutta), the geography of crime)

Year 10/11 (age 14-16)
Population and settlement (e.g., population changes, local settlements, Nairobi, sustainability)
Geomorphic processes and landforms (e.g., coastal landforms, local and national processes)
Economic systems and development (e.g., Vine Farm Lincolnshire, Japanese and Italian farming)
International disparities and interdependence (e.g., terms of trade, varying living standards)

History:

Year 7 (age 11-12)
The Roman Empire (e.g., growth, the Colosseum, the Romans metalwork, life in Rome, Augustus)
Medieval Realms (e.g., changes, Battle of Hastings, the Black Death, Magna Charta, King John)
Native Americans (e.g., Pocahontas, Plains Indians, European involvement in America)

Year 8 (age 12-13)
The Renaissance (e.g., explorers Columbus and da Gama, anatomy, astronomy, surgery, Italy, art)
Britain 1500-1750 (e.g., Tudors and barons, Henry VIII and the church, Mary I, Elizabeth I)
Slavery (e.g., the triangular trade, the slave trade, trading for slaves, slave sales, Middle Passage)

Year 9 (age 13-14)
Britain 1750-1900 (e.g., population and agriculture changes, Industrial Revolution)
World War I (e.g., reasons, recruitment of soldiers, the Western Front, Field Marshall Haig)
20th Century (e.g., consequences of WWI, timeline WWII, Battle of Britain, Holocaust, Dunkirk)

Year 10/11 (age 14-16)
Germany 1918-1945 (e.g., Weimar Republic, the rise of the Nazi Party, Hitler and the Holocaust)
The USA 1918-1945 (e.g., US economy boom, Wall Street Crash, New Deal, societal changes)
International relations (e.g., origins of the Cold War, Cuba and Vietnam, League of Nations)

Source: Adapted from Schemes of Work (Darwin School).

Bibliography

Alba, R. 1990. *Ethnic Identity: The Transformation of White America*. New Haven: Yale University Press.

Alba, R. 2005. Bright vs. blurred boundaries: Second-generation assimilation and exclusion in France, Germany and the United States. *Ethnic and Racial Studies*, 28(1), 20-49.

Alba, R. 2009. *Blurring the Color Line: The New Chance for a More Integrated America*. Cambridge: Harvard University Press.

Alba, R. and Nee, V. 2003. *Remaking the American Mainstream: Assimilation and Contemporary Migration*. Cambridge: Harvard University Press.

Alba, R. and Silberman, R. 2009. The children of immigrants and host-society educational systems: Mexicans in the United States and North Africans in France. *Teachers College Record*, 111(6), 1444-75.

Alt, C. (ed.) 2006. *Kinderleben: Integration durch Sprache? Bedingungen des Aufwachsens von türkischen, russlanddeutschen und deutschen Kindern*. Wiesbaden: Verlag für Sozialwissenschaften.

Anderson, J.J. 1997. Hard interests, soft power, and Germany's changing role in Europe, in *Tamed Power: Germany in Europe*, edited by P.J. Katzenstein. Ithaca: Cornell University Press, 80-107.

Angvik, M. and von Borries, B. (eds) 1997. *Youth and History: A Comparative European Survey on Historical Consciousness and Political Attitudes among Adolescents*. Hamburg: Körber-Stiftung.

Archer, L. 2003. *Race, Masculinity and Schooling: Muslim Boys and Education*. London: Open University Press.

Archer, L. 2008. The impossibility of minority ethnic educational 'success'? An examination of the discourses of teachers and pupils in British secondary schools. *European Educational Research Journal*, 7(1), 89-107.

Auernheimer, G. 1990. 'How black are the German Turks?' Ethnicity, marginality and interethnic relations for young people of Turkish origin in the FRG, in *Childhood, Youth, and Social Change: A Comparative Perspective*, edited by L. Chisholm et al. Basingstoke: Falmer Press, 197-212.

Auernheimer, G. 1996. *Einführung in die interkulturelle Erziehung*. Darmstadt: Wissenschaftliche Buchgesellschaft.

Avni, S. and Koumbarji, F. 1994. *Turkish/Turkish Cypriot Communities Profile*. London Borough of Hackney: Directorate of Social Services.

Bade, K.J. (ed.) 1993. *Deutsche im Ausland, Fremde in Deutschland: Migration in Geschichte und Gegenwart*. München: C.H. Beck.

Bade, K.J. 2000. The German hub: Migration in history and the present. *Deutschland Magazine on Politics, Culture, Business and Science*, 6, 38-43.

Bade, K.J. 2007. Versäumte Integrationschancen und nachholende Integrations- politik, in *Nachholende Integrationspolitik und Gestaltungsperspektiven der Integrationspraxis*, edited by H.-G. Hiesserich. Göttingen: V&R unipress, 21-95.

Bagnoli, A. 2007. Between outcast and outsider: Constructing the identity of the foreigner. *European Societies*, 9(1), 23-44.

Ball, S.J. 2003. *Class Strategies and the Education Market: The Middle Classes and Social Advantage*. London: Routledge.

Bandulet, B. 1998. *Was wird aus unserem Geld?* München: Wirtschaftsverlag Langen Müller Herbig.

Banks, J.A. 1979. Shaping the future of multicultural education. *Journal of Negro Education*, 48(3), 237-52.

Banks, J.A. 1997. Multicultural education: Characteristics and goals, in *Multicultural Education: Issues and Perspectives*, edited by J.A. Banks and C.A.M. Banks. Boston: Allyn and Bacon, 3-31.

Banks J.A. 2004. Multicultural education: Historical development, dimensions, and practice, in *Handbook of Research on Multicultural Education*, edited by J.A. Banks and C.A.M. Banks. New York: Macmillan, 3-29.

Banse, D. and Laninger, T. 2005. Mordmotiv: Blut für die Ehre. *Die Welt* [Online: 16 February]. Available at: http://www.welt.de/data/2005/02/16/464432.html [accessed: 4 August 2009].

Barker, M. 1981. *The New Racism*. London: Junction Books.

Barrett, M. 1996. English children's acquisition of a European identity, in *Changing European Identities: Social Psychological Analyses of Social Change*, edited by G.L. Breakwell and E. Lyons. Oxford: Butterworth Heinemann, 349-69.

Barrett, M. 2007. *Children's Knowledge, Beliefs and Feelings About Nations and National Groups*. Hove: Psychology Press.

Barrett, M. and Short, J. 1992. Images of European people in a group of 5 to 10- year-old English schoolchildren. *British Journal of Developmental Psychology*, 10, 339-61.

Bauböck, R. 1994. *Transnational Citizenship: Membership and Rights in International Migration*. Aldershot: Edward Elgar.

Bauman, Z. 2001. Identity in the globalising world. *Social Anthropology*, 9(2), 121-29.

Beck, U. 2000. *What is Globalization?* Cambridge: Polity Press.

Beckmann, C. 2005. Özcan Mutlu: 'Alle haben versagt. *Die Welt* [Online: 21 February]. Available at: http://www.welt.de/data/2005/02/21/517683.html [accessed: 4 August 2009].

Behörde für Bildung und Sport (ed.) 2003. *Hamburgisches Schulgesetz vom 16.4.1997 geändert am 27.6.2003*. Hamburg: Behörde für Bildung und Sport.

Bell, G.H. (ed.) 1995. *Educating European Citizens: Citizenship Values and the European Dimension*. London: David Fulton Publishers.

Benedictus, L. 2005. Two years ago, we were more isolated, everyone was scared: Turks in Green Lanes. *The Guardian* [Online: 21 January]. Available at: http://www.guardian.co.uk/uk/2005/jan/21/britishidentity5 [accessed: 2 August 2009].

Benhabib, S. 2004. *The Rights of Others: Aliens, Residents and Citizens.* Cambridge: Cambridge University Press.

Benhabib, S. 2005. *The Right to Have Rights in Contemporary Europe* [Online]. Available at: http://www8.georgetown.edu/centers/cdacs/benhabibpaper.pdf [accessed: 1 August 2009].

Benton, T., Cleaver, E., Featherstone, G., Kerr, D., Lopes, J. and Whitby, K. 2008. *Citizenship Education Longitudinal Study Sixth Annual Report: Young People's Civic Participation In and Beyond School.* London: DCSF.

Benyon, J. (ed.) 1984. *Scarman and After: Essays Reflecting on Lord Scarman's Report, the Riots and their Aftermath.* Oxford: Pergamon Press.

Berry, J.W. 1997. Immigration, acculturation and adaptation. *Applied Psychology: An International Review*, 46(1), 5-34.

Berry, J.W. and Sam, D. 1997. Acculturation and adaption, in *Handbook of Cross-Cultural Psychology*, edited by J.W. Berry, M.H. Segall and C. Kagitçibasi. London: Allyn and Bacon, 291-326.

Berry, J.W., Phinney, J.S., Sam, D.L. and Vedder, P. 2006a. Immigrant youth: Acculturation, identity, and adaptation. *Applied Psychology: An International Review*, 55(3), 303-32.

Berry, J.W., Phinney, J.S., Sam, D.L. and Vedder, P. 2006b. *Immigrant Youth in Cultural Transition: Acculturation, Identity and Adaptation across National Contexts.* Mahwah: Lawrence Erlbaum Associates.

Bhabha, H.K. 1990. *Nation and Narration.* London: Routledge.

Bhabha, J. 1998. Get back to where you once belonged: Identity, citizenship and exclusion in Europe. *Human Rights Quarterly*, 20(3), 592-627.

Bhavnani, K.K. and Phoenix, A. (eds) 1994. *Shifting Identities, Shifting Racisms: Feminism and Psychology Reader.* London: Sage.

Bielefelt, H. and Follmar-Otto, P. 2005. *Diskriminierungsschutz in der politischen Diskussion.* Berlin: Deutsches Institut für Menschenrechte.

Bildungskommission Nordrhein-Westfalen 1995. *Zukunft der Bildung: Schule der Zukunft*, Neuwied: Luchterhand.

Birg, H. 2009. Integration und Migration im Spiegel harter Daten. *Frankfurter Allgemeine Zeitung*, 9 April, 37.

Birman, D. and Trickett, E.J. 2001. Cultural transition in first-generation immigrants: Acculturation of Soviet Jewish refugee adolescents and parents. *Journal of Cross-Cultural Psychology*, 32(4), 456-77.

Bîrzéa, C. 2000. *Education for Democratic Citizenship: A Lifelong Learning Perspective.* Strasbourg: Council of Europe.

Blair, M. and Arnot, M. 1993. Black and anti-racist perspectives on the National Curriculum and government educational policy, in *The Multicultural*

Dimension of the National Curriculum, edited by A.S. King and M.J. Reiss. London: Falmer, 259-74.

Bleek, W. 1997. Zur Kontinuität rechtsextremen Denkens, in *Bochumer Beiträge zur Nationalismusdebatte: Dokumentation einer Vortragsreihe in der Ruhr-Universität Bochum*, edited by B. Faulenbach, K. Rudolph and M. Schlösser. Essen: Klartext, 20-35.

Bloemraad, I. 2006. *Becoming a Citizen: Incorporating Immigrants and Refugees in the United States and Canada*. Berkeley: University of California Press.

Bofinger, P., Collignon, S. and Lipp, E.-M. 1993. *Währungsunion oder Währungschaos? Was kommt nach der D-Mark*. Wiesbaden: Gabler.

Bond, R. and Rosie, M. 2002. National identities in post-devolution Scotland. *Scottish Affairs*, 40, 34-53.

Boos-Nünning, U. 1986. Die schulische Situation der zweiten Generation, in *Zukunft in der Bundesrepublik oder Zukunft in der Türkei: Eine Bilanz der 25-jährigen Migration von Türken*, edited by W. Meys and F. Şen. Frankfurt: Dagyeli, 131-55.

Boos-Nünning, U. and Karakaşoğlu, Y. 2005. *Viele Welten leben: Zur Lebenssituation von Mädchen und jungen Frauen mit Migrationshintergrund*. Münster: Waxmann.

Boteram, N. (ed.) 1993. *Interkulturelles Verstehen und Handeln*. Pfaffenweiler: Centaurus.

Brah, A. 1996. *Cartographies of Diaspora: Contesting Identities*. London: Routledge.

Brantlinger, E. 2003. *Dividing Classes: How the Middle Class Negotiates and Rationalizes School Advantage*. New York: Routledge.

Brennan, T. 1981. *Political Education and Democracy*. Cambridge: Cambridge University Press.

Brettfeld, K. and Wetzels, P. 2007. *Muslime in Deutschland: Integration, Integrationsbarrieren, Religion sowie Einstellungen zu Demokratie, Rechtsstaat und politisch-religiös motivierter Gewalt*. Berlin: Bundesministerium des Innern.

Brindle, P. and Arnot, M. 2001. *Gender and the Teaching of Citizenship*. University of Cambridge: Faculty of Education.

Broadfoot, P. 1999. Not so much a context, more a way of life? Comparative education in the 1990s, in *Learning from Comparing: New Directions in Comparative Educational Research*, edited by R. Alexander, P. Broadfoot and D. Philipps. Oxford: Symposium, 21-32.

Brubaker, R. 1992. *Citizenship and Nationhood in France and Germany*. Cambridge: Harvard University Press.

Bryman, A. 2008. *Social Research Methods*. 3rd Edition. Oxford: Oxford University Press.

Bukow, W.-D., Nikodem, C., Schulze, E. and Yildiz, E. 2001. *Die multikulturelle Stadt: Von der Selbstverständlichkeit im städtischen Alltag*. Opladen: Leske und Budrich.

Bullock, A.L.C. 1975. *A Language for Life: Report of the Committee of Inquiry Appointed by the Secretary of State for Education and Science under the Chairmanship of Sir Alan Bullock*, London: HMSO.

Bundesministerium des Innern 2004. *Gesetz zur Steuerung und Begrenzung der Zuwanderung und zur Regelung des Aufenthalts und der Integration von Unionsbürgern und Ausländern*. (BGBl I Nr. 41), Bonn: BMI.

Bundesministerium des Innern 2007. *Das Gesetz zur Umsetzung aufenthalts- und asylrechtlicher Richtlinien der Europäischen Union*. (BGBl I Nr. 42), Bonn: BMI.

Bundesregierung Deutschland 2007. *Der Nationale Integrationsplan: Neue Wege, Neue Chancen*. Berlin: Presse- und Informationsamt der Bundesregierung.

Bundesverfassungsgericht [2003] 2 BvR 1436/02.

Butler, J. 1997. *The Psychic Life of Power: Theories in Subjection*. Stanford: Stanford University Press.

Butler, T. and Robsen, G. 2003. *London Calling: The Middle Classes and the Remaking of Inner London*. Oxford: Berg.

Butterfield, S.-A. 2004. 'We're just black': The racial and ethnic identities of second-generation West Indians in New York, in *Becoming New Yorkers: Ethnographies of the New Second Generation*, edited by P. Kasinitz, J.H. Mollenkopf and M.C. Waters. New York: Russel Sage Foundation, 288-312.

Byram, M. 1996. Introduction: Education for European citizenship. *Evaluation and Research in Education*, 10(2-3), 61-7.

Byrne, B. 2006. *White Lives: The Interplay of Race, Class and Gender in Everyday Life*. London: Routledge.

Caglar, A.S. 1997. Hyphenated identities and the limits of 'culture', in *The Politics of Multiculturalism in the New Europe: Racism, Identity and Community*, edited by T. Modood and P. Werbner. London: Zed Books, 169-85.

Caglar, A.S. 2007. Rescaling cities, cultural diversity and transnationalism. *Ethnic and Racial Studies*, 30(6), 1070-95.

Cantle, T. 2001. *Community Cohesion: A Report of the Independent Review Team*. London: Home Office.

Cantle, T. 2006. Multiculturalism: A failed experiment? *Index on Censorship*, 35(2), 91-2.

Carter, B., Harris, C. and Joshi, S. 1987. *The 1951-1955 Conservative Government and the Racialization of Black Immigration*. University of Warwick: Centre for Research in Ethnic Relations.

Cashmore, E.E. 1989. *United Kingdom? Class, Race and Gender since the War*. London: Unwin Hyman.

Castano, E. 2004. European identity: A social psychological perspective, in *Transnational Identities*, edited by R. Herrmann, T. Risse and M. Brewer. Oxford: Rowman and Littlefield, 40-58.

Castles, S. and Miller, M. 2003. *The Age of Migration: International Population Movements in the Modern World*. Basingstoke: Palgrave.

Cesari, J. 2004. *When Islam and Democracy Meet: Muslims in Europe and in the United States*. New York: Palgrave Macmillan.

Cheles, L., Ferguson, R. and Vaughan, M. 1995. *The Far Right in Western and Eastern Europe*. London: Longman.

Chisholm, L., Büchner, P., Krüger, H.H. and Brown, P. (eds) 1990. *Childhood, Youth, and Social Change: A Comparative Perspective*. Basingstoke: The Falmer Press.

Chisholm, L., Du Bois-Reymond, M. and Coffield, F. 1995. What does Europe mean to me? Dimensions of distance and disillusion amongst European students, in *European Yearbook on Youth Policy and Research: The Puzzle of Integration*, edited by Circle for Youth Research Cooperation in Europe. Berlin: de Gruyter, 3-31.

Cinnirella, M. 1997. Towards a European identity: Interactions between the national and European social identities manifested by university students in Britain and Italy. *British Journal of Social Psychology*, 36(1), 19-31.

Citrin, J. and Sides, J. 2004. More than nationals: How identity choice matters in the new Europe, in *Transnational Identities*, edited by R. Herrmann, T. Risse and M. Brewer. Oxford: Rowman and Littlefield, 161-85.

Clarke, T. 2001. *The Burnley Task Force Report*. Burnley: Burnley Borough Council.

Cleaver, E., Ireland, E., Kerr, D. and Lopes, J. 2005. *Citizenship Education Longitudinal Study Second Cross-Sectional Survey 2004: Listening to Young People*. London: DfES.

Cohen, P. 1988. The perversions of inheritance: Studies in the making of multi-racist Britain, in *Multi-Racist Britain*, edited by P. Cohen and H.S. Bains. London: Macmillan, 9-118.

Commission on Integration and Cohesion 2007. *Our Shared Future: Themes, Messages and Challenges: A Final Analysis of the Key Themes from the Commission on Integration and Cohesion Consultation*. London: HMSO.

Connolly, P. 1998. *Racism, Gender Identities and Young Children: Social Relations in a Multi-Ethnic Inner-City Primary School*. London: Routledge.

Convery, A., Evans, M., Green, S., Macaro, E. and Mellor, J. 1997a. *Pupils' Perceptions of Europe: Identity and Education*. London: Cassell.

Convery, A., Evans, M., Green, S., Macaro, E. and Mellor, J. 1997b. An investigative study into pupils' perceptions of Europe. *Journal of Multilingual and Multicultural Development*, 18(1), 1-16.

Convey, A. and Merritt, A. 2000. The United Kingdom, in *Education in a Single Europe*, edited by C. Brock and W. Tulasiewicz. London: Routledge, 377-403.

Coulby, D. 2000. *Beyond the National Curriculum: Curricular Centralism and Cultural Diversity in Europe and the USA*. London: Routledge.

Coulby, D. and Jones, C. 1995. *Postmodernity and European Education Systems*. Stoke-on-Trent: Trentham Books.

Council of Europe 1989. *Recommendation 1111 of the Parliamentary Assembly on the European Dimension of Education*. Strasbourg: Council of Europe.

Council of Europe 1991. *Resolution 1 on the European Dimension of Education: Teaching and Curriculum Content.* Strasbourg: Council of Europe.

Council of Europe 2002. *The New Challenge of Intercultural Education: Religious Diversity and Dialogue in Europe* (Document DGIV/EDU/DIAL 7). Strasbourg: Council of Europe.

Council of Europe 2003. *Declaration by the European Ministers of Education on Intercultural Education in the New European Context.* Strasbourg: Council of Europe.

Council of Europe 2004. *Education for Democratic Citizenship 2001-2004: Activity Report for 2003* (Document DGIV/EDU/CIT 32). Strasbourg: Council of Europe.

Council of Europe 2005. *Policies and Practices for Teaching Socio-cultural Diversity.* Strasbourg: Council of Europe.

Council of Europe 2007. *Final Declaration: Building a More Humane and Inclusive Europe: Role of Education Policies.* Strasbourg: Council of Europe.

Council of Ministers of Education 1988. *Resolution of the Council and the Ministers of Education Meeting within the Council on the European Dimension in Education of 24 May 1988.* Luxembourg: Office for Official Publications of the European Communities (C 177/5).

Council of Ministers of Education 1993. *Green Paper on the European Dimension of Education.* Luxembourg: Office for Official Publications of the European Communities.

Council of Ministers of Education 2006. *Recommendation of the European Parliament and the Council of 18 December 2006 on Key Competencies for Lifelong Learning.* Brussels: Official Journal of the European Union (L 394/10).

Council of Ministers of Education 2007. *Council Conclusions of 25 May 2007 on a Coherent Framework of Indicators and Benchmarks for Monitoring Progress Towards the Lisbon Objectives in Education and Training.* Brussels: Official Journal of the European Union (C 311/10).

Council of the European Communities 1992. *Treaty on European Union.* Brussels: Official Journal of the European Union (C 191).

Council of the European Union 1997. *Treaty of Amsterdam.* Brussels: Official Journal of the European Union (C 340).

Council of the European Union 2000a. *Council Directive Implementing the Principle of Equal Treatment Between Persons Irrespective of Racial or Ethnic Origin.* Brussels: Official Journal of the European Communities (L 180/22).

Council of the European Union 2000b. *Council Directive Establishing a General Framework for Equal Treatment in Employment and Occupation.* Brussels: Official Journal of the European Communities (L 303/16).

Council of the European Union 2004. *Treaty Establishing a Constitution for Europe.* Brussels: Official Journal of the European Union (C 310).

Council of the European Union 2006. *Recommendation of the European Parliament and of the Council of 18 December 2006 on Key Competences for Lifelong Learning.* Brussels: Official Journal of the European Union (L 394/10).

Council of the European Union 2007. *Treaty of Lisbon.* Brussels: Official Journal of the European Union (C 306/01).

Council of the European Union 2008. European Pact on Immigration and Asylum. [Online]. Available at: http://www.euractiv.com/docad/pacteEN.doc [accessed: 11 July 2009].

Crossley, M. and Broadfoot, P. 1992. Comparative and international research in education: Scope, problems and potential. *British Educational Research Journal*, 18(2), 99-112.

Crul, M. and Holdaway, J. 2009. Children of immigrants in schools in New York and Amsterdam: The factors shaping attainment. *Teachers College Record*, 111(6), 1476-507.

Crul, M. and Vermeulen, H. (eds) 2003. The future of the second generation: The integration of migrant youth in six European countries. Special issue of *International Migration Review*, 37(4), 965-1144.

Crul, M. and Vermeulen, H. 2006. Immigration, education and the Turkish second-generation in five European nations: A comparative study, in *Immigration and the Transformation of Europe*, edited by C. Parsons and T. Smeeding. Cambridge: Cambridge University Press, 235-50.

Damanakis, M. 2005. European and intercultural dimension in Greek education. *European Educational Research Journal*, 4(1), 79-88.

Davies, S. and Sobisch, A. (eds) 1997. *Developing European Citizens.* Sheffield: Sheffield Hallam University.

Dawkins, R. 2006. *The God Delusion.* London: Bantom.

Delanty, G. 2000. *Citizenship in a Global Age: Society, Culture and Politics.* Buckingham: Open University Press.

Delanty, G. 2005. The idea of a cosmopolitan Europe: On the cultural significance of Europeanization. *International Review of Sociology-Revue Internationale de Sociologie*, 15(3), 405-21.

Delanty, G. and Rumford, C. 2005. *Rethinking Europe: Social Theory and the Implications of Europeanization.* London: Routledge.

Demaine, J. 2005. The 'new' politics of education in Britain's changing times. *International Studies in Sociology of Education*, 15(2), 115-27.

Denzin, N.K. and Lincoln, Y.S. (eds) 2000. *Handbook of Qualitative Research.* London: Sage.

Department for Children, Schools and Families 2007. *Guidance on the Duty to Promote Community Cohesion.* (DCSF/00598/2007), London: HMSO.

Department for Children, Schools and Families 2009. *Independent Review of the Primary Curriculum: Final Report.* (DCSF/00499/2009), London: HMSO.

Department for Communities and Local Government 2006. *Improving Opportunity, Strengthening Society: One Year On – A Progress Summary.* London: HMSO.

Department for Education and Skills 2001. *Schools Achieving Success*. (Cmnd. 5230), London: HMSO.

Department for Education and Skills 2002. *Green Paper 14-19: Extending Opportunities, Raising Standards*. (Cmnd. 5342), London: HMSO.

Department for Education and Skills 2005. *Developing the Global Dimension in the School Curriculum*. (DfES/1409/2005), London: HMSO.

Department for Education and Skills 2007a. *Diversity and Citizenship in the Curriculum: Research Review*. (DfES/00045/2007), London: HMSO.

Department for Education and Skills 2007b. *Languages Review*. (DfES/00212/2007), London: HMSO.

Department of Education and Science 1977. *Education in Schools: A Consultative Document*. (Cmnd. 6869), London: HMSO.

Department of Education and Science 1981. *West Indian Children in Our Schools: Interim Report of the Committee of Inquiry into the Education of Children from Ethnic Minority Groups*. (Cmnd. 8273), London: HMSO.

Department of Education and Science 1985. *Education for All: Report of the Committee of Enquiry into the Education of Children from Ethnic Minority Groups*. (Cmnd. 9453), London: HMSO.

Department of Education and Science 1987. *Education Support Grants*. (Circular 1/87), London: HMSO.

Department of Education and Science 1988. *Education Reform Act 1988*. (c.40), London: HMSO.

Der Kultusminister des Landes Nordrhein-Westfalen 1985. *Richtlinien und Lehrpläne für die Grundschule in Nordrhein-Westfalen: Sachunterricht*. Frechen: Ritterbach.

Derricott, R. 2000. National case studies of citizenship education, in *Citizenship for the 21st Century: An International Perspective on Education*, edited by J.J Cogan and R. Derricott. London: Kogan Page, 23-92.

Derrida, J. 1981. *Positions*, translated by A. Bass. London: Athlone.

Devine, D. 2005. Welcome to the Celtic Tiger? Teacher responses to immigration and increasing ethnic diversity in Irish schools. *International Studies in Sociology of Education*, 15(1), 49-70.

Devine, D. and Kelly M. 2006. 'I just don't want to be picked on by anybody': Dynamics of inclusion and exclusion in a newly multiethnic Irish primary school. *Children and Society*, 20(2), 128-39.

Dickopp, K.H. 1982. *Erziehung ausländischer Kinder als pädagogische Herausforderung: Das Krefelder Modell*. Düsseldorf: Schwann.

Dinan, D. 2004. *Europe Recast: A History of European Union*. Basingstoke: Palgrave Macmillan.

Dolby, N. 2000. Changing selves: Multicultural education and the challenge of new identities. *Teachers College Record*, 102(5), 898-912.

Dolby, N.E. 2001. *Constructing Race: Youth, Identity, and Popular Culture in South Africa*. Albany: State University of New York Press.

Douglass, S.L. and Shaikh, M.A. 2004. Defining Islamic education: Differentiation and applications. *Current Issues in Comparative Education*, 7(1), 5-18.

Duval Smith, A. 2005. Fading liberal dream tears Dutch apart. *The Observer*, 13 February, 22.

Düvell, F. 2009. *Irregular Migration in Northern Europe: Overview and Comparison*, Clandestino Project Conference, London, 27 March 2009, Available at: http://clandestino.eliamep.gr/wp-content/uploads/2009/04/key_note_28_3_09_fd.pdf [accessed: 5 August 2009].

Dyer, R. 1997. *White*. London: Routledge.

Ehrenreich, B. 1997. *Fear of Falling: The Inner Life of the Middle Classes*. New York: Harper-Perennial.

Emmanouilidis, J.A. 2008. Das differenzierte Europa: Königsweg oder Sackgasse der Integration? in *Die Verfassung Europas: Perspektiven des Integrationsprojekts*, edited by F. Decker and M. Höreth. Wiesbaden: Verlag für Sozialwissenschaften, 344-66.

Emmanouilidis, J.A. 2009a. Deutschland in der EU, in *Europa von A-Z: Taschenbuch der europäischen Integration*, edited by W. Weidenfeld and W. Wessels. Baden-Baden: Nomos Verlagsgesellschaft, 108-14.

Emmanouilidis, J.A. 2009b. *Global Europe 2025*, Paper for the 6th ELIAMEP European Seminar 'The Delphic Oracle on Europe: Politics and Policies' Conference, Delphi, 25-28 June 2009, Available at: http://www.eliamep.gr/en/wp-content/uploads/2009/06/emmanouilidis_global-europe-2025.pdf [accessed: 5 August 2009].

Engel, L. and Hinderliter Ortloff, D. 2009. From the local to the supranational: Curriculum reform and the production of the ideal citizen in two federal systems, Germany and Spain. *Journal of Curriculum Studies*, 41(2), 179-98.

Enneli, P. 2002. Social exclusion and young Turkish-speaking people's future prospects: Economic deprivation and the culturalization of ethnicity, in *Ethnicity and Economy: Race and Class Revisited*, edited by S. Fenton and H. Bradley. Basingstoke: Palgrave, 142-59.

Enneli, P., Modood, T. and Bradley, H. 2005. *Young Turks and Kurds: A Set of 'Invisible' Disadvantaged Groups*. York: Joseph Rowntree Foundation.

Enquete-Kommission 2002. *Bürgerschaftliches Engagement: Auf dem Weg in eine zukunftsfähige Bürgergesellschaft*. Berlin: Deutscher Bundestag.

Erdenir, B. 2010. Islamophobia qua racial discrimination: Muslimophobia, in *Muslims in 21st Century Europe: Structural and Cultural Perspectives*, edited by A. Triandafyllidou. London: Routledge, 27-44.

Esping-Andersen, G. 1990. *The Three Worlds of Welfare Capitalism*. Cambridge: Polity Press.

Esser, H. and Friedrichs, J. 1989. *Kulturelle und ethnische Identität bei Arbeitsmigranten im interkontextuellen, intergenerationalen und internationalen Vergleich*. Opladen: Westdeutscher Verlag.

European Commission 1982. *The Young Europeans* (Special Eurobarometer 18), Brussels: European Commission.

European Commission 1989. *The Young Europeans in 1987* (Special Eurobarometer 38), Brussels: European Commission.

European Commission 1991. *The Young Europeans in 1990* (Special Eurobarometer 51), Brussels: European Commission.

European Commission 1996. *The White Paper on Teaching and Learning: Towards the Learning Society.* Luxembourg: Office for Official Publications of the European Communities.

European Commission 1997. *The Young Europeans in 1997* (Special Eurobarometer 114), Brussels: European Commission.

European Commission 2001a. *Europeans and Languages* (Special Eurobarometer 147), Brussels: European Commission.

European Commission 2001b. *The Young Europeans in 2001* (Special Eurobarometer 151), Brussels: European Commission.

European Commission 2002. *Detailed Work Programme on the Follow-Up of the Objectives of Education and Training Systems in Europe.* Brussels: Official Journal of the European Union (C 142/01).

European Commission 2007. *Young Europeans* (Flash Eurobarometer 202), Brussels: European Commission.

European Commission 2008. *Migration and Mobility: Challenges and Opportunities for EU Education System*s. [Online]. Available at: http://eur-lex.europa.eu/LexUriServ/LexUriServ.do?uri=COM:2008:0423:FIN:EN:PDF [accessed: 6 August 2009].

European Commission (2009) *The Bologna Process: Towards the European Higher Education Area.* [Online]. Available at: http://ec.europa.eu/education/higher-education/doc1290_en.htm [accessed: 4 August 2009].

European Monitoring Centre on Racism and Xenophobia 2005. *Attitudes Towards Migrants and Minorities in Europe.* Wien: Manz Crossmedia GmbH and Co KG.

European Parliament and Council of the European Union 2006. *Decision No. 1983/2006/ EC of the European Parliament and of the Council of 18 December 2006 concerning the European Year of Intercultural Dialogue.* Brussels: Official Journal of the European Union (L 412/44).

Evans, R.J. 1997. *Rereading German History: From Unification to Reunification.* London: Routledge.

Faas, D. (forthcoming). The Nation, Europe and migration: A comparison of geography, history and citizenship education curricula in Greece, Germany and England. *Journal of Curriculum Studies.*

Faas, D. 2010. Muslims in Germany: From guest workers to citizens? in *Muslims in 21st Century Europe: Structural and Cultural Perspectives*, edited by A. Triandafyllidou. London: Routledge, 59-77.

Faist, T. (ed.) 2007. *Dual Citizenship in Europe: From Nationhood to Societal Integration.* Aldershot: Ashgate.

Finney, N. and Simpson, L. 2009. *'Sleepwalking to Segregation'?: Challenging Myths About Race and Migration.* Bristol: Policy Press.

Foucault, M. 1980. Two lectures, truth and power, in *Power/Knowledge: Selected Interviews and Other Writings 1972-77*, edited by C. Gordon. Brighton: Harvester, 78-133.

Foucault, M. 1988. Technologies of the self, in *Technologies of the Self: A Seminar with Michel Foucault*, edited by L. Martin, H. Gutman and P. Hutton. London: Tavistock, 16-49.

Fraga, L.R. and Elis, R. 2009. Interests and representation: Ethnic advocacy on California school boards. *Teachers College Record*, 111(3), 659-82.

Fülöp, M. and Ross, A. (eds) 2005. *Growing Up in Europe Today: Developing Identities Among Adolescents*. Stoke-on-Trent: Trentham Books.

Fuss, D. and Boehnke, K. (2004) *Doing Europe: Languages, Travel and Mobility*. [Online]. Available at: http://www.sociology.ed.ac.uk/youth/docs/Briefing4.pdf [accessed: 8 August 2009].

Gándara, P. and Rumberger, R.W. 2009. Immigration, language and education: How does language policy structure opportunity? *Teachers College Record*, 111(3), 750-82.

Gans, H. 1973. Introduction, in *Ethnic Identity and Assimilation: The Polish Community*, edited by N. Sandberg. New York: Praeger.

García Bedolla, L. 2005. *Fluid Borders: Latino Power, Identity, and Politics in Los Angeles*. Berkeley: University of California Press.

Geddes, A. 1999. *Britain in the European Union*. Tisbury: Baseline Book Company.

Gibson, M.A. 1976. Approaches to multicultural education in the United States: Some concepts and assumptions. *Anthropology and Education Quarterly*, 7(4), 7-18.

Gibson, M.A. and Hidalgo, N.D. 2009. Bridges to success in high school for migrant youth. *Teachers College Record*, 111(3), 683-711.

Giddens, A. 2000. *Runaway World: How Globalization is Reshaping Our Lives*. London: Routledge.

Gillborn, D. 1990. *'Race', Ethnicity and Education: Teaching and Learning in Multiethnic Schools*. London: Routledge.

Gillborn, D. 1995. *Racism and Antiracism in Real Schools*. Buckingham: Open University Press.

Gillborn, D. and Mirza, H.S. 2000. *Educational Inequality: Mapping Race, Class and Gender*. London: Office for Standards in Education.

Gilligan, C. 1982. *In a Different Voice: Psychological Theory and Women's Development*. Cambridge: Harvard University Press.

Gilroy, P. 1987. *There Ain't No Black in the Union Jack: The Cultural Politics of Race and Nation*. London: Hutchinson.

Gilroy, P. 2004. *After Empire: Melancholia or Convivial Culture?* London: Routledge.

Gilroy, P. 2005. *Postcolonial Melancholia*. New York: Columbia University Press.

Glaab, M. 1992. *Neugierig auf Europa? Die junge Generation in den neuen Bundesländern*. Bonn: Europa Union Verlag.

Goetz, K. 1996. Integration policy in a Europeanized state: Germany and the intergovernmental conference. *Journal of European Public Policy*, 3(1), 23-44.

Gogolin, I. 2000. Interkulturelle Erziehung in der multikulturellen Gesellschaft, in *Multikulturalität, Interkulturalität: Probleme und Prespektiven der multikulturellen Gesellschaft*, edited by C.Y. Robertson-Wensauer. Baden-Baden: Nomos Verlagsgesellschaft.

Gogolin, I. 2002. Linguistic and cultural diversity in Europe: A challenge for educational research and practice. *European Educational Research Journal*, 1(1), 123-38.

Gogolin, I. and Neumann, U. (eds) 2009. *Streitfall Zweisprachigkeit [The Bilingualism Controversy]*. Wiesbaden: Verlag für Sozialwissenschaften.

Goodhart, D. 2004. 'Too Diverse?' *Prospect Magazine*, 95, 30-7.

Gordon, T., Holland, J. and Lahelma, E. 2000. *Making Spaces: Citizenship and Difference in Schools*. Basingstoke: Palgrave.

Graves, J. 2002. Developing a global dimension in the curriculum. *The Curriculum Journal*, 13 (3), 303-11.

Green, A., Preston, J. and Germen Janmaat, J. (eds) 2006. *Education, Equality and Social Cohesion: A Comparative Analysis*. Basingstoke: Palgrave Macmillan.

Green, S. 2000. Beyond ethnoculturalism? German citizenship in the new millennium. *German Politics*, 9(3), 105-24.

Green, S. 2005. Between ideology and pragmatism: The politics of dual nationality in Germany. *International Migration Review*, 39(4), 921-52.

Grundy, S. and Jamieson, L. 2007. European identities: From absent-minded citizens to passionate Europeans. *Sociology*, 41(4), 663-80.

Guibernau, M. 2007. *The Identity of Nations*. Cambridge: Polity Press.

Guiraudon, V. 2006. Different nation, same nationhood: The challenges of immigrant policy, in *Changing France: The Politics that Markets Make*, edited by P.D. Culpepper, P.A. Hall, and B. Palier. Basingstoke: Palgrave Macmillan, 129-49.

Gundara, J.S. 2000. *Interculturalism, Education and Inclusion*. London: Paul Chapman.

Gundara, J.S. and Jacobs, S. (eds) 2000. *Intercultural Europe: Diversity and Social Policy*. Aldershot: Ashgate.

Ha, K.N. 2009. *Integration kann nicht verordnet werden: Ohne gleiche Rechte und Selbstbestimmung keine Integration*. [Online]. Available at: http://www.migration-boell.de/web/integration/47_1307.asp [accessed: 29 July 2009].

Hage, G. 1998. *White Nation: Fantasies of Supremacy in a Multicultural Society*. West Wickham: Pluto Press.

Habermas, J. 1992. Citizenship and national identity: Some reflections on the future of Europe. *Praxis International*, 12(1), 1-19.

Habermas, J. 1994. Struggles for recognition in the democratic constitutional state, in *Multiculturalism: Examining the Politics of Recognition*, edited by A. Gutmann. Princeton: Princeton University Press, 107-48.

Habermas, J. 2003. Towards a cosmopolitan Europe. *Journal of Democracy*, 14(4), 86-100.

Hall, S. 1991. The local and the global: Globalization and ethnicity, in *Culture, Globalization and the World System: Contemporary Conditions for the Representation of Identity*, edited by A. King. Basingstoke: Palgrave, 19-40.

Hall, S. 1992a. New ethnicities, in *'Race', Culture and Difference*, edited by J. Donald and A. Rattansi. London: Sage Publications, 252-59.

Hall, S. 1992b. The question of cultural identity, in *Modernity and its Futures*, edited by S. Hall, D. Held and T. McGrew. Cambridge: Polity Press, 273-326.

Hall, S. 1996. Who needs identity, in *Questions of Cultural Identity*, edited by S. Hall and P. du Gay. London: Sage, 1-17.

Halm, D. and Sauer, M. 2005. *Freiwilliges Engagement von Türkinnen und Türken in Deutschland*. Essen: Zentrum für Türkeistudien.

Halm, D. and Sauer, M. 2007. *Bürgerschaftliches Engagement von Türkinnen und Türken in Deutschland*. Wiesbaden: Verlag für Sozialwissenschaften.

Hankel, W., Nölling, W., Schachtschneider, K.-A. and Starbatty, J. 2001. *Die Euro-Illusion: Ist Europa noch zu retten?* Berlin: Rowohlt.

Hanrieder, W.F. 1995. *Deutschland, Europa, Amerika: Die Außenpolitik der Bundesrepublik 1949-1994*. Paderborn: Schoeningh.

Hansen, P. 1998. Schooling a European identity: Ethno-cultural exclusion and nationalist resonance within the EU policy of 'The European dimension of education'. *European Journal of Intercultural Studies*, 9(1), 5-23.

Hantrais, L. and Mangen, S. 1996. Method and management of cross-national social research, in *Cross-national Research Methods in the Social Sciences*, edited by L. Hantrais and S. Mangen. London and New York: Pinter, 1-12.

Haque, Z. 2000. The ethnic minority 'underachieving' group? Investigating the claims of 'underachievement' amongst Bangladeshi pupils in British secondary schools. *Race Ethnicity and Education*, 3(2), 145-68.

Hardy, J. and Vieler-Porter, C. 1990. Race, schooling and the 1988 Education Reform Act, in *The Education Reform Act 1988: Its Origins and Implications*, edited by M. Flude and M. Hammer. London: Falmer, 173-85.

Harris, C. 1988. Images of blacks in Britain: 1930-1960, in *Race and Social Policy*, edited by S. Allen and M. Macey. London: ESRC.

Haug, S. and Diehl, C. (eds) 2005. *Aspekte der Integration: Eingliederungsmuster und Lebenssituationen italienisch- und türkischstämmiger junger Erwachsener in Deutschland*. Wiesbaden: Verlag für Sozialwissenschaften.

Haug, S. Müssig, S. and Stichs, A. 2009. *Muslimisches Leben in Deutschland*. Nürnberg: Bundesamt für Migration und Flüchtlinge.

Hauler, A. 1994. *Die europäische Dimension in der schulischen Wirklichkeit: Eine quantitative Analyse des Europa-Unterrichts im historisch-politischen Unterricht an baden-württembergischen Realschulen*. Weingarten: Forschungsstelle für politisch-gesellschaftliche Erziehung.

Haw, K. 1998. *Educating Muslim Girls: Shifting Discourses*. Buckingham: Open University Press.

Haywood, C. and Mac an Ghaill, M. 1997. Materialism and deconstructivism: Education and the epistemology of identity. *Cambridge Journal of Education*, 27(2), 261-72.

Heater, D. 1990. *Citizenship: The Civic Ideal in World History, Politics and Education*. London and New York: Longman.

Heater, D. 1996. *World Citizenship and Government: Cosmopolitan Ideas in the History of Western Political Thought*. Basingstoke: Palgrave.

Heater, D. 2001. The history of citizenship education in England. *The Curriculum Journal*, 12(1), 103-23.

Heath, A. 2007. Crossnational patterns and processes of ethnic disadvantage, in *Unequal Chances: Ethnic Minorities in Western Labour Markets*, edited by A. Heath and S.Y. Cheung. Oxford: Oxford University Press, 639-95.

Heath, A. and Brinbaum, Y. (eds) 2007. Explaining ethnic inequalities in educational attainment. Special issue of *Ethnicities*, 7(3), 291-474.

Heath, A. and Roberts, J. 2008. *British Identity: Its Sources and Possible Implications for Civic Attitudes and Behaviour*. [Online]. Available at: http://www.justice.gov.uk/reviews/docs/british-identity.pdf [accessed: 1 July 2009].

Heath, A., Martin, J. and Elgenius, G. 2007. Who do we think we are? The decline of traditional social identities, in *British Social Attitudes: The 23rd Report – Perspectives on Changing Society*, edited by A. Park, M. Johnson, J. Curtice, K. Thomson and M. Phillips. London: Sage, 1-34.

Heckmann, F. and Schnapper, D. (eds) 2003. *The Integration of Immigrants in European Societies: National Differences and Trends of Convergence*. Stuttgart: Lucius and Lucius.

Herbert, U. 2003. *Geschichte der Ausländerpolitik in Deutschland*. Bonn: Bundeszentrale für politische Bildung.

Hewer, C. 2001. Schools for Muslims. *Oxford Review of Education*, 27(4), 515-27.

Hills, J. and Stewart, K. 2005. *A More Equal Society? New Labour, Poverty, Inequality and Exclusion*. Bristol: Policy Press.

Hinderliter Ortloff, D. 2005. Becoming European: A framing analysis of three countries' civics education curricula. *European Education*, 37(4), 35-49.

Hiro, D. 1991. *Black British, White British*. London: Grafton.

Hoff, G.R. 1995. Multicultural education in Germany: Historical development and current status, in *Handbook of Research on Multicultural Education*, edited by J.A. Banks. New York: Macmillan, 821-38.

Holdaway, J. and Alba, R. 2009. Introduction: Educating immigrant youth: The role of institutions and agency. *Teachers College Record*, 111(3), 597-615.

Holdaway, J., Crul, M. and Roberts, C. 2009. Cross-national comparison of provision and outcomes for the education of the second generation. *Teachers College Record*, 111(6), 1381-403.

Holmes, B. 1981. *Comparative Education: Some Considerations on Method*. London: Allen and Unwin.

Home Office 2002. *Nationality, Immigration and Asylum Act 2002*. (c.41), London: HMSO.

Home Office 2003. *The New and the Old: The Report of the 'Life in the United Kingdom' Advisory Group*. London: HMSO.

Home Office 2005. *Improving Opportunity, Strengthening Society: The Government's Strategy to Increase Race Equality and Community Cohesion*. London: HMSO.

Howard, M.M. 2008. The causes and consequences of Germany's new citizenship law. *German Politics*, 17(1), 41-62.

Huntington, S.P. 2004. *Who Are We? The Challenges to America's National Identity*. New York: Simon and Schuster.

Husén, T., Tuijnman, A. and Halls, W.D. 1992. *Schooling in Modern European Society*. London: Pergamon Press.

Hussain, Y. and Bagguley, P. 2005. Citizenship, ethnicity and identity: British Pakistanis after the 2001 'riots'. *Sociology*, 39(3), 407-25.

İçener, E. 2007. Privileged partnership: An alternative final destination for Turkey's integration with the European Union? *Perspectives on European Politics and Society*, 8(4), 415-38.

Ireland, E., Kerr, D., Lopes, J., Nelson, J. with Cleaver, E. 2006. *Active Citizenship and Young People: Opportunities, Experiences and Challenges in and Beyond School*. London: DfES.

Issa, T. 2005. *Talking Turkey: The Language, Culture and Identity of Turkish Speaking Children in Britain*. Stoke-on-Trent: Trentham Books.

Jamieson, L. 2002. Theorising identity, nationality and citizenship: Implications for European citizenship identity. *Slovak Sociological Review*, 34(6), 507-32.

Jann, W. 2003. State, administration and governance in Germany: Competing traditions and dominant narratives. *Public Administration*, 8(1), 95-118.

Jetten, J., Branscombe, N.R., Schmitt, M.T. and Spears, R. 2001. Rebels with cause: Group identification as a response to perceived discrimination from mainstream. *Personality and Social Psychology Bulletin*, 27(9), 1204-13.

Joppke, C. 2004. The retreat of multiculturalism in the liberal state: Theory and policy. *British Journal of Sociology*, 55(2), 237-57.

Joppke, C. 2007. State neutrality and Islamic headscarf laws in France and Germany. *Theory and Society*, 36(4), 313-42.

Kagitçibasi, C. 1991. Türkische Migranten aus der Sicht des Herkunftslandes, in *Türkische Jugendliche und Aussiedlerkinder in Familie und Schule*, edited by P. Bott, H. Merkens and F. Schmidt. Hohengehren: Schneider, 31-43.

Kandel, I.L. 1933. *Studies in Comparative Education*. Boston: Houghton Mifflin.

Karlsen, G.E. 2002. Educational policy and educational programmes in the European Union: A tool for political integration and economic competition, in *Education in Europe: Policies and Politics*, edited by J.A. Ibanez-Martin and G. Jover. Dordrecht: Kluwer, 23-52.

Karolewski, I.P. and Suszycki, A.M. (eds) 2007. *Nationalism and European Integration: The Need for New Theoretical and Empirical Insights*. London and New York: Continuum.

Kasinitz, P., Mollenkopf, J.H. and Waters, M.C. (eds) 2004. *Becoming New Yorkers: Ethnographies of the New Second Generation*. New York: Russel Sage Foundation.

Kasinitz, P., Mollenkopf, J.H., Waters, M.C. and Holdaway, J. 2008. *Inheriting the City: The Children of Immigrants Coming of Age*. Cambridge: Harvard University Press.

Kastoryano, R. 2002. *Negotiating Identities: States and Immigrants in France and Germany*. Princeton: Princeton University Press.

Kastoryano, R. 2006. French secularism and Islam: France's headscarf affair, in *Multiculturalism, Muslims and Citizenship: A European Approach*, edited by T. Modood, A. Triandafyllidou and R. Zapata Barrero. London: Routledge, 57-69.

Katzenstein, P.J. 1997. United Germany in an integrating Europe, in *Tamed Power: Germany in Europe*, edited by P.J. Katzenstein. Ithaca: Cornell University Press, 1-48.

Keating, A. 2009. Nationalizing the post-national: Reframing European citizenship for the civics curriculum in Ireland. *Journal of Curriculum Studies*, 41(2), 159-78.

Kerr, D. 1999. *Re-Examining Citizenship Education: The Case of England*. Slough: National Foundation for Educational Research.

Kerr, D., Cleaver, E., Ireland, E. and Blenkinsop, S. 2003. *Citizenship Education Longitudinal Study First Cross-Sectional Survey 2001-2002*. London: DfES.

Kerr, D., Ireland, E., Lopes, J., Craig, R. and Cleaver, E. 2004. *Citizenship Education Longitudinal Study Second Annual Report: Making Citizenship Education Real*. London: DfES.

Kesidou, A. 1999. *Die europäische Dimension der griechischen und baden-württembergischen Lehrpläne und Schulbücher der Sekundarschule: An den Beispielen Geographie, politische Bildung, Geschicht und Literatur*. Frankfurt am Main: Lang.

Kincheloe, J. and Steinberg, S. 1997. *Changing Multiculturalism*. Buckingham: Open University Press.

King, R. and Bridal, J. 1982. The changing distribution of Cypriots in London. *Etudes Migrations*, 19(65), 93-121.

King, A.S. 1993. Introduction, in *The Multicultural Dimension of the National Curriculum*, edited by A.S. King and M.J. Reiss. London: Falmer, 2-20.

Klein, G. 1993. *Education Towards Race Equality*. London: Cassell.

Koopmans, R., Statham, P., Giugni, M., Passy, F. 2005. *Contested Citizenship: Immigration and Cultural Diversity in Europe*. Minneapolis: University of Minnesota Press.

Kristen, C. and Granato, N. 2007. The educational attainment of the second generation in Germany: Social origins and ethnic inequality. *Ethnicities*, 7(3), 343-66.

Kristen, C., Reimer, D. and Kogan, I. 2008. Higher education entry of Turkish immigrant youth in Germany. *International Journal of Comparative Sociology*, 49(2-3), 127-51.

Krumm, H.J. 2009. Die Bedeutung der Mehrsprachigkeit in den Identitätskonzepten von Migrant(inn)en, in *Streitfall Zweisprachigkeit [The Bilingualism Controversy]*, edited by I. Gogolin and U. Neumann. Wiesbaden: Verlag für Sozialwissenschaften.

Küçükcan, T. 1999. *Politics of Ethnicity, Identity and Religion: Turkish Muslims in Britain*. Aldershot: Ashgate.

Kultusministerkonferenz 1950. *Vorläufige Grundsätze zur politischen Bildung an den Schulen und Hochschulen: Beschluss der Kultusministerkonferenz vom 15.6.1950*. Bonn: Sekretariat der Ständigen Konferenz der Kultusminister der Länder in der Bundesrepublik Deutschland.

Kultusministerkonferenz 1990. *Europa im Unterricht: Beschluss der Kultusministerkonferenz vom 08.06.1978 in der Fassung vom 07.12.1990*. Bonn: Sekretariat der Ständigen Konferenz der Kultusminister der Länder in der Bundesrepublik Deutschland.

Kultusministerkonferenz 1992. *Zur europäischen Dimension im Bildungswesen: Beschluss der Kultusministerkonferenz vom Juni 1992*. Bonn: Sekretariat der Ständigen Konferenz der Kultusminister der Länder in der Bundesrepublik Deutschland.

Kultusministerkonferenz 1996. *Interkulturelle Bildung und Erziehung in der Schule: Beschluss der Kultusministerkonferenz vom 25.10.1996*. Bonn: Sekretariat der Ständigen Konferenz der Kultusminister der Länder in der Bundesrepublik Deutschland.

Kultusministerkonferenz 2004a. *Vereinbarung über Bildungsstandards für den Primarbereich: Beschluss der Kultusministerkonferenz vom 15.10.2004*. Bonn: Sekretariat der Ständigen Konferenz der Kultusminister der Länder in der Bundesrepublik Deutschland.

Kultusministerkonferenz 2004b. *Vereinbarung über Bildungsstandards für den Hauptschulabschluss: Beschluss der Kultusministerkonferenz vom 15.10.2004*. Bonn: Sekretariat der Ständigen Konferenz der Kultusminister der Länder in der Bundesrepublik Deutschland.

Kultusministerkonferenz 2004c. *Vereinbarung über Bildungsstandards für den Mittleren Schulabschluss: Beschluss der Kultusministerkonferenz vom 15.10.2004*. Bonn: Sekretariat der Ständigen Konferenz der Kultusminister der Länder in der Bundesrepublik Deutschland.

Kultusministerkonferenz 2004d. *Standards für die Lehrerbildung: Beschluss der Kultusministerkonferenz vom 16.12.2004*. Bonn: Sekretariat der Ständigen Konferenz der Kultusminister der Länder in der Bundesrepublik Deutschland.

Kultusministerkonferenz 2006. *Bericht 'Zuwanderung': Beschluss der Kultusministerkonferenz vom 24.05.2002 in der Fassung vom 16.11.2006*. [Online]. Available at: http://www.kmk.org/fileadmin/veroeffentlichungen_beschluesse/2002/2002_05_24-Zuwanderung.pdf [accessed: 6 August 2009].

Kultusministerkonferenz 2008. *Europabildung in der Schule: Beschluss der Kultusministerkonferenz vom 08.06.1978 in der Fassung vom 05.05.2008*. [Online]. Available at: http://www.kmk.org/fileadmin/veroeffentlichungen_beschluesse/1978/1978_06_08_Europabildung.pdf [accessed: 8 August 2009].

Kuus, M. 2004. Europe's eastern expansion and the re-inscription of otherness in East Central Europe. *Progress in Human Geography*, 28(4), 472-89.

Kymlicka, W. 1989. *Liberalism, Community and Culture*. Oxford: Oxford University Press.

Kymlicka, W. 1995. *Multicultural Citizenship*. Oxford: Oxford University Press.

Kymlicka, W. 1998. *Finding Our Way*. Ontario: Oxford University Press.

Kymlicka, W. 2001. *Politics in the Vernacular*. New York: Oxford University Press.

Landeshauptstadt Stuttgart 2003. *A Pact for Integration: The Stuttgart Experience*. [Online]. Available at: http://www.stuttgart.de/img/mdb/publ/4843/25686.pdf [accessed: 5 August 2009].

Lash, S. and Urry, J. 1987. *The End of Organized Capitalism*. Cambridge: Polity Press.

Lee, S.S. 2004. Class matters: Racial and ethnic identities of working- and middle-class second-generation Korean Americans in New York City, in *Becoming New Yorkers: Ethnographies of the New Second Generation*, edited by P. Kasinitz, J.H. Mollenkopf and M.C. Waters. New York: Russel Sage Foundation, 313-38.

Lee, T. 2008. Race, immigration, and the identity-to-politics link. *Annual Review of Political Science*, 11, 457-78.

Lentin, R. 2001. Responding to the racialisation of Irishness: Disavowed multiculturalism and its discontents. *Sociological Research Online*, 5(4). [Online]. Available at: http://www.socresonline.org.uk/5/4/lentin.html [accessed 31 January 2010].

Levitt, P. and Waters, M.C. 2002. *The Changing Face of Home: The Transnational Lives of the Second Generation*. New York: Russel Sage Foundation.

Lewicka-Grisdale, K. and McLaughlin, T.H. 2002. Education for European identity and European citizenship, in *Education in Europe: Policies and Politics*, edited by J.A. Ibanez-Martin and G. Jover. Dordrecht: Kluwer, 53-82.

Louie, V. 2004. *Compelled to Excel: Immigration, Education and Opportunity Among Chinese Americans*. Stanford: Stanford University Press.

Louie, V. 2006. Second-generation pessimism and optimism: How Chinese and Dominicans understand education and mobility through ethnic and transnational orientations. *International Migration Review*, 40(3), 537-72.

Louie, V. and Holdaway, J. 2009. Catholic schools and immigrant students: A new generation. *Teachers College Record*, 111(3), 783-816.

Luchtenberg, S. 1996. The European dimension and multicultural education: Compatible or contradictory concepts, in *Challenges to European Education: Cultural Values, National Identities, and Global Responsibilities*, edited by T. Winther-Jensen. Frankfurt am Main: Peter Lang, 281-93.

Luchtenberg, S. 1997. Stages in multicultural theory and practice in Germany, in *Cultural Democracy and Ethnic Pluralism: Multicultural and Multilingual Policies in Education*, edited by R.J. Watts and J. Jerzy. Bern: Peter Lang, 125-48.

Mac an Ghaill, M. 1988. *Young, Gifted and Black*. Milton Keynes: Open University Press.

Mac an Ghaill, M. 1994. *The Making of Men: Masculinities, Sexualities and Schooling*. Buckingham: Open University Press.

Mac an Ghaill, M. 1999. *Contemporary Racisms and Ethnicities: Social and Cultural Transformations*. Buckingham: Open University Press.

MacDonald, I. 1983. *Immigration Law and Practice in the United Kingdom*. London: Butterworth.

MacLure, M. 2003. *Discourse in Educational and Social Research*. Maidenhead: Open University Press.

Malik, K. 1998. Race, pluralism and the meaning of difference. *New Formations*, 33, 125-35.

Malmborg. M. and Stråth, B. (eds) 2001. *Meanings of Europe: Variety and Contention Within and Among Nations*. Oxford: Berg.

Mandel, R. 2008. *Cosmopolitan Anxieties: Turkish Challenges to Citizenship and Belonging in Germany*. Durham: Duke University Press.

Marques, M.M., Valente Rosa, M.J. and Lopes Martins, J. 2007. School and diversity in a weak state: The Portuguese case. *Journal of Ethnic and Migration Studies*, 33(7), 1145-68.

Marshall, B. 2000. *The New Germany and Migration in Europe*. Manchester: Manchester University Press.

Marshall, H. 2007. Global education in perspective: Fostering a global dimension in an English secondary school. *Cambridge Journal of Education*, 37(3), 355-74.

Martin, P.L. 1994. Germany: Reluctant land of immigration, in *Controlling Immigration: A Global Perspective*, edited by W.A. Cornelius, P.L. Martin and J.F. Hollifield. Stanford: Stanford University Press, 189-226.

May, A. 1999. *Britain and Europe since 1945*. Harlow: Addison Wesley Longman.

May, S. 1994. *Making Multicultural Education Work*. Clevedon: Multilingual Matters.

May, S. 1999. *Critical Multiculturalism: Rethinking Multicultural and Antiracist Education*. Philadelphia: Falmer.

McCrone, D. and Kiely, R. 2000. Nationalism and citizenship. *Sociology*, 34(1), 19-34.

Meer, N. and Modood, T. 2009. The multicultural state we are in: Muslims, 'multiculture' and the 'civic re-balancing' of British multiculturalism. *Political Studies*, 57(3), 473-97.

Mehmet Ali, A. 2001. *Turkish Speaking Communities and Education: No Delight*. London: Fatal Publications.

Mercer, K. 2000. A sociography of diaspora, in *Without Guarantees: In Honour of Stuart Hall*, edited by P. Gilroy, L. Grossberg and A. McRobbie. London: Verso, 233-45.

Modood, T. 1992. *Not Easy Being British: Colour, Culture and Citizenship*. Stoke-on-Trent: Trentham Books.

Modood, T. 1997. Introduction: The politics of multiculturalism in the new Europe, in *The Politics of Multiculturalism in the New Europe: Racism, Identity and Community*, edited by T. Modood and P. Werbner. London: Zed Books, 1-25.

Modood, T. 2000. Anti-essentialism, multiculturalism and the 'recognition of religious groups', in *Citizenship in Diverse Schools*, edited by W. Kymlicka and W. Norman. Oxford: Oxford University Press, 175-98.

Modood, T. 2005a. A defence of multiculturalism. *Soundings*, 29(1), 62-71.

Modood, T. 2005b. *Multicultural Politics: Racism, Ethnicity and Muslims in Britain*. Edinburgh: Edinburgh University Press.

Modood, T. 2007. *Multiculturalism: A Civic Idea*. Oxford: Polity Press.

Modood, T., Berthoud, R. and Lakey, J. 1997. *Ethnic Minorities in Britain: Diversity and Disadvantage*. London: Policy Studies Institute.

Modood, T., Triandafyllidou, A. and Zapata-Barrero, R. (eds) 2006. *Multiculturalism, Muslims and Citizenship: A European Approach*. London: Routledge.

Moore, J. 1997. Brief candle or light through yonder window? Multicultural education in Britain in the eighties and nineties, in *Cultural Democracy and Ethnic Pluralism: Multicultural and Multilingual Policies in Education*, edited by R.J. Watts and J. Jerzy. Bern: Peter Lang, 149-64.

Morgan, D.L. 1988. *Focus Groups as Qualitative Research*. Beverly Hills: Sage.

Moscovici, S. 1984. The phenomenon of social representations, in *Social Representations*, edited by R.M. Farr and S. Moscovici. Cambridge: Cambridge University Press, 3-69.

Mullard, C. 1982. Multicultural education in Britain: From assimilation to cultural pluralism, in *Race, Migration and Schooling*, edited by J. Tierney, P. Dickinson and M. Syer. London: Holt, 120-33.

National Association of Schoolmasters Union of Women Teachers 2003. *Islamophobia: Advice for Schools and Colleges*. Birmingham: NASUWT.

Natterer, A. 2001. *Europa im Schulbuch: Die Darstellung der europäischen Einigung in baden-württembergischen Schulbüchern für Geschichte und Gemeinschaftskunde der Sekundarstufe I*. Grevenbroich: Omnia.

Nayak, A. 1999. White English ethnicities: Racism, anti-racism and student perspectives. *Race Ethnicity and Education*, 2(2), 177-202.

Nayak, A. 2001. Ice white and ordinary: New perspectives on ethnicity, gender and youth cultural identities, in *Investigating Gender: Contemporary Perspectives in Education*, edited by B. Francis and C. Skelton. Buckingham: Open University Press, 139-51.

Neave, G. 1984. *The EEC and Education*. Stoke-on-Trent: Trentham Books.

Nieto, S. and Bode, P. 2007. *Affirming Diversity: The Socio-Political Context of Multicultural Education*. 5th Edition. Boston: Allyn and Bacon.

Nigbur, D., Brown, R., Cameron, L., Hossain, R., Landau, A.R., Le Touze, D.S., Rutland, A. and Watters, C. 2008. Acculturation, well-being and classroom behaviour among white British and British Asian primary-school children in the south-east of England: Validating a child-friendly measure of acculturation attitudes. *International Journal of Intercultural Relations*, 32(6), 493-504.

Nuffield Foundation 2002. *Response from the Steering Group of the Nuffield Languages Programme to the Consultation Document 14-19: Extending Opportunities, Raising Standards*. [Online]. Available at: http://languages.nuffieldfoundation.org/filelibrary/pdf/response_to_14to19_green_paper.pdf [accessed: 28 July 2009].

Olsen, L. 1997. *Made in America: Immigrant Students in Our Public Schools*. New York: The New Press.

Olsen, J. 1999. *Nature and Nationalism: Right-Wing Ecology and the Politics of Identity in Contemporary Germany*. Basingstoke: Palgrave.

Olsen, L. 2009. The role of advocacy in shaping immigrant education: A California case study. *Teachers College Record*, 111(3), 817-50.

Organization for Economic Co-operation and Development 2006. *Where Immigrant Students Succeed: A Comparative Review of Performance and Engagement in PISA 2003*. Paris: OECD.

Organization for Economic Co-operation and Development 2007. *Naturwissenschaftliche Kompetenzen für die Welt von Morgen: OECD Briefing Note für Deutschland*. Paris: OECD.

Organization for Economic Co-operation and Development 2008. *Thematic Review on Migrant Education*. [Online]. Available at: http://www.oecd.org/ [accessed: 10 August 2009].

Osler, A. 1994. Education for development: Redefining citizenship in a pluralist society, in *Development Education: Global Perspectives in the Curriculum*, edited by A. Osler. London: Cassell, 32-49.

Osler, A. 1995. Citizenship, schooling and teacher education, in *Teaching for Citizenship in Europe*, edited by A. Osler, H.F. Rathenow and H. Starkey. Stoke-on-Trent: Trentham Books, 3-14.

Osler, A. 1999. Citizenship, democracy and political literacy. *Multicultural Teaching*, 18(1), 12-5.

Osler, A. and Starkey, H. 2001. Citizenship education and national identities in France and England: Inclusive or exclusive? *Oxford Review of Education*, 27(2), 287-305.

Osler, A. and Starkey, H. 2003. Learning for cosmopolitan citizenship: Theoretical debates and young people's experiences. *Educational Review*, 55(3), 243-54.

Osler, A. and Vincent, K. 2002. *Citizenship and the Challenge of Global Education*. Stoke-on-Trent: Trentham Books.

Ouseley, H. 2001. *Community Pride Not Prejudice: Making Diversity Work in Bradford*. Bradford: Bradford Vision.

Pagels, N. 2008. *Neue Ohrfeigen für das AGG: Vertragsverletzungsverfahren der EU-Kommission gegen die Bundesrepublik Deutschland.* [Online]. Available at: http://www.migration-boell.de/web/diversity/48_1623.asp [accessed: 31 July 2009].

Papoulia-Tzelpi, P. and Hegstrup, S. and Ross, A. (eds) 2005. *Emerging Identities Among Young Children: European Issues.* Stoke-on-Trent: Trentham Books.

Parekh, B. 2000. *Rethinking Multiculturalism: Cultural Diversity and Political Theory.* Basingstoke: Palgrave.

Parekh, B. 2008. *A New Politics of Identity: Political Principles for an Interdependent World.* Basingstoke: Palgrave.

Peil, F. and Ernst, S. 2005. Mord an junger Türkin. *Spiegel Online* [Online: 19 April]. Available at: http://www.spiegel.de/panorama/0,1518,342484,00.html [accessed: 27 July 2009].

Pepin, B. 2005. Can we compare like with like in comparative educational research? Methodological considerations in cross-cultural studies in mathematics education, in *Researching and Teaching the Learning of Mathematics II*, edited by B. Hudson and J. Fragner. Linz: Trauner, 39-54.

Philippou, S. 2007. Re-inventing 'Europe': The case of the European dimension in Greek Cypriot curricula of history and geography. *Curriculum Journal*, 18(1), 57-88.

Philipps, M. 1999. *Windrush: The Irresistible Rise of Multiracial Britain.* London: HarperCollins.

Phoenix, A. 1997. 'I'm white! So what? The construction of whiteness for young Londoners, in *Off White: Readings on Race, Power and Society*, edited by M. Fine, L. Weis, L. Powell and L. Mun Wong. New York: Routledge, 187-97.

Pichler, F. 2009. Cosmopolitan Europe: Views and identity. *European Societies*, 11(1), 3-24.

Piepenschneider, M. 1992. *Die europäische Generation: Europabilder in der Bundesrepublik Deutschland.* Bonn: Europa Union Verlag.

Pieterse, J.N. 1995. Globalization as hybridization, in *Global Modernities*, edited by M. Featherstone and S. Lash. London: Sage, 45-68.

Piper, N. 1998. *Racism, Nationalism and Citizenship: Ethnic Minorities in Britain and Germany.* Aldershot: Ashgate.

Pong, S. and Hao, L. 2007. Neighbourhood and school factors in the school performance of immigrants' children. *International Migration Review*, 41(1), 206-41.

Portes, A. and Rumbaut, R.G. 2001. *Legacies: The Story of the Immigrant Second Generation.* Berkeley: University of California Press.

Portes, A. and Zhou, M. 1993. The new second generation: Segmented assimilation and its variants. *Annals of the American Academy of Political and Social Science*, 530(1), 74-96.

Portes, A., Fernández-Kelly, P. and Haller, W. 2005. Segmented assimilation on the ground: The new second generation in early adulthood. *Ethnic and Racial Studies*, 28(6), 1000-40.

Priddat, B. and Wilms, H. 2008. *Nutzen und Kosten des Allgemeinen Gleichbehandlungsgesetzes (AGG)*. Berlin: Antidiskrimminierungsstelle des Bundes.

Qualifications and Curriculum Authority 1998. *Education for Citizenship and the Teaching of Democracy in Schools*. London: QCA.

Qualifications and Curriculum Authority 2000. *Citizenship at Key Stages 3 and 4: Initial Guidance for Schools*. London: QCA.

Qualifications and Curriculum Authority 2009. National Curriculum. [Online]. Available at: http://curriculum.qca.org.uk [accessed: 9 August 2009].

Rassool, N. 1999. Flexible identities: Exploring race and gender issues among a group of immigrant pupils in an inner-city comprehensive school. *British Journal of Sociology of Education*, 20(1), 23-36.

Raveaud, M. 2008. Culture-blind? Parental discourse on religion, ethnicity and secularism in the French educational context. *European Educational Research Journal*, 7(1), 74-88.

Raymond, G.G. and Modood, T. 2007. *The Construction of Minority Identities in France and Britain*. Basingstoke: Palgrave Macmillan.

Reay, D. 2008. Psychosocial aspects of white middle-class identities: Desiring and defending against the class and ethnic 'other' in urban multi-ethnic schooling. *Sociology*, 42(6), 1072-88.

Reay, D., Hollingworth, S., Williams, K., Crozier, G., Jamieson, F., James, D. and Beedell, P. 2007. 'A darker shade of pale?' Whiteness, the middle classes and multi-ethnic inner city schooling. *Sociology*, 41(6), 1041-60.

Reay, D., Crozier, G., James, D., Hollingworth, S., Williams, K., Jamieson, F. and Beedell, P. 2008. Re-invigorating democracy? White middle class identities and comprehensive schooling. *Sociological Review*, 56(2), 238-55.

Reeves, F. 1983. *British Racial Discourse*. Cambridge: Cambridge University Press.

Riemann, W. and Harrassowitz, O. 1990. *Über das Leben in Bitterland: Bibliographie zur türkischen Deutschlandliteratur und zur türkischen Literatur in Deutschland*. Wiesbaden: Harrassowitz.

Riesgo Alonso, V. 2009. *Chancen für den Nationalen Integrationsplan durch Mobilisierung und Partizipation*. [Online]. Available at: http://www.migration-boell.de/web/integration/47_1353.asp [accessed: 25 July 2009].

Risse, T. 2004. European institutions and identity change: What have we learned? in *Transnational Identities*, edited by R. Herrmann, T. Risse and M. Brewer. Oxford: Rowman and Littlefield, 247-71.

Risse, T. and Engelmann-Martin, D. 2002. Identity politics and European integration: The case of Germany, in *The Idea of Europe: From Antiquity to the European Union*, edited by A. Pagden. Cambridge: Cambridge University Press, 287-316.

Ritchie, D. 2001. *Oldham Independent Review Panel Report*. Oldham: Oldham Metropolitan Borough Council and Greater Manchester Police.

Ros, M. and Grad, H. 2004. *Who Do You Think You Are? Regional, National and European Identities in Interaction*. [Online]. Available at: http://www. sociology.ed.ac.uk/youth/docs/Briefing 2.pdf [accessed: 2 July 2009].

Roxburgh, A. 2002. *Preachers of Hate: The Rise of the Far Right*. London: Gibson Square.

Runnymede Trust 2000. *The Future of Multi-Ethnic Britain: Report of the Commission on the Future of Multiethnic Britain*. London: Profile Books.

Ryba, R. 1992. Toward a European dimension in education: Intention and reality in European Community policy and practice. *Comparative Education Review*, 36(1), 10-24.

Ryba, R. 1995. Unity in diversity: The enigma of the European dimension in education. *Oxford Review of Education*, 21(1), 25-36.

Ryba, R. 2000. Developing the European dimension in education: The roles of the European Union and the Council of Europe, in *Problems and Prospects in European Education*, edited by E.S. Swing, J. Schriewer and F. Orivel. London: Praeger, 244-61.

Sadler, M. 1964. How far can we learn anything of practical value from the study of foreign systems of education? *Comparative Education Review*, 7(3), 307-14.

Sander, W. 2003. *Politik in der Schule: Kleine Geschichte der politischen Bildung*. Bonn: Bundeszentrale für Politische Bildung.

Santel, B. and Weber, A. 2000. Zwischen Ausländerpolitik und Einwanderungspolitik: Migrations- und Ausländerrecht in Deutschland, in *Migrationsreport 2000*, edited by K.J. Bade and R. Münz. Bonn: Bundeszentrale für Politische Bildung, 109-40.

Sarup, M. 1986. *The Politics of Multiracial Education*. London: Routledge.

Sarup, M. 1991. *Education and the Ideologies of Racism*. Stoke-on-Trent: Trentham Books.

Sarup, M. 1993 *An Introductory Guide to Post-structuralism and Postmodernism*. London: Harvester.

Sauer, M. 2007. *Perspektiven des Zusammenlebens: Die Integration türkischstämmiger Migrantinnen und Migranten in Nordrhein-Westfalen*. Essen: Stiftung Zentrum für Türkeistudien.

Savage, T. 2004. Europe and Islam: Crescent waxing, cultures clashing. *The Washington Quarterly*, 27(3), 25-50.

Savvides, N. and Faas, D. (forthcoming) 'Does Europe matter? A comparative analysis of young people's European identities at a state school and a 'European school' in England. *Compare*.

Sayad, A. 2004. *The Suffering of the Immigrant*. Cambridge: Polity Press.

Scarman, L. 1981. *The Brixton Disorders: 10-12 April 1981, Report of an Enquiry by the Right Honourable The Lord Scarman*. (Cmnd. 8427), London: HMSO.

Schäfer, T. and Brückner, G. 2008. Soziale Homogenität der Bevölkerung bei alternativen Definitionen für Migration: Eine Analyse am Beispiel von

Bildungsbeteiligung, Erwerbstätigkeit und Einkommen auf der Basis von Mikrozensusdaten. *Wirtschaft und Statistik*, 12, 1046-66.

Schiffauer, W. 2006. Enemies within the gates: The debate about the citizenship of Muslims in Germany, in *Multiculturalism, Muslims and Citizenship: A European Approach*, edited by T. Modood, A. Triandafyllidou and R. Zapata-Barrero. London: Routledge, 94-116.

Schiffauer, W., Baumann, G, Kastoryano, R. and Vertovec, S. (eds) 2004. *Civil Enculturation: Nation-state, School and Ethnic Difference in Four European Countries*. Oxford: Berghahn Books.

Schissler, H. and Soysal, Y.N. (eds) 2005. *The Nation, Europe and the World: Textbooks and Curricula in Transition*. Oxford: Berghahn Books.

Schulte, A. 1999. Demokratie als Leitbild einer multikulturellen Gesellschaft, in *Medien und multikulturelle Gesellschaft*, edited by C. Butterwege, G. Hentges and F. Sarigöz. Opladen: Leske and Budrich, 187-206.

Schwarz, H.-P. (ed.) 1975. *Konrad Adenauer: Reden 1917-1967. Eine Auswahl.* Stuttgart: Deutsche Verlags-Anstalt.

Seibert, H. 2008. *Junge Migranten am Arbeitsmarkt: Bildung und Einbürgerung verbessern die Chancen.* Nürnberg: Institut für Arbeit und Berufsforschung.

Şen, F. and Goldberg, A. 1994. *Türken in Deutschland: Leben zwischen zwei Kulturen*, München: C.H. Beck.

Şen, F. and Sauer, M. 2006. *Islam in Deutschland – Einstellungen der türkischstämmigen Muslime: Religiöse Praxis und organisatorische Vertretung türkischstämmiger Muslime in Deutschland.* Essen: Zentrum für Türkeistudien.

Sewell, T. 1997. *Black Masculinities and Schooling*. Stoke-on-Trent: Trentham Books.

Shennan, M. 1991. *Teaching About Europe*. London: Cassell-Council of Europe.

Siedler, D. 2002. *Islamunterricht an deutschen Schulen: Erste Erfahrungen im nordrhein-westfälischen Schulversuch*. [Online]. Available at: http://www.uni-leipzig.de/~rp/vortraege/siedler.html [accessed: 21 July 2009].

Skeggs, B. 1997. *Formations of Class and Gender: Becoming Respectable.* London: Sage.

Skinner, G. 2002. Religious pluralism and school provision in Britain. *Intercultural Education*, 13(2), 171-81.

Skrobanek, J. 2009. Perceived discrimination, ethnic identity and the (re-) ethnicization of youth with a Turkish ethnic background in Germany. *Journal of Ethnic and Migration Studies*, 35(4), 535-54.

Sleeter, C. 1993. How white teachers construct race, in *Race Identity and Representation in Education*, edited by C. McCarthy and W. Crichlow. New York: Routledge, 157-71.

Smith, M.P. 2007. The two faces of transnational citizenship. *Ethnic and Racial Studies*, 30(6), 1096-116.

Solomos, J. 1992. The politics of immigration since 1945, in *Racism and Antiracism: Inequalities, Opportunities and Policies*, edited by P. Braham, A. Rattansi and R. Skellington. London: Sage.

Solomos, J. 1993. *Race and Racism in Britain*. London: Macmillan.

Song, M. 2009. Is intermarriage a good indicator of integration? *Journal of Ethnic and Migration Studies*, 35(2), 331-48.

Sonyel, S.R. 1988. *The Silent Minority: Turkish Muslim Children in British Schools*. Cambridge: The Islamic Academy.

Soysal, Y. 1994. *Limits of Citizenship: Migrants and Postnational Membership in Europe*. Chicago: University of Chicago Press.

Soysal, Y. 2002a. Locating European identity in education, in *Fabricating Europe: The Formation of an Education Space*, edited by A. Nóvoa and M. Lawn. Dordrecht: Kluwer, 55-68.

Soysal, Y. 2002b. Locating Europe. *European Societies*, 4(3), 265-84.

Soysal, Y., Bertilotti, T. and Mannitz, S. 2005. Projections of identity in French and German history and civics textbooks, in *The Nation, Europe and the World: Textbooks and Curricula in Transition*, edited by H. Schissler and Y. Soysal. Oxford: Berghahn Books, 13-34.

Spannring, R., Wallace, C. and Haerpfer, C. 2001. Civic participation among young people in Europe, in *Youth, Citizenship and Empowerment*, edited by H. Helve and C. Wallace. Aldershot: Ashgate, 32-8.

Spohn, W. and Triandafyllidou, A. (eds) 2003. *Europeanization, National Identities and Migration*. London: Routledge.

Stalker, P. 2002. Migration trends and migration policy in Europe. *International Migration*, 40(5), 151-79.

Statistisches Bundesamt 2008a. *Ausländische Bevölkerung*. (Fachserie 1 Reihe 2). Wiesbaden: Statistisches Bundesamt.

Statistisches Bundesamt 2008b. *Bevölkerung und Erwerbstätigkeit: Einbürgerungen 2007*. (Fachserie 1 Reihe 2.1). Wiesbaden: Statistisches Bundesamt.

Süssmuth-Kommission 2001. *Zuwanderung gestalten, Integration fördern*. Berlin: Bundesministerium des Innern.

Sunier, T. 2009. Teaching the nation: Religious and ethnic diversity at state schools in Britain and the Netherlands. *Teachers College Record*, 111(6), 1555-81.

Tajfel, H. 1974. Social identity and intergroup behaviour. *Social Science Information*, 13(2), 65-93.

Taylor, B. and Thomson, K. (eds) 1999. *Scotland and Wales: Nations Again?* Cardiff: University of Wales Press.

Taylor, W.H. 1995. Ethnic relations in all-white schools, in *Ethnic Relations and Schooling: Policy and Practice in the 1990s*, edited by S. Tomlinson and M. Craft. London: Athlone Press, 97-117.

Ter Wal, J. 2007. The Netherlands, in *European Immigration: A Sourcebook*, edited by A. Triandafyllidou and R. Gropas. Aldershot: Ashgate, 249-62.

Thomson, M. and Crul, M. (eds) 2007. The second generation in Europe. Special issue of *Journal of Ethnic and Migration Studies*, 33(7), 1025-193.

Thränhardt, D. 2008. *Einbürgerung: Rahmenbedingungen, Motive und Perspektiven des Erwerbs der deutschen Staatsangehörigkeit*. Bonn: Friedrich Ebert Stiftung.

Tizard, B. and Phoenix, A. 2002. *Black, White or Mixed Race? Race and Racism in the Lives of Young People of Mixed Parentage.* London: Routledge.

Todd, E. 2004. *After the Empire: The Breakdown of the American Order.* New York: Columbia University Press.

Tomlinson, S. 1990. *Multicultural Education in White Schools.* London: B.T. Batsford Ltd.

Tomlinson, S. and Craft, M. 1995. *Ethnic Relations and Schooling: Policy and Practice in the 1990s.* London: Athlone Press.

Triandafyllidou, A. (ed.) 2010. *Muslims in 21st Century Europe: Structural and Cultural Perspectives.* London: Routledge.

Troyna, B. 1992. Can you see the join?: An historical analysis of multicultural and antiracist education policies, in *Racism and Education: Structures and Strategies,* edited by D. Gill, B. Mayor and M. Blair. London: Sage, 63-91.

Troyna, B. 1994. Reforms, research and being reflexive about being reflective, in *Researching Education Policy: Ethical and Methodological Issues,* edited by D. Halpin and B. Troyna. London: Falmer, 1-14.

Troyna, B. and Williams, J. 1986. *Racism, Education and the State.* London: Croom Helm.

Tsoukalis, L. 2003. *What Kind of Europe?* Oxford: Oxford University Press.

Tulasiewicz, W. 1993. The European dimension and the national curriculum, in *The Multicultural Dimension of the National Curriculum,* edited by A.S. King and M.J. Reiss. London: Falmer, 240-58.

Tulasiewicz, W. and Brock, C. 2000. Introduction: The place of education in a united Europe, in *Education in a Single Europe,* edited by C. Brock and W. Tulasiewicz. London: Routledge, 1-48.

Turner, J.C. 1987. A self-categorization theory, in *Rediscovering the Social Group: A Self-Categorization Theory,* edited by J.C. Turner, M.A. Hogg, P.J. Oakes, S.D. Reicher and M.S. Wetherell. Oxford: Basil Blackwell, 42-67.

Vasta, E. 2007. From ethnic minorities to ethnic majority policy? Multiculturalism and the shift to assimilationism in the Netherlands. *Ethnic and Racial Studies,* 30(5), 713-41.

Verhofstadt, G. 2006. *The United States of Europe.* London: Federal Trust for Education and Research.

Vertovec, S. 1999. *Migration and Social Cohesion.* Aldershot: Edward Elgar.

Vertovec, S. 2007. Super-diversity and its implications. *Ethnic and Racial Studies,* 30(6), 1024- 54.

Vertovec, S. and Wessendorf, S. (eds) 2010. *The Multiculturalism Backlash: European Discourses, Policies and Practices.* London: Routledge.

Von Borries, B. 1999. A cross-cultural comparison of students' concepts of Europe, in *Intercultural Reconstruction: European Yearbook of Youth Policy and Research,* edited by S. Hübner-Funk, L. Chisholm, M. du Bois-Reymond and M. Sellin. Berlin: De Gruyter, 33-50.

Wachter, B. 2004. The Bologna Process: Developments and progress. *European Journal of Education,* 39(3), 265-73.

Wakenhut, R., Martini, M. and Forsterhofer, R. 1998. Ethnic consciousness and inter-ethnic relations in adolescents and young adults of South Tyrol, in *Ethnic and National Consciousness in Europe*, edited by M. Martini. Florence: Angelo Pontecorboli Editore, 51-66.

Walkington, H. 1999. *Theory into Practice: Global Citizenship Education*. Sheffield: The Geographical Association.

Wallace, W. (ed.) 1990. *The Transformation of Western Europe*. London: Pinter.

Wallach Scott, J. 2007. *The Politics of the Veil*. Princeton: Princeton University Press.

Warikoo, N. 2004. Cosmopolitan ethnicity: Second-generation Indo-Caribbean identities, *Becoming New Yorkers: Ethnographies of the New Second Generation*, edited by in P. Kasinitz, J.H. Mollenkopf and M.C. Waters. New York: Russel Sage Foundation, 361-91.

Warner, W.L. and Srole, L. 1945. *The Social Systems of American Ethnic Groups*. New Haven: Yale University Press.

Waters, M.C. 1990. *Ethnic Options: Choosing Identities in America*. Berkeley: University of California Press.

Waters, M.C. 1999. *Black Identities: West Indian Immigrant Dreams and American Realities*, Cambridge: Harvard University Press.

Watts, M.W. 1999. Xenophobia among young Germans in the nineties, in *Intercultural Reconstruction: European Yearbook of Youth Policy and Research*, edited by S. Hübner-Funk, L. Chisholm, M. du Bois-Reymond and M. Sellin. Berlin: De Gruyter, 117-39.

Weidenfeld, W. and Piepenschneider, M. 1990. *Junge Generation und europäische Einigung: Einstellungen, Wünsche, Perspektiven*. Bonn: Europa Union Verlag.

Weil, P. 2004. Lifting the Veil. *French Politics, Culture and Society*, 22(3), 142-9.

Wessendorf, S. 2007. 'Roots migrants': Transnationalism and 'return' among second-generation Italians in Switzerland. *Journal of Ethnic and Migration Studies*, 33(7), 1083-102.

Westdeutscher Rundfunk 2009. *Rückgang um 20 Prozent*. [Online]. Available at: http://www.wdr.de/radio/wdr2/rhein_und_weser/514600.phtml [accessed: 31 July 2009].

Werbner, P. and Yuval-Davis, N. 1999. Introduction: Women and the new discourse of citizenship, in *Women, Citizenship and Difference*, edited by P. Werbner and N. Yuval-Davis. London: Zed Books, 1-38.

Wetherell, M. 1998. Positioning and interpretive repertoires. *Discourse and Society*, 9(3), 387-412.

Whitty, G. 1989. *The New Right and the National Curriculum: State control or market forces? Journal of Education Policy*, 4(4), 329-41.

Whitty, G. 1997. Education policy and the sociology of education. *International Studies in Sociology of Education*, 7(2), 121-35.

Whitty, G. 2008. Twenty years of progress? English education policy 1988 to the present. *Educational Management Administration and Leadership*, 36(2), 165-84.

Whitty, G. and Menter, I. 1989. Lessons of Thatcherism: Education policy in England and Wales 1979-1988. *Journal of Law and Society*, 16(1), 42-64.

Wilhelm, R.W. 1998. Issues in multicultural education. *The Curriculum Journal*, 9(2), 227-46.

Wilpert, C. 2003. Racism, discrimination, citizenship and the need for anti-discrimination legislation in Germany, in *Challenging Racism in Britain and Germany*, edited by Z. Layton-Henry and C. Wilpert. Basingstoke: Palgrave, 245-69.

Wilson, V. 1997. Focus groups: A useful qualitative method for educational research? *British Educational Research Journal*, 23(2), 209-24.

Wood, P., Landry, C. and Bloomfield, J. 2006. *Cultural Diversity in Britain: A Toolkit for Cross-Cultural Co-operation*. York: Joseph Rowntree Foundation.

Woodard, S. 1998. Britain and Europe: History of a relationship, in *Britain in Europe*, edited by M. Fraser. London: Strategems, 128-31.

Wyn Jones, R. 2001. On process, events and unintended consequences: National identity and the politics of Welsh devolution. *Scottish Affairs*, 37, 34-57.

Yin, R.K. 2009. *Case Study Research: Design and Methods*. 4th Edition. London: Sage.

Youdell, D. 2003. Identity traps or how black students fail: The interactions between biographical, sub-cultural and learner identities. *British Journal of Sociology of Education*, 24(1), 3-20.

Young, J.W. 2000. *Britain and European Unity 1945-1999*. Basingstoke: Palgrave.

Yuval-Davis, N. 1997. Ethnicity, gender relations and multiculturalism, in *Debating Cultural Hybridity: Multi-Cultural Identities and the Politics of Anti-racism*, edited by P. Werbner and T. Modood. London: Zed Books, 193-208.

Zirkel, S. 2008. The influence of multicultural educational practices on student outcomes and intergroup relations. *Teachers College Record*, 110(6), 1147-81.

Zolberg, A.R. and Woon, L.L. 1999. Why Islam is like Spanish: Cultural incorporation in Europe and the United States. *Politics and Society*, 27(5), 5-38.

Index